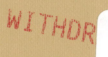

Henry the Liberal

THE MIDDLE AGES SERIES

Ruth Mazo Karras, Series Editor
Edward Peters, Founding Editor

A complete list of books in the series
is available from the publisher.

HENRY THE LIBERAL

Count of Champagne, 1127–1181

Theodore Evergates

UNIVERSITY OF PENNSYLVANIA PRESS

PHILADELPHIA

Published by
University of Pennsylvania Press
Philadelphia, Pennsylvania 19104-4112
www.upenn.edu/pennpress

Printed in the United States of America on acid-free paper
1 3 5 7 9 10 8 6 4 2

Library of Congress Cataloging-in-Publication Data
ISBN 978-0-8122-4790-9

Contents

Preface

Count Henry the Liberal of Champagne (1127–81) was justly celebrated in his own time for his generosity (hence "the Liberal"), for his unusually inquisitive mind, and for balancing the practical arts of governance with learning. And that is how he is generally remembered today. As I delved into the details of his life, however, those characterizations seemed inadequate to encompass the experiences and accomplishments of one of the most engaging princes of twelfth-century France. Tutored in the liberal arts from an early age, mentored in the practice of rulership from the age of seven, leader at twenty of the Champenois contingent on the Second Crusade, and count of two of his father's counties from twenty-two to twenty-five, he was by then an experienced and well-traveled prince who would rule the county of Champagne for the next three decades. As the most reliable of King Louis VII's great lords, Henry served the king in military affairs and on diplomatic missions, and he married Louis and Queen Eleanor's eldest daughter, Marie. His brother Thibaut was royal seneschal for more than three decades, another brother, William, was archbishop successively of Sens and Reims, and his sister Adele became Louis VII's third wife and mother of the future Philip II. Henry knew all the major political and religious figures of his time—three popes, the emperors of Germany and Constantinople, Henry II of England and his sons, and a long list of archbishops, bishops, and abbots, not to mention learned clerics with whom he shared a love of books and history.

It is curious that no contemporary writer saw fit to pen a biography or even a significant portrait of Henry, who lived so large in the public sphere. Obituaries remembered him primarily for his benefactions, and one simply noted his name, *Henricus dictus Largus*. Three lengthy praise letters by Philip of Harvengt (ca. 1160), Nicholas of Montiéramey (ca. 1160), and Guy of Bazoches (1170s) laud Henry as a literate and generous prince but offer few details about his life, and the brief remembrances after his death are anecdotal rather than substantive. Pierre Pithou, who wrote the first history of the counts of Champagne (1572), had little to say about the counts themselves, despite the title of his book.[1] The first substantial account of Henry and his rule appeared in 1861, as volume 3 of Henry d'Arbois de Jubainville's seven-volume history of the counts of Champagne.[2] Beyond being a font of information about Henry and his world, it provides a catalogue of the count's acts and establishes a framework for understanding Henry's life and the evolution of his county. A century later, in 1959, John F. Benton revisited Arbois de Jubainville's work preparatory to a study of the court of Champagne under Henry and Countess Marie, and although Benton was unable to complete the project, he made two enduring contributions.[3] The first was to begin a critical edition of Henry's known acts, which Michel Bur recently has brought to fruition with the publication of more than 550 acts.[4] Benton also proposed that we reconceptualize the twelfth-century "court" of Champagne by extending the concept of the court beyond the vernacular writers to include a galaxy of writers in Latin, the *literati* clerics and prelates who were intimately part of the "twelfth-century renaissance," thus enlarging our understanding of the cultural achievements of twelfth-century Champagne.[5]

The world of Henry the Liberal is much better known today than only a generation ago thanks to the vigorous and probing scholarship devoted to medieval Champagne, its art and architecture, monasticism (especially Cistercian), aristocratic families and their practices, the trade fairs, and literature both Latin and vernacular. Critical editions are now available of letter collections, ecclesiastical and comital cartularies, library catalogues, and the registers of the High Court that describe the customs of the principality. Among the significant new subjects opened to inquiry are Patricia Stirnemann's identification of Count Henry's personal library and her recovery of southern Champagne as a center of book-making and manuscript painting from the mid-twelfth century.[6] Within that broad cultural context the friendship networks linking *literati* prelates in Champagne with their colleagues across northern France and England assume new significance, as does Count Henry's singular tomb commissioned from Mosan craftsmen. Without exaggeration it can be said that the rise of Champagne as one of the more important princely states of twelfth-century France and its cultural efflorescence can be attributed largely to the interests, vision, and policies of Henry the Liberal.

This study traces Henry through the distinct stages of his life in order to capture the contingent events compelling his attention at those specific moments. It is based on the premise that Henry was not the same person in his early twenties, when he led a company of Champenois barons and knights on the Second Crusade, that he was in his forties, when he commissioned copies of books by ancient authors in concert with Thomas Becket, then in exile in Sens. The stages-of-life approach is especially useful for understanding Henry's life and policies as a bachelor prince, the thirteen years (1152–64) when the county of Champagne took shape as a new political entity. Seen from a distance of almost nine centuries, that was Henry's singular achievement, to construct a major new polity, the county of Champagne, and to endow it with the institutions and identity as a province in early modern France that would survive his dynasty.

It should be said at the start that in the absence of contemporary accounts of Henry's life we must rely primarily on several types of non-narrative sources to reconstruct his life and works: his sealed letters patent, the letters written by *literati* clerics to or about him, his chancery's administrative registers (the rolls of fiefs), the fragmentary catalogue of his library, and the remains or later sketches of his material works (his tomb, residences and chapels, and books). We also can learn something about Henry from his decision to construct a new capital in Troyes, to found chapters of secular canons, and to make the trade fairs the economic motor of his county's economy. The chroniclers who mention Henry's military expeditions, crusades, and diplomatic missions beyond the county do so almost in passing, yet they testify to the considerable range of Henry's travels and engagement in "foreign affairs." This study consequently is highly contextual in that it locates Henry within the events of his time, even when he was not immediately involved, and often deals more with the individuals who directly influenced him than with Henry himself. From these disparate materials emerges the portrait of an engaging personage, as original and captivating as the better-known monarchs, prelates, and intellectuals of the time with whom he interacted.

Count Henry and His Relatives

William The Conqueror king of England 1066-87

Henry I king of England 1100-35

Adela countess of Blois d.1137 = Stephen count of Blois d.1102

Blois

Stephen king of England 1135-54

Henry bishop of Winchester 1129-71

Agnes = Hugh III of Le Puiset d.1132

Thibaut IV count of Blois-Champagne 1120-52

Evrard IV of Le Puiset viscount of Chartres 1129-90

Hugh bishop of Durham 1153-95

Hugh abbot of Lagny 1163-71

Mathilda countess of Blois 1126-52 d.1160

Henry bishop of Troyes 1145-68

Carinthia

Ida countess of Nevers d.1179 = William III count of Nevers 1147-61

William IV count of Nevers 1161-68

Henry bishop of Autun 1148-70

Walter bishop of Langres 1163-79

Burgundy

Sibyl = Roger II king of Sicily 1140-54

Roger of Apulia = Elizabeth of Champagne d.1149

Elizabeth = Roger of Apulia d.1149

Mathilda = Rotrou count of Perche 1144-91

Agnes countess of Bar-le-Duc 1165-70 d.1207 = Renaud II count of Bar-le-Duc 1149-70

Henry I count of Bar-le-Duc 1170-90

France

Marie = Henry I 1152-81

Alice countess of Blois 1165-98 = Thibaut V count of Blois 1152-91

Stephen count of Sancerre 1152-90

William archbishop of Sens, 1168-75 archbishop of Reims, 1176-1202

Adele queen of France 1160-80 d.1206 = Louis VII king of France 1137-80

Marie = Odo II duke of Burgundy 1143-62

Philip II king of France 1180-1223

Hugh III duke of Burgundy 1165-92

Henry II count of Champagne 1187-90/97

Thibaut III count of Champagne 1198-1201

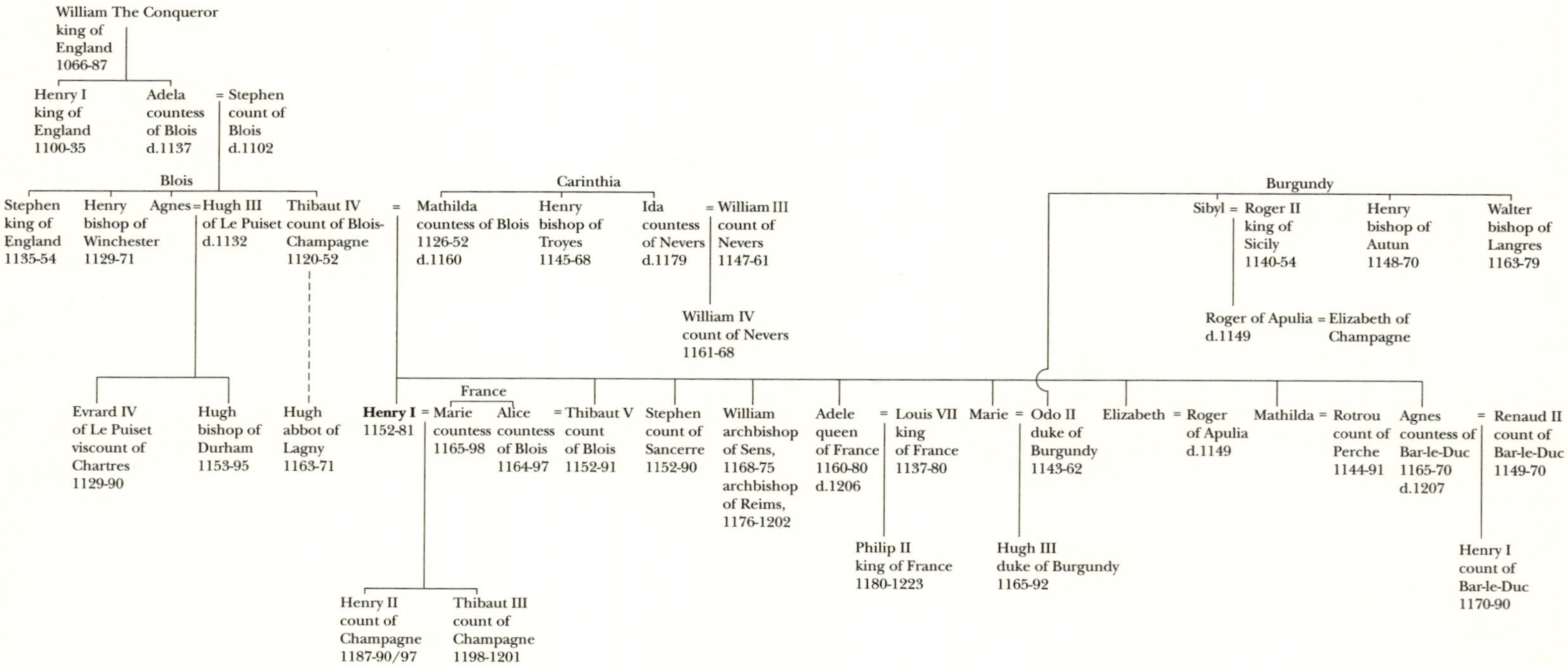

Figure 1. Genealogy: Count Henry and his relatives.

Chapter 1

The Young Count, 1127–1145

We know the date of Henry's birth, December 1127, only because his father, Count Thibaut, was so overjoyed that he franchised a certain Walter, his wife Emeline, and their children from all taxes and personal service, including guard duty at the walls and towers of Vitry and service in the count's army.[1] The original castle (*castrum*) of Vitry was built in the late ninth century on a natural elevation dominating the Saulx valley, where two towers and a wall protected a compound of brick buildings containing the count's residence, a bakery, storehouses, stables, and ancillary residences and shops.[2] Directly below the fortress, which was accessed by a single road passing through a gate and incline to the upper ridge, a small town (*burgus*) was surrounded by a moat. Count Thibaut had acquired Vitry only two years earlier, in 1125, and apparently upgraded the site for his new bride, for Robert of Torigni later called Vitry "a very fine fortress."[3]

Count Thibaut (1120–52) was one of the most powerful princes of northern France, esteemed by laymen and religious alike for his honesty, piety, and personal comportment. According to a sober writer like Orderic Vitalis, he was renowned among knights, a lover of peace and justice, and distinguished among the princes of France by wealth and character.[4] Before 1125 his vast assortment of lands extended from his ancestral counties of Blois and Chartres in western France (he was always called count of Blois) to the northern plains of Champagne east of the royal domain, in what later would be called Brie. His eastern lands included one episcopal town, Meaux, which he shared with its bishop but seldom visited. Thibaut favored rather his castle-towns located on rivers, notably Château-Thierry on the Marne, Bray-sur-Seine, and Montereau-fault-Yonne, and a few inland towns: the centrally located Sézanne, where he often held court with his barons; Coulommiers, a favorite

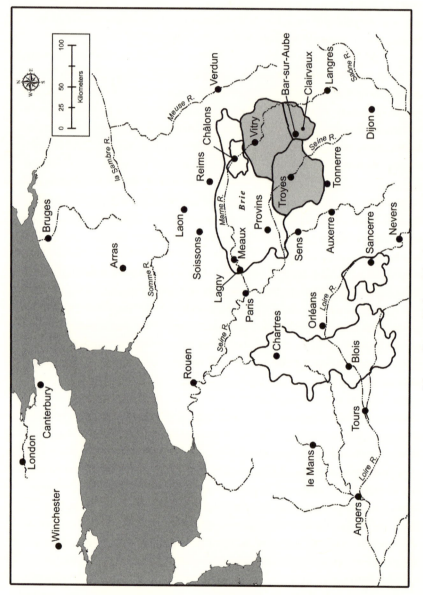

Map 1. Count Thibaut's lands in 1150.

retreat of his mother, Countess Adela of Blois; and especially Provins, his most important commercial center. The fertile plains of Brie supported many of the count's knights who rendered castle-guard in his towns in return for their fiefs, but beyond the castellans who administered the count's fortified sites, Brie harbored relatively few castle lords.

In 1125 Thibaut acquired his uncle Count Hugh's three contiguous counties of Troyes, Bar-sur-Aube, and Vitry in southern Champagne, which controlled the upper reaches of the Seine, Aube, and Marne Rivers and included the old episcopal city of Troyes (Map 1).[5] It was with good reason that Thibaut was regarded as the most powerful lord in northern France and royal sympathizers cast him as the chief rival to King Louis VI. The chronicler of Morigny, writing in the early 1130s, called Thibaut "count of Chartres, Blois, Meaux, and many other provinces, who was count palatine and within France second only to the king."[6] Not only did his lands bracket the royal domain and dwarf it in size, Thibaut was, at thirty-three, the most eligible bachelor prince of the realm in 1125. But the count was not interested in marriage, having turned from his youthful bellicosity to an inner life after the White Ship (1120) sank with his sister and brother-in-law and many noble-born men and women.[7] He considered becoming a monk in the manner of Godfrey of Cappenberg, who famously dismantled his castles in order to follow Norbert of Xanten, founder of the Premonstratensian monks. But Norbert advised Thibaut to become instead a responsible prince and to beget descendants, and so Thibaut sent emissaries to Regensburg (November 1125), where with the assistance of Bishop Hartwich of Regensburg and Archbishop Frederick of Cologne, he obtained the hand of their niece Mathilda, the eighteen-year-old daughter of Duke Engelbert II of Carinthia.[8] The couple married in 1126 and took up residence in Vitry, which provided a secure and tranquil home for a family that would grow to nine children.

Thibaut's acquisition of Count Hugh's lands brought him into direct contact with the new order of Cistercian monks, especially with the charismatic Abbot Bernard of Clairvaux (1115–53), who became a personal friend of the count and his family during the quarter century of explosive growth in Cistercian houses.[9] Thibaut provided substantial material support to Clairvaux, Signy, and Pontigny in the 1130s and facilitated the Cistercian takeover of several existing but materially or spiritually deficient monastic communities. "He bought land, built new monasteries, and gave money everywhere that the servants of God established new colonies," wrote Bernard's biographer in eulogizing Thibaut.[10] The count's support extended to the Cistercians' stepchild, the Knights Templar, the band of knights founded in part by a local baron, Hugh of Payns, to defend Christian pilgrims from the depredations of Muslim bandits while traveling from the Mediterranean coast to Jerusalem.[11] On 31 October 1127, only weeks before Henry's birth, Count Thibaut donated a house and land at Barbonne near his castle-town of Sézanne for use by Hugh's knights, and confirmed the donations his barons had made to "the knights of the Temple of Solomon."[12] At the Council of Troyes on 13 January 1129 Thibaut and his seneschal André of Baudement heard Hugh of Payns, fresh from a recruiting tour in western France, Flanders, England, and Scotland, present his case for the recognition of his knights as a new religious order.[13] Bernard of Clairvaux had prepared a tract, *In Praise of the New Knighthood*, reconciling a deep personal aversion to violence with current needs to protect pilgrims and early Christian sites in the holy land, thus justifying the concept of a new monastic order dedicated to sacred violence.[14] In the cathedral church of Troyes the papal legate Cardinal Mathieu of Albano, the archbishops of Reims and Sens, ten bishops, and eight abbots heard Hugh of Payns's proposal. There followed an animated discussion joined by Count Thibaut and his lay companions.[15] Ultimately the council accepted the constitution of a militarized monastic order based on the Benedictine Rule. Bernard's tract promoting the Knights Templar was instrumental in recruiting knights to the new order, which soon evolved into the premier military organization of the West, far beyond what Hugh of Payns could have imagined in 1129.[16] But Hugh had planted the idea of permanent armed confrontation in the Holy Land, a worldview that two decades later would draw the Cistercians into all-out support for the Second (the Cistercian) Crusade, in what would prove to be a formative experience for young Henry.

The Education of a Prince

Henry was five in 1132, when first mentioned in a document. His parents had taken him to Coulommiers, one of his grandmother Adela's favorite retreats in the middle of the plains of Brie, where they renewed her grants to the priory of Ste-Foy in honor of a saint known for her miracles. A hand-drawn cross at the end of the document, identified as "the *signum* of Henry, son of Count Thibaut," indicated the boy's consent.[17] Henry's tutor Stephen accompanied the family, suggesting that Henry had begun a program of study from an early age. Philip of Harvengt, abbot of Bonne-Espérance, later congratulated Henry on being educated in the liberal arts and reminded him of what he owed his father, who although not so well educated himself wanted his son to excel through the "knowledge of letters."[18] Peter of Celle, who came to know Henry well, attested to Henry's "most tenacious memory," a capacity admired by the prelate-authors of the time, but which failed him, Peter intimated, when it suited.[19]

Henry's training as count began in earnest in 1134 at seven, when he appeared at his father's court in Troyes to witness an act "done in public." Abbot Walter of Larrivour presented a charter of Count Hugh of Troyes to suppport his claim to certain mills built in the pastures between his recently founded Cistercian monastery and the older house of St-Martin-ès-Aires. At court and witnessing were the bishop of Troyes, three abbots, several prominent canons of Troyes cathedral, six castle lords, and the provost of Troyes. But Abbot Walter, fearing that he had lost the case on its merits (Count Hugh left Champagne in 1125, before Larrivour was founded), departed before the count announced his judgment. Insulted, the count decided for the canons of St-Martin. The scribe of the document recording the count's decision noted that young Henry "marked his *signum*." It survives as Henry's earliest extant autograph cross.[20]

The next year, 1135, eight-year-old Henry accompanied his parents to their western lands, where Count Thibaut discussed the English succession with the disgruntled Norman barons, who encouraged him to claim the throne at the imminent death of his uncle King Henry I (see Figure 1).[21] But Thibaut was outmaneuvered by his younger brothers Stephen and Henry, who were prominent fixtures in England. Stephen had been sent there at a young age by Countess Adela and became, according to someone who knew him, the "dearest of all the nephews of King Henry," both for his "close family relationship" and for "many conspicuous virtues," for he was "rich and at the same time unassuming, generous, and courteous . . . bold and brave, judicious and patient."[22] Henry ("of Blois") arrived in England in the 1120s after spending twenty years as a Cluniac monk, and he, too, became close to his uncle the king, whose patronage made him abbot of Glastonbury (1126–71), bishop of Winchester (1129–71), and one of the wealthiest and most powerful prelates in England.[23] He was, according to a protégé, "a man of inexpressible eloquence as well as wonderful wisdom."[24] It was Bishop Henry who convinced the prelates and barons of England to support Stephen as King Henry's successor instead of the king's daughter Matilda, whom they had sworn earlier to accept.[25] After Stephen was crowned king of England on 22 December 1135,

Thibaut left Normandy angry, according to Orderic Vitalis.[26] But he had to accept the inevitable, for Stephen had spent most of his life in service to his uncle, while Thibaut's influence and reputation were located in the French lands beyond Normandy. Count Thibaut, then in his early forties with a young family, was not up to challenging his brother and embarking on a novel and risky venture in a foreign land.[27]

While the comital family was still in Chartres, the abbot of Marmoutier asked Henry, then nine years old, to confirm his father's earlier charter, which Henry did in a postscript added by a monastic scribe to the count's original charter.[28] Thereafter Henry often accompanied his father, and occasionally his mother and brothers, on their peregrinations between castle-towns, where he met his father's provosts and local castle lords and observed his art of governance. At Épernay he confirmed his father's gift to the abbey of St-Martin and witnessed a case involving the illicit alienation of a fief.[29] In the spring of 1137 he likely accompanied his father to pay their last respects to Henry's grandmother Adela, who died at Marcigny on 8 March 1137. Soon afterward his father traveled to Evreux in Normandy to renounce his claim to the throne of England in return for 2,000 marks of silver from King Stephen.[30] Bishop Henry of Winchester facilitated what must have been a delicate family matter before the three brothers rode on to Rouen, where Stephen confirmed an annual donation of 100 marks of silver from his treasury to the nuns at Fontevraud for the souls of his family.[31] Even Louis VI had to accept a fait accompli. In mid-May 1137 he invested Stephen's son Eustace with Normandy, then asked Innocent II to recognize Stephen as king of England.[32] Count Thibaut did the same.[33]

There is no mention of young Henry at any of these events, but as a ten-year-old count-in-training, and partly an English royal himself, he must have been apprised of the acts of his two formidable uncles in England at the very moment that another pivotal event was playing out in France. In mid-June 1137 Louis VI contracted the marriage of his eldest son, Louis, with Eleanor, the thirteen-year-old heiress of Duke William X of Aquitaine. Within weeks Count Thibaut, then about forty-four, and a handful of other great French barons, including the royal seneschal Ralph of Vermandois, Counts William II of Nevers and Rotrou II of Perche, together with Abbot Suger of St-Denis and Bishop Geoffroy of Chartres, accompanied sixteen-year-old Prince Louis to Bordeaux for the marriage on 25 July.[34] Whether or not Henry accompanied his father to Bordeaux or witnessed the entry of Louis VII and Eleanor into Paris after the death of Louis VI (1 August), his life became inextricably linked with the new king for more than four decades, until their deaths only months apart (Louis VII in November 1180, Henry in March 1181).

Later that fall Henry witnessed his father renew the Fair of Saint Martin in Provins. The count defined the limits of the marketplace ("from the tower of my seneschal Girard [of Provins] to my tower") and asserted his right to half of the rents and taxes paid by the merchants, who had to buy and sell their goods within that prescribed area. Since Provins had been assigned as dower to Countess Adela and then to Countess Mathilda, as the document states, both Mathilda and Thibaut had their seals placed on the document, while Henry marked his consent with a *signum*, implicitly recognizing his mother's rights in Provins.[35] On most occasions Count Thibaut had his seal affixed to documents prepared by the recipients, usually monasteries.[36] Even when he made a judicial determination or confirmed a third-party act, the beneficiary institution usually drafted the document in his name for him to seal, in one case after young Henry and his mother had drawn their crosses.[37] But since the townsmen of Provins did not possess a corporate notary in 1137, Thibaut's own cleric William drew up the document and his chaplain Ralph affixed the count's pendant seal.[38] Young Henry already had witnessed his father's benefactions, adjudications, and arbitrations; the charter of 1137 introduced the future count to the important role of markets and fairs in the economic life of his father's towns.

Louis VII

Henry's eleventh through sixteenth years, 1138 to 1144, were dominated by his father's troubled relations with the new king. Henry may well have met Louis VII in the spring of 1138, when his father accompanied the king to Langres and Auxerre to receive "homages and fidelity" from local castle lords and to intrude in the disputed episcopal election in Langres.[39] Count Thibaut's initial good relations with Louis were due in part to the departure of the seneschal and the dowager queen Adelaide from the royal court and the restoration of Abbot Suger of St-Denis as the king's chief adviser. Suger fostered close ties between Thibaut and Louis because, he said, the king was so young and inexperienced.[40] But an omen of rocky times ahead came in September 1138 when Louis, perhaps misreading Thibaut's attentions, summoned the count to come "immediately" to help suppress the commune in Poitiers (within the queen's lands), warning Thibaut that he would bear responsibility for any misadventure, should he not come. The count replied that "he could do nothing without first consulting with his barons," clearly a diplomatic excuse.[41]

Pacific relations between the king and the count lasted for three years. In late 1140 Thibaut cooperated with Louis in suppressing the commune in Reims, no doubt because it offered a dangerous example to his own towns.[42] The next spring Louis, Thibaut, and William II of Nevers attended the Council of Sens (25–26 May 1141), where in the presence of a large number of barons and prelates, including the archbishops of Reims and Sens and their suffragan bishops, Peter Abelard's writings were condemned as heretical.[43] It is likely that fourteen-year-old Henry accompanied his father to Sens, if not to observe the Council, at least to see the relics of Saint Stephen displayed in the expansive new cathedral being built in honor of the saint.[44] Sens cathedral would be the model for Henry's own chapel built in Troyes a decade later and likewise dedicated to Saint Stephen. Counts Thibaut and William of Nevers are not known to have participated in the Council's deliberations as they did at the Council of Troyes in 1129, but they may have used the occasion to arrange a marriage between Thibaut's sister-in-law, Ida of Carinthia, and William's eldest son, William (III).[45] About the same time Thibaut sent his daughter Elizabeth/Isabelle, then about twelve, to marry the son of King Roger II of Sicily. Bernard of Clairvaux may have had a hand in that alliance, since two Cistercian monks accompanied the girl to Sicily, where Roger had invited them to found a monastery.[46]

Relations between Thibaut and Louis became openly hostile when the king decided to impose his chancellor Cadurc as archbishop of Bourges after the death of Archbishop Alberic (1136–41), the distinguished former master of the school of Reims.[47] The cathedral canons were divided, with most preferring Peter de la Châtre, the local candidate also favored by Pope Innocent II. Louis granted the chapter his license to elect anyone except Peter, but the canons, resenting that intrusion in their affairs, elected Peter as archbishop on the very day (26 May 1141) that Louis witnessed Abelard's condemnation in Sens. Louis "became very angry" and swore on Scriptures that as long as he lived, Peter would neither enter Bourges nor assume the archiepiscopal office. The pope consecrated the archbishop in Rome, placed the king's lands under interdict, and prohibited all religious services in Louis's presence.[48] Adding insult to injury, the pope was quoted as remarking, "The king is a child [actually twenty-one] who must be instructed, and prevented from assuming bad habits."[49] Count Thibaut offered the new archbishop refuge in Champagne. "Indignant at this," wrote William of Nangis, "the king convoked all his great men to join him in warring against Count Thibaut."[50]

Thibaut naturally declined to join Louis's expedition to Toulouse in June 1141, just as earlier he had refused to accompany the king to Poitiers on the queen's behalf. But this time his refusal began the definitive unraveling of his on-and-off relationship with Louis.[51] Robert of Auxerre, who wrote an account of regional events not long afterward, linked the two conflicts, over Aquitaine and Bourges, as having poisoned relations between Louis and Thibaut, and wondered whether the count had ventured too far in opposing the king.[52] In fact Thibaut was much troubled by the recent turn of events. He "urgently and continually pestered me with his affairs," wrote Bishop Hato of Troyes to Abbot Peter the Venerable of Cluny.[53] Not mentioned but perhaps also weighing on the count was the fact that his brother King Stephen was still held prisoner after losing the battle of Lincoln (2 February 1141) and seemed on the verge of losing the throne of England.[54]

If relations between Thibaut and Louis were contentious during the Bourges affair, they turned toxic in late 1141 and 1142 after the king's seneschal and distant cousin, Ralph of Vermandois, repudiated his wife Eleanor in order to marry the queen's sister Alice/Petronilla.[55] Ralph had married Eleanor, Thibaut's niece, as part of a peace agreement Louis VI arranged between Ralph and Thibaut in 1135, and so Ralph's contrived divorce obtained on the grounds of consanguinity from three compliant bishops was a personal affront to Thibaut, who appealed to Innocent II. The papal legate Ivo convened a council at Lagny, that is, within Thibaut's lands, where the count presented his case before a group of sympathetic prelates that included Bernard of Clairvaux. The bishops affirmed the validity of Ralph's first marriage (the couple was not, in fact, related within the prohibited degrees of consanguinity), and the legate excommunicated Ralph and Alice and suspended the three prelates who had granted the sham divorce.[56] Thus three seemingly unrelated issues—an illegitimate summons to military service in the queen's lands, a disputed episcopal election in Bourges, and a fraudulent divorce—became entangled around one common thread: in all three cases Count Thibaut had actively opposed the king. The king's anger, apparently stoked by Queen Eleanor, led to a complete breakdown of royal-comital relations, and soon young Henry learned a hard lesson on dealing with an impetuous monarch.

The death of the bishop of Châlons (6 May 1142) provided Louis the opportunity for revenge. He ordered his brother Robert to occupy the episcopal lands, in effect, to exercise the traditional *regalia* over a vacant see, this one conveniently located as a staging point for an attack on Thibaut's lands. Louis was more than angry; he was playing a complicated game against the count,

the pope, and episcopal chapters within his realm. The canons of Châlons rose
to the challenge: with royal troops occupying Châlons and in the absence of
the king's license to elect, they chose a Champenois, Guy of Montaigu, as
their new bishop. In the summer or fall of 1142 Louis personally led an army
into Count Thibaut's lands, laying waste to what he could and destroying the
count's castle at Vitry, an event widely recounted in the chronicles.[57] Robert of
Torigni reports that the king ravaged Thibaut's lands and that a large number
of men and women perished in the conflagration at Vitry.[58] A continuation of
Sigebert of Gembloux furnishes the most detailed account of events: "With
many troops he [Louis] attacked the fortress called Vitry, where he captured
or killed the residents and the soldiers who resisted. The town having been
put to the torch, the fire spread so fast that the castle itself, which was strongly
built, burned at the same time at great peril to those inside it. In the fighting
and the fire, those who were killed or who perished in the flames numbered
1500."[59] Arnold of Bonneval was even bleaker: "Almost all that belonged to
the count was pillaged, burned, and depopulated."[60] Arnold surely recalled
that shortly after he became abbot of Bonneval (1129), Louis VI burned down
the town of Bonneval as a lesson to Count Thibaut, who as royal advocate of
the monastery had built a personal residence on the abbey's lands.[61] The events
at Vitry thus played out against long memories. Peter, prior of Jully, had a
more positive outlook, predicting to the count's chaplain that Thibaut, if he
protected the church, would emerge victorious in his conflict with the king.[62]
It was the same Peter whose vision before 1135 had predicted that Thibaut
would not pass over to England to claim the English crown.[63]

The destruction of Vitry, where Thibaut and Mathilda had raised a family
in tranquility, was an especially vile blow, and a traumatic experience for
fifteen-year-old Henry, who was born and spent his early boyhood years there.
Thibaut made a number of countermoves to protect his family and lands. He
sent his youngest son, William, then about seven, to England to be raised in
the household of his brother Bishop Henry of Winchester for a career in the
church. That probably occurred in the spring, during a lull in the civil war
following King Stephen's release from captivity (1 November 1141). After William's
departure from Champagne the rest of the comital family gathered in
Sézanne, where the three remaining sons—Henry, Thibaut, and Stephen—
each marked a *signum* on their father's charter for the canons of Val-Chrétien.[64]
At the same time Thibaut married his daughter Marie, then about thirteen or
fourteen, to Odo II, the new duke of Burgundy.[65] More significantly, Thibaut
took young Henry with him to Augustines, just below Bar-sur-Seine at the

border with Burgundy, to witness his homage to the duke of Burgundy for the county of Troyes and the castle-towns of Ervy, Isle-Aumont, and St-Florentin, and for five castles held from him by his barons: Villemaur, Chappes, Plancy, Arcis, and Ramerupt (see Map 3).[66] It appears that in the aftermath of the royal incursion in Champagne, Thibaut sought to strengthen his relationship with the Burgundian duke for the lands he had acquired from Count Hugh in southern Champagne.[67] The duke and the count both understood the significance of the event and had identical documents drawn up describing the homage and naming the castles at issue.[68] That was the earliest known homage recorded between laymen in eastern France—there is no evidence that Thibaut had done homage to the king or any other lord—and it was a reminder to young Henry that his father's lands were held from lords other than the king.[69] Returning from Augustines, Thibaut and Henry stopped at Clairvaux, where the count made a donation. On arriving at the comital residence in Bar-sur-Aube, a scribe recorded the donation and Henry drew his cross on the parchment to mark his consent.[70] Increasingly, young Henry appeared with his father in the absence of his mother, as if the count were involving his sixteen-year-old son and presumptive heir more directly in the practice of lordship.

The continuator of Sigebert of Gembloux's chronicle reports that the kingdom suffered "a great disruption by war because of the dispute between the king and the princes, of whom Count Thibaut of Blois was most prominent."[71] Bernard of Clairvaux and Suger attempted a reconciliation with the help of the king's trusted adviser Jocelin, bishop of Soissons. Bernard convinced Thibaut to seek the lifting of the royal seneschal's excommunication in return for the restitution of Vitry and the king's acceptance of the newly elected bishop of Châlons, but Pope Innocent II refused to lift the excommunication until Ralph left his new wife. Then Louis hardened his position and seemed ready to invade Thibaut's lands again.[72] Bernard warned the king against risking a schism within the church.[73] Sixteen-year-old Henry became a pawn in those political machinations when Thibaut contracted Henry's marriage with Laurette, daughter of Thierry of Alsace, count of Flanders.[74] Whether Henry gave his formal consent to the marriage is not known, but the threat was not lost on the king: the union of Blois-Champagne and Flanders would literally encircle the royal domain and hold the king hostage to an all-powerful count. Louis protested to the pope that the couple was too closely related for a canonically valid marriage, but Pope Celestine II, a confidant of Bernard of Clairvaux, responded coolly to Louis's advocate, Bishop Alvisius of Arras:

I have received your letter explaining the consanguineous relationship between the son of the count of Blois and the daughter of the
noble Count Thierry of Flanders; but since we have found that the
bishops of France were lax in pursuing the Holy See's mandate [in
interdicting the king's land], and since they failed to do justice in
Count Thibaut's case against Ralph of Vermandois [i.e., they
granted a divorce on fraudulent grounds], I have reserved the question to the Holy See. If you wish to pursue that or any other case,
you may present it to me by 12 March 1144, when it will be decided
in the presence of both parties according to canon law.[75]

Ultimately Henry's marriage did not occur, but the prospect of marrying
under those circumstances must have brought home to him in a very personal
way something about how power politics was played in northern France.

Suger and St-Denis

With the new pope, Lucius II, amenable to resolving a very complicated affair, Count Thibaut sent two allies, Bishop Geoffroy (of Lèves) of Chartres
and Abbot Arnold of Bonneval, to Rome to seek a relaxation of ecclesiastical
censures against the king and the royal seneschal. The pope annulled the interdict weighing on Louis and relieved the king of his oath taken in anger
against the archbishop of Bourges. He also lifted the seneschal's excommunication, but only after Ralph left his wife, a compromise that ultimately took
effect with her death in 1147.[76] On 22 April 1144, Bernard, Suger, and Bishop
Hugh of Auxerre convinced Louis to make a definitive peace with Thibaut.
That may have occasioned the count's gift in thanks to Clairvaux of the inlaid
gemstones from two very heavy and fine gold vases that had belonged to King
Henry I of England, who used to display them on a banquet table during his
crown wearing. Thibaut gave the gemstones, said Bernard's biographer, so that
the Cistercians could sell them to fund their building program.[77] Suger crowed
about the sapphires, emeralds, topazes, rubies, and hyacinths that he purchased for 400l., far below their actual value. Thibaut had obtained them
from his brother Stephen in 1137, said the abbot, in quitclaim to the throne of
England, so they ultimately came from the extraordinary collection that
Henry I had amassed, a fact that gave Suger special satisfaction.[78]
    Discussions between the parties continued at St-Denis two months later
at the dedication of the remodeled abbey church on 11 June 1144. Abbot Suger

had invited all the principals to what was, in effect, a "surreptitious summit" to conclude the resolution of a complicated set of issues that threatened to destabilize the realm.[79] The presence on that festive occasion of a large contingent of bishops, abbots, and princes facilitated reconciliation. In his memoirs Suger names a few of those who attended the dedication ceremonies: five archbishops (Reims, Sens, Rouen, Bordeaux, Canterbury), thirteen bishops, and two laymen—King Louis and Count Thibaut.[80] Suger does not mention any abbot by name, not even Bernard, nor does he note any of the many lay *optimates* in attendance, but surely they included young Henry, then seventeen, and Countess Mathilda, as well as Queen Eleanor; it was simply too special an occasion to be missed. And it was here that Henry must have seen how Suger had created an entire monastic complex of singular presence, an example of what could be done through force of will and vision.

Suger had recruited a small army of craftsmen—masons, stone carvers, goldsmiths, enamelers, glaziers, and painters—from Burgundy, Poitou, Lotharingia, and even Italy, to work on his grand project.[81] The great gold cross that stood next to the altar required a team of five to seven Mosan goldsmiths two years to craft.[82] The profusion of Sugerian luxury extended to three portals filled with exquisite stone carvings; the tympanum featuring a prominent figure of Suger himself; life-size column-statues of Old Testament prophets and kings and queens of France (Merovingian, Carolingian, Capetian) dressed in the latest twelfth-century fashion; and elaborate columns with human and animal figures. Those portal sculptures, the earliest of their type in northern France, constituted an intricate theological program with powerful scenes for visitors entering the abbey church.[83] The large, finely crafted bronze doors of the central portal, in which Suger is represented and his name inscribed on the lintel, must have stunned visitors with their magnificence and intricate metalwork. The *literati* who knew how to read the artfully crafted stained glass windows would have been impressed by their complex exegetical program.[84] A new dormitory, refectory, cloister, and hospice were also Suger's work.[85] The entire monastic compound, in fact, was a monument to the abbot, who had his image imprinted or his name inscribed on every conceivable object: on the lintel of the central portal, the doors, windows, altars, vases, and liturgical vessels.[86] It was a spectacular performance in art and architecture. The entire project was largely completed between 1137 and 1144, testimony to Suger's drive, not to mention his aesthetic sensibilities. It was unlikely that Henry had seen anything comparable in his father's lands. Less than a decade later he would emulate Suger's achievement in a suburb of Troyes named, appropriately enough, St-Denis.

The visiting dignitaries in 1144 brought gifts that they placed on the new altar at St-Denis. The bishops deposited their pontifical rings, wrote Suger, while the king gave emeralds, Count Thibaut brought hyacinths and rubies (no doubt from the same cache he had acquired from his brother), and the other princes gave emeralds.[87] But Louis and Thibaut, the two preeminent laymen, also brought personal, exotic gifts of antique provenance. Louis regifted the rock crystal "Eleanor Vase" that Eleanor had given him on their marriage.[88] Count Thibaut, for his part, regifted an equally dazzling vase, the rock crystal ewer he had received from Roger II of Sicily on the occasion of his daughter Elizabeth's marriage to Roger's son. Suger was particularly impressed by the fact that the vase came "in the same box in which the king of Sicily sent it."[89]

Of the many private discussions that took place at St-Denis, one of the most consequential was Queen Eleanor's meeting with Bernard of Clairvaux. The austere abbot might well have felt out of place amid Suger's extravagance and was in a gruff mood when Eleanor complained that, except for her early miscarriage, she had failed to conceive a child. Bernard promised that if she convinced Louis to make peace with Thibaut, her prayers would be answered.[90] In the spirit of the occasion Louis agreed, and four months later, on the feast of Saint Denis (9 October 1144), the parties met again at the abbey to ratify their final accord.[91] Louis recognized the archbishop of Bourges and agreed to do penance for his intemperate oath, while Thibaut abandoned the proposed marriage between Henry and Laurette of Flanders. Louis also agreed to stop supporting his seneschal Ralph, who remained excommunicate for his bigamous marriage.[92] Suger and Bernard had forced Louis and Thibaut to join against their new common rival, Count Geoffroy of Anjou, who had conquered virtually all of Normandy.[93]

The end of four contentious years between Count Thibaut and Louis VII coincided with Henry's coming of age in December 1145, when he turned eighteen and acquired his first seal. A round seal of white wax depicts him on a horse galloping to the right (in contrast to his father's seal, which has the count riding to the left).[94] He wears a conical helmet with nasal protector, and holds a long shield in his left hand and a lance with banner raised vertically in his right hand. It is inscribed "Seal of Henry, son of Count Thibaut."[95] Among the earliest documents he authenticated with it was one for his friend Peter, a noble-born monk recently returned from his studies in Paris to became abbot of the Benedictine monastery of Montier-la-Celle (1145–62), located just beyond the gates of Troyes.[96] At issue was the intermarriage of their respective tenants: to which lord did the children belong? Usually a lord surrendered his rights over the woman and her children in exchange for comparable rights over a woman of her husband's lord; but in a few cases the two lords of the new couple might claim lordship over half the future children, which is what Henry allowed here: "Henry, son of Count Thibaut, to his friend (*dilectis suis*) Peter, abbot of Montier-la-Celle, and to its chapter, greetings. According to your request, I concede the marriage between Hugh, brother of Thibaut of Bouilly, and Dulcia, sister of my *serviens* Gobraud, . . . together with half of their children. . . . My father Count Thibaut concedes this . . . and I have ordered this letter to be authenticated by my seal."[97] Witnesses included several monks, minor court personnel, and "William, my father's cleric" (later Henry's chancellor), who probably drafted the letter. That was Henry's first independent act (none of his father's great men were present) for which he used his personal seal.[98]

Henry at eighteen was the eldest son in a growing household of siblings. His sisters Marie and Elizabeth/Isabelle already had married, Marie to Odo II of Burgundy and Elizabeth to Roger of Apulia. His two brothers living in England were being mentored by their paternal uncle, Bishop Henry of Winchester: ten-year-old William lived in the episcopal household, while an older half-brother Hugh (a child of Count Thibaut's premarital liaison) was abbot of St. Benet of Holme.[99] Five siblings were still at home in 1145: Thibaut (about fifteen or sixteen), Stephen (perhaps thirteen), Mathilda (about eight), Agnes (about seven), and Margaret (of unknown age).[100] The youngest daughter, Adele (future queen of France), was born mostly likely around 1145 and thus was about the same age as Marie of France, who was born to Queen Eleanor in March or April 1145, one year after Bernard of Clairvaux's purported intervention at St-Denis in the matter of her infertility.[101] If, as is likely, young Henry met Eleanor at St-Denis in 1144, he could not have imagined that three years later she and King Louis would promise him their infant daughter Marie in marriage, that twenty-one years later he would marry her, and that after his death Countess Marie would preserve his principality for almost two decades for their sons.

Chapter 2

The Second Crusade, 1146–1151

On 1 December 1145, shortly before Henry turned eighteen, Pope Eugenius III addressed a bull, *Quantum praedecessores*, to King Louis VII and the great lords of France with a full bill of particulars justifying a crusade to shore up the Latin crusader states after the fall of Edessa and the destruction of its Christian community by Zengi (23 December 1144).[1] The death of Pope Lucius II (15 February 1145) and the elevation of Eugenius III three days later delayed the Curia's response to a looming threat to the very presence of Latins in the Holy Land.[2] But by late spring 1145, after news of Edessa arrived in France, Louis VII decided to undertake a pilgrimage to Jerusalem, for reasons that are not entirely clear. William of Nangis claims that Louis sought to expiate the wanton killing of innocents at Vitry, while the Chronicle of Morigny states that he was moved by the stories of Edessa's fall and the afflictions of its Christian community as reported by legates sent from Antioch and Jerusalem.[3] It may well be that Louis seized the occasion to expunge the memory of several unsavory deeds, including his intemperate oath taken against the elected bishop of Bourges and his meddling in episcopal elections.[4] By late 1145 the royal and papal motives converged with the Cistercians' call for a holy war, especially by Bernard of Clairvaux and Bishop Geoffroy of Langres. Young Henry of Champagne was soon drawn into a vortex of events that would consume his life for the next three years and ultimately mark him and a generation of young companions for the rest of their lives.

Louis VII and the Cistercians

The king celebrated Christmas at Bourges in 1145. After a crown wearing, he announced his plan to go to Jerusalem. Then Bishop Geoffroy gave a fiery speech recounting the destruction of Edessa that elicited a "great lamentation," according to Odo of Deuil, the king's chaplain.[5] The bishop had just returned from southern France, where Bernard of Clairvaux preached against a certain monk Henry, who had been condemned at the Council of Pisa (1135) for speaking against the church establishment.[6] Bishop Geoffroy, a cousin and close associate of Bernard since 1113, had served as prior of Clairvaux and indeed as Bernard's alter ego before being elected the first Cistercian bishop of Langres (1138–63), thanks to Bernard's intervention in a sharply contested election.[7] That the bishop spoke so fervently about a mission to the East suggests that a crusade project had crystallized within Cistercian circles and was known to Bernard, who easily moved from fulminating against heretics to preaching against the heathen. But the bull authorizing an armed expedition to combat the infidel had not yet arrived in France when Louis announced at Bourges what was troubling him—"the business of God, namely the expedition to Jerusalem."[8] The attending barons, mindful of the king's recent acts, were disinclined to accompany him overseas and gave a cool response. Without papal sponsorship and a coherent rationale, the king's proposal appeared to be an ill-conceived personal quest. In light of that indecisive meeting, it was decided to reconvene three months later at Vézelay. In the intervening months, between Christmas 1145 and Easter 1146, the nature of the king's venture changed, as his pilgrimage, the pope's crusade, and the Cistercian war against dissident Christians merged into one great undertaking against the "heathen." In the end, the barons were swept up by the call of the Cistercians, who made the crusade their own.[9]

In response to Louis's request, the pope reissued *Quantum praedecessores* (1 March 1146) in time for the king's Easter Council (31 March) at Vézelay.[10] Louis, appearing with a prominently displayed cross, made an impassioned speech: "We are men of virtue who will resist the heathen," he pronounced, according to the chronicler of Morigny, thus transforming his personal pilgrimage into a full-blown military expedition against the Muslims.[11] In a field outside the church, Bernard gave a characteristically powerful sermon in support of the expedition. So many lords and knights had come to Vézelay to take the cross, the king's chaplain reported, that the precut crosses did not suffice and clothing had to be torn into crosses on the spot. A large contingent of Champenois barons and prelates attended, with the notable exception of Count Thibaut, who was, as a scribe from St-Denis discreetly put it, "still living at the time."[12] It is not clear whether he was still angry over the destruction of Vitry and did not wish to be under the king's command, or whether his age (fifty-five) was a factor. But it would have been unthinkable, given Thibaut's close friendship with Bernard of Clairvaux, that a count of Champagne not support the Cistercian enterprise, and so young Henry, then nineteen, took the cross in his father's stead. Henry's presence at the council, in fact, was remarked. One writer described him on that occasion as "a young man, generous (*largius*), wise, and of magnanimous heart."[13] Otto of Freising named only two of the "great and illustrious men" at Vézelay, Count Thierry of Flanders and Henry, "son of Thibaut, count of Blois."[14]

A number of young nobles from southern Champagne accompanied Henry to Vézelay, including Anselm and Garnier of Traînel, Jacques and Anseric of Chacenay, Walter II of Montjay/Châtillon, William III of Nevers and Renaud of Tonnerre, and many unnamed others.[15] Among the prelates was Thibaut of Payns, abbot of Ste-Colombe of Sens and son of Hugh of Payns, founder of the Templars.[16] Young Henry also met a number of regional princes who would become close to him on that expedition: Count Thierry of Flanders; the king's brothers Robert (count of Dreux) and Peter of Courtenay; Count Renaud of Joigny and his brother Guy; and a host of barons from Burgundy, including the seneschal Renier of La Roche-Vanneau (brother of Bishop Geoffroy of Langres) and Josbert of Laferté-sur-Aube, the viscount of Dijon who already had made a substantial donation to Clairvaux, which Henry witnessed, in anticipation of Vézelay.[17] The one important lord missing from Vézelay, and from the expedition, was Henry's brother-in-law Odo II, duke of Burgundy, who like Count Thibaut may not have been able to overcome a deep antipathy toward the king after the destruction of Vitry, the home of his wife Marie of Champagne.

The assembled barons and knights took the cross after a reading of the papal bull. Beyond the remission of sins, it promised them several concrete privileges for undertaking the expedition, notably protection of their properties and families during their absence, and exemption from judicial suit and the repayment of debts until their return from the East. The bull also allowed crusaders to mortgage their fiefs, after duly informing their relatives and lords, to religious communities and to individual ecclesiastics as well as to laymen. That attention to detail struck just the right chord to lure a reluctant laity to a problematic venture. The pope sounded one note of caution, however. Echoing Bernard of Clairvaux's treatise in praise of the "new knighthood," Eugenius reminded those who had taken the cross to dress appropriately and to forswear fancy apparel and gilded or silvered arms; they should be sober and focused on fighting the infidel. They would meet the next spring to depart from St-Denis on the Fair of Lendit, 11 June 1147, exactly three years after the dedication of St-Denis.

Bernard and a host of preachers took copies of the papal bull as they set out to recruit crusaders. Preaching in the Rhineland, Bernard famously critiqued heretics and secular clerics in Cologne, implicitly conflating religious nonconformists with Muslims as enemies.[18] In August he toured Flanders before proceeding through Brabant and Namur; by November he had passed through Liège, Worms, and Mainz. He met Emperor Conrad III at Frankfurt and later at Speyer, where Conrad took the cross (27 December).[19] Through personal charisma and his letters, Bernard effectively transformed the crusade from an exclusively French enterprise, as framed in the papal bull, into a larger French-German one.[20] In the meantime, Louis wrote to the Byzantine emperor, Manuel Komnenos, announcing the expedition and requesting permission for his forces to traverse the emperor's lands and visit markets along the way. In August 1146 Manuel promised Louis and his army a warm welcome during their journey through his lands in order to fight the Turks.[21]

By the time Bernard returned to Clairvaux on 6 February 1147, the momentum of preparation was palpable. On 2 February Louis met Conrad at Châlons to coordinate their expeditions, and on 16 February he met with his great lords and prelates at Étampes to set the route of march. Ambassadors of Roger II of Sicily promised support for a maritime passage in the Mediterranean, but the decision was made to take the overland route, to follow the Danube to Constantinople. Another delicate question regarded the appointment of a guardian of the realm in the king's absence. It must have been an awkward moment for both Louis and Count Thibaut, who apparently was present at Étampes.[22] A decade earlier Thibaut had accompanied young Louis to Bordeaux for marriage, and he still ranked among the most esteemed princes of northern France after the debacle of Vitry. In a face-saving gesture, the king allowed the assembled barons and prelates to choose a guardian; they selected Suger and Count William II of Nevers. But since William already had decided to join the Carthusians and could not be dissuaded, Suger became the sole guardian.[23] Only in June, after the expedition was underway and in the absence of Count Thibaut, did Louis name a secular colleague to act with Suger, none other than the seneschal Ralph, count of Vermandois and Thibaut's nemesis. It must have been a bitter moment for Thibaut, and further evidence that the king's resentment still ran deep despite their formal reconciliation. The next spring at the Council of Reims (March 1148), Thibaut was heard to predict that Ralph, who continued to defy ecclesiastical sanctions for repudiating his legitimate wife, Thibaut's niece, would not be long for the world and would lack progeny. John of Salisbury recalled ca. 1164 that many still alive at that time could vouch for that prediction, which had come to pass.[24]

The Crusade

In the spring of 1147 Pope Eugenius came to France to launch the crusade. He stopped at Clairvaux on 6 April to meet with his old friend and mentor Abbot Bernard, and five days later, on 11 April, he arrived in Troyes, where he preached an expansive version of crusade, of Christian war against non-Christians, Slavs as well as Muslims.[25] Henry certainly heard the pope's speech, and as leader of the Champenois contingent, he must have met Eugenius in private. Ever since Vézelay, Henry had been preparing for the expedition, sealing documents as "son of Count Thibaut" for barons and knights selling property, including fiefs, for their crusade expenses. In one case he and his father together passed through their hands a fief given to Clairvaux by two brothers with the consent of their wives, sons, and daughters, and their lord Hugh, viscount of Laferté-sur-Aube, just as prescribed by the papal bull authorizing the alienation of fiefs to religious institutions.[26] Castle lords, too, sold, mortgaged, and leased their properties to raise cash for the expedition. Henry and his father witnessed Milo I, lord of Nogent-sur-Seine, sell property and revenues to the nuns of the Paraclete for the substantial sum of 120*l.*[27] In the second week of June 1147, on the eve of his departure, Walter II of Brienne and his wife and two sons confirmed his grandfather's gift to the priory of Notre-Dame of Ramerupt; the next day, before he and his eldest son set out, Walter sealed a second document, consenting to any future gifts by his fief-holders to the priory, proving the force of the papal bull in encouraging the transfer of fiefs to religious houses.[28] The widespread alienation of landed fiefs, few of which were ever recovered by their knightly proprietors, was one unintended consequence of the papal bull in Champagne.[29]

Henry arrived at St-Denis with a large force of Champenois barons and knights in early June 1147. Some fathers came with their sons, like Walter II of

Châtillon and his son Guy, and Count Walter II of Brienne and his son Erard. Several came with their brothers, like Anselm and Garnier of Traînel, Jacques and Anseric of Chacenay, Renaud and Odo of Pougy, and Count Renaud and Guy of Joigny. Others came alone: Count Milo III of Bar-sur-Seine, Clarembaud III of Chappes, Geoffroy III of Joinville, Anseric I of Montréal, Bartholomew of Vignory, and newly married Hugh III of Broyes-Commercy.[30] The recently widowed Milo I of Nogent-sur-Seine was among the few mature men from distinguished local families. With virtually every baronial lineage represented, the Champenois made up a sizable contingent of castle lords and knights (there is no evidence of women from this region on the crusade, perhaps reflecting the strong Cistercian presence in Champagne). Henry, just twenty, developed very close friendships with several young barons from southern Champagne in their twenties and thirties, particularly the Traînel and Pougy brothers and Geoffroy of Joinville. By virtue of their crusade experiences and subsequent prominence in Champagne through Count Henry's rule and beyond, they were "the generation of '47."

The Overland March

On 11 June 1147 the crusaders met at St-Denis for the ceremonial departure. Dignitaries included Pope Eugenius, King Louis, Queen Eleanor, the dowager queen Adelaide, Abbots Suger and Bernard, and a crowd of dukes, counts, castle lords, and knights.[31] After the king received the standard (*oriflamme*) of St-Denis, the long column of carts, mounted men and their wives, and an assortment of hangers-on set out for Metz, the designated jumping-off point for the overland journey to Constantinople (see Map 2).[32] According to a later report, Henry and Louis together led a force of two hundred nobles, suggesting that they traveled together.[33] Henry, the youngest regional prince, was accompanied by his chaplain Martin and carried a personal letter of introduction from Bernard of Clairvaux addressed to the emperor of Constantinople, asking Manuel to gird Henry with his sword.[34] Arriving at Metz (15 June), Louis and Henry were greeted by Archbishop Adalberon, who gave them gifts in appreciation for his own earlier reception in Paris.[35] Louis gave the order of march and received oaths of loyalty from the principal leaders, but discipline proved problematic from the start, presaging internal problems that continued to plague the expedition.[36] The French passed through a succession of prosperous German towns—Worms on the Rhine (29 June), Würzburg, Regensburg, and Passau—before arriving in Hungary in mid-July. Louis wrote to Suger that they had arrived safely but, as he mentioned in all his subsequent letters, he needed money.[37] On 4 October, after a difficult journey of almost four more months, Louis reported, the army arrived at Constantinople.[38]

Emperor Manuel Komnenos received the king with honor, Louis wrote, perhaps because he was appropriately deferential but also because the French army was, despite several incidents, better disciplined than the Germans who had preceded them.[39] The two monarchs established an immediate rapport on learning that they were the same age—twenty-seven—and same height.[40] The king and his entourage were quartered in the imperial summer residence in the Philopation park, just beyond the city walls and the imperial palace of Blachernae. We do not know where Count Henry was quartered. But when Manuel escorted Louis on a tour of the city and its religious monuments, Henry surely must have been among the princes invited to accompany the two monarchs.[41] He would have seen the real splendor of the imperial residence, which, as the king's chaplain Odo of Deuil put it, "surpasses anything I can say about it."[42] Odo marveled at the beauty of the many churches with their troves of relics, and was particularly impressed by the relics in the chapel of Constantine's palace, the church of the Virgin of Pharos, which held the Holy Lance, the Cross, the Crown of Thorns, and the Shroud.[43] The emperor then honored Louis with a great banquet, again probably attended by Henry and the leading French lords.

The French spent ten days camped outside of Constantinople before setting out for Asia Minor. At some point Henry presented the emperor his letter of introduction from Bernard of Clairvaux. After requesting that Manuel aid the French army in its passage through Asia Minor, Bernard praised young Henry as "the son of the illustrious prince Count Thibaut, a young man, noble and of fine character, who has devoted his early years under arms (*militia*) to the pursuit of justice rather than maliciousness (*malitia*). He is the son of a man whose love of truth, kindness, and justice has made him loved and honored among princes." Drawn up "in the name of Bernard" by the abbot's secretary, Nicholas of Montiéramey, the letter captures the contrast between the true ideals of knighthood, which Bernard had ascribed to the Templars, and the rough comportment of secular knights.[44] Bernard asked the emperor to gird Henry with the sword against the enemies of Christ. Reminding him that many venues were available for such a ceremony, Bernard asked Manuel to confer that special honor on Henry at the Byzantine court so that "he will remember it for the rest of his life." In light of subsequent events, it appears

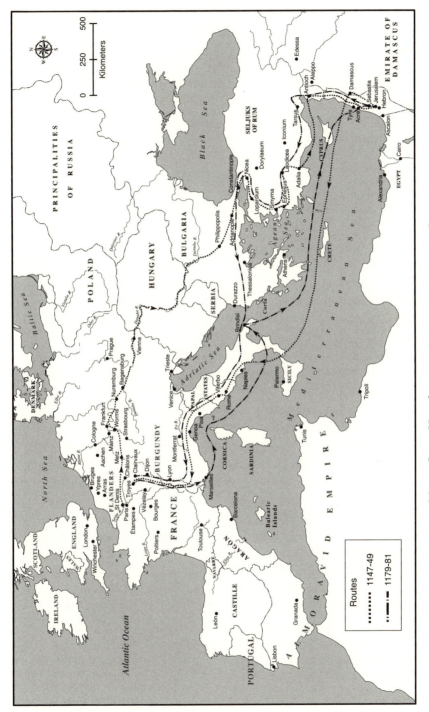

Map 2. Count Henry's overseas journeys, 1147–49, 1179–81.

that Manuel did ceremonially gird Henry in a traditional giving of arms before the French army crossed over to Asia Minor.[45]

After being transported across the Bosporus, the king and emperor came to terms regarding passage of the crusaders through imperial lands. The barons finally did homage to the emperor, as he demanded, after discussion revealed that homages for multiple fiefs were perfectly acceptable in France, and so a homage to the emperor would in no way diminish their loyalty to King Louis.[46] The Champenois would have recognized it as "homage saving fidelity" to one's primary lord. In return, the emperor offered the barons gifts. If Henry received a piece of the "true cross," which he later gave to his chaplain, it would suggest that the twenty-year-old count had charmed the emperor just as he had the king and queen of France (all in their mid-twenties) during their overland journey.[47]

The French and German armies took separate routes in Asia Minor, with Conrad III's forces heading directly eastward and Louis's army taking the southern coastal route, to arrive at Ephesus by Christmas. A few days later Henry distinguished himself in the first serious engagement against the Turks. Odo of Deuil gives a detailed account of the event, which became one of the expedition's few memorable moments. The Turks had set an ambush, sending three mounted archers to confront the French who were crossing the swollen waters of the Meander, while the rest of Turkish troops created a distracting din. Counts Henry, Thierry of Flanders, and William IV of Mâcon with their respective contingents charged the archers, pushing through the river to the other bank and forcing the Turks to retreat. King Louis did the same against the enemy in the rear.[48] William of Tyre cited that engagement in his history of the Western occupation of the Levant, noting that the crusading army took much booty after that encounter, and Niketas Choniates later expanded its significance as marking the beginning of the Frankish army's success.[49] The only misfortune signaled by Odo of Deuil was the drowning of Milo of Nogent, an esteemed Champenois castle lord and benefactor of the nuns at the Paraclete under Abbess Heloise.[50]

Henry's close contact with Louis during the march to and beyond Constantinople, and his exploit at the Meander, forged a bond that survived the disastrous ascent of Mount Cadmus in the first days of January 1148, when Louis lost control of his army, which was almost annihilated.[51] Louis later wrote to Suger of the many who died there, mentioning Walter II of Montjay (Châtillon) and Count Renaud I of Tonnerre, younger brother of William II of Nevers.[52] Mount Cadmus was a defining event of the expedition, comparable to the destruction of the German army at Dorylaeum the previous October. Louis surrendered command of his army to the Templars, who were comprised largely of barons and knights from the six commanderies founded in Champagne.[53] After reorganizing the remnants of the French forces, the Templars led the march to the port of Adalia, where they arrived on 20 January 1148.

It is not clear whether Henry accompanied the king and queen, who sailed from Adalia with a number of barons and prelates directly to Antioch, or took the land route with his companions and knights to meet the king there in March.[54] The prince of Antioch, Eleanor's uncle Raymond of Toulouse, wanted the depleted and dispirited French forces to move against the Turks in the north, whereas Louis was determined to see Jerusalem, the ultimate goal of his pilgrimage. The stay in Antioch was further complicated by Eleanor's intimate talks with Raymond, which incited malicious rumors in the army and led to the king's precipitous departure for Jerusalem in May.[55] Since the recovery of Edessa seemed unlikely, and indeed pointless given its destruction, it was agreed to hold a council of war at Palmarea near Acre (24 June) to decide on the next course of action. William of Tyre describes the most prominent French barons in attendance beside Emperor Conrad, his half-brother Otto, bishop of Freising, and Frederick, duke of Swabia (and future emperor). The list includes Count Thierry of Flanders ("a magnificent count"), Count Ivo (of Nesle) of Soissons ("a wise and faithful man"), Robert of Dreux ("count of Perche and the king's brother"), and Henry of Champagne, "the eldest son of Lord Thibaut, count of Troyes, son-in-law of the lord king, and a young man of fine character." In identifying Henry as Louis's son-in-law (*gener*), the chronicler suggests that Louis and Eleanor already had promised Henry their three-year-old daughter Marie in marriage.[56] Two years earlier Count Geoffroy of Anjou had pressed Louis to betroth the infant Marie to his own son Henry, then thirteen, but that project failed to materialize after Bernard complained that the couple was too closely related.[57] By a curious turn of fate, Henry of Anjou would marry instead Marie's mother Eleanor after her divorce in 1152 and make her queen of England.

The attack on Damascus, which had been decided at Palmarea after much debate, did not go well in the face of stiff resistance and an influx of fresh Muslim forces.[58] By mid-July it was abandoned, and most crusaders, including Henry and his companions, prepared to return home after visiting the obligatory sites in Jerusalem and Sebastia, where the bones of John the Baptist had recently been discovered (1145) in the church of St John.[59] Louis and

Eleanor decided to linger at the holy sites, and as a parting gift Louis gave Henry an exceptionally laudatory letter of appreciation addressed to Count Thibaut. Louis spoke of his friendship with Henry, who had displayed "devotion at all times" and whose "loyal service" had earned his gratitude and affection.[60] In light of their later close relationship, the king's letter expressed a genuine attachment to Henry. But the letter had another purpose as well. It notified Thibaut that Louis would return after the next Easter (3 April 1149) and therefore asked the count, by virtue of his fidelity and respect for the crown, to serve as guardian of the realm and to see that no harm came to it until Louis returned. The conflation of the language of friendship with the language of duty signaled the king's attempt to mend his frayed relationship with Thibaut.[61]

The Return Voyage

It took Henry about five months to reach Champagne by early March 1149 (see Map 2). Only one thing is certain about his return voyage: it was perilous. The bishop of Troyes later remarked that Henry described the dangers he encountered on land and sea while returning from Jerusalem, and that "fearing death, he swore an oath to God and to St Nicholas" to fund three canons in the church at Pougy. The three brother-lords of Pougy—Odo, Renaud, and Manasses—agreed to endow two canons, making for a chapter of five canons. According to the bishop of Troyes, Henry fulfilled his vow shortly after becoming count of Troyes.[62] Why Pougy? Probably because Henry was traveling with Odo of Pougy, soon to become his constable, and perhaps also with his brother Manasses, a cathedral canon who became the first provost of Henry's chapel (and later bishop of Troyes).[63] Henry was not the only one to suffer a stormy return: Count William III of Nevers had a similar experience and made a similar vow in order to escape burial at sea.[64]

It is highly probable that Henry returned via Sicily and spent several weeks in Palermo with King Roger II before proceeding northward. That was the preferred route of returning crusaders. Louis took it in the fall of 1149 and wrote to Suger that he was entertained by Roger in Palermo for several weeks while waiting for Eleanor's ship.[65] Henry had personal reasons, as well, to visit Roger. His oldest sister, Elizabeth/Isabelle, then about twenty, had married Roger's son, Roger of Apulia, several years earlier (1140/43).[66] Besides seeing her again, Henry might have wanted to visit the ruler who had sent Count Thibaut the sumptuous crystal ewer on the occasion of her marriage, and which Thibaut presented to Suger at the dedication of St-Denis in 1144.[67] There was another possible reason. Roger's name had been mentioned often in the course of the crusade: his ambassadors had offered to transport Louis and his barons by sea from southern France to the Levant, and in Constantinople the French certainly heard stories of Roger's exploits against the Greeks in the Mediterranean, especially the capture of Thebes and Corinth in the fall of 1147, shortly before the French arrived in Constantinople.[68] Roger II was clearly a person to be reckoned with in the eastern Mediterranean, and a future count of Champagne might well profit from meeting him.

If Henry did visit his sister and Roger II, he would have witnessed the construction of a new palace in Palermo with its attached church, the Capella Palatina, as the capital of an expanding Sicilian kingdom. Construction began in 1143 and was well advanced by the late 1140s when Henry saw it.[69] It would have given the young count a sense of the ambitions of one of the more prominent rulers in the Mediterranean. Constantinople and Jerusalem were of course impressive cities, but they were of ancient and inimitable provenance. If there was any model for the construction of an entirely new capital for a new state, it was Palermo and Sicily under Roger II. After visiting Palermo, Henry likely traveled to Rome to meet with Pope Eugenius, whom he had met earlier in Troyes and at St-Denis at the beginning of the crusade, then took the "French road" from Rome over the Alps to Dijon and ultimately to Champagne.

An Apprentice Count

With the king still abroad in the spring of 1149, the regent Suger was troubled by the easy violence of the returning veterans. He urged Louis to return as soon as possible because "the barons and princes of the realm" were "perturbing" the kingdom, "wolves" were seizing lands, and the realm was exposed to the rapacious.[70] Suger implicated the king's brother Robert, who was stirring some barons to rebellion in hopes of usurping the throne, even though Suger assured Louis that he had preserved the king's courts, tallages, and revenues in anticipation of his return.[71] Suger faced an equally serious challenge in the tournaments being conducted by returning crusaders. Ecclesiastical councils at Clermont (1130), Reims (1131), the Lateran (1139), and most recently at Reims (March 1148) severely condemned jousts and tournaments, which had been suspended during the Second Crusade.[72] But with the return of seasoned combatants, those diverting events resumed in the spring of 1149. It is not known why Henry joined the king's brother in sponsoring a tournament at that time, for he risked alienating Bernard of Clairvaux, a close friend of the family. Bernard was well known for having railed against tournaments, especially in his *In Praise of the New Knighthood* justifying the new order of Knights Templar at the Council of Troyes (1129). He painted a devastating picture of knights decked out in their finery and luxurious trappings while engaged in gratuitous violence.[73] Bernard protested to Suger, asking him to "take the sword of the spirit" and prohibit the scheduled tournament. The kingdom is at peace, but those two (Robert and Henry) are troubling the realm in the king's absence, complained Bernard, and since you, Suger, are in charge, you should prevent it. Bernard advised Suger that he was sending the same letter to the archbishops of Reims and Sens, the bishops of Soissons and Auxerre, and to Counts Thibaut and Ralph of Vermandois, in effect, putting Suger on notice that his actions, or lack thereof, would bear scrutiny.[74]

Nevertheless a *tornamentum* was held at the traditional opening of the tournament season after Easter (11 April). Technically it violated the prohibition of tournaments during the crusade, for the king was still overseas and his realm was still under papal protection.[75] The outcome of the tournament was singularly inconvenient for Henry, whose companion Anseric of Montréal was captured by Suger's man, Renaud of Pomponne. In an exceedingly deferential letter to Suger, Henry mentioned their friendship and mutual affection, and he asked to meet Suger at Meaux to resolve the matter.[76] Perhaps the issue at hand had less to do with a ransom than with Renaud's unchivalrous tactics leading to Anseric's defeat, for Renaud's subsequent murder was taken to illustrate how the wheel of fortune could turn against the high and mighty.[77]

The prospect of ex-crusaders about in the land prompted Suger to convoke an assembly of prelates in Soissons on 8 May 1149 to discuss the grave state of affairs threatening the peace of the realm in the king's continued absence.[78] Two months later the pope authorized Archbishop Hugh of Sens to summon the troublemakers to determine whether they had changed their behavior, and if contemptuous, they were to be excommunicated.[79] That may well have occasioned Countess Matilda's complaint to Bernard of Clairvaux about her son's bad behavior. Bernard tried to console the countess with the thought that young men are prone to evil deeds, and counseled her continued maternal love for him despite his lack of filial piety. The abbot concluded, "I wish he would treat others as he has treated me, for he has always done whatever I requested."[80] Duly chastised by both Suger and Bernard, Henry soon turned from tournaments to state building, a task that consumed him for the next two decades. By 11 November 1149 Louis had returned to Paris by way of Cluny, and Henry settled in to acting like a responsible young count within his father's lands.

Henry was twenty-two in the spring of 1149 when his father, then fifty-seven, transferred his two easternmost counties, Vitry and Bar-sur-Aube, to Henry. During the next two years Count Henry sealed under both titles, but he preferred to hold court at Bar-sur-Aube, where he began to construct a new residence in the walled town astride an old Roman road connecting Langres, Châlons, and Reims to Flanders in the north.[81] He continued to appear with his father, as if they were exercising a transitional, condominium type of lordship preparatory to Henry's full succession. At Igny abbey they heard the suit brought by the abbot of St-Médard of Soissons against the mayor of Igny in a complex case vented in the presence of five local provosts.[82] At Florent-en-Argonne, Thibaut and Henry, "who now has part of my land," said the old count, confirmed Clairvaux's earlier acquisition of their fiefs, and both sealed in the presence of Countess Mathilda and her younger sons Thibaut and Stephen, who marked their *signa*.[83] But another court session, in which Henry judged alone, pointed to the future. The case involved a "very serious dispute" between Belin, the mayor of Bar-sur-Aube, who had built mills on the Aube River, and the monks of the priory of Mont-Bar, who held the monopoly of milling within Bar-sur-Aube.[84] Henry reached a face-saving resolution: Belin would surrender half of the mills to the monks in the form of an annual payment of milled grain, which his miller would swear to the monks and the count to render honestly. Witnesses included key members of Henry's future court: Peter the Bursar, the marshal Geoffroy (of Chartres), Henry's chaplain Nicholas (of Montiéramey), the notary William, who made the stenographic record of the court session and wrote the final document, and the chancellor William, who presented the document to the monks at Bar-sur-Aube. Count Thibaut and Bernard of Clairvaux observed but did not otherwise participate in the proceeding.

The Death of Count Thibaut

Count Thibaut was about sixty when he died on 10 January 1152 at Lagny, where he had often sought spiritual renewal with the Benedictine monks of St-Pierre.[85] For Thibaut, Lagny was not just a quiet retreat. The monastery housed the bones of Saint Thibaut, who died in 1066 and was sanctified in 1073. The saint's brother Arnold, abbot of Lagny, had the remains translated to Lagny and placed in the church of St-Thibaut-des-Vignes at the gate of the abbey.[86] A late twelfth-century *vita* celebrated the saint as a noble-born son from Provins who renounced his family's wealth and worldly temptations for a monastic life, the very model that had tempted Count Thibaut himself before he was dissuaded by Norbert of Xantan.[87] Count Henry later repaid the monks of Lagny for the many expenses they had incurred during his father's frequent visits, and he recalled with appreciation that his father had been buried with great respect in a worthy tomb.[88] It was a porphyry tomb, seven to eight feet long by four feet wide; eight columns on a double-tiered base supported a single plain slab devoid of any inscription or religious symbol. It was placed over the bones of the count's namesake Saint Thibaut.[89]

Count Henry founded an anniversary Mass for "my father, the illustrious count of Blois," at the nearby cathedral of Meaux, where the canons enjoyed a special meal of bread, wine, and meat on that occasion.[90] Monastic obituary notices throughout the region remembered the old count for his piety and good lordship, as well as for his benefactions. "A most Christian man and illustrious prince," recalled the canons of St-Loup of Troyes.[91] William, the monk at St-Denis who wrote a biography of Suger, passed over Thibaut's long, contentious strife with Louis VII with a quote from Ecclesiastes 44:17: "In the time of anger, he fostered reconciliation."[92] Abbot Arnold of Bonneval, who had known Thibaut since the 1130s, penned a long encomium at the end of his biography of Bernard of Clairvaux. "No one dared to say or to do anything unseemly in his presence," he wrote.[93] Arnold mentioned the count's perseverance while the king subjected his lands to fire, rapine, depopulation, and widespread devastation (in 1142), and he placed Thibaut in the company of Job, Solomon, and Absalom. For Arnold, Thibaut was the Cistercians' most powerful and constant benefactor. He purchased land, constructed houses, and contributed money to the abbey. He made charitable contributions and gave clothing to the poor; his court was open to the needs of religious; and his lands were a port for all who sought refuge, perhaps an allusion to Abelard's exile in Provins and at the Paraclete, where Heloise was still abbess. Arnold concluded by describing Thibaut's two magnificent gifts to Clairvaux, the first consisting of "two immensely heavy and wonderfully crafted gold vases" acquired from the treasury of his uncle, Henry I of England, and the second a collection of Thibaut's own jewels, which the abbey was supposed to sell to pay for its needs.[94] But the most extravagant memorial to Thibaut was an allegorical miniature painting in a copy of Hugh of Fouilloy's *De avibus*, composed not long after Thibaut's death. Much copied in Cistercian circles, *De avibus* depicts Christ as a cedar tree. But in this unique copy the figure of Christ is replaced by a layman seated in majesty, with hands extended in a gesture of generosity, surrounded by sparrows in front of a tree inscribed "This cedar was Count Thibaut." That Thibaut symbolically displaced Christ testifies to the old count's stature within reformed monastic circles.[95]

Contemporary chroniclers were struck by Thibaut's division of his lands among his three sons in that it severed the lands in Blois-Chartres from all the lands east of the royal domain, and by the fact that his eldest son did not take his father's title and paternal inheritance in western France. Henry instead took all of Thibaut's lands east of the royal domain, in effect attaching Brie to Count Hugh's three southern counties of Troyes, Bar-sur-Aube, and Vitry (see Map 1). The county of Blois and its title passed to the second son, Thibaut (V), while the lands ("honor") of Sancerre went to the third son, Stephen, who appropriated a new title, "count" of Sancerre.[96] If the tripartite division of Thibaut's lands seemed unconventional at the time, it appears that Thibaut had decided it under the influence of several imperatives. The first was a structural problem inherent in his vast array of lands. Could a rambling collection of lands extending from Chartres in the west to Vitry in the east remain a viable political entity in mid-twelfth-century France, even in the hands of a vigilant and forceful prince? The answer was clear. The future belonged to more compact territorial states. The division of Thibaut's lands into relatively cohesive entities was a recognition of how the political environment in France had changed in the previous half century. But how would those entities be allocated among the three inheriting sons? Again, the answer was clear. The eldest would take the more valuable share, not necessarily the paternal inheritance. By the mid-1140s the unstoppable expansion of the Angevins, culminating in the conquest of Normandy and dominance in western France, portended an unenviable future for the county of Blois, boxed in as it was between the royal domain and the Angevins, even though Thibaut had made peace with Count Geoffroy of Anjou and dubbed his eldest son in 1149.[97] The county of Blois had passed its apogee; the future lay in Thibaut's lands east of the royal domain, where Henry was born and spent his formative years.

The chroniclers did not mention it, but Thibaut himself had planned to decouple his western and eastern lands. The rapid economic development of the rural economy of Champagne and its commercial fairs already was evident, principally in Provins, which was attracting foreign merchants. Thibaut paid close attention to the security of roads leading to his fairs and to the fairs themselves as venues for commercial exchange. He shifted the fair at Épernay to Troyes (1136), renewed the fair of St-Martin in Provins (1137), and established a second fair in the upper town of Provins (1140s), making for three fairs in Provins. At the same time he fostered three commercial fairs in Troyes.[98] Taken together, those acts constituted an economic policy that looked forward to developing the potential of his eastern lands. The chroniclers noted only the anomalous inheritance division, not its rationale.

The *eruditi* and *literati* prelates of the time remembered Thibaut rather for his character: he was a model prince. John of Salisbury recalled that Count Thibaut was known for "his pursuit of justice and reputation for uprightness, a reverence for the church and generosity toward the poor," while Robert of Torigni remembered him as "a prince of great sanctity and generosity to the poor.[99] Gerald of Wales, in his *Book on the Instruction of Princes* written ca. 1193, draws a portrait of Thibaut that any reader would instantly recognize as the antithesis of the formidable "tyrant," Henry II of England.[100] For Gerald, who was born ca. 1146 and knew of Count Thibaut only from what he had heard or read decades later, Thibaut's persona had acquired almost mythic standing. That is, Count Thibaut still stood as a real-life model prince four decades after his death: religious and pious, conspicuous supporter of the poor, and a countermodel to the English king. Robert of Auxerre, writing about the same time in the 1190s, summed up the most widely repeated image of Thibaut:

> There flourished at that time Thibaut, count of Champagne, father of orphans and protector of widows, eyes of the blind, feet of the deformed; singularly generous in supporting the poor, in fostering the monastic life, and in exhibiting an incomparable largess toward religious of all kinds. . . . Words do not suffice to describe the profuse generosity of his gifts, his love of the religious, and his encouragement of excellence.[101]

There was something else about Thibaut that Arnold of Bonneval captured inadvertently by linking Thibaut and Bernard of Clairvaux: their deaths marked the end of an age. The great era of Cistercian expansion peaked at midcentury. The Cistercian crusade ended in failure. And Bernard and Eugenius III died within weeks of each other in 1153. The age of Bernard's charismatic religious leadership, and of Count Thibaut's quiet piety, was over.

Perhaps Abbot Arnold had seen the swagger of the returning crusaders, a co-hort of high-energy young veterans who had "seen the world" and had en-countered diverse peoples, religions, customs, foods, and architecture—as Count Thibaut had not. Count Henry and his twenty-some companions were on the cusp of a new age.

Chapter 3

Count Palatine of Troyes, 1152–1158

Count Thibaut died at Lagny on 10 January 1152, just weeks after Henry turned twenty-five. Among those present at the interment was Prior Odolric of Ste-Foy of Coulommiers, which had received substantial benefactions from Thibaut and his mother, Adela. After the funeral, as Henry passed through Coulommiers, Odolric made the customary request of a new lord: would he confirm the letters his father and grandmother had sealed on behalf of the priory? The prior retrieved Thibaut's letter of 1132 with Henry's *signum* made as a five-year-old boy and asked an additional favor, which Henry graciously allowed, that "no one, except in my or my wife's presence, may chant in my chapel at Coulommiers without the consent of the said monks." A priory monk recopied Count Thibaut's earlier document with Henry's added concession, and Chancellor William presented the new letter to the prior after affixing Henry's seal.[1] That was exactly what was expected of a new lord.

Later that spring Henry attended a memorial service in Provins with his mother Countess Mathilda and his three brothers, Count Thibaut of Blois, Stephen (without title), and William (identified as a cleric). After the service Abbot Geoffroy of Lagny reminded Henry of the great expenses his monastery had incurred during his father's "very frequent visits." Thibaut found Lagny a perfect retreat, convenient for its location between his lands in Champagne and his ancestral lands in western France, and for its association with his namesake Saint Thibaut, whose relics were housed there. Acknowledging Lagny's hospitality, and in appreciation of "the great honor with which my father Thibaut was buried," Henry abolished the right of visitation long enjoyed by the comital family, provided that he and his three brothers and their entourages (but not their heirs) retained that right during their lifetimes. As an additional gift, Henry remitted 20 of the 108 *modii* of wine owed him by the abbey's new tenants so that the monks would celebrate his father's anniversary. Bishop Manasses of Meaux and a large contingent of his canons witnessed, as did four abbots, Henry's cousin Evrard of Le Puiset (viscount of Chartres), and two of Henry's crusade companions, Walter of Montmirail and Anseric of Montréal.[2]

Count Thibaut's death signaled the passing of a generation of rulers and prelates within a few short years: Abbot Suger of St-Denis and Count Geoffroy of Anjou in 1151, Emperor Conrad of Germany in 1152, Pope Eugenius III and Abbot Bernard of Clairvaux in 1153, and Roger II of Sicily and King Stephen of England in 1154. Touched by the deaths of so many pillars of the pre-crusade world, Henry commissioned Simon Aurea Capra, prior of St-Ayoul of Provins and a leading Latin poet of the day, to compose epitaphs for those he especially admired: his father Thibaut, Suger of St-Denis, and three prominent Cistercians—Bernard of Clairvaux, Pope Eugenius III, and Hugh of Mâcon (first abbot of Pontigny, who died 10 October 1151 as bishop of Auxerre).[3] Henry understood that he lived in a time of transition. He belonged to a cohort of young veterans bonded in the crucible of the Second Crusade, of prelates who began their careers around midcentury, and of secular canons who would staff the episcopal and princely governments of the post-crusade world. At the level of high politics, Henry would learn to maneuver between three young and exigent monarchs: Louis VII (1137–80), Henry II of England (1154–89), and Frederick I of Germany (1152–90).

Constructing a New Capital

During his first few months as count, Henry attended to the unfinished business of his father's last days. His earliest extant letters patent (20 February 1152) certified what his father "and his entire court" had decided in a suit brought by the cathedral canons of Troyes against Henry's crusade companions, the brothers Anselm II and Garnier of Traînel, regarding tenants in three villages. Since the decision had yet to be written up, the old count's chaplain, the physician William who had drafted Thibaut's letters since 1137, wrote Henry's letter and verified it by reading it aloud, in effect placing it in the public record, before adding Henry's seal.[4] The letter contains the earliest datable use of Henry's new title, "count palatine of Troyes." It was an invented title, obtained by adding his father's honorific "palatine" to Count Hugh's title "count of Troyes." Although "palatine" was long associated with the counts of

Blois, Thibaut's own scribes referred to him only by his ancestral title "count of Blois," even after he acquired Count Hugh's three counties in Champagne.[5] Henry might reasonably have adopted the more accurate and encompassing title "count of Champagne," which contemporaries used informally. In opting for the exclusive "palatine," he announced his special standing among the princes of the realm, as prospective son-in-law of the king of France, and as great-grandson of William the Conqueror and nephew of King Stephen of England. At the same time, "count of Troyes" shifted the locus of his comital authority from his father's inherited lands in Blois to Champagne, specifically to the county of Troyes, for which his father had done homage in 1143. It also anchored Henry in the city he intended to make his primary residence and the administrative center of his principality. "Count palatine of Troyes" remained his only title thereafter.

With his new title came a new round seal, typical of the equestrian pendant seals sported by a generation of barons after the Second Crusade.[6] Its main elements remain unchanged from his preaccession seal: he still rides his horse to the right and wears the same conical helmet with nosepiece, and his left hand holds a shield close to his body. But engravers altered the seal matrix so that his right arm no longer holds a lance with standard close to his body; rather, his arm extends outward, holding a sword pointing upward.[7] The inscription, too, was modified, from "seal of Henry, son of Count Thibaut" to "seal of Henry, count palatine of Troyes." His chancellor, who carried the seal matrix, used it to authenticate the count's acts by affixing it to wax on silk threads passed through slits in a parchment document, so that the seal was pendant and the document "patent."[8] Henry used that seal, with one slight change in 1176, for the rest of his life.[9]

Henry met his first serious challenge as count on 25 February 1152, barely six weeks after his succession. His chancellor drafted a letter describing it.[10] Appearing in the cathedral church of St-Pierre of Troyes, Henry expressed regret for having the bishop's man named Otranus seized within the suburb of St-Denis, just beyond the walls of the old city of Troyes where the cathedral was located (Figure 2). He had acted in anger, he admitted. His ancestors had given the suburb to the cathedral canons with exemption from his jurisdiction and taxes, and both he and his father had confirmed that privilege.[11] On reflection, and on the advice of Bernard of Clairvaux, he humbly recognized his misdeed in the chapter hall before the assembled canons, the bishop of Troyes (his maternal uncle Henry of Carinthia), and the abbots of Montier-le-Celle (his friend Peter), Clairvaux (Bernard), and Bonneval (Arnold, who was traveling with Bernard).[12] Present on Henry's behalf were several clerics and knights of his household staff as well as his crusade companions Anseric of Montréal, Hulduin of Vendeuvre, Hugh of Romilly, Odo of Pougy (the future constable), and William of Dampierre. Henry promised in the hand of the chapter's provost Odo (nephew of the former bishop) to pay a fine. And then, in a dramatic gesture, he turned a scene of contrition into one of triumph, as he presented his cap to the chapter's archdeacon and treasurer Guirric (another nephew of the former bishop) as a sign (*memoria*) that he recognized the ancient liberty and immunity of that suburb. It was an astute performance, and a hallmark of Henry's rule. It explains why he was so well liked, so well connected, and ultimately successful as count. Henry's cap became a kind of secular relic that would remain in the cathedral's treasury for six hundred years.[13]

The chancellor's letter passes over the reason for Henry's anger: the bishop's men had trespassed on ground being prepared for the construction of a new palace complex in the suburb of St-Denis, a prime undeveloped urban site, vacant except for the small rural parish church serviced by the cathedral canons. Recognizing the explosive nature of the issue—defending an old privilege against the project of an energetic young count—the canons asked Bernard of Clairvaux, as a longtime friend of the comital family, to intercede with Henry. The clash over jurisdiction within weeks of Thibaut's death suggests that work had already begun on the construction of a new comital residence to replace the antiquated one in the northwest corner of the Gallo-Roman city. The old half-hectare compound, with buildings dating to the tenth century, contained a private residential quarter, a public hall, a chapel, and a small donjon (twelve meters square) and tower.[14] But neither Thibaut nor Henry frequented what must have been an incommodious, claustrophobic place "with the air of a prison," which it later became.[15] Especially for Henry, who had visited far grander palaces during the crusade, notably the Great Palace in Constantinople and the palace and Cappella Palatina under construction in Palermo, the decrepit comital buildings in the old town of Troyes must have seemed quite unworthy of a palatine prince. The suburb of St-Denis, adjacent to both the old city and the commercial district just beyond the Seine, was an ideal location for a new princely residence. In constructing an entirely new urban quarter, Henry changed the topography of the city, transforming Troyes from an episcopal to a comital city and capital of his nascent principality.

The construction of a new princely compound was Henry's most visible

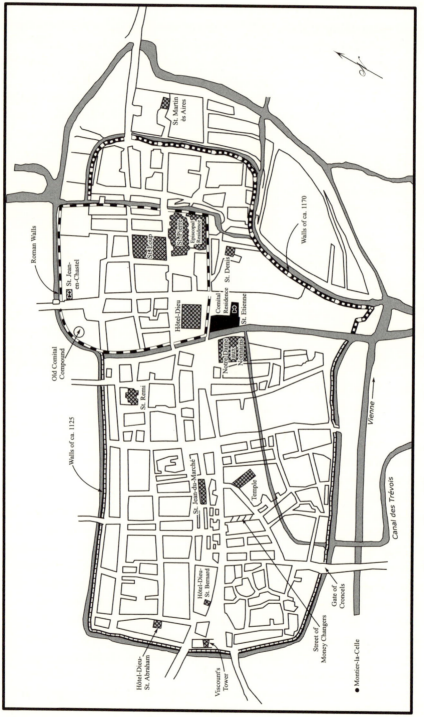

Figure 2. Plan of Troyes, based on Chapin, *Les villes de foires de Champagne*, planche 2.

St. Martin ès Aires

Roman Walls

Walls of ca. 1170

St. Jean-en-Chastel

St. Loup

Episcopal Residence

Old Comital Compound

St. Denis

Hôtel-Dieu

Comital Residence

St. Etienne

St. Remi

Notre-Dame aux Nonnains

Walls of ca. 1125

St. Jean-du-Marché

Temple

Hôtel-Dieu-St. Bernard

Vienne →

Canal des Trévois

Gate of Croncels

Street of Money Changers

Viscount's Tower

Hôtel-Dieu-St. Abraham

• Montier-la-Celle

Figure 3. Count Henry's residence and chapel, from Arnaud, *Voyage archéologique*, 25.

and symbolic act as new count, and it announced an ambitious ruler. Although the exact stages of construction cannot be determined, the project
appears to have been conceived as an integrated campus built around the
count's residence with a great hall and an attached chapel (Figure 3).[16] Twenty-
five house plots of identical size (20 x 50 meters), with gardens in the rear,
were laid out along a street five hundred meters long (later known as the
Street of the Close) for the resident canons who would staff the chapel and
serve in the count's administration (Figure 4). Since the entire complex fit
between two branches of the Seine River, it initially lacked an encircling wall.
In many respects the campus conformed to ninth-century models of a princely
palace.[17]

During the next five years the suburb of St-Denis was a busy construction
site, much like Suger's St-Denis a decade earlier, as the count's residence and
chapel gradually emerged from the ground and the canons built their individual houses. The significance of the count's project must have been apparent

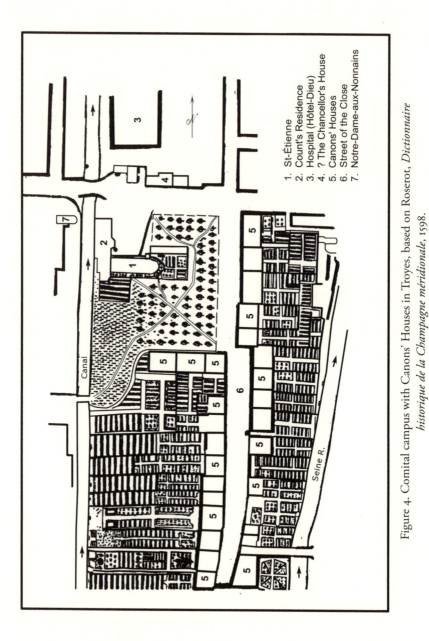

1. St-Étienne
2. Count's Residence
3. Hospital (Hôtel-Dieu)
4. ? The Chancellor's House
5. Canons' Houses
6. Street of the Close
7. Notre-Dame-aux-Nonnains

Figure 4. Comital campus with Canons' Houses in Troyes, based on Roserot, *Dictionnaire historique de la Champagne méridionale*, 1598.

from the start. The most powerful lord east of the royal domain was establishing his primary residence in an old episcopal town on the major trade route between the Mediterranean and northern Europe. That Henry would undertake such an ambitious program so soon after his succession is not surprising. Substantial new buildings were rising across France, not only at St-Denis and Sens, which furnished models for the new Gothic architectural style, but even in Paris, where Abbot Suger had restored the royal palace in the king's absence overseas.[18] The Cistercians, who had established a ubiquitous presence in Champagne, were still building their churches and granaries while in England, as Henry's brother William would have reported on his return, their uncle Bishop Henry of Winchester was investing huge resources in building manor houses, the most resplendent being Wolvesey, his primary episcopal residence in Winchester, dubbed "almost a palace."[19] Count Henry's project was of greater significance, however, in that like Roger II in Palermo, he was constructing a new capital for his principality. It would shift the center of gravity in Champagne from the northern plains, which his father had ruled through constant itineration, to a fixed center in the county's only episcopal town in the south.

While construction progressed, Henry immersed himself in the internal affairs of his principality. As he had on a smaller scale as count of Vitry and Bar-sur-Aube, he traveled through his lands holding court, confirming his father's acts, and, most important, presenting himself to his barons, townsmen, and prelates. In the spring of 1152 he visited Épernay, Châlons, and Reims. In Épernay he confirmed the Templars' rights over a mill and a fish pond at Neuville-au-Temple "in thanks for the service and honor that the brothers rendered me and my men in the Holy Land." He gave them as well a two-part letter announcing the resolution of a dispute that he and his father had decided earlier but not yet confirmed by letters patent.[20] At Châlons he confirmed the forfeiture of Guy of Possesse's fief at St-Amand to the canons of Châlons as penalty for the damages that Guy had inflicted on them.[21] In Reims, the largest and most important of the episcopal towns that ringed his lands, Henry gave the canons of St-Remi abbey the monopoly of fishing along the banks of the Marne at Condé, which his provosts would enforce. He did it, he said, "for the salvation of the soul of my father Count Thibaut and my ancestors, and also for my [own] prosperity and salvation."[22] In the presence of witnesses, he placed that gift symbolically on the high altar, where the relics of Saint Remi were flanked by two recently sculpted monumental stone tombs of Carolingian kings. Pope Urban II, a native of nearby Châtillon, had granted

St-Remi the right to crown the kings of France, and now Abbot Odo sought to bury them as well; the two monumental figures were part of his campaign, in competition with Suger at St-Denis, to obtain that privilege.[23]

With the King

Within weeks of his accession, Henry was drawn to events beyond the county. On 21 March 1152 at Beaugency, a council of ecclesiastics under Archbishop Hugh of Sens heard a number of prelates and relatives of the king and queen swear that the couple was too closely related for a canonical marriage, and so Queen Eleanor was granted the divorce she had sought three years earlier while on the Second Crusade. Leaving her two daughters, seven-year-old Marie and two-year-old Alice, in Paris, Eleanor headed south, managing to elude Count Thibaut V, who had taken a fancy to her in Paris (he later married her daughter Alice), to join and then marry young Henry of Anjou (18 May). Louis claimed that her failure to seek his permission to marry was a *casus belli*, and he confiscated Eleanor's lands.[24] Inevitably Count Henry was drawn into the conflict. He joined his cousin Eustace IV of Boulogne (son of King Stephen of England, who earlier had done homage to Louis for Normandy), and the king and his brother Count Robert of Dreux in attempting to capture Henry of Anjou, who was about to embark from Barfleur for England. Louis expected to conquer and divide Normandy and Aquitaine among his supporters, but his forces were checked and had to withdraw under a truce (19 July), leaving Normandy firmly in the hand of the Angevins.[25] Count Henry returned to Champagne, probably in late August, no doubt with a healthy respect for the count of Anjou's military skills.

Soon after the debacle at Barfleur, Henry was implicated in an affair involving his close companion Anselm II of Traînel. It arose because Henry had brokered a marriage for Anselm that went awry. We know about it because Anselm's cousin Guy Gasteblé, a young knight at the time and witness to the event, testified about it more than a half century later as a monk "ill and aged and fearing death."[26] As Guy recalled, Anselm married Alice of Donzy at Henry's suggestion, but after the ceremony (perhaps involving only the couple's consent to marry) Anselm failed to consummate the union, perhaps because Alice was still very young, and left her in the custody of her father, Geoffroy of Donzy. A short time later, according to Guy, Geoffroy gave Alice in marriage to Count Henry's own brother Stephen, count of Sancerre, with the castle of Neuilly and half of the town of Oulchy in Champagne as dowry. Deprived of his wife and her dowry, and publicly dishonored, Anselm complained to Henry, who in turn appealed to the king. Louis and Henry besieged and soon captured the castle of St-Aignan, where the couple was celebrating their nuptials, forcing Geoffroy of Donzy to give Anselm the dowry promised for a legitimately contracted but unconsummated marriage.

Henry's joint action with Louis at Barfleur and at St-Aignan strengthened the ties they had forged on the crusade and led at some point in 1153 to Henry's formal betrothal to Louis's eldest daughter, Marie, then eight years old, confirming a promise made during the crusade. A notary quoted Henry, then twenty-six, as saying that he made a grant to St-Pierre of Coincy "in the year [1153] in which I betrothed (*affiduciavi*) the daughter of the king."[27] The queen mother, Adelaide, most likely had cared for Eleanor's two abandoned daughters before taking the veil at the convent of St-Pierre of Montmartre.[28] At that point Marie was sent away. She may have entered the old Benedictine convent at Avenay, just north of Count Henry's castle-towns along the Marne and not far from Archbishop Samson of Reims, who had close ties with Louis. Or, more likely, she was placed in the custody of the viscountess of Mareuil, near Avenay.[29] It would be another eleven years before Marie would cohabit with Henry; in the interim he appeared among the king's closest and most loyal princes of the realm.

On 6 January 1153 Henry of Anjou landed in England to claim the throne as the grandson of King Henry I, and through the spring and summer, by force and negotiation, he gradually imposed his claim.[30] His case was bolstered when Eleanor delivered a son, William, on 17 August, and by November, King Stephen recognized Henry of Anjou as his successor, for which Henry did homage and paid his proper respects. Within a year Stephen was dead (25 October 1154), and on 19 December 1154 the count of Anjou was crowned king of England. Eleanor was a queen again, a turn of affairs that compelled the king of France to recalibrate his own alliances. The brother-counts Henry of Troyes and Thibaut of Blois figured prominently in that new equation. Thibaut became the king's seneschal and likely betrothed Louis's younger daughter Alice, a child of three or four.[31] Henry and Thibaut proved steadfast vassals of their prospective father-in-law, with their lands on either side of the royal domain serving as a counterweight to the block of lands controlled by the Angevins in Normandy and western France.

After returning from a pilgrimage to St. James of Compostella in the spring of 1155, Louis convened an assembly of prelates and princes in Soissons

(10 June 1155) to institute a peace of the realm, specifically "for reducing the fever of malignancy."[32] Count Henry attended, as did his brother-in-law Odo II, duke of Burgundy, and the counts of Flanders, Nevers, Soissons and many unnamed barons in addition to Archbishops Hugh of Sens and Samson of Reims and their suffragan bishops. Of the prominent lay lords listed in the official record of the convocation only "Count Henry" was mentioned by name, an indication of his estimation in the eyes of the king. For ten years after next Easter (March 1156), the king declared, he and the signatories to the peace would protect all churches in the kingdom and their possessions, all farmers with their animals, and merchants and all other travelers. Henry and the great lords followed Louis in swearing an oath to that effect, while the prelates bowed before relics and "promised" to help the king and the princes carry out this mission. It was the first time a king of France had attempted to enact legislation for the entire realm, in effect to transform the church's Peace of God into a royal peace. Count Thibaut already had established a kind of territorial peace in protecting merchants passing through Champagne, and his forceful complaint to the regent Suger in Louis's absence overseas, about merchants being abused en route to his fairs, suggests that the king, too, had been safeguarding the roadways within the royal domain.[33] The council also heard the cathedral canons of Soissons defend their right to interdict, which the bishop denied but which the council upheld. At the conclusion of the council Louis dispatched Henry to inform Pope Adrian IV personally of its decisions.[34] Henry no doubt followed the "French Road" across the Alps to Rome (June/July 1155), the very route he had taken six years earlier on returning to France from the crusade.[35] In all these matters, Henry was the only great lord mentioned by name, as if he, like his father, was regarded as the first, and indeed only palatine, prince of the realm.

In these same early years of his rule Henry regularized the feudal status of his towns of Vertus and Provins. The canons of Reims reminded him that "according to an old agreement," his father had held the town (*castrum*) of Vertus only for his lifetime.[36] In fact Henry's grandmother Adela had received Vertus (ca. 1100) for a single lifetime plus the life of one heir (that is, Count Thibaut).[37] Although that document did not mention it, Henry apparently resisted doing homage to the chapter for a castle-town he regarded as his rightful inheritance in the heartland of his county. A homage to a sympathetic prelate like Archbishop Samson of Reims was much more acceptable.[38] "Since this conflict had lingered for some time," he declared in 1154, "I came to the court of my lord [Samson] archbishop of Reims, and on the day that I did homage (*feci hominium*) and recognized the prior right of the church of Reims, the canons unanimously re-granted that castle for my lifetime on condition that I pay them 40*s.*, money of Provins, annually on the feast of Saint Remi in addition to the 40*s.* they used to collect from my ancestors by the old custom."[39] Henry made a similar payment in recognition for holding the "fief of Provins" from the archbishop of Sens, 40*l.* worth of wax each year on the feast of Saint Stephen.[40] There is no reference to a homage for Provins, but his homage for Vertus—the only homage Henry is known to have done—certified his de facto hereditary right to the town, much like the homage of royal heirs in England validated their hereditary rights to their Continental possessions.[41]

Palace, Chapel, and Canons

The construction of the new comital residence and chapel was substantially completed by 1157 when Henry, then thirty, confirmed the chapter's possessions in what appears to have been the dedication of the church.[42] Henry said that he founded the chapel for his soul and the soul of his father and ancestors with the consent of "my brothers and my friends and barons." One year later, on 22 November 1158, he appeared "before the altar of Saint Stephen in my chapel" to promise his friend Abbot Peter of Montier-la-Celle not to alienate any more of the salt tax collected by the abbey in Troyes.[43] Two months after that, on 1 February 1159, Henry's grant to the canons of St-Loup was noted as having been "done in public in Troyes in the church of St-Étienne." Fourteen named canons of St-Étienne—the dean, four priests, three deacons, two canons, three subdeacons, and the treasurer—witnessed "on my behalf," said the count.[44] By that time the chapter was formally constituted, its endowment confirmed, and the chapel substantially built and roofed, if not entirely finished.[45] The speed of construction, six to seven years from breaking ground, was unusual but not exceptional. Bishop Geoffroy of Langres began a similar project on returning from the crusade, with a new church and canons' compound partially completed by 1157.[46] Suger's earlier rebuilding of St-Denis was stunningly fast, and like Count Henry's project, it was remarkable as much for its ambitious conception as for its speed of execution.[47]

Suger, Geoffroy of Langres, and Henry of Winchester were models of entrepreneurial prelates, but Henry surely had other models in mind on returning to Champagne in 1149. He had seen magnificent cities and palaces abroad, but of all the princely residences he had visited, the one that I think most influenced him, because it matched his own ambitions, was Palermo, where Roger II was building a palace-chapel complex as the capital of his newly enlarged kingdom. Although we lack an explicit reference to Henry's visit to Palermo, it seems highly likely that on returning from the Holy Land in late 1148 he passed through Sicily to visit his sister Elizabeth, who had married Roger II's eldest son eight years earlier.[48] Roger had been building the Cappella Palatina since 1143, and it survives today as a powerful testament to his political and dynastic ambitions. Even if it was not completed by 1148, the construction was well enough along for Henry to envision Roger's magnificent chapel and residential quarters as the capital of a new principality.

Since Henry's new residence and chapel in Troyes were dismantled after the French Revolution, we must rely on the eighteenth-century sketches made after their demolition for a sense of Henry's project (see Figure 3). The residence was a rectangular, two-storied building of 600 meters in length sited along the Seine.[49] The ground floor contained a kitchen, storage, and service area.[50] Above, accessed by an exterior stairway of thirty steps, was a great hall, 13 x 30 meters long, for sessions of the count's court and other public events [A] (Figure 5). A series of interconnected rooms along the rear of the building [B] served as the living quarters, with Henry's large personal chamber [D] offering a direct view of the Seine and, beyond it, the wealthy Benedictine convent of Notre-Dame-aux-Nonnains.[51] It was a residence worthy of an ambitious count and his future royal wife.

The chapel abutting the residence was named St-Étienne in honor of the first martyr Stephen, according to the canon-poet Evrat.[52] Modeled after the cathedral of St-Étienne of Sens, it was the first Gothic church built in southern Champagne and one of the largest.[53] Its massive double-column pillars, large nave, and lack of a transept were especially noteworthy.[54] A fragmentary Corinthian capital, the only surviving element of the building, gives a sense of its sumptuous stonework.[55] Like the Cappella Palatina in Palermo, St-Étienne of Troyes was more than a princely chapel; it was a cathedral-sized church that dwarfed the Carolingian cathedral in the old city of Troyes (St-Étienne was 1.5 times larger in width and length). And like the Cappella Palatina, St-Étienne was joined to the count's palace in such a way that the tribune, an enclosed balcony [C], opened to the chapel to afford Henry a direct view of the altar and a private place to listen to liturgical chants, which he is reported to have much enjoyed. While his chapel was under construction he frequented monastic churches in and near Troyes, like Montier-la-Celle, where his friend

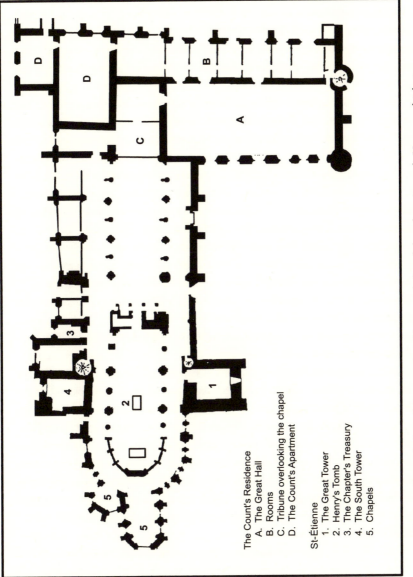

The Count's Residence
  A. The Great Hall
  B. Rooms
  C. Tribune overlooking the chapel
  D. The Count's Apartment

St-Étienne
  1. The Great Tower
  2. Henry's Tomb
  3. The Chapter's Treasury
  4. The South Tower
  5. Chapels

Figure 5. Ground plan of the count's residence and chapel, based on Arnaud, *Voyage archéologique*, 25.

Peter was abbot. As he remarked on one occasion, he placed a gift on the monastery's altar of Saint Frodobert on a Sunday "while the monks were chanting the matinale Mass."[56] Philip of Harvengt noted Henry's lifelong appreciation of liturgical music: "When the solemn liturgy is sung, when the concordant melody of hymns and canticles and sweet organa sound out, you [Henry] are delighted, they say, as if by a harmony of the firmament and stars, indeed, as I would say more correctly, by a prophecy of the angelic symphony and supercelestial song."[57]

For his chapel Henry recruited canons with the technical expertise necessary for a government based on written records. The resident canons built their stone houses within the count's compound on twenty-five identically sized plots along the Street of the Close, running from the walls of the old city to a cul de sac (see Figure 4). Some of the houses were habitable by the time the endowment charter drawn up in 1157. Henry recalled that he had promised to build the church of St-Étienne "next to my house" and to endow it with "many possessions and various sumptuous gifts." With the chapel built, he confirmed the chapter's endowment, namely, what he already had given ("what I gave"), including the use of his forests for the construction of the church and the canons' houses; what he gave on this occasion (the liberty of the chapter's cloister and church); what the canons had purchased on their own account ("what you have bought"), including houses and merchant stalls in the market; and what the chapter had received from others (Thibaut the Scribe and three associates, for instance, had given their five stalls in the marketplace).[58] In all, St-Étienne possessed two ovens, three and a half merchant lodges, fifteen houses, three mills, and six commercial stalls, most being exempt from the count's taxes and jurisdiction. Most unusual, and perhaps most lucrative, was the chapter's exclusive right to the revenues from the fifteen-day Fair of the Close that opened on 22 January, when the canons collected tolls on goods sold during the fair as well as half the rents from houses in St-Étienne's close.[59] The count did not license the chapter to acquire his fiefs, and in fact the endowment did not include any feudal property; its patrimony amassed in the preceding six years depended entirely on commercial activity and the trade fairs in Troyes.

The fourteen canons of St-Étienne mentioned in 1159 did not include five canons particularly close to the count: his chancellor William, his chaplain Nicholas of Montiéramey, the notary William, the provost Manasses of Pougy, and Haice of Plancy. The existence of nineteen identifiable canons in 1159 suggests that the chapter might have attained its initial limit of about twenty-five canons by 1163, when there was a waiting list for the next five available prebends.[60] A later site plan of the count's campus indicates that some canons subsequently acquired or built additional houses across the street in the old city and elsewhere in Troyes to accommodate an enlarged chapter.[61] Two of the comital buildings also were located inside the walls of the old city. One was "the house of the chancellor," where the careful work of drafting the count's letters took place beyond the coming and going of the count's campus.[62] Next to it was the hospital (*Domus Dei*) that Henry had founded concurrently with St-Étienne. Originally called the Hospital of St-Étienne because the chapter's canons administered it in accordance with the Capitulary of Aix (816), which required every chapter to be responsible for a hospital, it also was known as the Hospital of the Count in recognition of its foundation under Henry.[63] Master Herbert, a physician and canon of St-Étienne and "procurator of the poor," administered it as a shelter for the ill and a hospice for poor travelers.[64] Lepers, the blind, and invalids needing long-term care without hope of recovery were sent to the local leper house just outside the gate of Croncels.[65] The fact that the hospital collected an *annualia*, or first-year's income, from each new prebendary of St-Étienne suggests its importance as a highly visible social service funded by the count.[66]

The chapel-residence complex, canons' houses, and hospital comprised a highly symbolic group of structures in Troyes. Except for the hospital and chancellor's house, the count's buildings were in an open campus devoid of walls and towers. Even after it was enclosed ca. 1170, the campus retained its original character as an administrative center devoted to the count's business, set apart from both the old city and the commercial quarter of Troyes.[67] Henry appointed the canons of St-Étienne and endowed their prebends.[68] The canons witnessed at court on his behalf, and their houses virtually embraced his residence and chapel. They were, in effect, the count's men, making for a powerful symbiotic relationship between the secular and the religious. Anyone having business with Henry, his court, or his officials could have no doubt, walking into his compound, of having entered the count's domain. The cathedral canons drew Henry's ire in February 1152 precisely because they threatened his grand plan for a new residential-administrative quarter in Troyes as the capital of his principality.

In October 1157, about the time that Henry sealed St-Étienne's endowment charter, King Louis assembled an army in Troyes as a precaution against threatening maneuvers by Frederick Barbarossa. The emperor had just held a diet in Besançon, where in the presence of the papal chancellor, Cardinal

Roland Bandinelli, the archbishops of Vienne and Lyons and the bishops of Valence and Avignon pledged fidelity and did homage to Frederick for the benefices they held from him. That was an extraordinary event, wrote Bishop Otto of Freising, "which men now living cannot recall having ever occurred before." Frederick was to meet Louis at Dijon, said Otto, but the king, fearing that Frederick was planning to attack him, gathered his own forces in Troyes. There, for one night, marveled Bishop Henry of Troyes, the city lodged nine bishops with their troops.[69] It was the perfect occasion for Count Henry to show off his new campus, his "garden city."[70] Perhaps on that occasion Louis, seeing the count's canons enjoying their "most excellent prebends" and new quarters, made his famous quip: "Truly, count, you must be mad," he chided, "you are squandering the patrimony of your heirs on effeminate clerics."[71] Sparring with the king, Henry replied that Louis surely knew of cases where a single person responsible for a church's resources dissipated them to the misfortune of the entire community; it was much preferable, he said, that each prebendary be responsible for his own acts and not jeopardize the interests of the others. The count responded wisely, commented the writer of this anecdote. But of course Henry had artfully deflected the sting, for the king had missed the point. Henry was not squandering his wealth but rather investing in what we would call "human resources," a pool of talented and loyal candidates for administrative and religious offices. Beyond that, he was establishing a new literate community in Troyes and soon in his other commercializing towns. It was precisely the chapters of secular canons, appointed and endowed by the prince, that accounted in great part for the cultural flowering of Champagne in the second half of the twelfth century. Henry's generosity appears not so much an expenditure as a shrewd investment in the cultural life of his principality.

At Court

Sometime around 1160 two *literati* clerics wrote short treatises celebrating Count Henry's character and achievements. His chaplain and intellectual mentor, Nicholas of Montiéramey, penned an effusive thanks for Henry's many benefactions to the church, to his knights, and to Nicholas himself, without which, said the chaplain, his career would not have been the same (he had just been appointed to a priorship in Troyes). Recalling Plato's prescription for a well-ordered state, he flattered Henry for being at once a "philosopher prince" and a "princely philosopher":

For this reason I should say that the happiness of our age is most noteworthy in your principality (*principatum*), by which the clergy are enriched and churches are endowed and embellished. Nor are the knights envious, since you also gratify them. . . . Thus seated between the literary and equestrian order, you glorify both, magnificent and munificent to each. . . . The Lord gave you intellect and an erudite tongue so that your noble blood might shine in its eloquence and intelligence (*ingenium*). . . . Since coming of age I have found favor with the magnates and the greatest princes of this world, but to you alone, because of your natural lordship, I owe what I am and, because of your friendship, what I am able to be.[72]

Addressed to "his most serene prince and dearest lord Henry, count of Troyes," the letter was more than an obsequious performance by "brother Nicholas, sinner in life and garbed as a monk." It was an allusive thanks for a perfect life sinecure as prior of St-Jean-en-Châtel in Troyes. Located just opposite the antiquated comital residence in the old city, and in close proximity to good libraries and communities of canons whose bookish interests paralleled his own, St-Jean provided Nicholas, in his early forties, with a privileged institutional space and the *otium*, free of monastic discipline, to pursue his personal interests within a vibrant cityscape.

The second, more subtle praise letter was written by Philip of Harvengt, abbot of Bonne-Espérance (Premonstratensian) near Cambrai, who did not know Henry personally and indeed may never have met him.[73] Written in the tradition of the "mirror of the prince" and free of Nicholas's ingratiating tone—Philip was about sixty years of age and recently elected abbot—the letter extols Henry as a rarity among princes for having acquired a knowledge of letters (*scientia litteralis*) that provided him the moral grounding necessary to rule his county proficiently.[74] For that, you should thank your father, wrote Philip, for providing the education and guidance that he himself lacked. You excel in the study of letters, which you pursued for many years, he continued, and although you love the military life and respect your knights, when you withdraw from the business of governance (*negotium*), you take up a book, either pagan or Christian. Henry's reading and rereading of scripture drew Philip's special praise, for the count skillfully discerned what was valuable and what was not. Far from diminishing him as a prince, Philip observed, reading refreshed the count with the "liberal waters" of the ancients.

Like Nicholas of Montiéramey, Philip of Harvengt dwelled on the knight-cleric topos, the inherent contrast between the military and the learned life, the life of action and the life of the mind. They flattered Henry in stating that he melded the two—he was a prince who governed well precisely because he was educated. Providing for the church as well as for his knights, and caring for the downtrodden and infirm, he was an ideal prince, at once a knight and a cleric. By an interesting coincidence John of Salisbury completed his *Policraticus*, a similarly idiosyncratic mirror of the prince dedicated to his friend Thomas Becket, the English royal chancellor, in 1159.[75] John's treatise powerfully tied personal conduct to public office, the good of the polity being dependent on the comportment of the prince.[76] Who could have missed the devastating portrait of King Henry II as the "tyrant" in the *Policraticus*? In stark contrast, Count Henry, like his father, received accolades as a model prince, one whose intellectual qualities were matched by moral scruples, generosity, and the art of compromise. But if the idealized portraits of Count Henry attest to his high repute among the learned of his time, they fail to capture the day-to-day activities that consumed his life, often at court where he was engaged—and was seen to be engaged—in the governance of his principality. His 552 letters patent surviving either as originals (209) or as copies paint a vivid picture of Henry at court, where he adjudicated disputes, received petitions for his benefactions and interventions, oversaw transactions involving his fiefs, and certified nonlitigious transactions. As the most powerful and prestigious regional lord, he drew to his court laymen of all ranks as well as ecclesiastics seeking resolution of their disputes or validation of their property transactions.[77]

Court sessions called "days" took place most often in his great hall in Troyes or in Provins. Since chancery scribes usually noted only when and where a document was delivered (*datum*), not the time or place where an act or decision was "done" (*actum*), the count's letters patent are not a reliable guide to his actual itineraries. In fact Henry seems not to have followed a fixed circuit through his towns or a routine schedule of "days," and a few sessions were clearly ad hoc affairs. André of Montmirail, for example, was summoned to answer charges that he had exacted hospitality unjustly from a local priory. "The prior complained to me," said the count, "and I summoned André forthwith." Appearing at court, André admitted his error, paid the abbot a 6*l*. fine, and then was grilled by the count about his rights in the village at issue.[78] Count Hugh of Roucy, too, was summoned to answer charges: "I informed him of the day that issue would be pleaded in my court," said the count, "but he did not come," and so Henry summarily decided for the plaintiff.[79]

The court's routine business was witnessed or reviewed by a small but variable group of about six men drawn from the core of Henry's highest officials (seneschal, butler, constable), technical staff (bursar, treasurer, marshal), and chancery personnel responsible for preparing the written records of the proceedings (notary, chancellor). The team Henry assembled by the spring of 1152 would remain with him through his bachelor years, the critical period for the construction of his new capital and principality (see Table 1 in Appendix 1). His highest officers were crusade companions. The butler Anselm II of Traînel, his most trusted companion of about the same age whom he "greatly treasured," witnessed more than 150 of Henry's acts.[80] Odo of Pougy, who was with Henry during their perilous return voyage from the East, became his constable.[81] William I of Dampierre witnessed a number of Henry's acts without portfolio before succeeding Odo as constable.[82] The most senior member of that cohort, and of the most distinguished lineage, was the seneschal Geoffroy III of Joinville.[83] For more technical matters, Henry relied on his father's officials whom he had known as a boy. Peter the Bursar had served Count Thibaut as chamberlain (*camerarius*) since 1138 and continued in that capacity.[84] Two marshals from prominent Provinois families, Walter (Burda) and William Rex (Breban), witnessed almost two hundred of Henry's acts. Several prominent pluralist canons from St-Étienne also appeared routinely at court, almost as if they were working from a duty roster (see Table 2 in Appendix 1). They included the provost Manasses of Pougy (the constable's brother), Roric of Ramerupt (archdeacon of Meaux), Haice of Plancy (master of the school of St-Étienne), and Rainald of Provins (treasurer of St-Quiriace and de facto treasurer of the count). Four knights who frequently witnessed—the brothers Peter and Drogo (Bristaud) of Provins, Daimbert of Ternantes, and Girard Eventat of Bray—qualified as "court knights" in the sense that they held several comital fiefs and were sufficiently worthy to sit at court and even to accompany Henry on his tours.[85] Periodically the count's trusted friends attended, particularly his chaplain Nicholas and his butler Anselm of Traînel's brother Garnier and brother-in-law Hugh II of Plancy.[86] That relatively small and stable group witnessed and vetted every act of the count "done in public," occasionally in the presence of a visitor like Peter of Blois.[87] The court was not a consultative body of barons that met to share in governance with the count; it was rather the count's business meeting with his officers and staff, an occasion for Henry to get things "done."

Dispute Resolution

We see dispute resolution at Henry's court primarily through successful litigation by religious institutions, in most instances against laymen. Often Henry
simply confirmed what the parties to a dispute already had resolved. The canons of Toussaints-en-l'Île of Châlons, for example, sent their provost Martin
to Henry's court at Vitry (1153) seeking confirmation of their settlement with
the knight Peter of Frignicourt regarding milling charges.[88] After the court
vetted the agreement, Henry reminisced that Martin had been "my chaplain
who served me well during the journey to Jerusalem," then presented Martin
with "a piece of the holy cross which I obtained by the grace of God." The
court notary recorded Henry's confirmation and gift, drafted and sealed the
count's letter, and presented it to Martin in Vitry so that he could return to
Châlons with both the letter and the relic.

   In mediating disputes Henry revealed a talent for forging compromises.
In some cases he appointed a trusted mediator to convene the parties, obtain
testimony, and arrange an agreeable settlement for his confirmation. He delegated the aged baron Hulduin of Vendeuvre, who had served Count Thibaut
since the 1120s, to settle a dispute between Stephen of Bar-sur-Aube and the
monks of Beaulieu-sur-Aube over the use of fields and woods, then ordered
the resolution written up without vetting by his council.[89] In another dispute
two arbiters had local men walk off property lines before presenting the terms
of the settlement at court: "This division of parishes was accepted by both
parties in my presence," said Henry, and "after letters were exchanged, I directed that they be sealed with my seal."[90] In a few cases Henry intervened
personally. He pressured two powerful lay lords to give up their rights over
four villages to the abbey of Signy, then invested the monks *per manum*.[91] And
when the abbot of Cormery complained that the count's butler Anselm of
Traînel had established a chapter of canons in his castle, to the detriment of
the abbey, Henry mediated a compromise by which the abbey preserved its
parish rights but Anselm retained his canons.[92] On one occasion Henry acted
jointly with Bartholomew, lord of Vignory, in settling a dispute between the
Cistercians at La Crête and the knight Walter Calderun, but instead of sealing
his own letter, Henry let Bartholomew announce the knight's quitclaim.[93] In
all these cases Henry seems to have delighted in crafting face-saving exchanges
of properties or revenues.[94] At court, just as in the arena of high politics, he
was the consummate practitioner of the art of reconciliation.

   In adjudicating challenges to his own rights Henry proved remarkably accommodating. Responding to the immigrants from Lotharingia living in Wassy who protested a provost's maltreatment, Henry confirmed their privileges—since they had settled there, as they reminded him, "because of my father's righteousness"—and at their request established a "new village" and had its customs put to parchment.[95] Accused of illicitly collecting a *taille* from the villages of St-Médard of Soissons, he ordered an inquiry, and on finding that his agents admitted he had no right to that tax, he quit his claim.[96] Monasteries whose villages were threatened by predatory local lords placed their tenants under Henry's custody (*custodia, advocatio*) in return for an annual protection tax.[97] Earlier, Counts Hugh and Thibaut had granted their monastic advocacies to their barons in fief, but that proved problematic because lay advocates acting in the count's name often exceeded their authority and resorted to violent extorsions.[98] Having the count as a personal protector was the reason why monastics were so insistent that Henry not alienate that responsibility. As he promised the canons of St-Pierre-aux-Monts of Châlons, who placed their village of Sogny under his protection, "I will never abandon that custody nor will I give it to anyone in fief."[99] In fact, Henry is not known to have enfeoffed any advocacy, and he replied testily to the provost of St-Martin of Tours, who accused him of alienating his custody over the village of Chablis. The canons of St-Martin of Tours, who possessed Chablis, "heard that I gave what I had there to Anseric [of Montréal] and insisted in very strong language that I revoke what I had done." Henry denied the accusation. "I responded that the custody and procuration [tax] of that village are paid to me once annually, and that I did not give the fidelity (*fidelitatem*) of the men there to Anseric of Montréal, nor did I grant it to anyone else, because I am not able nor do I have the right to transfer that custody from my hand."[100] But Henry had learned a lesson. It was no longer acceptable to privatize his advocacy or custody over monastic lands; thereafter he delegated the protection of monastic villages to his own provosts, who served as de facto advocates answerable directly to him.[101] In later years he formalized co-lordship agreements in which he shared lordship over monastic villages through his mayors or provosts. That represented a dramatic shift in the exercise of comital authority in the countryside, from privatizing the count's advocacy through fiefs granted to barons, to exercising it directly through his agents.

One lingering issue that troubled monasteries was the ancient right of hospitality enjoyed by the counts. Count Thibaut was barely interred when the abbot of Lagny asked Henry to abolish that obligation, of which the old count had frequently availed himself, said the abbot. Henry willingly remitted what had become an onerous obligation to lodge and feed the count and his retinue.[102] What disturbed the monks even more was the claim of hospitality by the count's household, provosts, and agents in the count's absence. After the abbot of Montier-la-Celle complained about that during one of Henry's visits, the count authorized the brothers to deny hospitality to anyone of his household unless they "see my sealed letters and directives" and provisions were sent in advance.[103] Similarly at Molesme, "none of my men, neither knight nor cleric nor any of my sergeants, may be housed or fed in any manner" in the abbey's villages, except those accompanying the count while leading the villagers in military service.[104]

Nonlitigious Confirmations

Since the court also served as a venue for authenticating nonlitigious transactions, mostly relating to property not affecting him directly, Henry was drawn into the smallest details of life in his county. If the extant documents are indicative, those cases consumed much of his time at court. Petitioners like the widow Elia of Villemaur and her three sons, daughter, and grandson sought Henry's confirmation of her gift (a mill) to the Premonstratensians at Dilo, where her husband Odo was buried.[105] Geoffroy of Vendeuvre, his wife Havidis, and her son and daughter from her first marriage appeared at court to present land to the monks at Châlons.[106] Odo of Lagery and his sister Helvide asked Henry to guarantee their sale of a village to the abbot of Igny.[107] The count readily confirmed those transactions formalized in his presence. He even confirmed prior oral transactions on the basis of testimony alone. Abbot Louis of St-Pierre-aux-Monts of Châlons found Henry at Isles-sur-Marne, where he asked for letters patent to certify a gift made long ago by a knight, now deceased, of an entire village with its tenants, which the abbey had held peacefully for many years, he said. In the presence of witnesses Henry ordered a document written and his seal affixed; later, according to the notary who drafted it, the letter was vetted by the seneschal Geoffroy of Joinville, the constable Odo of Pougy, the butler Anselm of Traînel, the treasurer Peter the Bursar, and the marshal Walter of Provins.[108] The prior of Cormey asked Henry for a similar confirmation of the rights it had enjoyed in its town market under Count Thibaut, that is, the right to tax mills and the sale of salt, wine, and bread. He asked for a written record of their rights, said the prior, in order to preclude the imposition of new customs.[109]

In a few instances Henry certified the written records of earlier transactions, in effect validating documents rather than the transactions themselves. The nuns at Fontaines-les-Nonnes near Meaux asked him to "confirm by writing and to authenticate by my seal" a long list of domain lands and fiefs described in his father's sealed confirmation, which they presented to Henry; a chancery scribe recopied the substance of the document, to which Henry added several benefactions.[110] The nuns of Andecy likewise asked him to confirm their prewritten *pancartes* listing benefactions dating from their foundation by Count Thibaut.[111] Cases like these illustrate how the demand for written records in the middle decades of the century increased the workload of the count's court and chancery from what it had been under Count Thibaut.

The Business of Fiefs

By the end of his thirty-year rule, Henry had about 1,900 knights holding property or revenue directly from him in fief tenure in his thirty or so castellanies.[112] How many of those fiefs he himself granted, when, and under what conditions remains an open question. Although Counts Hugh and Thibaut had granted fiefs earlier, we detect them only when they passed to religious communities, in effect, when they ceased being fiefs. We know very little about the creation or prevalence of fiefs as tenures before the mid-twelfth century; in fact, there are no examples of Henry explicitly receiving homage at court for a fief before 1165. The known cases aired at court dealt primarily with transfer of fiefs to monasteries by sale or donation (in effect, their conversion to allods), which required the count's license. But fiefs were malleable tenures. They could be annuitized (de facto alienations), diminished (partial alienations), and increased (augmented with new property or revenues), as well as alienated outright.[113] The variety of those transactions suggests the existence of a flourishing market in fiefs by the mid-twelfth century, and indeed since the 1120s.[114] By 1150 the traffic in fiefs was quite routine: buying, giving, mortgaging, and converting fiefs to allods (and vice versa) were unremarkable property transactions.[115]

In most cases Henry readily confirmed the alienation of his fiefs, in effect consenting to the reversion of fiefs to allodial status and the elimination of any attached service obligation.[116] A fiefholder like Diet of Traînel would promise his fief to a monastery, in his case Vauluisant, then solicit Henry's letter of consent, which the count gave in a sealed letter for the beneficiary.[117] When both parties were present at court, Henry participated in a ceremonial transfer, the fiefholder investing Henry with the fief, and he in turn investing the recipient abbot.[118] On the rare occasion when he refused his consent, it was only until the proper formalities had been observed in recognition of his rights, as when he initially disallowed the sale of a fief to the canons of Soissons because the seller had not obtained either his or his father's license; on appeal by the canons, he of course consented.[119] In the absence of any sustained confiscation known from his bachelor years, it appears that Henry, true to his reputation for generosity, routinely ratified the sale and donation of fiefs to religious institutions, just as he and his father had done in 1147 before the Second Crusade. Still more valuable than those one-off confirmations were his open-ended licenses encompassing all past acquisitions of his fiefs "up to this day," and the future acquisition of his fiefs "by gift or purchase" or "by gift, purchase, or exchange" without need of further approval.[120] To the beneficiary, an open-ended license obviated the need to secure Henry's consent for each acquired fief, a simplification that responded to the increasing mobility of fiefs and facilitated their transfer to religious institutions. There is no evidence that Henry ever sought to restrict the alienation of his fiefs or the service attached to them, at least not before 1165.

Henry's Letters Patent

In the absence of a register of the count's acts at court, the beneficiaries or recipients assumed the responsibility for preserving his letters patent drawn up by the chancery and sealed and presented by the chancellor. Since most of the letters given to laymen have disappeared from the family strongboxes where they were stored, the court's deliberations are known largely from documents preserved in the archives of ecclesiastical institutions pertaining to their acquisitions and successful litigations. Yet the handful of Henry's letters for laymen that do survive confirm the long reach of his court into the strictly secular affairs of his county. Some letters survive because they subsequently were conveyed with property to monastic institutions. In one of his earliest extant letters (ca. 1152) Henry recalled that he had promised, while his father was still alive, to augment the fief of Hugh Eventat of Bray, the knight who "served me faithfully," perhaps during the Second Crusade. The original letter, which Hugh presumably received in evidence, survives because it later passed with the property to the nuns of Foissy.[121] Henry's letter granting his sergeant Peter a house in the market of Troyes (1158) survives because the property later was sold to the nuns of Notre-Dame-aux-Nonnains, who kept the letter as a title deed.[122] His letter stating the terms for the repayment of a 120*l*. fief-rent mortgaged by his cousin Archambaud, lord of Sully (1158), remained in the Sully family coffers for forty-five years before being returned to the chancery.[123]

The chancery also drafted half-part chirographs, documents containing two identical texts, one for each party. The knight Gorman of Mareuil received the count's chirograph (1152) recording the resolution of his dispute with the Templars at Neuville-au-Temple.[124] Gervais of Châtillon (1155), too, received a half-part document for his exchange of property with the monks at Chézy-sur-Marne: "I [Henry] ordered my sealed letters for the church and for Gervais," quoted the notary who drafted the document.[125] We know that Gorman and Gervais received the documents only because the Templars and the monks at Chézy preserved their halves of the chirographs. Even more surprising than the letters given to his knights in the 1150s are the ones that Henry presented to rural communities, which preserved them locally for more than two centuries. The villagers of Rozay-en-Brie, who appeared before the count to deny owing *tailles* and *corvées* to the canons of Notre-Dame of Paris, kept Henry's sealed letter affirming their rights (1153) until royal officials copied it in 1382.[126] The immigrants at La Neuville-à-Remy, who asked for protection against the demands of the count's provost at Wassy, preserved Henry's letter of privileges (1156) until 1377, when it, too, disappeared after being copied.[127] The chance survival of these letters from the 1150s, whether originals or copies, suggests that from the very start of his rule, and in the midst of constructing his new compound in Troyes, Henry dealt with a wide range of issues involving only laymen, and his court was a far busier place than reflected by the records preserved in ecclesiastical archives.[128]

*   *   *

Henry was an exceptionally active and innovative ruler during his first seven years as count of Troyes. His most visible acts were the construction of a new capital in Troyes and the foundation of a wealthy and influential chapter of canons in his chapel next to his new residence. Both announced new directions, his palace-chapel-campus complex because of its location in Troyes rather than in the more commercially developed Provins, and the chapter of St-Étienne because of its secular canons and their close personal ties with Henry. Henry also appeared prominently with King Louis on the field of battle and in high profile conferences regarding the peace of the realm. All that represented a radical break from his father's support of reformed monasticism and his contentious, and recently violent, relations with the king.

Beyond campaigning with the king and overseeing construction in Troyes, Henry devoted considerable time to exhibiting good lordship at court, whether it involved the resolution of disputes, the recognition of private transactions dealing with his fiefs, or the granting of benefactions, privileges, and exemptions from his exactions. The fact that only 241 of Henry's sealed letters survive, as originals or copies, from his thirteen years as bachelor prince, roughly 1.5 letters per month, suggests that we have recovered only a fraction of his acts.[129] Despite the bias of the surviving records, Henry appears to have dealt as much with strictly secular affairs as with conflicts between laymen and religious institutions, and to have immersed himself in the details of very local matters with seemingly boundless energy. If Philip of Harvengt is to be believed, Henry sought respite from his responsibilities in the writings of the ancients and in the close reading of Scriptures. On turning thirty-one in December 1158, the bachelor count was midway through the process of transforming his father's lands into a modern twelfth-century principality.

Chapter 4

The Late Bachelor Years, 1159–1164

By the time he turned thirty-two in December 1159, Henry's new residence was habitable, the fabric of his cathedral-size chapel in the latest architectural style was substantially completed, his generously endowed chapter of St-Étienne was functioning, and the houses of his well-schooled canons dotted the formerly open field of St-Denis. No other castle lord had anything comparable in size or splendor to the count's campus. It not only enlarged the urban space of Troyes; it also shifted the topography of power away from the old walled city where the bishop shared lordship with the count. At the same time Troyes emerged as the capital city of Henry's principality, the epicenter of his extensive portfolio of lands and thirty or so towns and fortresses. It was where he held court most frequently and where his chancery drafted most of his documents. Although his seal proclaimed him "count of Troyes," the old county of Troyes and the other counties he inherited no longer served as political or administrative entities; Henry was in fact count of Champagne. And, in an altogether remarkable turn of affairs that would have amazed his father, Henry was close to the king, as crusader companion, political ally, and prospective son-in-law. It was a singular achievement for a bachelor prince who had ruled for less than a decade.

Henry also formalized his betrothal to Marie of France, who turned fourteen in 1159 and was, according to canon law, of age to consent to marriage. It is not known whether she and Henry had met earlier, perhaps during one of his passages through Paris on the king's military ventures, but the couple is attested together only in 1159. It is unclear where they met. Her guardian, Alice of Mareuil, may have brought her to Troyes to see the new comital residence and chapel, or, more likely, the couple met in the count's residence in Vertus, where Henry arrived with a small riding party consisting of his butler

Anselm of Traînel, marshal William of Provins, and notary William.[1] We
know about that meeting only because Marie's guardian asked Henry to give
the nuns of Avenay a gift in appreciation of their hospitality, which he did,
granting them eight *setiers* of grain rent from his nearby mills at Auberive.
Henry spoke of Marie as "the countess, my betrothed (*sponse mee*)," but the
notary who placed her name in the witness list before the count's three companions identified her as "Marie, countess of Troyes," which in a canonical
sense she was if she had given her consent to marriage.[2] But it would be another five years before she cohabited with Henry in Troyes.

The Count's Canons

Just as the new palace-chapel complex in Troyes was coming to fruition in
1159, Henry became involved in the refoundation of two chapters of canons in
his fair towns of Provins and Bar-sur-Aube, the consequence of an intense
conflict that erupted in the 1150s over the proper lifestyle of canons. The Capitulary of Aix (816), which formalized the constitutions of canons originally
drawn up by Bishop Chrodegang of Metz (754), allowed clerics performing
liturgical services in cathedrals the right to live in individual houses within a
cloister, to eat meat, to possess property, and to receive individual revenues.[3]
But from the late eleventh century Gregorian reformers sought to make the
canons more like monks, that is, "regular" in the sense that they would follow
a strict rule (*regula*) of a common life, and in the subsequent war of words the
"regular" canons wrote disparagingly about the loose living of canons they la-
beled as "secular."[4] A writer from Liège who devoted an entire treatise to the
varieties of religious delivered a scathing critique: some seculars are responsible, content with a simple diet and clothing, and care for the poor, he admitted, but others pamper themselves with costly dress, decorate their houses
lavishly, and engage in wordly affairs more than seemed fitting. They would
be better off, he suggested, if they lived communally and gave up the "superfluous things of life."[5] With support from reforming prelates and sympathetic
princes, chapters were forcibly converted to regular status, often after bitter
conflict. Count Thibaut had actively sponsored the conversion of secular
chapters in his towns of Oulchy, Château-Thierry, Épernay, Provins, Chantemerle, and Troyes, in what was a general movement in northern France closely
tied to the spread of the new religious orders, primarily the Premonstratensians and Cistercians.[6] But forced conversions in Champagne ended with

Henry, whose religious sensibilities lay elsewhere. The canons of his new chapel were of course secular, like the cathedral canons of Troyes, in a pointed reversal of his father's antisecular policy. By the time Countess Marie took up residence in Troyes, Henry had founded or refounded five chapters of thirty to forty canons each, comprising altogether about one hundred and fifty secular canons in his most important urban centers. The creation of an entirely new class of clerics within his principality, which he had not envisioned in 1152, had ramifications extending far beyond the new canons' quarter in the suburb of St-Denis in Troyes.[7]

The issue of secular versus regular came to the fore at St-Quiriace, the largest and most prominent urban chapter in Provins, located next to the comital residence (see Figure 6). Count Thibaut had attempted to convert the canons to regular status, but after a fierce internal conflict the seculars were allowed to remain until replaced by regulars through attrition.[8] It was the solution he first adopted in 1122 when he installed regular canons in his chapel at Oulchy.[9] St-Quiriace became in effect a mixed chapter of secular and regular canons. Perhaps encouraged by Henry's foundation of St-Étienne in Troyes, the remaining seculars in St-Quiriace sought the restoration of their chapter's original status.[10] The new pope, Adrian IV, delegated the archbishop of Sens (Hugh of Toucy) and the bishops of Paris (Thibaut) and Orléans (Manasses of Garlande) to resolve the dispute, which they did in September 1157, about the time that Count Henry confirmed St-Étienne's endowment.[11] The regular canons left St-Quiriace, and during the next two years Count Henry cooperated with the three prelates in dividing the chapter's property, revenues, and rights between the seculars remaining in St-Quiriace and the departed regulars. Archbishop Hugh made good use of his brother William, archdeacon of Sens, who appears in all the final documents crafted in Count Henry's residence in Provins on 27 September 1159.[12] They ratified the restoration of St-Quiriace to its former status and the transfer of the regulars to St-Jacques of Provins, a hospital founded by Count Thibaut I (ca. 1050) to care for pilgrims and the infirm. Count Henry generously endowed the relocated regular canons, exempting them from all taxes and rents related to commercial transactions within their houses during the fairs, and licensing them to acquire freely from his lands and fiefs.[13] Two years later, in 1160, the two parties reconvened in the episcopal palace in Sens to ratify their agreement in the presence of Count Henry and Archbishop Hugh.[14]

St-Quiriace's restored chapter consisted of at least twelve canons and three identifiable officers: the dean Mathieu Burda of Provins (also precentor of Sens cathedral), the provost William of Champagne (the count's brother), and the treasurer Rainald (archdeacon of Provins and canon of Meaux).[15] The dean Mathieu, in fact, may have been the driving force behind the restoration of the seculars in a well-executed reversal of Count Thibaut's imposition of regular status two decades earlier. As son of Herbert Burda the Elder, provost of Provins, and Margaret, viscountess of Provins, Mathieu represented one of the most powerful families in Provins, and as precentor of Sens cathedral under whose jurisdiction St-Quiriace fell, he wielded great influence in both Provins and Sens.[16] Count Henry's foundation of secular canons in St-Étienne of Troyes presented the perfect occasion for Mathieu to reopen the issue at St-Quiriace, and the removal of regulars proved to be a durable and mutually beneficial solution.[17] St-Quiriace would furnish canons to the count's court, his next chancellor (Master Stephen), and the next bishop of Troyes (Mathieu himself).

St-Quiriace was not physically connected to the count's residence in Provins and did not formally constitute a comital chapter; Henry simply sponsored the restoration of its earlier status and actually endowed a chapter of regular canons at St-Jacques in order to facilitate their removal from St-Quiriace. But the restored seculars soon emerged as a de facto comital chapter, with the count enhancing its already substantial endowment. Beyond confirming the possessions of the "secular canons," he granted them the sales tax on woolen cloth, the tax paid by his mint house in Provins (just below St-Quiriace), and 20 percent of the revenue he collected during the fairs of May and St-Martin.[18] The next year he gave a 16*l.* revenue in support of the building campaign to enlarge and restyle St-Quiriace's church into the largest Gothic church in Champagne.[19] With a nave (13 x 30 meters) larger than the just-built St-Étienne of Troyes (13 x 20 meters), it was second in size only to its model, Sens cathedral (15.25 x 40 meters).[20] Henry also had the comital residence in Provins rebuilt according to the same general model as his new residence in Troyes, with due consideration to site differences. The great hall of Provins (16.5 x 42 meters) had a similar layout but was slightly larger than the hall in Troyes (13 x 30 meters).[21] At the same time an interior wall enclosed St-Quiriace and the count's residence, making the southeastern projection of the upper town of Provins a virtual campus like the one in Troyes, and an old tower in the upper town was reconfigured into the idiosyncratic tower-fortress that remains to this day one of the city's identifying features.[22] By the time he married, Henry had indelibly marked the topography of his two principal cities, with his princely compounds and their Gothic-style chapels adjacent to his most important commercial fairs.

Whereas he was drawn into the internal chapter politics of St-Quiriace, Henry himself took the initiative in refounding the chapter of St-Maclou in the chapel next to his residence in Bar-sur-Aube, which he may have begun to upgrade a decade earlier as count of Bar-sur-Aube. In 1159 he endowed a chapter of secular canons in St-Maclou with the consent of the abbot of St-Oyand, whose monks had serviced his chapel there, and Bishop Geoffroy of Langres, whom he had known on the crusade.[23] It was the only conversion Henry sponsored, St-Étienne being an entirely new foundation and St-Quiriace a restored chapter. He provided St-Maclou with 10 percent of all his tolls and sales taxes in Bar-sur-Aube, payable each week "by those who collect my revenues." He licensed the chapter to acquire his fiefs by gift or purchase from his fiefholders, and granted jurisdiction over immigrants who chose the chapter's lordship after residing one year and one day in Bar-sur-Aube.[24] Despite those resources, St-Maclou's early years were difficult. Six years later the chapel was still under construction, and the canons had not found sufficient housing in the vicinity.[25] Ultimately St-Maclou could not rival the wealth of St-Étienne and St-Quiriace, nor match the close ties those chapters formed with the episcopal chapters of Sens, Meaux, and Troyes.

Networking the Count's Chapters

While his uncle Henry was bishop of Troyes, Count Henry granted prebends in St-Étienne to several influential cathedral canons to create a web of overlapping personal, familial, and institutional relationships (see Table 2 in Appendix 1). Canons Manasses of Pougy (brother of the constable) and Archdeacon Manasses (son of the lord of Villemaur) became respectively the first provost and dean of St-Étienne.[26] Canons Haice of Plancy (brother of Hugh II of Plancy) and Guirric Boceps (treasurer and nephew of Bishop Henry) received prebends, as did two canons of Meaux cathedral, Rainald (also treasurer of St-Quiriace) and Roric (brother of the count's knight Nevel of Ramerupt).[27] By co-opting a few key cathedral canons, Count Henry created a symbiotic relationship between the cathedral and his chapters in Troyes and Provins, providing him with a reservoir of talented, well-educated, and loyal officials, and a community of stakeholders in the fortunes of his county. The pluralists constituted, in modern parlance, an interlocking directorship. St-Étienne would furnish two chancellors and two bishops of Troyes, while St-Quiriace would provide a chancellor, a bishop of Troyes, and an archbishop of Sens and Reims.

The most significant but elusive canon was the count's brother William, provost of the cathedral since ca. 1156 and also of St-Quiriace after its restoration. He was about seventeen when he returned from England after his father's death. The decade he spent with his uncle Bishop Henry of Winchester, by all accounts the wealthiest, most influential, and most cultured churchman in England, laid the foundation for a brilliant ecclesiastical career.[28] Earlier Count Thibaut had asked Bernard of Clairvaux to find William a suitable position in the church, but the old Cistercian declined because of William's age and because it was not right, said Bernard, for someone "to hold benefices in many churches," indicating that William already held or was promised prebends before his return.[29] Count Henry appealed to his friend Peter of Celle, who sent a strong letter of recommendation to the pope, asking that young William be appointed provost of Soissons. Peter mentions William's distinguished ancestry, his father's "virtues and probity," and his powerful brothers Counts Henry and the royal seneschal Thibaut, who would give him "aid and counsel in all things." In sum, "we most eagerly commend him to you."[30] Peter said nothing about William's personal qualifications; in fact he may not even have known the newly arrived William. The pope, an experienced reader of letters of recommendation, recognized this as pure puffery, and nothing came of the matter.

But Count Henry and Bishop Henry could make things happen for William in Champagne. It is likely that William received a cathedral prebend shortly after arriving in Troyes for his father's memorial service and soon became provost of the cathedral and St-Quiriace.[31] He had inherited considerable financial interests from his father's properties and revenues in Provins, and the fact that the count's primary mint was located next to St-Quiriace must have weighed in his selection as provost of St-Quiriace. As provost of both the cathedral in Troyes and St-Quiriace in Provins, he acquired an intimate knowledge of both chapters and of the financial affairs in the count's two primary fair towns. Whether he routinely consulted with Count Henry is unknown, but given his prominence, he must have been regarded as the count's eyes and ears in Troyes and Provins, as well as in Meaux, where he also held a prebend.[32]

Henry's policy of networking his canons extended to other chapters in Troyes. In 1161, when regranting the use of his waters along the Seine in Troyes to the regular canons of St-Martin-ès-Aires, he required them to process with the canons of St-Étienne ("my church," he said) every year on the feast of Saint Stephen (3 August) and at the death of every canon of St-Étienne.[33]

St-Martin already possessed the water rights, but as a fief granted by Count Thibaut in return for unspecified service, which Henry now defined as the obligation to join his canons in liturgical processions. One can imagine the satisfaction of the seculars of St-Quiriace at that comeuppance, two decades after the canons of St-Martin had forced St-Quiriace to become a regular chapter. Two years later, in 1163, Henry promised the fifth available prebend at St-Étienne to the regular canons of St-Loup, located just opposite the cathedral of Troyes, if they, too, would join the canons of St-Étienne in procession. "In order to bind the two chapters in community and closeness," said the count, "it is enacted that both chapters will participate in the burial of each other's deceased brothers" and will celebrate together the annual feast days of Saints Stephen and Lupus.[34] The canons of St-Étienne must have appreciated that gesture, since the count's father had imposed regular canons in St-Loup with the help of André of Baudement, his long-time seneschal turned Cistercian.[35] Thus within a decade of Henry's accession, the regulars had been brought to heel in Champagne. More charitably we might say that Henry repaired the contentious relations between regulars and seculars by forcing prominent regulars in Troyes to join "his" seculars in public procession around his chapel inside the comital campus.[36]

St-Étienne was not entirely finished in 1160. It still lacked glazing, interior adornments, and a collection of relics that would make it a pilgrimage destination. Having seen the spectacular collection of relics in the chapel of Constantine's palace in Constantinople, Henry knew that a chapel's display of ornaments and relics adorned the prince as much as his church. He partially remedied that lack in 1161 by purchasing a cache of relics from the monks at Rebais: a piece of the shroud of Christ, a fragment of the prophet Elijah's arm, a tooth of Lazarus, and two teeth of Saint Geneviève. "On the very day that I carried away the relics," he recalled at court, he assigned the monks a 60s. annual rent, payable by his toll collector at Rebais during the fairs at Bar-sur-Aube.[37] Mention of the count's goldsmith that same year suggests that Henry commissioned reliquaries for displaying the new objects in his chapel.[38] All four relics were still at St-Étienne a century and a half later: the tooth of Saint Lazarus was stored in the Large Treasury (in "a jewel-studded crystalline vase, decorated above and below in gold") along with the "shroud of the Lord," while the teeth of Saint Geneviève (in a "crystalline vase covered with silver") and the relics of the prophet Elijah (in a "long green crystalline vase decorated above and below with silver") were in the Small Treasury.[39] It is not known how many additional relics Count Henry procured for his chapel, but in the fourteenth century St-Étienne possessed more than 240 reliquaries of all types.[40]

Henry's chapters quickly grew into substantial communities. By 1163 St-Étienne had twenty-three identifiable canons, not counting the chancellor, chancery scribes, and nonresident canons, and a waiting list for the next five available prebends.[41] St-Quiriace had more than forty-four canons by 1176 (reduced from the hundred authorized) and St-Maclou about thirty.[42] The demand for his prebends prompted Henry to found a chapter of seculars in Sézanne, a traditional site of his father's court.[43] But Sézanne, lacking the vitality and amenities of Troyes and Provins, was fated to remain an agricultural center and its chapter a quiet retreat for canons. Even so, by 1176 the chapter of St-Nicholas had at least thirty-four canons and a waiting list for the next seven available prebends.[44] The chapter at Bray-sur-Seine, too, was filled by 1173, leading Henry to increase its resources for additional canons.[45] A prebend promised in the count's chapter might take years to materialize, however: of the five prebends Henry promised in St-Étienne by 1163, only three had been received ten years later.[46] Yet the prestige of the count's chapters was so great that Thomas Becket, on arriving in France in late 1164, was advised to seek prebends from Count Henry as well as from the king in order to ease his life in exile.[47] Awarding prebends appealed to Henry's practical interests as much as to his generosity. As Philip of Harvengt observed to Henry, "in those churches you delight in appointing clerics who because of a certain lifestyle are customarily called 'secular,' and in furnishing them with sumptuous provisions and ample revenues, they willingly and eagerly offer themselves to your service."[48] With thirty to forty prebends each, the count's five chapters supported at least 150 secular canons (the cathedral of Troyes had about thirty resident canons).[49] The count's chapters, like his court, were staffed with men who shared a strong regional identity and a personal loyalty to him.

Royal and Papal Politics

Early in his rule Count Henry had been drawn into the skirmishes between Louis VII and Henry II of England, but relations between the two monarchs seemed to stabilize in 1158, after Henry II swore fidelity to Louis VII and proposed a marriage between their children. In June Thomas Becket, the English royal chancellor, made a magnificent entry into Paris in a long train bearing luxurious gifts that dazzled his French hosts.[50] It was agreed that the infant

Margaret of France, barely months old, would marry young Henry of England, then three years old, and bring the Vexin as her dowry. Count Henry was among the many distinguished laymen and bishops who witnessed the two kings sign the marriage treaty in Rouen in May 1160.[51] But the political climate changed abruptly four months later, after Queen Constance died in childbirth (4 October). The barons pressed Louis to remarry: "It was especially feared that the kingdom might lack an heir," which is to say a male heir, since Louis's two daughters by Eleanor were betrothed to the brother-counts of Champagne and Blois. It was decided that Louis would marry their youngest sister, Adele, who was fifteen or sixteen and described as praiseworthy by nature, radiating good sense, and possessed of an elegant, virtuous body.[52] Henry and Thibaut surely attended Adele's marriage (3 November) in the cathedral of Notre-Dame of Paris. Archbishop Hugh of Sens officiated, since Archbishop Samson of Reims refused to perform the ceremony on the grounds that the couple was too closely related.[53] After crowning Adele, Archbishop Hugh celebrated Mass. Stephen, chanter (later bishop) of Meaux, read from the epistle, while William, archdeacon of Sens (later bishop of Auxerre), read from the gospel.[54] Then Mathieu, precentor of Sens and dean of St-Quiriace of Provins (later bishop of Troyes), led the choir in procession.[55]

That seemingly fortuitous event for the royal and comital families unsettled Henry Plantagenet, who could had not have imagined, when he betrothed his son to Louis's daughter the previous May, that Louis would remarry only months later, and to a sister of the counts of Champagne and Blois. The prospect of a French royal heir, instead of young Henry of England, upset his political calculus, and so he preempted Louis's scheduled remarriage by advancing the marriage of his son and Margaret of France to 2 November. Executing the marriage contract, Henry II took immediate possession of Margaret's dowry in the Vexin, which the Templars held pending her marriage.[56] Once again Count Henry was drawn into what was becoming a never-ending contest of guile and wits, and occasionally of brute force, in what has been called a generation-long "cold war" between the two monarchs.[57]

One month after Adele's marriage to the king, Countess Mathilda died (11 December 1160).[58] She had been countess of Blois for a quarter century (1126–52) and dowager countess for almost a decade. In retirement she led a quiet life on her dower lands, perhaps in or near the castle-town of Chantemerle, with a small household staff and her daughters, Agnes and Adele until they married and Margaret until she entered Fontevraud.[59] Her last days were spent at La Pommeraye, the priory she founded with Abbess Heloise a decade earlier in the presence of her sons Henry, Thibaut, and Stephen. On her deathbed she was visited by Count Henry and William, her brother Bishop Henry of Troyes, and two close friends of the family, Archbishop Hugh of Sens and Count Henry's old tutor Stephen. She died at about fifty after making her last bequest to the nuns from her dower property in Provins and was buried at La Pommeraye.[60] Of her funeral, there is no mention, but Abbess Heloise most likely met the comital family at some point during Mathilda's last illness. Shortly afterward, Henry visited Lagny to endow an eternally burning lamp at his father's tomb.[61]

The Papal Schism

A schism arose when Roland Bandinelli, papal chancellor and distinguished canonist, was elected pope by a majority of cardinals (7 September 1159) as Alexander III.[62] Within days a rival conclave elected Octavian of Monticelli (Victor IV), and soon Frederick Barbarossa convoked a council of sympathetic cardinals in Pavia to reaffirm Victor's election and excommunicate Alexander. But Louis VII and his brother Bishop Henry of Beauvais were staunch supporters of Alexander, who was preferred by most of the French prelates, and in July 1160 Bishop Henry hosted a council of prelates, with the kings of England and France in attendance, to hear the legates of Alexander and Victor and the envoys of Frederick Barbarossa present their cases.[63] Given the gravity of the issue and his personal tie to Louis, it is likely Count Henry was among "the crowd of princes and nobles" present at Beauvais, where the two kings declared for Alexander, thus pitting France and England against the empire.[64]

During the next three years Count Henry, always the mediator and perhaps naive or disingenuous, became deeply entangled in the schism by attempting to mediate a highly charged international conflict. In the spring of 1162 the king convinced Alexander to meet with Frederick Barbarossa, then authorized Count Henry and Bishop Manasses of Orléans to arrange a general meeting of prelates on both sides in order to end the schism.[65] Henry and Manasses traveled to Pavia, probably in early May, where they arranged for Louis and Frederick to meet on 19 September at St-Jean-de-Losne, the Burgundian border town that led to the Great Saint Bernard Pass and the "French road" to Rome. Henry was familiar with the route, having taken it in 1148 on returning from the crusade and in 1155 to report the Peace of Soissons to the pope. It was agreed that Louis and Frederick, accompanied by prelates and great lords from each side, would decide which pope would be accepted by all.

Henry returned from Pavia with a letter from Frederick dated 31 May. Addressed to Louis, it lauded his "dear relative [Count] Henry, your faithful man," who could establish friendship and good relations between "our two related realms."[66] Of course Alexander had not agreed to submit to a judgment by council—he had been duly elected pope, after all—and he asked the archbishop of Reims to warn the king about the perils of such a meeting. But to no avail, for by early September Louis was in Dijon.[67] Only at that point did Count Henry reveal what he had accepted on Louis's behalf, including a provision that if Louis did not bring Alexander to the meeting with the emperor, Henry would do homage to Frederick, in effect, transfer the *mouvance* of the land he held in fief from the king. Hugh of Poitiers, who wrote the most detailed account of the event, which he may have witnessed, quoted Count Henry: "I swore an oath that I would transfer to him [Frederick] whatever I hold in fief from the king's domain and henceforth will hold that from him."[68] The king was "stunned" to hear of that proviso made without his consent; he had agreed only to a meeting, not to conditions. Henry is reported to have replied that Louis, angered by Alexander's earlier intransigence, in fact had authorized Henry through the bishop of Orléans to arrange such a conference with Frederick and agreed to abide by all of Henry's arrangements.[69]

The meeting at St-Jean-de-Losne on 20/21 September did not go as planned. Frederick was expected to arrive with Victor, and Louis with Alexander, but duplicity abounded on all sides, and much that was agreed to in private was not set to writing. Frederick regarded his own attendance at the meeting as a concession to Louis, who was expected to embrace Victor IV.[70] Count Henry apparently saw himself as a good faith interlocutor, although it appeared to some observers that he favored Victor, who was related to his mother, Countess Mathilda.[71] Henry arrived with a small company that included his uncle Bishop Henry of Troyes, his chaplains Drogo and Nicholas of Montiéramey, and Thibaut (the Scribe) of Fismes, his notary from St-Étienne who would draft any resultant document.[72] The emperor's contingent arrived on 8 September with Count Henry's maternal cousin Herman, duke of Carinthia, but since Victor did not come, Frederick was strictly in default.[73] The king asked for a delay, but the imperial emissaries refused, and Louis returned to Dijon. At the duke of Burgundy's palace Count Henry informed Louis that since he had violated the accord, Henry was bound "to transfer to the emperor all the land that he held in fief from the king, and would receive it back after doing homage to the emperor."[74] Crestfallen, the king went to St-Jean-de-Losne where he waited for the emperor on the bridge over the border between France and Germany from 3:00 p.m. to 9:00 p.m. before leaving in humiliation.[75] Frederick himself appeared at midnight, as if to keep within the letter of the agreement, but by then Louis was gone.[76]

What actually happened at St-Jean-de-Losne is not entirely clear, but it shows Count Henry, then thirty-five, acting confidently as an intermediary between the monarchs of France and Germany. Girard Eventat, one of the count's trusted knights who accompanied him to meet Frederick, later confirmed that Henry had guaranteed the king's acceptance of whatever he negotiated with Frederick, and that if Louis failed to agree, Henry would place himself in captivity until he, Henry, accepted the *mouvance* of several castles from Frederick. Girard recalled (ca. 1201) the names of only four castles, although he knew that there were others. The count's chancery registers later identified nine baronial castles that Henry held in fief from the emperor, all located on the eastern border between the county and the empire (Map 3).[77] Just what Henry and Frederick arranged has never been adequately explained, since Henry in fact held only one fief from the king, the county of Meaux (Brie) bordering the royal domain. It appears that Frederick was trying to fix the frontier between France and the empire according to the border established by the Treaty of Verdun (843), which was generally understood to fall in the zone between the Marne and Meuse Rivers.[78] In any event, St-Jean-de-Losne was a boon to Henry, as it formalized the first extension of his overlordship eastward beyond the traditional limits of his father's lands.

Henry, Louis, and Frederick had taken the measure of each other during the Second Crusade, but at St-Jean-de-Losne the emperor outwitted both the king and the count until the very end. Shortly after the aborted meeting with Frederick, Louis met Henry Plantagenet at Chouzy-sur-Loire, where they publicly recognized Alexander III as pope. Louis then met Count Henry at Châlons and at Moret to repair their frayed relationship, perhaps in anticipation of the general ecclesiastical council convened by Alexander III.[79] The Council of Tours (19 May 1163) is said to have drawn more than 500 prelates— at least 105 bishops and archbishops and 400 abbots—including Thomas Becket, the new archbishop of Canterbury (consecrated 3 June 1162) and a full contingent of prelates from Champagne.[80] Despite failing to end the schism, the Council did solidify support for Alexander, who soon settled in the archiepiscopal palace in Sens for the next two and a half years (30 September 1163– April 1165).[81] Sens was a centrally located royal town close to the well-traveled road between France and Italy. It possessed a newly completed cathedral, one of the largest at the time and a rival to St-Denis in architectural innovation.

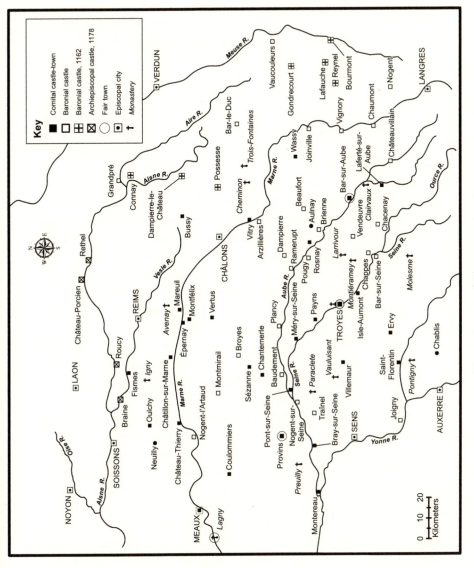

Map 3. County of Champagne in 1181.

Key

- Comital castle-town
- Baronial castle
- Baronial castle, 1162
- Archiepiscopal castle, 1178
- Fair town
- Episcopal city
- Monastery

NOYON

SOISSONS

LAON

Oise R.

Aisne R.

Aisne R.

Braine

Neuilly

Oulchy

Château-Thierry

Nogent-l'Artaud

Coulommiers

MEAUX

Lagny

Provins

Pont-sur-Seine

Preuilly

Montereau

Bray-sur-Seine

Nogent-sur-Seine

Traînel

Paraclete

Vauluisant

Villemaur

SENS

Joigny

AUXERRE

Chablis

Pontigny

Saint-Florentin

Ervy

Bar-sur-Seine

Isle-Aumont

TROYES

Montiéramey

Chappes

Payns

Méry-sur-Seine

Baudement

Plancy

Chantemerle

Sézanne

Broyes

Montmirail

Vertus

Montfélix

Épernay

Mareuil

Avenay

REIMS

Fismes

Roucy

Château-Porcien

Rethel

Grandpré

Conray

Dampierre-le-Château

Bussy

Vitry

Arzillières

Dampierre

Ramerupt

Rosnay

Pougy

Larrivour

Aulnay

Brienne

Beaufort

Vendeuvre

Chacenay

Clairvaux

Laferté-sur-Aube

Bar-sur-Aube

Molesme

Châteauvillain

Chaumont

Vignory

Bourmont

Reynel

Lafauche

Nogent

LANGRES

Joinville

Wassy

Cheminon

Trois-Fontaines

Possesse

Bar-le-Duc

Vaucouleurs

Gondrecourt

VERDUN

Meuse R.

Aire R.

Aisne R.

Vesle R.

Marne R.

Marne R.

Aube R.

Seine R.

Seine R.

Seine R.

Ource R.

Yonne R.

CHÂLONS

Igny

Châtillon-sur-Marne

N
E   W
S

0 10 20
Kilometers

Its experienced and hospitable archbishop, Hugh of Toucy, recently had celebrated the marriage of Louis and Adele of Champagne, and was close to both
the king and Count Henry. Six months after Alexander arrived in Sens the
schism ended with the death of Victor IV (22 April 1164). The German emperor tried to enlist Count Henry's support for another rival pope, Guy of
Cremona (antipope Paschal III), but Henry instead went to Paris, where he
and Louis reaffirmed their support for Alexander.[82]

Family Affairs

Shortly after the misadventure at St-Jean-de-Losne, Henry confronted the lingering troubles at the abbey of Lagny, where his father was buried. After a fire
had seriously damaged the abbey church, he directed the abbot to build a
tower on the abbey's land; rebuffed, ostensibly because the pope refused to
allow it, Henry vented his anger, according to the chancery scribe who quoted
him.[83] Abbot Geoffroy (1148–62) was a difficult person. Accused on several
occasions of mistreating the monks, he managed to evade rebuke until papal
judges delegate of Pope Alexander III finally deposed him.[84] The next abbot
lasted barely a year before being shot through the eye by an arrow while trying
to seize a malefactor.[85] At that point either Count Henry or Alexander III at
his behest took matters into his own hand by appointing the count's half-
brother Hugh (II) as abbot of Lagny (1163–71).[86] Hugh had been living quietly
in Champagne since 1155 after spending almost twenty years in England, the
last ten as abbot of St. Benet Holme and Chertsey.[87] Counts Henry and Thibaut and canon William attended Hugh's installation as abbot.[88]

   The next year, 1164, proved especially auspicious for the three brothers. In
September William was elected bishop of Chartres in a disputed election. Not
only was he an outsider who upset a half-century of local domination of the
chapter, he was at twenty-nine under the minimum age for consecration as
bishop.[89] Having spent the last decade as provost of the cathedral of Troyes
and five years as provost of St-Quiriace of Provins, he was poised to ascend the
ecclesiastical hierarchy and might well have waited a short while for another
opening. But Chartres was an irresistible prize, the most important see in his
father's ancestral lands and the principal city of his brother, the royal seneschal, who described William's election in detail for the king.[90] We can only
guess that Louis VII and Counts Henry and Thibaut interceded with Alexander III, who owed his success during the schism to the French party. The pope
ordered a new election, to be held before 13 January 1165.[91]

At about the same time in September or October, Count Thibaut, then about thirty-four, married Alice of France, the younger daughter (about fourteen) of Louis VII and Eleanor of Aquitaine. All that we know about the wedding is Thibaut's brief mention to the king that Count Henry "did not attend my wedding."[92] Neither, apparently, did Louis or Eleanor. In those same fall months of 1164 or spring of 1165, Marie of France came to live with Henry in Troyes. The two marriages culminated a Capetian-Champenois alliance begun on the Second Crusade and strengthened by a decade of shared experiences in the 1150s. Henry had served Louis in foreign affairs against the monarchs of England and Germany, and Thibaut, as royal seneschal, had attended virtually all the king's court sessions, where he acquired an intimate knowledge of the king's affairs. By early 1165 Henry and Thibaut were married to the king's daughters, William of Champagne was bishop-elect of Chartres, their sister Adele was queen (since 1160), and King Louis's brother Henry was archbishop of Reims (since 1162). When Queen Adele delivered an heir to the throne in the summer of 1165 she completed the stitching of an interfamilial fabric in the making for almost two decades, one that would endure for more than a century and culminate in another marriage, between Jeanne, heiress of Champagne (1284–1305), and Philip IV of France, who finally merged the comital and Capetian dynasties.

The Fairs

It was Henry's good fortune that the Fairs of Champagne became centers of international commerce and finance during his years as a bachelor prince. His father had promoted fairs in Provins and Troyes, luring merchants from the episcopal cities of Reims and Châlons to his smaller and less-developed towns, which became centers of regional exchange.[93] Those initiatives, and later Henry's, coincided with persistent internal conflicts between the townsmen and archbishops of Reims, which made Reims a less desirable venue for commercial activity than the quiet towns of southern Champagne.[94] Count Thibaut offered well-policed markets and a secure network of roads under his protection, especially on the secondary roads passing through Troyes and Provins across Brie to the royal domain and the cloth-producing towns of northern France and Flanders.[95] By the 1130s cloth merchants from northern France were coming to Provins, the most commercially developed of Thibaut's towns in Champagne.[96] It was there in 1137 that ten-year-old Henry witnessed his father renew the Fair of St-Martin (beginning 6 November) held in the "old market" at the church of St-Thibaut, just beyond the count's walled compound in the upper town (see Figure 6).[97] Merchants were required to lease lodgings and halls for their goods there, with the exception of merchants from Arras and Flanders, who were permitted to take quarters beyond the limits of the old market.[98] That is the earliest mention of foreign merchants at the fairs. About the same time Thibaut established the Fair of May, located in the "new market" at the church of St-Laurent, and had the entire upper town beyond his own residential compound enclosed with walls, thus creating a single commercial space for the May and November fairs.[99] When Henry renewed the Fair of May in 1164, he addressed "the churches, clerics, knights, townsmen, and all men having houses within the fairgrounds," which included both the old and the new markets, in effect, most of the upper town of Provins. Henry reminded the residents that merchants lodged and doing business within the limits of the fairgrounds had to remove their stalls and display cases before nightfall, and that he was entitled to half of all rents collected during the fairs.[100]

The suburban priory of St-Ayoul of Provins, where the saint's relics made it a destination for pilgrims, sponsored a third fair (in September) that came under the count's protection.[101] We know that the three fairs of Provins were vibrant in the 1140s because Count Thibaut complained to Suger that the money changers of Vézelay en route to his fairs in Provins had been seized on the royal road between Sens and Bray and despoiled of 700*l.*[102] Reminding Suger that he was responsible for the security of the roads in the absence of the king overseas, Thibaut demanded the release of the money changers and the restitution of their possessions: "I cannot let this injury pass because it threatens my fairs," he wrote.[103] Provins with its fairs clearly held pride of place among Thibaut's towns. Located on his inherited lands in Brie and lacking a resident bishop (unlike Meaux), Provins served as de facto capital of his lands east of the royal domain. It was there that the first abbot of St-Marien of Auxerre frequently visited the count on business and was received with great respect, reported the chronicler Robert of Auxerre.[104]

Troyes, too, had three fairs by 1150, but they were less developed than those in Provins. All three—the "hot" fair of St-Jean (mid-July), the "cold" fair of St-Remi (November), and the Fair of the Close (January)—were held in the "new town," the marshland enclosed in the 1120s as a commercial and industrial center beyond the old walled city and entirely under the count's jurisdiction (see Figure 2).[105] Troyes did not achieve commercial parity with

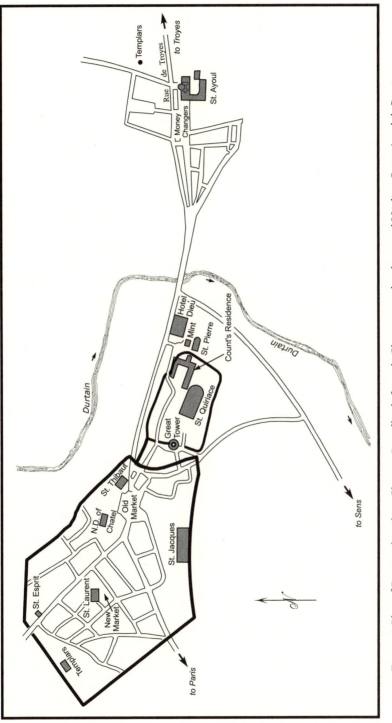

Figure 6. Plan of Provins, based on Chapin, *Les villes de foires de Champagne*, planche 4, and Verdier, *Saint-Ayoul de Provins*, 141.

Provins until Henry made it his primary residence and capital. The fact that he tried to limit the fair at Lagny in 1154 by restricting the merchants and money changers to ten days of commercial activity suggests that he was attempting to extend his father's policy of concentrating the fairs in his two most important towns.[106] Lagny was a small monastic border town, a port of entry from the royal domain, and although the count authorized its fair and protected merchants frequenting it, just as he did at St-Ayoul of Provins, the fair revenues at Lagny were collected by the abbey and thus not as vital to the count as the revenues from Troyes and Provins.

Troyes and Provins, only a day's journey apart, offered complementary periods for commercial exchange six times through the year, from May (Provins) and July (Troyes) to September (Provins), November (Troyes and Provins), and January (Troyes), with the Lenten fair in nearby Bar-sur-Aube (late February/early March) providing a bridge between the winter and summer fairs. The count's coin minted in Provins, the *provinois*, soon became the preferred coin and money of account for commercial exchanges, in effect, the "dollar" of the twelfth century, both at the fairs and well beyond Champagne.[107] A fixed annual cycle of clustered fairs, with an internationally recognized currency, was a boon for Henry. It provided a stream of sales taxes, tolls, and rents independent of the agricultural seasons, and it shifted the financial basis of the county to commercially generated revenues.

If Count Thibaut was the primary architect of the fairs, it was Henry who transformed them from regional exchanges into international centers of commerce and finance. Indirect evidence suggests that he built on his crusade connections to obtain treaties with regional princes to protect merchants traveling to Champagne.[108] A consortium of castle lords and regional princes who oversaw merchant traffic in their lands already was in place by December 1152 when Pope Eugenius III addressed Count Henry, Duke Odo II of Burgundy, the counts of Joigny and Chalons, the viscount of Sens, and the lords of Bourbon, Donzy, Luzy, Montréal, Mont-St-Jean, Rougemont, Thil, and Vergy, asking them to prohibit the townsmen of Vézelay from participating "in the fairs and markets in your lands" because they had been excommunicated for opposing Abbot Pons of Vézelay.[109] The pope assumed that those lords controlled both their markets and their roadways, just as Henry asserted in 1154 in confirming privileges for St-Ayoul of Provins and St-Pierre of Lagny: merchants attending those fairs "are under my protection, going and coming under my safeguard and security at all times throughout my land."[110]

The next year at Soissons (1155), King Louis announced a peace by which regional princes swore to secure the roads in their lands and to protect "merchants and all others."[111] With the king were Count Henry, the duke of Burgundy (Henry's brother-in-law Odo II), and their crusade companions Counts William III of Nevers (Henry's uncle) and Thierry of Flanders, and unnamed barons, who together ruled a contiguous swath of lands extending from Burgundy to Flanders. Although crafted as a royal initiative for the betterment of the realm, the Peace of Soissons effectively strengthened existing bilateral accords among the regional lords who had created a single commercial zone linking northern France and Germany with Italy and the Mediterranean ports.[112] The chief beneficary of that protected corridor was Count Henry, whose centrally located fairs in Champagne already were serving as the venue of choice for northern French and, increasingly, Italian merchants. By the end of his bachelor years, Henry's fair towns were welcoming a steady stream of merchants, ecclesiastics, and travelers passing through Champagne along the great trunk route between the Mediterranean and northern Europe. Thomas Becket's emissary, Henry of Houghton, wrote in 1163 that in going from Soissons to Rome, he passed through the lands of Count Henry "partly because the route was more direct," and, he might have added, partly because it was more secure, which most long-distance travelers must have found as well.[113]

Spreading the Wealth

Secure roads, regulated markets, and a regular cycle of fairs at clustered venues were of course critical to the success of the fairs. But just as important was Henry's insight to make religious communities and his knights and barons stakeholders in the new commercial economy. He was not the first to exempt religious houses from his tolls and commercial taxes. Decades earlier Count Hugh had exempted the canons of St-Loup from sales taxes on their commercial transactions in Troyes, and the monks of Montier-la-Celle from taxes on the goods they sold "in market and out of market."[114] But Henry expanded those benefits and privileges on a massive scale. By 1161 St-Loup's exemptions included all tolls and duty taxes (*pedagium*) at his gates and bridges, the sales tax (*telonium*) on goods purchased or sold for the brothers' own use (not for resale), and the so-called "customary taxes," which covered a variety of fees, commissions, rents, and arbitrary exactions.[115] A standard form of Henry's letter-mandates addressed to his agents reads: "the brothers shall not pay any toll, duty, or customary payment anywhere in my land; they may freely buy and sell at my fairs for their own use without payment; they may not suffer any molestation or injury or impediment by my officials or agents; and they will be treated peacefully by my men in all places."[116] Bernard of Clairvaux had obtained similar mandates from Louis VI and the count of Flanders to facilitate his order's long-distance commercial transactions; Henry extended those exemptions from his tolls and taxes in all his lands so that Clairvaux and its associated abbeys "might freely buy and sell at my fairs exempt from all taxes on whatever is necessary for their own use."[117] Many if not most religious houses acquired those privileges, which assured a regular flow of monastic middlemen bearing letters of exemption to the fairs.

Even more lucrative were the exemptions of merchant halls from the count's sales tax. As a favor to his chaplain Nicholas, prior of St-Jean-en-Châtel, Henry freed the priory's hall in the market of Troyes from his taxes on the sale of fustian, woolens, and other cloth, in effect allowing the priory to retain any taxes it collected.[118] He favored his bursar's son with a similar privilege in the hall where fustian was sold in Provins during the Fair of St-Martin.[119] Abbot Peter of Celle requested the same exemption for St-Ayoul's three houses and two halls in Provins, that is, the right to keep the entire sales tax on commercial transactions, which was in essence an annual contribution for rebuilding the priory's church, which had recently burned to ashes.[120] Henry presented that exemption at the dedication of the new church's foundation on 30 August 1159 in the presence of the archbishop of Sens and the abbot of St-Pierre-le-Vif of Sens.[121] What made tax exemptions especially valuable is that they tended to increase in value with the volume of commercial transactions.

Besides granting exemptions from his tolls and sales taxes, Henry assigned annual rents from fair revenues, which were disbursed in one of two ways. The first was point-of-collection disbursement, in which the count assigned a fixed sum to be paid from a specific toll house, sales tax, weighing fee, or money-changing table. At Vitry, for example, he assigned the canons of Ste-Geneviève 20s. rendered annually at Christmas by the toll collector of Vitry, and at Ramerupt he founded an anniversary Mass for his friend Walter II of Brienne at the priory of Notre-Dame, payable by the toll collector there.[122] To pay for the relics he purchased from Rebais abbey, Henry directed his toll collector at Rebais to pay the abbey's treasurer 60s. annually during the Fair of Bar-sur-Aube.[123] Money changers, too, disbursed mandated payments. In Provins each money-changing table rendered 40s. to the priory of St-Ayoul during its fair, and 5s. to the hospital of Provins during the May Fair.[124] A money-changing table and a toll station would be called today a "cost center," the point at which revenue is collected, accounted for, and expended. Point-of-collection disbursement eliminated the need for the collector to transport monies to the treasury in Provins, and for the recipient to travel to Provins to collect the cash. But it did necessitate some form of accounting, for the assessment and collection of the revenues, for the disbursement of sums as directed by the count's mandates, and for the transfer of balances less expenses to the treasury. Unfortunately, no account survives from the twelfth century, and very little is known about Henry's toll and duty collectors. But they must have been financially successful if Hubert, the toll collector at Provins, is any indication, for he placed his daughter in the aristocratic convent of Fontaines-les-Nonnes, a house long favored by the counts and later by Countess Marie.[125]

More complex were disbursements from general revenues, assigned either as percentages of total revenues or as specific encumbrances. When Henry directed "those who collect my revenues" in Bar-sur-Aube to deliver 10 percent of his tolls and sales taxes each week to the canons of St-Maclou, he expected that sum to be calculated on his total weekly revenues.[126] Similarly, the canons of St-Quiriace received 20 percent of all his tolls and taxes from the two fairs in Provins, while the monks of St-Ayoul enjoyed three-quarters of the revenues from their fairs, in both instances the percentage being calculated on the total take.[127] Henry also placed encumbrances on specific fairs. The Templars, for example, received 12*l.* from the sales taxes at each Fair of St-Remi and St-Jean of Troyes, in effect a 24*l.* encumbrance on those fair revenues in Troyes.[128] The nuns of the Paraclete similarly collected 35*l.* annually from the three fairs at Provins.[129] Knights, too, collected fief rents from the fair revenues. The abbot of Lagny went so far as to complain to the pope that Henry was molesting his abbey by "assigning its [*sic*] revenues to knights as fiefs [*beneficia*]."[130] From these examples we can infer the existence of separate accounts for tracking revenues at each fair by source: from commercial sales taxes (in merchant halls), rents (for lodging), and fines, as well as tolls, entry fees, and transaction costs (for changing money). In effect, there must have existed both point-of-collection accounts as well as detailed general accounts recording each fair's revenues, encumbrances, and expenses as well as disbursements.

To maintain the good order of the fairs and to collect sales taxes and rents, Henry created a new official, the bailiff (*ballivus*), first mentioned in 1161, about the same time that bailiffs appeared in Flemish cities.[131] Earlier, hereditary viscounts, members of lordly families with urban tower residences, had monitored commercial activities in the count's towns, policed the roads leading to them, collected sales taxes and duties, and administered justice related to commerce.[132] Their replacement by directly accountable bailiffs and wardens of the fairs (first mentioned in 1174) was another of Henry's contributions to the effective administration of the fairs.[133]

Henry's Chief Financial Officer and Treasurer

Despite the surge in economic activity in the 1150s and 1160s and the consequent increase in the count's revenues, Henry's finances remain opaque in the absence of any extant financial register from twelfth-century Champagne. Even the function of his *camerarius*, who was a regular member of his inner council, is obscure. Modern historians depict him either as a minor personage "primarily in charge of the finances of the household" or as "a kind of minister of finances."[134] In fact his role may well have evolved from one to the other. Peter the Bursar (*bursaudus*), who had served the count's father since 1138, continued to oversee Henry's financial affairs with the title of financial officer (*camerarius*) until 1166. Under an itinerant Count Thibaut, Peter had been responsible for securing the count's treasure box, but with the increasing volume and complexity of the count's finances after 1152, the bursar's role shifted from the physical custody of the count's liquid assets to accounting for general revenues.[135] Peter's replacement, Artaud (of Reims), served as *camerarius* for more than three decades and figured more as the count's chief financial officer than as custodian of his treasure box.[136] Like the chancellor, whose oversight extended to the count's incoming and outgoing letters as well as to internal records, the bursar monitored the flow of the count's revenues and expenditures, much like Abbot Suger, who kept a record of the royal finances in the king's absence on crusade.[137] That Artaud became the butt of biting anecdotes more than a century later attests to his role as keeper of the count's finances. It is not known whether Count Henry held special sessions of his court devoted to audits of the provosts' and bailiffs' accounts, as was the case in Flanders after 1157.[138] But the fact that financial accounts survive from twelfth-century Flanders and England makes it highly likely that similar accounts existed for the equally complex financial regime in Champagne under Count Henry.[139]

If the count's *camerarius* oversaw Henry's finances, the treasurer (*thesaurarius*) of St-Quiriace, Rainald of Provins, assumed responsibility for the count's treasure boxes located deep within the crypt of St-Quiriace.[140] Consisting of two rooms cut from the rock cliff directly under St-Quiriace and later joined by a corridor, the crypt was an ideal location for the count's treasury, being both secure and close to the fairs in Provins, which at the time generated most of Henry's revenues.[141] It also was near the count's mint house, where the *provinois* was produced on St-Quiriace's property just below the cliff of the high town, and where the chapter collected a tax on every coin struck.[142] Given the proximity of the count's treasury to his mint, it made sense for Henry to appoint the chapter's treasurer to serve him in that same capacity, especially since Troyes lacked a natural, comparably secure site for the count's treasury. In confirming St-Quiriace's possessions following the restoration of the secular canons in 1161, Henry granted the treasurer Rainald, "for the administration of the treasury," the sales tax from hemp, linen, and rope for making bellpulls.[143] As a canon of Meaux and of both St-Quiriace and St-Étienne, Rainald was typical of the pluralist canons Henry relied on to administer his principality and was richly rewarded for his services. As the count's treasurer he tracked the inflows and outflows of specie from the count's coffers in Provins, while the bursar, who sat at court as the count's chief financial officer, kept a record of the count's global revenues and expenses. The sheer volume, variety, and complexity of cash flows at the fairs necessitated written accounts by toll collectors, money changers, bailiffs, provosts, and the count's treasurer in order to account for revenues, encumbrances, exemptions, and authorized disbursements.[144] The count's officials were as dependent on written records as the merchants who frequented his fairs.

The Principality in 1164

In December 1164 Count Henry turned thirty-seven. Since his accession thirteen years earlier he had created a distinctly new polity from his father's lands lying east of the royal domain, what fairly can be called a principality. The term *principatus*, meaning "a state or polity of the prince," was rarely used at the time and was restricted to the discourse of *literati* prelates. If Henry's chaplain Nicholas of Montiéramey once applied *princeps-principatus* to Henry and his county, the chancery did not employ either term.[145] Nevertheless, Henry had created a territorial state, a polity quite different from his father's. Although he traveled frequently, both within his lands and far beyond, he was not an itinerant prince like his father. The new comital campus, with his residence, attached chapel, and "his" canons, rooted Henry in Troyes, where he most often held court and his chancery drew up most of his letters patent.

And his new seal proclaiming him count palatine of Troyes symbolically placed Troyes, rather than his father's preferred city of Provins, at the center of his realm.

Henry is not known to have engaged in any military action within his lands during his bachelor years; all his military and diplomatic ventures were in service to the king beyond Champagne. Within his principality he was most visible through his acts at court, where a train of petitioners—prelates, monks, and nuns; barons, widows, knights with their families; townsmen, villagers, and immigrant settlers—sought something from him, whether benefactions, licenses, confirmations of property transactions, or the resolution of disputes. In all these Henry continued his father's legacy of exhibiting good lordship, even taking cases against himself when the facts warranted. Whether his court met at Troyes or Provins or in another castle-town, it was the locus of his authority and the occasion for its display. Philip of Harvengt reminded Henry of what he owed his father for his education, but the abbot might have pointed out that Henry also was indebted to his father for his early training in the craft of lordship.

The trade fairs, which became international precisely during these years, were critical to the economic development of Henry's principality, and indeed they became one of its pillars. By 1165 the cycle of fairs was fully operational, with the six primary ones being located in Troyes and Provins, and the *provinois* had emerged as an international currency and money of account. In addition to the various commercial revenues flowing to the count's beneficiaries must be added the indirect revenues stimulated by the fairs, such as the rents from lodgings and halls and the sale of provisions (food and wine), which most monastic institutions and many canons and townsmen enjoyed. Unlike merchants in Mediterranean lands who enjoyed extraterritorial status within urban enclaves, in Champagne merchants rented their lodgings, storage facilities, and trading halls from local proprietors, including the count. It can be said that Count Henry, building on his father's precedents, capitalized on the post-crusade surge in regional and long-distance commerce, not only by fostering the fairs but also by sharing their fruits broadly with the several constituents of his county, creating in effect a general community of stakeholders in the success of the fairs and his principality.

If the fairs generated a new economic prosperity in Champagne, the establishment of a resident chancery in Troyes was equally transformative for the administration of a polity comprised of thirty or so castellanies.[146] The term castellany (*castellaria, castellania*) was not new in the 1150s, but the sense of the term was, as it came to mean an administrative district surrounding the count's town or fortress, encompassing not only his lands, rights, and revenues, but also the communities, knights, and tenants within it.[147] The rolls of fiefs (1178) listing the count's fiefholders—his "castellany knights" (*milites castellarie*)—according to the castellany where they owed castle-guard presented a new cognitive map of Henry's principality (see Map 3).[148] A case from 1163 illustrates that new reality. After one of his recently impoverished knights alienated his landed fief to a local priory, Henry invested the prior with the fief. But when Adam Bridaine, a knight from Épernay, offered to hold the fief from the count in return for six months of annual castle-guard at Vitry, Henry paid the prior to recover the fief and its service. Fifteen years later, in 1178, Adam was listed among the count's fiefholders in the castellany of Vitry, not in the county of Vitry, which Henry had ruled as count of Vitry before 1152.[149] The old county of Vitry, like the counties of Troyes, Bar-sur-Aube, and Meaux, had ceased to exist as polititcal or administrative entities after 1152. If the county of Troyes disappeared, Henry's title, "count of Troyes," took on new meaning as "count of Champagne."

The castellany template that Henry imposed on the ad hoc collection of counties, lordships, and disparate properties he inherited from his father effectively redefined those lands as belonging within a single polity comprised of castellanies. Inherited castle lordships and small counties like Brienne and Bar-sur-Seine were reconceived as privileged enclaves existing *within* the count's principality, much like autonomous monastic lands, rather than as coexisting with it. The castellany template was just as essential to the formation of the principality as the new capital, the new chapters with almost 200 secular canons, and the consolidation of the trade fairs, all of which crystallized during Henry's thirteen years as a bachelor prince. It was a stunning achievement.

Chapter 5

The Culture of Count Henry

Count Henry was reputed above all for his generosity, primarily in the form of benefactions, exemptions, and commutations to religious communities. Many of those acts occurred in the course of his travels, when he, as the wealthiest and most powerful regional lord, was expected to bestow his largess on his hosts. His notary William carefully recorded those solicitations, noting, for instance, that Henry gave the Cistercian monks of La Crête a forge and forest rights at Wassy in appreciation for spending a feast day with them.[1] He made many smaller commemorative donations as well, like anniversary Masses for his father and mother and for Walter II of Brienne, his crusade companion. Peter Riga, the canon-poet of Reims, captured that aspect of Henry's character in a poem seemingly recited in 1165 at a banquet to celebrate the birth of King Louis's son Philip (II).[2] The poet devoted the last twelve lines of his 80-line poem to an extravagant eulogy of Henry, the guest of honor, making a play on *dare* twelve times (not always with equal grace) in what amounted to base flattery at a public event. Of course it cost nothing for a poet to laud the queen's brother and the infant's uncle for his widely known acts of generosity.

Walter of Châtillon, a poet of even greater distinction, addressed Henry on another occasion as the "the count of liberality (*comes libertatis*)."[3] Indeed, John of Salisbury identified "conspicuous liberality" (*liberalitas insignis*) as one of Henry's two distinctive traits, the other being "admirable humility" in matters of scriptural interpretation.[4] As applied to Henry, *largus* and *liberalitas* captured more than his material generosity; they conveyed an expansive sense of "open," "approachable," "receptive," and "honest." That trait, combined with his inquisitive mind, allowed Henry to develop close relations with leading *literati* prelates and clerics of the time.

A Circle of *Eruditi*

Having been "home schooled" by private tutors, Henry had all the character-istics of an autodidact, without the benefit or limitation of an institutional education in a monastic or cathedral school. Peter of Celle cited Henry's "most tenacious memory," a quality admired by *literati* prelates, especially Bernard of Clairvaux, whose own extraordinary memory was legendary.[5] Al-though Bernard remained a tireless supporter of Count Thibaut and knew Henry from his earliest years, he had no apparent influence on Henry's reli-gious or intellectual formation. Nor did another renowned preacher, Gebuin of Troyes, who had served as Bernard's secretary and worked on Bernard's sermons before becoming chanter at the cathedral of Troyes (1128) and bish-op's chancellor (1146–61).[6] Henry had known Gebuin since 1134, when as a seven-year-old he marked a cross on his father's letter in Gebuin's presence, and while still young he must have heard Gebuin's widely admired sermons. John of Salisbury, who heard them during his stay with Peter of Celle, was so impressed that he asked Peter for a copy of the sermons, as did royal chancel-lor Thomas Becket.[7] Henry endowed the cathedral chanter with a 3*l.* revenue, but it is doubtful whether the sermons made any lasting impression on him.[8]

It was another of Bernard's secretaries, Nicholas of Montiéramey, who had the strongest intellectual influence on Henry.[9] Born near Troyes and edu-cated at the Benedictine monastery of Montiéramey just outside Troyes, Nicholas became secretary to Bishop Hato of Troyes (1138) while still in his early twenties and already known to Abbot Peter the Venerable of Cluny.[10] Nicholas accompanied Bishop Hato to the Council of Sens (1141), then trav-eled to Rome to report the council's proceedings to the pope.[11] Young Henry had encountered Nicholas in the episcopal household in Troyes before Bishop Hato retired to Cluny in September 1145. Nicholas then joined the Cistercians at Clairvaux and became Abbot Bernard's secretary, with a private room for writing.[12] At Clairvaux in 1146 Nicholas witnessed Louis VII's younger brother Henry, outfitted in his finery, succumb to Bernard's charismatic presence and become a Cistercian on the spot.[13] During the next three years Nicholas and Henry shared a love of books in what was a treasured moment for Henry of France, who in appreciation bequeathed to Clairvaux his personal library of luxury volumes acquired earlier while he was a student in Paris.[14]

For five years Nicholas drafted Bernard's letters, which he delivered along with more confidential oral reports, in effect acting as Bernard's emissary, and

it is likely that he wrote Bernard's letter of introduction for Henry addressed
to Manuel Komnenos in the spring of 1147. He also wrote out, and perhaps
partly composed, Bernard's sermons. "I am sending you two volumes of sermons," he wrote to Abbot Peter of Montier-la-Celle, whom he had known in
Troyes, "copy them quickly and return the exemplars to me as soon as they are
copied."[15] At the same time Nicholas was procuring books from Cluny, where
he charmed Abbot Peter the Venerable.[16] Among the books Nicholas copied
for Clairvaux's library was a rare volume of Freculf's *History of the Franks*.[17]
Apparently Nicholas was a heavy borrower, and on one occasion Peter had to
remind him to return the originals of Augustine's *Contra Julian* and a history
of Alexander the Great after copying them, and to bring to Cluny "any other
good ones (*bona*) [that is, books] that you might have."[18] All the while Nicholas maintained an extensive correspondence on his own account.[19] In a flattering letter to Peter Comestor, a cathedral canon and master in Troyes, he
recalled their mutual "love of Scriptures, charming conversations, and graceful manners" before pointedly asking for a copy of the letters of Hildebert of
Le Mans, presumably available in the cathedral library, for him to copy for
Clairvaux's library.[20] Unfortunately Nicholas abused his cordial relations with
Bernard by misusing the abbot's seal, perhaps on an unauthorized letter. On
being expelled from Clairvaux "there was found on his person," Bernard informed the pope, "besides books, money, and much gold, three seals—his
[Nicholas's] own, the prior's, and mine—not my old seal but the new one I
was obliged to have made on account of his cunning and frauds."[21] Peter the
Venerable observed in mitigation that Nicholas had a wide knowledge of sacred and profane writings and was, moreover, an interesting conversational-
ist.[22] Count Henry, similarly charmed, immediately made Nicholas his
personal chaplain in 1151, even before Count Thibaut died.[23]

As Henry's chaplain, Nicholas occasionally witnessed at court and accompanied the count on his travels.[24] Henry's frequent mention of "my chaplain" Nicholas, "my dearest friend" Master Nicholas, once even "my dear and
familiar Master Nicholas," suggests that Nicholas was more than a chaplain,
that he was the count's intimate and intellectual mentor.[25] Nicholas would
have found in Henry a kindred spirit, someone imbued with letters—Henry
read closely (*codices prescruteris*), according to Philip of Harvengt—while immersed in worldly affairs.[26] For Bishops Hato and Henry of Troyes and Abbots Peter of Cluny and Bernard of Clairvaux, Nicholas was an accomplished
and engaging personality. Popes Adrian IV and Alexander III, too, were taken
with him. Alexander called him "a special son of the church" whose *opera* he

knew well, and sent letters of commendation to Archbishop Hugh of Sens and Count Henry.[27] The infectious charm of Nicholas led to a friendship with Henry lasting three decades, during which Henry supported Nicholas's bookish pursuits and received in turn anthologies and copies of books (see below).

Another of Henry's close friends was Peter of Celle, who came from a family of substantial means near Provins with long-standing ties to the counts.[28] After entering Montier-la-Celle, just south of Troyes, Peter continued his education at the Cluniac priory of St-Martin-des-Champs in Paris, where he developed friendships with Prior Thibaut (future bishop of Paris), John of Salisbury, and perhaps Suger at St-Denis. Peter returned to Champagne as abbot of Montier-la-Celle in 1145 and soon hosted John of Salisbury at the abbey's priory of St-Ayoul in Provins. As John later recalled to Peter, "I possess more [now] than we two possessed when we were together at [St-Ayoul of] Provins [in 1147–48]."[29] Although the role of St-Ayoul in the intellectual life of Provins has yet to be fully revealed, the priory seems to have functioned like St-Jean-en-Châtel in Troyes, where the priors, freed of monastic oversight, pursued bookish interests virtually as secular clerics within an urban environment. St-Ayoul acquired that role earlier, as Abelard wrote ca. 1130: "I fled secretly to the land of Count Thibaut [ca. 1121], where once earlier I had stayed in a monastic cell [at the priory of St-Ayoul]. I was slightly acquainted with the count personally, but when he heard of my afflictions, he took pity on me. There I began to live in the town of Provins in a community of monks from Troyes [Montier-la-Celle] whose prior [Ralph, 1098–1122] had long been my close friend and loved me dearly. He was overjoyed by my arrival and made every provision for me."[30]

John of Salisbury and Peter of Celle stayed in regular communication through the 1150s, exchanging books as well as letters across the Channel.[31] Their letters contain the most explicit evidence of the intellectual life of erudite clerics in Champagne and their ties with like-minded clerics beyond the county. In April 1157, while in Thomas Becket's service, John wrote to Peter in Troyes: "When you find a reliable messenger, please send me the [collection of] letters of Bernard; I beg you also to have an anthology made of his works as well as your own and those of the precentor [Gebuin] of Troyes and anything else that is similar."[32] John added: "Give my greetings to my dearest Thomas, your provost," an Englishman who was prior of Montier-la-Celle's priory of La Celle-sous-Chantemerle.[33] Peter replied that he was looking for Gebuin's sermons and would assign a scribe to make a copy as soon as he found them.[34] Shortly after, Peter sent John a copy of Bernard's letter collection as well as a copy of his own *De panibus*, a treatise on breads mentioned in the Bible. In thanks, John suggested that Peter write a sequel on wine mentioned in the Bible to complement, as he put it, the dryness of the bread.[35]

It was about that time, in the summer of 1157, that a fire destroyed the century-old church and buildings of St-Ayoul of Provins. "Nothing was saved except the books and relics of the saints," wrote Peter.[36] Reminded of the books he had left in Champagne, John asked for the return of his Boethius, *On the Trinity*, which he had left with Peter (at Montier-la-Celle), as well as the other books he had left with "lord Simon (Aurea Capra), prior (of St-Ayoul) of Provins."[37] To soften his request for the return of books, always a delicate matter among friends, John sent Peter a silver salt cellar by special courier.[38] If the conflagration at St-Ayoul reminded John of the books he left in Champagne, it led Peter of Celle, as the prior's superior, to organize a relic tour in England as part of the campaign to rebuild the priory church. John may have instigated the tour, since he specifically requested the relics of Saints Ayoul, Savina, and Frodobert, "on whose bread I was nourished [during his earlier stay at St-Ayoul]," and asked Peter to send an accompanying letter of authenticity.[39] Peter wrote that he was sending John the relics of Ayoul in a costly reliquary.[40] It was their close friendship that made possible a relic tour in England, a rare event approved by the archbishop of Canterbury.[41] Two years later, in 1159, John sent Peter a draft of his *Policraticus* for a critical reading, with instructions to edit and then forward it, if Peter thought it good enough, to the dedicatee, chancellor Thomas Becket.[42] Peter, for his part, replied that he was rereading John's letters (in the first letter collection) for their "charm and style" and their "perfect arrangement of the narrative," a most welcome appreciation for any writer.[43] The exchange of letters, books, and relics reveals a wide network of friends who shared early educational and institutional experiences. That network of *eruditi*, extending from Cluny and Clairvaux through Troyes and Provins to Paris and Canterbury, included Benedictine and Cistercian monks, bishops and abbots, as well as secular canons.[44]

It is unclear what role the cathedral chapter of Troyes and its school played in the cultural life of the city, since the fire of 1188 that razed the cathedral destroyed the chapter's library as well.[45] The bishop of Troyes, the count's uncle Henry of Carinthia, had studied in Paris before joining the Cistercians at Morimond (1123) in the county's eastern borderland, which was attracting a number of Germans, and then became founding abbot of a daughter house at

Weiler-Bettnach (1132).[46] When Bishop Hato of Troyes died in early 1146, Countess Mathilda, perhaps with Bernard of Clairvaux's encouragement, lobbied the pope for her brother Henry's election as bishop.[47] It was a propitious moment, after the election of Eugenius III (15 February 1145), the first Cistercian pope, while Bernard was generating support for a crusade. Bishop Henry apparently tolerated well a chapter of secular canons that included several luminaries besides the chancellor Gebuin, notably Master Peter Comestor, dean of the cathedral chapter since 1140 and an intimate of Nicholas of Montiéramey.[48] Peter Comestor was also a canon of St-Loup of Troyes, which supposedly had an ample library, and received a prebend in St-Étienne from Count Henry.[49] He began his most famous work, the *Scholastic History*, a compendium of biblical history, while teaching in Troyes and completed a first "edition" after becoming chancellor of the cathedral school of Notre-Dame of Paris in 1168.[50] In dedicating the *History* to his old friend William of Champagne, former provost of the cathedral of Troyes, Peter identifies himself as a "priest of Troyes."[51] Since Peter Comestor was among the handful of cathedral canons with prebends in St-Étienne, which Count Henry dispensed (see Table 2 in Appendix 1), it is highly likely that Henry was familiar with Peter's work on biblical history.

A cathedral canon with an even closer relationship with Henry was his childhood tutor Stephen of Provins, brother of the marshal William Rex of Provins.[52] Canon Stephen witnessed "on behalf of the count" in 1153, was among the original prebendaries of St-Étienne, and accompanied Count Henry and his brother William to Countess Mathilda's deathbed in 1160.[53] Stephen was typical of Henry's *eruditi* friends who remained in the background, working for the count without portfolio until Henry appointed him chancellor in 1176. It is striking how many accomplished canons were in Henry's employ, in the sense that he funded their prebends. Just as Philip of Harvengt had observed, Henry surrounded himself with talented, highly educated, and well-connected canons available for his service.

A Literate Prince

The letters of Count Henry's friends and acquaintances describe the routine exchange of books within an international network of clerics from the late 1140s through the early 1160s. John of Salisbury, Peter of Celle, Nicholas of Montiéramey, and Peter the Venerable were part of a friendship network that actively sought books in monastic libraries and exchanged exemplars for making institutional and personal copies.[54] John of Salisbury's letters are especially valuable in revealing how as a young student, "while poor and in a foreign land," he carried books with him, including a classic, Boethius's *On the Trinity*, and a recent treatise, Hugh of St-Victor's *Commentary*.[55] The production and circulation of manuscript books spiked in midcentury, reflecting the demand created by new institutional libraries and by prelates, clerics, and laymen like Count Henry who were building personal collections. Certainly St-Remi of Reims and Ste-Colombe of Sens possessed fine libraries from Carolingian times, as did the cathedral chapters in Reims, Sens, and Auxerre, whose scriptoria produced their books. By the 1130s and 1140s books were also being produced by professional scribes for both individuals and religious institutions. John of Salisbury acquired books while at school in Paris, as did Prince Henry of France, who had the means to purchase luxury volumes from high-end Parisian copy shops in the 1140s.[56] St-Victor of Paris, which emerged as a major intellectual center in the 1120s and 1130s, contracted with professional scribes to make and illustrate the books it could not produce internally. The chapter's rule of 1139 (*Liber ordinis*) required the librarian to distribute ink and parchment to external scribes and pay them for their work.[57] Like other new religious communities, St-Victor needed an entire library, and as soon as possible, to support canons interested in advancing their intellectual interests; they could not wait the decades required for in-house copying to create a working library. It was a similar convergence of institutional and personal needs in Champagne in the 1150s and 1160s that created an almost insatiable demand for books of all types.

In southern Champagne it was the foundation of new monastic communities, especially the Cistercians at Pontigny, Clairvaux, Vauluisant, and Larrivour, that spurred the production of books. After devoting their first years to the construction of abbey churches and claustral buildings, the brothers turned their attention to their libraries, making copies of biblical, liturgical, and patristic as well as ancient secular works from exemplars borrowed from older Benedictine houses.[58] At Clairvaux in the late 1140s, Nicholas of Montiéramey copied books from Cluny's library, both at Clairvaux from borrowed exemplars and at Cluny. At Pontigny, after the claustral buildings and church were completed by 1151, Abbot Guichard (1136–65) spent the rest of his abbacy developing a sizable library.[59] Pontigny's first catalogue, drawn up in 1165/75, lists about 150 volumes made in-house or purchased within the preceding fifteen years.[60] Vauluisant under Abbot Peter (1159–79), who may have been

English, acquired a collection of books in part from Pontigny's exemplars of the church fathers, historians, and contemporary monastic writers.[61] Like the canons of St-Victor of Paris, the Cistercian monks at Pontigny and Vauluisant purchased some of their books from professional copy shops in nearby Sens, which had become a major book-producing center by midcentury.[62]

There is evidence of professional scribes in Troyes and Bar-sur-Aube in those same years. William "the Englishman" lived in Bar-sur-Aube in a house owned by the Fontevrist priory of Foissy. Prioress Helisend, widowed mother of the butler Anselm of Traînel, asked Count Henry to exempt William from the provosts of Bar-sur-Aube, that is, from collecting the count's sales taxes, for as long as he lived there.[63] Although William's exact activities are unknown, a "William the Englishman" later held a prebend in St-Quiriace, copied two volumes of classical authors for Count Henry in 1167 and 1170, and was identified as a scribe/notary (*scriba*) of Provins in 1175.[64] A reasonable inference is that he was the same professional scribe, tasked to make liturgical books for the nuns at Foissy in the 1150s but available thereafter to make books for others, including the count.

In Troyes, as already noted, one of the count's chief scribes was Thibaud "the Scribe" (of Fismes), who earlier had served Count Thibaut as "scribe of the count."[65] Thibaut the Scribe owned five stalls in the main market of Troyes in partnership with three other canons of St-Étienne, one being the Englishman Walter Gilbert. A canon with three business associates in the chapter, who lived in a stone house in the chapter's close, and who "made many good things (*bona*) for us" (as noted in his obituary), Thibaut surely must have used his skills in making books for the chapter's library.[66] An entirely new chapter like St-Étienne needed at the very least a basic collection of liturgical texts, gospel books, and patristic commentaries. And a wealthy, high-profile chapter affiliated with the count would expect to possess a well-stocked library of cultural and intellectual interest as well; it would be surprising if the canons who were overseeing the construction of their individual residences in the 1150s did not assemble a chapter library to match the scale and extravagance of the count's chapel. Henry "spared no expense" in furnishing his chapel, observed Philip of Harvengt, and providing it with chalices, vestments—and books.[67] The demand for institutional and personal libraries, and the availability of talented scribes and illuminators, created a bull market for Latin books of all kinds after 1150.

It is difficult to determine when Henry began to build a personal library. He inherited from his father a handful of books, including a large, luxurious

two-volume Bible known as the "Bible of the Counts of Champagne."[68] Copied at Chartres in the mid-1140s and painted by Master Thierry of Chartres, it
was one of two sets commissioned by Count Thibaut, the second being the
"Bible of Saint Bernard," apparently Count Thibaut's gift to the abbot.[69]
Henry also may have inherited a volume containing Bernard's sermons and a
treatise of advice (*On Consideration*) addressed to Pope Eugenius III. Produced at Clairvaux and painted between 1148 and 1152, it may have been Bernard's gift to Count Thibaut, a token of appreciation for all the count had
done for the Cistercians.[70] An exquisite ninth-century Psalter made in the
same Hautvillers workshop as the Utrecht Psalter and later known as the Psalter of the Count also may have been a gift, either to Count Thibaut from the
abbot of Hautvillers or to Count Henry from Peter of Celle on becoming
abbot of St-Remi in 1162.[71] There is no evidence that Count Thibaut collected
books for his own enrichment; in fact, he regarded his intellectual formation
as deficient, and it was one reason that he provided Henry with a quality education. Even if Henry read from the "Bible of the Counts," his father's books
were primarily heirlooms rather than resources for expanding Henry's intellectual horizons.

Henry is known to have commissioned original works only from Simon
Aurea Capra, an esteemed Latin poet and prior of St-Ayoul of Provins (1148–
54).[72] Peter of Celle, Simon's superior who may have known him from their
student days in Paris, spoke of Simon as "the light of my eyes."[73] Early in
Henry's rule, perhaps in 1153, Simon composed a set of well-turned Latin epitaphs for the recently deceased whom Henry especially esteemed: his father
Thibaut, Suger of St-Denis, Bernard of Clairvaux, Pope Eugenius III, and
Hugh of Mâcon (first abbot of Pontigny).[74] Henry then commissioned Simon
to write *Ylias*, a 430-line Latin verse condensation of the *Aeneid*, which Simon
completed before leaving St-Ayoul in 1155 to join the canons at St-Victor of
Paris.[75] Henry's copy of the *Ylias* (the "short version," relating only the history
of Troy) contains a unique colophon: "Here ends [the poem of] Aurea Capra
on the Iliad, [written] at the request of Count Henry."[76] Later at St-Victor,
Simon "wonderfully corrected and amplified" the *Ylias* to include the adventures of Aeneas, with materials from Ovid and a fourth-century compendium,
Excidium Troie, among others.[77] One of the earliest copies of that "long version" was acquired by Bishop Philip of Bayeux (1142–63), a serious book collector, who left it with his 140-volume library to the abbey at Bec.[78] Both the
short and long versions of the *Ylias* are highly rhetorical exercises in con-
densed Latin, an unabashed display of Simon's poetic craftsmanship.

Having seen "Greece" in Constantinople and having heard Greek still spoken in those lands, Henry and his crusade veterans, with vivid memories of their own war journey to the eastern Mediterranean, would have been keenly interested in similar experiences of the ancients. But a 430-line abstract of the *Aeneid* was not an obvious choice for a book in the early 1150s, a time when Geoffrey of Monmouth had just completed a lively account of the Trojan origins of England in his *History of the Kings of Britain*. That was an instant success in Normandy, where a conscientious librarian like Robert of Torigni at Bec acquired a copy only a few years after Geoffrey finished writing in the 1130s.[79] But Geoffrey's *History* apparently did not reach Champagne before the 1160s.[80] Nor does Henry seem to have read or collected the vernacular versions of ancient epics popular in the mid-1150s, notably the "romances of antiquity" (*Roman de Thèbes, Roman d'Enéas*) and Wace's adaptation of Geoffrey's *History* (*Roman de Brut*).[81] Henry was less attracted to the chronology and details of historical events than to useful anecdotes, essentially teaching moments, for what they offered leaders like him, and the *Ylias* fit perfectly. It provided a close reader like Henry with a virtual anthology of exempla of personal conduct that he could explore under the guidance of his learned chaplain Nicholas.[82] For an inquisitive bachelor prince in his late twenties and early thirties, the company of a charming, erudite chaplain was a most welcome diversion from the business of governance.

Nicholas presented Henry with several of his own compilations in the 1150s, including collections of letters, sermons, liturgical sequences, and an anthology of classical texts—all examples, as he himself pointed out, of his keen eye for fine texts and his hard work in rendering them in pleasurable language. In fact, Nicholas freely mixed his own compositions with borrowed (unattributed) materials. His long-honed expertise as secretary to Bishop Hato of Troyes and Abbot Bernard of Clairvaux was precisely in gathering, reworking, and repackaging cultural products, whether ancient texts or recently written letters or sermons, which he offered with flattering dedications to important personages. One of his earliest collections for Henry was a miscellany, probably a presentation copy (dedicated "to his singular lord and benefactor Henry, count palatine of Troyes"), consisting of nineteen sermons by Bernard and several others, brief commentaries on the Psalms lifted from Hugh of St-Victor, several liturgical responses, and ten musical sequences.[83] Nicholas was of course intimately familiar with the sermons of Bernard of Clairvaux, some of which he may have written while in the abbot's service, and freely interspersed them with his own compositions. He made

two other copies of the miscellany, one dedicated to his fellow monks at Montiéramey and the second dedicated to an unnamed pope, most likely Adrian
IV.[84] Only Henry's copy contains the liturgical sequences, which were probably intended for use in his new chapel. Ever the proficient compiler and an-
thologizer, Nicholas based his sequences on earlier models at about the same
time that Andrew of St-Victor was composing his highly esteemed sequences.
The Victorines were reinventing the sequence repertoire in the 1140s and
1150s, and by introducing those new forms in Troyes, Nicholas was bringing
the latest style in Gothic song to the earliest example of Gothic architecture in
southern Champagne.[85] The new sonority emanating from St-Étienne was
soon shared with the regular canons of St-Martin-ès-Aires and St-Loup who
accompanied the seculars of St-Étienne in procession on their saints' days and
on the anniversaries of their deceased canons.

Nicholas's most influential compilation for Henry, now known as the *Florilegium Angelicum*, is an anthology of maxims and aphorisms drawn from
classical authors but edited and revised into a concise, elegant style.[86] As with
his sermon collection, Nicholas made multiple copies, which were subsequently recopied as choice, readily accessible anthologies of canonical authors.
Henry's copy became the exemplar for a presentation volume dedicated to an
unnamed pope, again most likely Adrian IV.[87] During a visit to Rome in
1157/59, ostensibly on Montiéramey's business, Nicholas captivated the English pope, who found him "delightful and agreeable" and obliged his request
for letters of credence addressed to the archbishop (Samson) of Reims and the
bishop (Henry of France) of Beauvais, Nicholas's fellow bibliophile a decade
earlier at Clairvaux.[88] Just what Nicholas's "business" was remains a matter of
conjecture, but it might not be too far fetched to see him scouting the fine
libraries in Beauvais and Reims for books to copy. Given his reputation for
lifting books and valuables from Clairvaux, librarians might have been reluctant to admit him, a situation rectified by a papal letter. If so, the *Florilegium*
was an offering to the pope on the occasion of Nicholas's visit, or after, in
thanks for the pope's letters. In his dedication Nicholas claims that he selected, edited, and drew up the collection "by my own labor" so that it would
delight and give pleasure.[89] He had the volume illuminated by the same talented painter or paint shop in Troyes that illustrated several other volumes for
Montiéramey in the early 1160s.[90] There is no evidence, in the 1150s, that
Count Henry commissioned or that Nicholas copied any single-authored volume for the count like the books Nicholas had copied earlier for Clairvaux's
library.

The History Project

About the time that his new residence and chapel were habitable, around 1160, Henry decided to build a personal library of works by historians, in what has been called the "history project."[91] His chaplain Nicholas located exemplars and even transcribed copies for Henry. In order to facilitate his task, Nicholas was appointed prior of St-Jean-en-Châtel (1160–79), Montiéramey's priory located in the old town of Troyes directly across the street from the abandoned residence of the counts. Henry provided Nicholas with a life income from a commercial hall where merchants sold fustian, woolen cloth, and other goods.[92] The next year Henry sealed two letters for Nicholas, "for the love of my dearest Master Nicholas." In the one addressed to the abbot of Montiéramey, Nicholas's nominal superior, the count exempted the abbey's three houses (merchant halls) in Bar-sur-Aube from his sales tax, meaning that the monks could keep any tax they collected, specifically to support Nicholas "for doing his business."[93] The second letter, a mandate for Nicholas to present to the count's officials in Bar-sur-Aube, announced that the count had exempted Nicholas from his justice and sales taxes, both during and after the fairs.[94] Nicholas's "business," here as in Beauvais and Reims, surely must have involved the acquiring and copying of books, and it is not coincidental that an assistant, a "subchaplain" Drogo, appears at the priory, most likely to cover for Nicholas during his absences in the quest for books.[95] Given his experience as acquisition librarian and copyist at Clairvaux, it is likely that Nicholas procured books for St-Étienne as well as for Henry, since the new chapter was in need of an entire collection of liturgical and educational books.

Henry's history books, each a single-authored work, were copied by a few hands from exemplars in nearby monastic libraries.[96] Nicholas himself copied at least three of the half-dozen identifiable volumes. One contains Josephus's *Jewish Antiquities* (*Antiquitates Judaicae*, Jewish history from its origins to 66 A.D.) and *The Jewish War* (*Bellum Judaicum*, on the revolt of 66).[97] Those sixth-century Latin translations of the original Greek books may well have been available at the cathedral school of Troyes, where Peter Comestor was drawing heavily on Josephus, especially the *Antiquities*, for his *Historia scolastica*.[98] Peter states in his introduction to the *Historia* that he wrote it at the urging of his colleagues (*socii*), who found the available glosses too brief and insufficiently explanatory of biblical history; they wanted to understand "the truth of history" (*veritas historiae*).[99] Josephus's *Antiquities*, with its expansive and imaginative reading of Old Testament history, appealed to Henry for the same reason. We must wonder whether Count Henry, given his proclivities, was among those who asked Peter Comestor to provide more historical background for a better reading of scripture.[100]

Nicholas also made a copy of Quintus Curtius Rufus's *History of Alexander of Macedon*, a Latin account of Alexander's life consisting of imagined speeches and romanticized incidents, probably from the same exemplar at Cluny that he had used to make Clairvaux's copy in the late 1140s.[101] He did the same in transcribing Freculf's universal *History* (from the creation to the coming of the Franks), copying the exemplar at Cluny that he had used earlier for Clairvaux's copy.[102] Like the *History of Alexander*, Freculf's *History* was a kind of "mirror of the prince," a commentary on moral political action, specifically on the conduct of a prince, with examples of what he should and should not do.[103] It is likely that Henry also acquired a copy of Hugh of Fleury's *History of the Franks* (*Historia Francorum*) in these same years as well as a copy of Baudri of Bourgeuil's *History* of the First Crusade, made from a volume at Vauluisant.[104] Baudri's *History* would have been doubly relevant to Henry, for its account of events in places that he had visited two decades earlier, and for what Baudri has to say about his grandfather Stephen, count of Blois and one of the leaders of the First Crusade, who died at Ramla in 1102.

The historical works that Nicholas copied exclusively for Count Henry—Josephus, Quintus Curtius Rufus, Freculf, Hugh of Fleury, and Baudri of Bourgeuil—were made in the years around 1160, after Nicholas became prior of St-Jean-en-Châtel and while Henry was subsidizing the prior's "business." Nicholas procured the exemplars, copied them in his own hand, and contracted with a local painter or workshop for their illumination, as he did for four other works copied for Montiéramey.[105] In overseeing the entire process of book production Nicholas served as a kind of literary agent for Count Henry and the chapter of St-Étienne, as well as for Montiéramey, where he was still nominally a monk. Even a connoisseur of fine books like Archbishop Henry of Reims sent his copy of Sigebert of Gembloux's *Universal Chronicle* to Troyes for illumination after being alerted to the existence of high-end Flemish or Mosan painters in Troyes, either by his old friend Nicholas or by Peter of Celle, who arrived at St-Remi of Reims from Troyes in 1162.[106]

Count Henry was surrounded by literate canons and prelates with whom he shared a culture of the book, that is, the Latin book. It was precisely Henry's erudition in Latin that Philip of Harvengt praised, stressing several times that it was Latin learning as opposed to Hebrew and Greek and, he might have added, French.[107] As Henry's chaplain and intellectual mentor, Nicholas of Montiéramey fed Henry a steady diet of anthologies, truly bouquets of cut flowers, until 1160 when the "history project" yielded historical narratives more to Henry's taste.[108] What inspired that undertaking is unknown, but perhaps one factor was conversation with learned canons like Peter Comestor and his colleagues at the cathedral school of Troyes, who also sought more history. What Henry absorbed from his books of history beyond their anecdotes, exempla, and memorable imagined speeches, all part of the cultural baggage of his learned canons, is not clear. But Philip of Harvengt may have captured the essence of Henry's book learning in remarking that the count sought relief from his duties by reading, secular as well as religious works. Peter of Celle, who knew the count well, confirmed that observation, as did John of Salisbury, who wrote to Henry that "He [Peter of Celle] assured me that you [Henry] enjoy nothing more than in having discussions with learned men on literary matters, and he added—for my private ear—that you often offend the unlettered because they cannot pull you away from your studies in order to immerse you in the tempest of practical affairs."[109]

Chapter 6

Pesky Prelates and English Exiles, 1165–1170

On turning thirty-seven in December 1164, Henry entered a new phase of his life. For the first time he was drawn into several abrasive, overlapping conflicts with neighboring prelates. In Langres, Meaux, and Vézelay the issues remained largely local or regional, but the papal schism, involving the monarchs of France, Germany, and England and the episcopacy of northern France, was of greater moment. So, too, was the acrimonious clash between Henry II of England and Archbishop Thomas Becket, which had long-term repercussions in France. One unintended consequence of Becket's exile was the arrival of an accomplished band of English clerics in the archiepiscopal cities of Reims and Sens at the very borders of Champagne; their learning and personal connections with like-minded prelates and clerics within the county fanned a regional bibliomania that consumed Henry and his chaplain Nicholas. Throughout these events the count continued to be fully engaged in governing his principality. He also acquired a wife and soon had children.

Countess Marie

Marie arrived in Troyes in late 1164 or spring 1165, about the time her sister Alice married Henry's brother Thibaut. We have no details about the date and place of her marriage, if a formal wedding was celebrated at all, since her consent to marry Henry, given in 1159 at fourteen, was sufficient in canon law to constitute a legitimate marriage. From that point Henry regarded Marie as his wife and countess. In a curious way their lives had been entwined ever since her birth in 1145, a fulfillment of Abbot Suger's promise to Queen Eleanor that she would bear a child if she convinced her husband to make peace with Count Thibaut. Offered in marriage to Henry during the crusade, Marie was betrothed at eight in 1153, after the royal divorce, and sent away before the king remarried in late 1154.[1] That was a typical convenience to a remarrying parent, to send away the children of a first marriage in order to begin a new family. Marie spent the next eleven years either in or near the Benedictine monastery of Avenay, where Alice of Joinville, sister of the count's seneschal, was abbess.[2] Most likely Marie was placed in the custody of the viscountess of nearby Mareuil and enjoyed the educational and spiritual benefits of Avenay without actually living within its confines, which may explain why the viscountess suggested in 1159 that Henry make a gift to the convent in appreciation for its services.[3]

By the spring of 1165 Henry and Marie were cohabiting and her cleric Laurent was sitting at Henry's court.[4] She was about twenty when she entered the comital residence, with its chapel built in the latest architectural style facing the twenty-five canons' houses, each with a garden, giving the air of a pleasant open campus. Laurent would serve her secretarial needs for the next decade, writing and presenting her letters patent in the same manner that the chancellor prepared and presented the count's letters.[5] Henry tasked one of his knights, Nevel of Aulnay/Ramerupt, brother of Archdeacon Roric of Meaux, as Marie's personal escort, and one of his chaplains, Drogo, as her chaplain.[6] Her household included a lady-in-waiting, a certain Nigra, for whom she later expressed a "sincere affection."[7]

Marie's first child, Henry, was born on 29 July 1166, one year after Queen Adele delivered the future Philip II (21 August 1165). Count Henry was overjoyed. Breaking with the practice of naming a firstborn son after his grandfather (Thibaut), he instead named the boy after himself, and in celebration of his son's birth on the feast day of Saint Loup, he commissioned a luxurious gospel of John for the canons of Saint-Loup of Troyes, located in the old town directly opposite the cathedral.[8] The count had been most generous, wrote Abbot Guitier after Henry's death in 1181: "He also gave this very gospel book which I have in my hands and in which I am writing, and he stipulated that it never be alienated from our church for any reason, at any time; young Henry, his son, is depicted in it presenting the book, as it were, to Saint Loup, in commemoration of his birth, for which the book was given to the same Saint Loup."[9] The volume was bound with a cover of precious stones and a silver engraving of young Henry offering the book to the saint.[10] On that same occasion, "when my son Henry was born," the count gave a 10*l.* revenue to the Fontevrist nuns at nearby Foissy.[11]

Marie sealed her first letters patent as countess of Troyes in 1166, in a grant of two mills on her dower property to the canons of St-Quiriace.[12] Her seal, typical of highborn women, depicts her standing in a long robe with a large belt and long sleeves hanging from her outstretched arms; she holds a large fleuron in her right hand and a dove in her left. It reads: "Seal of Marie, daughter of the king of the Franks, countess of Troyes."[13] In a few instances she simply witnessed Henry's acts relating to her dower lands without sealing, and in others she appended her seal to Henry's letter, as when he granted the canons of St-Quiriace the use of woods on her dower property at Jouy.[14] Thereafter she paid close attention to her dower lands in Provins, Coulommiers, and Jouy, very likely the same properties and rents that Countess Mathilda had enjoyed, but without Mathilda's private residence in Provins, which Henry had disposed of shortly after his mother's death.[15] Marie even wrote a personal letter to her father, the king, defending her right to seize men from St-Denis for not paying tolls ("which are mine") at Coulommiers. Henry used to collect between 7*l.* and 10*l.*, she claimed, whereas the tolls now produced only 40*s.* to 60*s.*, that is, barely half their former yield. So she was entirely in her right to apprehend toll evaders, she said, and asked Louis not to trouble Henry with this matter.[16]

Marie played no discernible role in the governance of the county. Henry's officials had been working together since their initial appointments in 1152, and the chapters of St-Étienne and St-Quiriace furnished his administrative and secretarial staff. Nor did Marie accompany Henry on his travels between his secondary residences, unlike Henry's mother Mathilda, who occasionally accompanied Count Thibaut. In fact, Henry and Marie's family life remains obscure. They were eighteen years apart in age, and had radically different formative experiences. Henry had grown up the eldest of four boys and six girls, had accompanied his parents on their journeys, and from an early age had been groomed in the arts of governance (which he did not provide to his own son). Despite the itinerant nature of his father's life, Henry had the strong emotional support of a large conjugal family, and none of his siblings predeceased him, making for a thick familial network that lasted his entire life. Marie's early years, by contrast, lacked a secure grounding. Eleanor had left her as an infant of two in Paris during the Second Crusade, and then abandoned seven-year-old Marie and her two-year-old sister Alice after the royal divorce in 1152. There is no evidence that Marie ever met her mother again, but even if she did, it seems unlikely that they developed lasting emotional ties. Marie and Alice may have met for the Christmas holiday in 1166, when Count Thibaut sat at Henry's court in Troyes (see below), but otherwise they seem to have led entirely separate lives, even in their later years as widows and regents.

Pesky Prelates

As a bachelor prince, Henry had very good relations with the four prelates whose sees surrounded his lands (Reims, Châlons, Langres, Sens) and the two (Meaux and Troyes) within his lands. But shortly before Marie arrived in Troyes, Henry and his brothers Thibaut and William became entangled in a series of conflicts involving the king, the regional prelates, and Pope Alexander III, who was residing in the episcopal palace in Sens. In September 1164 William, who was provost of both St-Quiriace and the cathedral in Troyes, was elected bishop of Chartres under unusual circumstances. As described in Thibaut's letter to the king, a handful of canons in the absence of the dean entered the church at dawn before the deceased bishop was buried and elected the chapter's provost as bishop.[17] The dean then convened the other canons and elected William, who was a serious contender by virtue of his multiple family connections—son of the old Count Thibaut, brother of the royal seneschal and the queen, and nephew of Bishop Henry of Winchester, who had graced the cathedral with many fine gifts, including an exquisite cross heavy with gold and gemstones.[18] Each side appealed to the king, who had not granted a license to elect, and Count Thibaut cautioned Louis against condoning an illegal election. On 8 October the pope ordered a new election to be held before 13 January 1165.[19] Not surprisingly, William again was elected bishop of Chartres, the primary episcopal see in his father's ancestral lands, despite being under the requisite age for consecration as bishop.[20] The pope permitted him to remain provost of St-Quiriace of Provins until his consecration, with the understanding that he would resign as provost of the cathedral chapter of Troyes. As the next provost, the pope recommended Herbert of Bosham, who had just arrived in France with Thomas Becket, as someone "outstanding in his knowledge of letters and in honest manners."[21] But William and the cathedral chapter disregarded that advice, and he remained provost of both the cathedral of Troyes and St-Quiriace of Provins. The pope, needing reliable allies for his own political maneuverings with Becket in France, let the matter drop.

Becket in France

Archbishop Thomas Becket of Canterbury had crossed the channel on 2 November 1164 to escape Henry II's wrath in the aftermath of the Constitutions of Clarendon and the Council of Northampton.[22] King Louis and the northern French lords received him with great honor and promises of material aid. All of Paris, in fact all of northern France, remembered Becket's spectacular entry into Paris six years earlier, in the summer of 1158, as Henry II's ambassador sent to lubricate the projected marriage treaty between the English king's three-year-old son and the French king's infant daughter. Becket's sartorial extravagance (twenty-four changes for himself) and all manner of sumptuousness was matched by the sheer magnitude of his train, consisting of two hundred gentlemen with their liveried attendants and wagons heaped with goods and presents, marching in serried ranks accompanied by squires and falcons before the chancellor brought up the rear of the grand procession.[23] No wonder Becket in exile was received so generously, at least at first. Within weeks he reached Sens (29 November), where he sought the support and protection of Pope Alexander III, himself an exile who had arrived a year earlier.[24] Archbishop Hugh of Sens had his hands full during the last two months of 1164, hosting within his episcopal quarters both a pope and an archbishop of Canterbury, two exceptionally forceful personalities.

The trials of Becket in exile are told largely in terms of his relations with the kings of France and England, but on another, subterranean level a network of personal relationships operated concurrently beyond the sphere of the purely political. Becket was received warmly by the king in Soissons and by the pope in Sens in part because of earlier relationships linking the English exiles to old friends and colleagues in France. A whole generation of English clerics had studied in Paris in the 1130s and 1140s, including John of Salisbury and Herbert of Bosham. While John kept his distance from Becket by settling in Reims, Bosham shared Becket's privations as his closest intellectual adviser, writer of his letters, and majordomo of the primate's household in exile. Their reception in Sens was particularly cordial because William of Champagne, the newly elected bishop of Chartres, immersed himself in Becket's tribulations.[25] William had spent a decade in England (1142–52) in the household of his uncle Henry, bishop of Winchester, and had met Becket as well as Bosham, who later recalled that he had known William "as a boy" and remarked with seeming familiarity that William was indebted to the English church "for having suckled him as a child."[26] William was still provost of two important chapters in southern Champagne and had three prominent siblings in Queen Adele and Counts Henry and Thibaut. It was a formidable nexus of influence, and Becket's former colleague and friend, Bishop John of Poitiers, advised him to take advantage of it. Accept the benefices offered by the king and Count Henry, John counseled, for they will treat you better for it.[27] Becket failed to heed that advice, as each passing month stiffened his resolve to act without constraining ties.

By the end of December Becket and his companions had settled in the nearby monastery of Pontigny, where Abbot Guichard provided his guests separate housing on the monastic grounds of one of the most striking Cistercian churches of the time, and which remains today much as Becket found it.[28] The English would stay there almost two years, to 11 November 1166, during which Becket, with Herbert of Bosham as his intellectual guide, improved his grasp of the sacred word and command of Latin.[29] The presence of an embattled Roman pontiff in Sens, an intransigent English primate at nearby Pontigny, and a bellicose archbishop in Reims made for powerful exemplars of prelate conduct at the very borders of Champagne, as a new generation of emboldened bishops challenged Count Henry on a host of issues dealing with episcopal-comital relations.

Two clashes with neighboring prelates in 1165 announced a new era of difficulties. In the spring of 1165 the bishop of Langres, Walter of Burgundy, brought suit at the royal court, accusing Count Henry of violently usurping episcopal lands, pillaging the village of Gevrolles in particular, and accepting the homage of Rainard of Montsaugeon for the village of Condes, which was "dishonest," said the bishop, because Rainard "was my liegeman."[30] The bishop even accused Henry's envoys of lying to the king about the matter. The king summoned Henry to a hearing at Gisors, where he had scheduled a meeting with Henry Plantagenet on other matters (11 April 1165), including a possible reconciliation with Becket. The count replied that he could not respond to such an important issue "without taking counsel" of his barons. He had convened them for Easter, he said, and would notify the king by Easter Thursday (9 April) whether or not he would come to Gisors.[31] Henry did not go to Gisors, and the outcome of the bishop's case is unknown.

In the same year Bishop Stephen of Meaux accused Henry of trying to ruin the bishop's coinage by minting debased versions of his coins.[32] Henry had enjoyed good relations with the previous bishop of Meaux, Manasses of Cornillon, and Archdeacon Roric of Ramerupt, who was Henry's confidant. Although Henry had a residence in Meaux where he occasionally held court, neither he nor his father had intruded in the city they shared with the bishop. Just why Henry counterfeited the bishop's coin is not clear, unless he was try-ing to make his own coin, the *provinois*, the exclusive coin circulating within his lands shortly after renewing the Fair of May.[33] Bishop Stephen, a former canon of Provins and Sens, and a resolute supporter of Becket, proved a for-midable adversary. In reconciling with the bishop, Henry admitted abjectly:

> I made coins similar to the coins of Meaux in my lands, causing the coins of Meaux to lose their value, for which I admit my error; and wishing to correct that error, I swore on holy relics that henceforth I will not allow the making of the coin of Meaux, either good or bad copies, nor will I permit the coin of Meaux to be debased in any way but will allow it to circulate throughout the counties of Provins and Troyes [that is, at the fairs] with the same value as the coins of Provins and Troyes and to be accepted without having to be ex-changed [by money changers].[34]

Three of Henry's closest companions ("my barons")—the butler Anselm of Traînel, Hugh II of Plancy, and the constable Odo of Pougy—swore on his behalf that he would abide by this agreement with the bishop.[35] Henry's effu-sive apology and corrective action indicate that he knew the danger of befoul-ing the image of good lordship that he, like his father before him, had assiduously fostered. But the ascendance of the *provinois* as the de facto coin of international exchange from the middle decades of the century and the consequent demise of the coin of Troyes effectively nullified the equivalence of the coins of Meaux, Provins, and Troyes, rendering moot any defense of the bishop's coin.

Vézelay

More entangling for Henry was the conflict between the new abbot of Véze-lay, William of Mello, and the new count of Nevers, Henry's nephew William IV, who intensified a long-standing conflict over the abbot's jurisdiction and taxing authority in the town of Vézelay.[36] The town had outgrown its original location within the abbey complex to become a substantial commercial center by the 1140s, when its money changers were frequenting the fairs in Provins. The previous abbot had tried to tax the merchants in Vézelay, but Henry's aunt Countess Ida of Nevers, in her husband's absence overseas, prohibited the merchants from doing business in the abbot's town, all of which earned her Bernard of Clairvaux's rebuke.[37] Encouraged by the countess, the townsmen of Vézelay revolted against the abbot, established a commune, and organized a militia (1152–55). The king ultimately suppressed the commune and restored an unquiet peace, but the fundamental issues regarding the relative rights of the abbey, the townsmen, and the count of Nevers remained unresolved. In 1161 the new count of Nevers reopened the conflict by prohibiting the monks from electing a new abbot on the grounds that he, as the abbey's protector, had not granted permission to elect. The monks claimed they had enjoyed immunity from secular jurisdiction since the abbey's foundation in the ninth century. An initial reconciliation broke down through a series of small missteps, and all attempts to appease the parties failed. The monks vilified Countess Ida for inciting the townsmen to violence, but this time the king was reluctant to intervene, perhaps because Ida was the maternal aunt of his new queen, Adele. Count Henry made excuses for William and Ida, forestalling intervention by the royal army and allowing the bishop of Langres to attempt arbitration, but Count William, encouraged by his mother, insisted on his rights. After being excommunicated, he and Ida occupied the abbey (25 November 1165), claiming the right of hospitality. At that point the sixty or so monks abandoned the abbey and walked to Paris to appeal to the king. On their arrival (5 December), Louis delegated Counts Henry and Thibaut to pressure William to make amends.

It is curious how the Vézelay affair, a local and regional conflict over rights, privileges, and revenues, became a flash point in the great clash over religious liberties in England. In April 1166, while Count Henry was still trying to mediate between the parties in Vézelay, the pope restored Becket as primate of England. Becket sent Herbert of Bosham to meet King Henry at Angers (1 May 1166), and then met John of Salisbury at Château-Thierry before traveling to Vézelay. There, at Sunday Mass on 12 June 1166, Becket unexpectedly thundered excommunications of Henry Plantagenet's supporters, calling them out by name to the dismay of all present.[38] King Henry responded in kind, threatening to expel the Cistercians from England and all his lands in France if Becket did not leave Pontigny, and so the Cistercian General Chapter (14 September 1166) advised Becket to leave. In those same months Count Henry and Archbishop Henry of Reims mediated a settlement between the abbot of Vézelay and Count William of Nevers that was formalized in November in Paris. Kneeling before the gospels, a cross, and relics, William swore to uphold the accord written in a chirographic letter placed

before him. Ida refused to swear but promised to abide by her son's understanding and had a knight take an oath on her behalf. The abbot and the
count concluded their settlement in a "great friendship," said the abbot's secretary, "and there was no distance between them."[39]

Just as the conflict at Vézelay was resolved, Louis VII escorted Becket
from Pontigny to the old monastery of Ste-Colombe in a suburb of Sens,
where the archbishop and his companions-in-exile would spend the next four
years (11 November 1166 to late November 1170).[40] It was an ideal location.
Alexander III had recently consecrated Ste-Colombe's new church (26 April
1164) in the presence of Archbishop Hugh of Sens, King Louis, and Count
Thibaut. The abbey enjoyed special papal protection, and it had a well-stocked
library that appealed to the *eruditi* in Becket's company.[41] Herbert of Bosham
spoke for many in Becket's company who gladly exchanged the spare life in
Pontigny for the pleasures of living in Sens.[42]

Reims

If November 1166 saw the resolution of the conflict in Vézelay and the transfer
of Becket to Ste-Colombe of Sens, it also witnessed an emerging crisis in
Reims, where Archbishop Henry had introduced the same combative style of
management he had exhibited as bishop of Beauvais. One year younger than
King Louis, he was on a fast track to a brilliant ecclesiastical career when he
experienced a religious conversion on encountering Bernard of Clairvaux in
1146. His brief stay at Clairvaux, besides introducing him to a fellow bibliophile, Nicholas of Montiéramey, made him a hard-edged Cistercian. Elected
bishop of Beauvais in 1149 with Suger's influence, Henry proved a contentious
ecclesiastical prince.[43] He incurred the enmity of his knights by refusing to
pay their customary fief rents, and his imperious manner troubled both the
cathedral canons and townsmen of Beauvais. Shortly after his election to
Reims (14 January 1162), he intruded in the contested episcopal election at
Châlons, where both candidates were from distinguished old Champenois
lineages.[44] Count Henry, the king, Pope Alexander III, and a majority of the
chapter supported Guy of Joinville, younger brother of Henry's seneschal
Geoffroy. Archbishop Henry alone sided with Guy of Dampierre, whose
death a year later ended that conflict, but his delay in consecrating Guy of
Joinville was a portent of his tenure in Reims.[45]

John of Salisbury, who had been residing at St-Remi in Reims since 1164
by invitation from Abbot Peter of Celle ("my dearest friend"), wrote an

account of the communal revolt in Reims.[46] St-Remi was a suburban monastic complex in a major archiepiscopal city, and like Ste-Colombe in Sens it possessed an excellent library. But it was a stressful time, and John drew a severe portrait of the archbishop.[47] He alienated his castle lords, who were in open rebellion.[48] He clashed with the cathedral chapter, which resented his heavy hand, and was reprimanded by the pope, who appealed to the king to reason with his brother.[49] The archbishop also withheld the fief rents owed to his knights and imposed, in John's words, "new and intolerable taxes" on the townsmen, who were determined to resist them. John's eyewitness account of the revolt in October 1167 is all the more valuable in that his host Abbot Peter, having assumed episcopal powers in Reims in the archbishop's absence, was at the very center of events.[50]

While the archbishop was in Rome, the burghers took over the city, occupied his towers and fortified houses, and expelled his officials and supporters in an attempt to force the restoration of their former liberties.[51] Abbot Peter recalled the archbishop from Rome, but he refused to dialogue with the rebels and fined them 2,000*l.* for their insolence.[52] The townsmen appealed to Count Henry, who was well known as a sympathetic mediator, but he declined to intervene within an episcopal principality in a matter involving the king's brother. Perhaps also remembering his father's role in acting with the king to suppress the commune in 1140, when he was thirteen, Henry advised the townsmen to consult with the king. But Louis rebuffed them and instead came to the aid of his brother and demolished fifty town houses of the commune's leaders, who in revenge destroyed the properties of the archbishop's collaborators. The archbishop then sought the intervention of Count Philip of Flanders, who reportedly entered the city with 1,000 knights. But the townsmen had taken the precaution of wasting the countryside, making it inhospitable to an occupying army. At that point cooler heads prevailed, and Count Henry joined Count Philip in counseling the archbishop to make peace with the townsmen.[53] The king was upset by his brother's intransigence, said John of Salisbury, so the archbishop ultimately called on their brother Robert of Dreux to mediate a settlement by which the old customs were allowed to stand in return for a 450*l.* fine to cover damages, far less than the actual value of destroyed property.[54] It is highly likely that Count Henry had a hand in the final settlement, given his reputation as a mediator and his friendship with Robert extending back to the Second Crusade. Meanwhile in Champagne, the count's castle-town of Vertus burned down, the "entire town," according to the count.[55] Whether the conflagration of Vertus was related to the revolt in Reims is unknown, but the fact that Henry had done homage to the archbishop of Reims for Vertus in 1154 suggests arson.

In these same months, according to John of Salisbury, Count Henry tried to mediate a long-term peace between the kings of France and England at the frontier between Gisors and Trie, where Becket and the English king attempted to reconcile their differences (around 19 November 1167). John reports that Count Henry and King Henry tried to outdo one another in cleverness.[56] It was during these negotiations that Count Henry met King Louis at Mantes and presented the fief of Savignies to Bishop Bartholomew of Beauvais, who had one of his knights promise service to the count.[57] Working behind the scenes with Count Philip of Flanders, Henry finally arranged a provisional agreement at Soissons (March 1168), and he must have been present when the two kings met again in Mantes in May.[58] But the English king made excuses and delayed accepting the proposed settlement, all the while ravaging Brittany. He even tried to manipulate the bishop-elect of Chartres, known to be close to Louis, but William saw through the duplicity.[59] It was during these on-and-off negotiations beyond Champagne that Count Henry appeared with bishop-elect William in Chartres, shortly before William's election as archbishop of Sens.[60]

Sens

William of Champagne was elected archbishop of Sens in late October 1168, and on 18 December, weak from fasting, was promoted to deacon in preparation for his consecration.[61] Count Henry was present, as was Thomas Becket, who must have been reminded of his own extraordinary ascension from cleric and chancellor to archbishop of Canterbury. On 22 December Maurice of Sully, bishop of Paris, installed William as archbishop.[62] King Louis had requested that William not go to Rome for a papal consecration because of the flux of current events, and so William was consecrated instead by his own suffragans in the presence of the king and queen and the "leading men" of the realm, including no doubt Counts Henry and Thibaut and their wives.[63] John of Salisbury, who had advocated for William's promotion, described him as "a person in whom great hope was placed, of noble reputation, and of high authority and influence in the French kingdom. After the king of France it is he who gives patronage, advice, and aid to the archbishop of Canterbury . . . for there is no one among the clergy of France who surpasses him in good sense and eloquence."[64] William Godel, an English monk living in Sens who probably witnessed the installation and later may have entered the archbish-op's service, called the new archbishop "a most splendid young man"—he was thirty-three.[65]

Archbishop William resigned as provost of St-Quiriace of Provins and chose Master Stephen as his successor.[66] He also resigned as provost of the cathedral chapter in Troyes, but only after reminding the canons (including Peter Comestor) assembled in the chapter hall, with his brother Count Henry in attendance, that he had received "the provostship with all its honor, dignity, and authority in elections, with jurisdiction over the cloister and the investi-ture of houses, and over fiefs, for as long as I live."[67] In recognition of that lifetime right, he retained a 20*l.* revenue on the understanding that the office of provost would not be filled after his death.[68] At the same time, William re-mained bishop-elect of Chartres through an exceptional papal permission, a token of his special relationship with Alexander III. In holding two episcopal sees concurrently, he rivaled his uncle Henry, who for four decades had been bishop of Winchester and abbot of Glastonbury.

Archbishop William immediately joined his brothers in attempting to resolve the issues embroiling Becket and the kings of France and England. On 6–7 January 1169 at Montmirail in the county of Chartres, Henry II finally accepted the terms worked out months earlier and renewed "the homage and fidelity" he already had done to Louis for Normandy (in 1151, before becom-ing king). Then the two kings "shook hands and kissed."[69] Young King Henry did "homage and fidelity" to Louis for Anjou and Maine (his father's inheri-tance), and Richard did the same for Poitou (his mother's inheritance). It was agreed in addition that Richard would marry Louis's daughter Alice, and that Margaret of France would be crowned with the Young King.[70] The matter of the archbishop of Canterbury had a different outcome. In the presence of the archbishops of Reims, Sens, and Rouen, and many bishops and abbots, Becket bowed to heavy pressure to end his conflict with King Henry and accepted all the agreed provisions. But at the last moment he uttered a reservation—"saving the honor of God"—which was taken as an insolence after all sides had devised a carefully scripted reconciliation.[71]

Meanwhile, Count Henry continued to act as an intermediary between Louis and Emperor Frederick, with the count's envoys in Lombardy propos-ing a marriage between Louis's two-year-old son Philip (Count Henry's nephew) and Frederick's daughter Sophie. John of Salisbury feared such an alliance, and the marriage did not materialize.[72] But Count Henry's involve-ment with these and other negotiations in the late 1160s reveals how deeply involved he was in the larger political events of his time, and how he played the great game of politics with the most important monarchs and religious leaders of western Europe. For the first time we might speak of a Champenois party around the king, with the new archbishop of Sens and his brothers Henry and Thibaut, soon joined by Stephen, acting in common with Louis in the business of the realm, just after their sister Queen Adele had provided the king with a male heir. It would remain a powerful alliance through the rest of Count Henry's life.

At Court

Despite his engagements beyond Champagne, Henry continued to devote himself to the local affairs of his county. In fact, much of his time was consumed by the ordinary, routine, and repetitive business of governance. As earlier, most of the evidence pertains to court cases involving religious institutions that preserved the records in their favor. But from the 1160s there also survive documents relating to transactions between laymen that lift a veil, if slightly, on the purely secular matters that must have occupied Henry far more than can be detected now. One of the more significant cases was heard on 29 December 1166 in Troyes in the presence of his brother Thibaut and several lords close to Henry. At issue was the fate of the castle and lordship of Possesse, which Jean of Possesse, then in his thirties, abandoned to become a Cistercian monk.[73] The case was unusual in several respects. Jean was a second son who inherited Possesse when his older brother, Guy II, died after mortgaging the castle to Count Henry.[74] During his eight years as lord of Possesse, Jean attended Henry's court when it met at nearby Vitry. But he seems not to have married, and after making substantial distributions of property to the Templars and five neighboring Cistercian houses, with the consent of his younger brother Hugh, Jean entered Clairvaux in 1166.[75] Thereafter until his death ca. 1192, he arbitrated disputes between monasteries and appeared in witness lists just after the abbot and prior of Clairvaux, a mark of his competence in practical matters.

Soon after Jean's brother Hugh succeeded to Possesse (minus its mortgaged castle), he mortgaged the rest of the lordship to Count Henry and left for the Holy Land. On the way, however, he married and settled in Italy, thus leaving the castle and lordship of Possesse in limbo without a direct heir. Count Henry might well have incorporated the mortgaged castle into his own domain lands, but instead he allowed the indirect heirs to present their claims at court. The court scribe captured the interplay between Henry and his barons in his own words:

> I, Henry, count palatine of Troyes, wish it to be known by this letter that Guy of Garlande and his son Anselm asked me to convene a court session regarding their right to the castellany of Possesse because Hugh of Possesse has married and remains in Calabria. At the appointed session in Troyes on the 29th of December, they [Guy and Anselm of Garlande] claimed the above mentioned castellany by right of inheritance, and I recognized their right. I pointed out, however, that when Hugh left for Jerusalem, he placed his land in my hand and later delegated me through legitimate nuncios to exercise custody over his land. Then my barons who were present, namely, my brother Count Thibaut [of Blois], lord Anselm of Traînel [butler] and his brother Garnier [of Marigny], Simon of Broyes, William of Dampierre, Hugh [II] of Plancy, the constable Odo [of Pougy], Girard of Châlons [lord of Nogent-sur-Seine], Drogo of Provins and his brother Peter [Bristaud of Provins], Peter the Bursar, the marshal William [of Provins], and many others decided that, to be fair about it, I should direct Hugh to return and retake his land within one year. If he does not, I will invest Guy and Anselm with their inheritance, excepting however Hugh's right, if he returns, and my own right for the redemption [of the mortgage] of my fief. The barons also decided that in the interim, if it was agreeable to me, I should commit the custody of the said land to Guy and Anselm.[76]

Since Hugh did not return, Count Henry allowed Guy of Garlande to redeem the mortgaged fief.[77]

The case of Possesse illustrates Henry's respect for the principles of inheritance within the baronage, where familial rights still trumped the count's prerogatives as the region's most powerful lord.[78] Clearly Henry saw his own interests as prince aligned with those of his barons in providing a legitimate successor to a substantial castle lordship. His successors would not accede so readily to the familial rights of the baronage, but a larger sense of collegiality prevailed in Henry's time and in fact characterized his rule. Possesse is also important in standing for the many strictly secular cases that came to Henry's

court, for which we lack extant records. The exact dynamic of the court's de-
liberation eludes us, but when the count speaks of "my barons," and the court
"directed that I should order" something, and the barons decided what the
count should do "if it was agreeable to me," the stenographer captures the
give-and-take of the court as Henry and the barons worked out an equitable
solution to an unusually complicated question of inheritance involving two
important castle lords, Jean of Possesse and Guy of Garlande, who were well
known to the court from having attended previous court sessions.

More dramatic was the excommunication of the count's constable and
close friend Odo of Pougy. Accused by the abbot of St-Germain-des-Prés of
abusively using the abbey's woods and contradicting the abbot's claim, he was
excommunicated by Archbishop Hugh of Sens. According to the court stenographer, "the abbot said that since the time of Charlemagne, who gave the
woods to the abbey in perpetual possession, the church had held them continuously and entirely, and had done there whatever it wished." No one dared
challenge the abbot's word at court in the absence of a written record of that
right, and so Odo, "fearing for his soul and on advice of his friends and of
me," Count Henry is quoted as saying, "quit his claim to the woods, retaining
only his right to use them to repair his bridge and fortress, and the right of his
men living within the walls of Marolles to use the woods."[79]

Most conflicts between religious houses and laymen were settled with less
drama on the simple recognition of established facts. When the nuns of the
Paraclete brought suit against the residents of Périgny-la-Rose, claiming that
Count Thibaut had required them to use the convent's banal mill, the matter
was quickly settled after Henry "recognized the truth of the matter" on the
word of the nuns in the absence of a written record.[80] Henry also accepted in
evidence a new type of document circulating in the decades after 1150, as well-
born men and women acquired personal seals that they used to authenticate
letters patent drafted by their household clerics.[81] Their seals carried the same
authority as those affixed by the comital or episcopal chancery, and were subject to the same scrutiny. At Sézanne in 1166, for example, "in the presence of
myself and my court," Henry heard the canons of St-Médard of Soissons accuse André of Montmirail, lord of La Ferté-Gaucher, of denying their tenants
the use of certain woods, and they presented André's sealed letter in evidence
of their right. After reading the letter "carefully" and verifying the authenticity
of its seal, the count confirmed the canons' right.[82] If the seal was a powerful
tangible expression of authority, it also could be made to testify against its
author.

Cases involving his fiefs continued to come to Henry's court. Peter of Origny, for example, brought his wife and two sons to a "day" at Château-Thierry because he had promised his fief to the convent of Valsery as an entry fee for his two daughters who wished to become nuns there; after hearing Peter explain the details of the feudal transfer, Henry consented and had letters patent drafted and sealed for the nuns.[83] The widow Aguidis of Montguillon and her three sons came to Provins seeking Henry's sealed letter confirming her perpetual gift to the nuns of Jouy of a fief that she and her husband had held from the count.[84] In these cases Henry authorized the conversion of his fiefs held by laymen to allodial property held by religious houses, as he routinely did since his accession, in effect relinquishing both the feudal property and the service owed for it; and he continued to confirm the acquisition of fiefs "up to the present day" and licensed unlimited future acquisitions without need of further consent.[85] But he also adopted a new practice in the late 1160s, of requiring the fiefholder to replace an alienated fief with his own allodial property, thus changing the tenurial status of the two properties, the count's fief becoming an allod, and the fiefholder's allod becoming a comital fief.[86] Only rarely, however, did Henry confiscate a fief alienated without his license, and then he usually relented after complaint from the monastic recipient.[87] The volume and variety of feudal transactions recorded by a fully functional chancery after 1160 confirm the scattered evidence of a complex circulation of fiefs before the 1150s, far beyond the widely documented alienation of fiefs to religious institutions.[88]

Bibliomania

The arrival of English exiles in Reims and Sens in 1164 fueled a frenetic quest for locating, copying, and illuminating books during the six years of Becket's residence in France. It was entirely fortuitous that the taste and expertise of the English, who came without their books, spurred Count Henry's book collecting. His predilection for works of history and moral instruction coincided with their tastes, which had been enriched by a generation of precocious Anglo-Norman historiographers in the 1130s and 1140s, chroniclers who combined an interest in ancient history with a sensitivity to issues regarding the moral conduct of political leaders. Both Nicholas of Montiéramey, on Count Henry's behalf, and Herbert of Bosham, for Becket, combined their frequent diplomatic missions with visits to old monastic libraries at Cluny,

Ste-Colombe of Sens, St-Denis, and St-Remi of Reims, and to cathedral libraries in Auxerre and Beauvais in order to copy or borrow exemplars. The
traffic in books already well under way by the 1150s reached a frenzy after 1164.

The English in Reims, Pontigny, and Sens

John of Salisbury described his return to France in the spring of 1164, fifteen
years after completing his studies in Paris, as almost a reverie. France was a
land of peace and prosperity, he observed, as he was greeted warmly at every
stage of his journey from the coast to Paris. The abundance of food, the happiness of the people, and respect for the clergy reminded him of Ovid's quip:
"A happy thing is exile in such a place as this."[89] Becket had urged John to stay
in Paris and resume an academic life, but John lacked sufficient resources—
Paris was expensive even then—and sold his horses for a year's rent, payable in
advance. John finally wrote to Peter of Celle, seeking an invitation to Reims.
Peter would have offered what he later proposed to Bishop Bartholomew of
Exeter: a furnished house, a large library, and the leisure (*otium*) for his stud-
ies.[90] For Peter and John it was the renewal of a friendship formed during their
student days in Paris in the early 1140s and continued briefly at St-Ayoul of
Provins in the late 1140s and in correspondence through the 1150s. St-Remi
proved an ideal refuge, both for a library reputed for its extensive holdings in
Greek and Latin, and for keeping John at some distance from Becket at Sens.[91]
Reims was close enough to Troyes to permit easy communication with Count
Henry, who in the summer of 1166 forwarded to John a letter sent to him by
Frederick Barbarossa, which John in turn sent on to Becket at Pontigny.[92]

Reims was comforting to John in another sense, in that it harbored a
community of English who served as teachers in the cathedral school and as
deans of the cathedral chapter. Master Fulk of the cathedral school became
dean of the chapter and figured prominently as papal judge delegate, often in
the company of Peter of Celle, abbot of St-Remi, during an expansive period
of papal delegations under Alexander III.[93] The distinguished jurist Ralph of
Sarre, who had ties to Reims even before Becket's exile, succeeded Fulk as
dean and subsequently bequeathed his large personal library to Canterbury
cathedral.[94] And Philip of Calne, who taught law, become archdeacon of the
cathedral chapter by 1170.[95] The fact that John of Salisbury and other English
clerics settled in Reims confirms the continuing prestige of its cathedral school
in the second half of the twelfth century.[96] Count Henry and Nicholas of
Montiéramey also had important personal ties to Reims. Archbishop Henry's

long-standing ties with Nicholas began in the late 1140s at Clairvaux, where they shared an interest in fine books. Peter of Celle, alter ego of the archbishop in his absence, had been Count Henry's closest prelate friend while abbot of Montier-la-Celle until 1162. Simon Aurea Capra, prior at the Carthusian priory of Mont-Dieu, a favorite retreat for weary prelates near Reims, had written the *Ylias* for Count Henry while prior of St-Ayoul of Provins, where John of Salisbury had stayed in 1148.[97] And so when John arrived in Reims in 1164, he passed seamlessly into an overlapping nexus of political, intellectual, and personal ties linking the archbishop, his brother the king, Peter of Celle, Simon Aurea Capra, and Thomas Becket with Count Henry and the *literati* clerics in Troyes, Clairvaux, and St-Victor.[98] Finding St-Remi conducive to writing, John immediately set to recording his recollection of events witnessed more than a decade earlier under the title *Memoirs of the Papal Court* (*Historia pontificalis*), dedicated to his host and friend Peter of Celle, all the while producing and receiving a voluminous correspondence.[99] On returning to England in December 1170, John remembered how happy he had been at St-Remi, "a place like paradise."[100]

Within months of John's arrival in Reims, Becket reached Sens (November 1164) after an almost celebratory march from the coast of France. He came to press his case with the pope, who had spent the last year in residence in the archbishop's palace, and soon settled with his entourage in the nearby Cistercian monastery of Pontigny.[101] Founded in 1114 as the second daughter of Cîteaux, it had grown to perhaps one hundred monks by 1165, not counting lay brothers, living in the monastic compound around the magnificent abbey church, the largest Cistercian church of the time.[102] Herbert of Bosham did not take to living in Pontigny, as he put it, "in solitude among stones [of the newly built church] and monks." It was a shock to Becket's household, accustomed as it was to fine dining and agreeable conversation with nobles and knights at Becket's generous table, although Bosham did admit that the monks allowed the exiles to eat meat and to enjoy "certain other indulgences."[103] Pontigny, only twenty kilometers from Auxerre, where Becket earlier had studied briefly, provided Becket with the tranquillity to rectify his knowledge of the scriptures under Bosham's guidance. It was here that Becket asked Bosham, who remained his most influential theological mentor during exile, to edit Peter Lombard's *Great Gloss and Commentary* on the Psalms and Epistles, which Becket was studying daily. Writing in his own hand, Bosham composed the pages to guide the reader by adding running titles, numbering the chapters, varying scripts by color and size, adding side notes, and inserting colored initials. Inventor of a highly original *mise en page*, Bosham was, in sum, a type-setter *avant la lettre*.[104] His project would take another decade to finish.[105]

It was at Pontigny, Bosham later reminisced, that church-state issues were discussed and were set to imagined dialogues between Becket and his *eruditi*, including Bosham himself.[106] Bosham recalled their study group, where Becket was particularly drawn to the Psalms and Epistles.[107] It is curious, though, that Bosham should furnish so much information about the exile years without mentioning his own role in procuring books for Pontigny and for Becket. Pontigny was in the midst of a programmatic copying of books for its library, an enterprise that may have prompted Bosham to act as its acquisitions librarian, an expert who knew what belonged in a proper library.[108] William Fitzstephen reports that Becket—actually Bosham on his behalf—searched for books far and wide: "there was not a church bookcase in all of France with an old book that he did not have copied."[109] When Becket left France in December 1170, he took with him a personal collection of sixty-nine volumes, which is to say, he had acquired about one volume per month during his six years of exile.[110]

Becket's move to Ste-Colombe of Sens (November 1166) was fortuitous, according to Bosham, in that it offered urban amenities within the tranquility of a suburban religious setting.[111] Sens was a royal town that Louis VII often visited, and an especially attractive one according to Bosham, who praised its bountiful countryside—the abundance of grain, wine, oil, forests, and rivers— and the exemplary character of its people, that is, liberally educated and urbane clerics, and hospitable, generous, and easygoing laymen.[112] Bosham did not mention two other recent enhancements in Sens: the towering, just-completed cathedral built in the latest style, and the professional book-making and illumination shops that made Sens a center of the book trade. Ste-Colombe thus gave access both to a well-stocked library and to professional copyists and illustrators working in Sens, which must have facilitated the production of books for Becket.[113] Archbishop Hugh of Sens was known as a collector of painted books as well as the builder of a spectacular cathedral, but it was the presence of three learned prelates—the pope, the archbishop, and Becket—with active chanceries and literate entourages that made Sens a major book-producing center by the 1160s. Bosham commissioned a number of books from commercial copy shops in Sens, as did nearby monasteries, especially of large, single-volume Bibles painted in Channel style. If the demand for copies of old books spiked in the 1160s, so did the need for copies of brand-new books, especially the glossed books of Peter Lombard, Peter Comestor, and Gratian.[114] Bosham failed to mention another factor that made Sens such an important regional center: the close personal ties between the archbishop and canons of Sens with canons in Champagne at the cathedral of Troyes, St-Étienne of Troyes, and St-Quiriace of Provins, where Mathieu, former preceptor of Sens, was dean of the chapter.

Despite Bosham's failure to mention Nicholas of Montiéramey, Bosham was well known in Troyes and cooperated with Nicholas in acquiring, exchanging, and producing books for their patrons in those years. Alexander's recommendation of Bosham to replace William of Champagne as provost of the cathedral of Troyes failed perhaps because of Bosham's prickly character and foppish manners. Well known as an eccentric foil to Becket, he was just as transgressive in his personal comportment as Nicholas of Montiéramey, who once wrote a presumptuously familiar letter to the bishop of Auxerre requesting a barrel of fine wine.[115] William Fitzstephen, who knew Bosham well, relates a telling anecdote. During an encounter between Henry II and Becket, the king remarked on Bosham's arrival with a sharp comment: "See, here comes a proud one, acting like a noble, splendidly attired, wearing a tunic and cloak of green cloth of Auxerre hanging from his shoulders in the German manner and falling to his ankles, with suitable adornments." Bosham harangued the king, said Fitzstephen, to which the exasperated king replied: "Why should my kingdom be disturbed and my peace unsettled by the son of a priest [referring to Bosham]." To which the ever impertinent Bosham responded: "I, at least, am not the son of a priest, for I was not born while my father was a priest, which he became only later; nor, in the same manner, is one the son of a king unless his father was born a king." That carried a sting, for Henry II was the son of a count.[116] Such a character was not destined for higher ecclesiastical office.

Count Henry's Library

Henry possessed about twenty books of various provenance before 1165.[117] From his father he inherited a large, two-volume Bible produced at Chartres ("Bible of the Counts of Champagne"), a volume of Bernard of Clairvaux's sermons, and perhaps a ninth-century Psalter. In the 1150s he commissioned or received as gifts—the distinction not always being clear when the copyist was in his employ or held a prebend through his good offices—Simon Aurea Capra's verse *Ylias* and several anthologies compiled by Nicholas of

Montiéramey of sermons, liturgical sequences, letters, and ancient texts, notably in the *Florilegium Angelicum*. After Nicholas became prior of St-Jean-en-Châtel in 1160, Henry acquired several works by historians: Josephus's *Jewish Antiquties* and *The Jewish War*, Quintus Curtius Rufus's *History of Alexander of Macedon*, Freculf's universal *History*, and probably Hugh of Fleury's *History of the Franks* and Baudri of Bourgueil's *History* of the First Crusade.

Between January 1165 and the late months of 1170 the English *eruditi* in Reims and in Becket's company in nearby Pontigny and Sens reinvigorated Henry's quest for books, with Nicholas of Montiéramy and Herbert of Bosham serving as scouts, copyists, and production managers of books reflecting the interests of the English. Henry acquired a copy of Geoffrey of Monmouth's *History of the Kings of Britain*, most likely made while Becket was in residence at Pontigny and from the same exemplar used for the copies made for Becket and for Pontigny.[118] Given Henry's historical bent and the popularity of Geoffrey's highly entertaining if imaginative tales of King Arthur and the magician Merlin, the *History of the Kings of Britain* was an ideal addition to Henry's eclectic collection of histories. It is likely that Henry also acquired Vegetius's *De re militari* in these same years, and from the same exemplar as Becket's copy.[119] John of Salisbury, writing from Reims in 1166 or 1167, alluded to it with humor in praising Henry for his learning and devotion to practical matters: "as your Vegetius says, no one ought to know more than a prince, whose knowledge can benefit all his subjects."[120] If Vegetius stimulated discussion about military training, the organization of military units, and siege warfare, it was John's *Policraticus* that popularized Vegetius as a kind of "mirror" for the prince, who might well ponder the role of skill, preparation, psychology, and intelligence in successful battles, but even more the role of a prince in an advanced civil society.[121] An enlightened ruler like Henry needed to know his Vegetius, and John implied that Henry already was familiar with the text.

Henry's curiosity extended far beyond historical anecdotes to probing questions about texts and correct readings. In 1167 he posed five questions to Alberic, master at the cathedral school of Reims: How many books comprised the Old and New Testaments? Who were their authors? What was the Table of the Sun that the philosopher Apollonius saw in the sand, as mentioned by Jerome in a letter to the priest Paulinus? What are the cantos of Virgil and Homer mentioned in the same letter of Jerome? And what is the source and meaning of the oft-quoted statement "Those things which do not exist are more God-like than those things that do exist"? Master Alberic asked John of Salisbury to respond, since he knew Henry. In a treatise-letter John begins with a gracious remembrance of Count Thibaut's support during John's student days, and flatters Henry by mentioning Peter of Celle's assurance that Henry's questions were genuine and the count took pleasure in intellectual exchange.[122] After a learned disquisition on the books of the Old and New Testaments and their authors, John provides an elegant explication of the Table of the Sun. Jerome had touched on the subject, said John, but Valerius Maximus offers a more detailed account in his *Memorable Deeds and Sayings* (*Facta et dicta memorabilia*), which John apparently consulted in St-Remi's library, citing "Book 4, chapter 1, under the rubric *On Moderation*."[123] In ancient Miletus, John recounts, a dispute arose between the fishermen and a man who had prepurchased the day's catch of fish. Since the fishermen hauled in a gold Delphic table with the fish, the purchaser naturally demanded it, too, since he had paid for the entire catch, that is, whatever was in the nets, whereas the fishermen argued that he had purchased only the fish. The dispute was submitted to the oracle of Delphi, who pronounced that the table would bring misfortune to the possessor unless he was the wisest of all men. Seven wise men in turn declined the tribute and the table. Finally Solon offered the table to Apollo, in whom the Sun was worshipped; and so, according to Valerius Maximus, the table was called the Table of the Sun. The story so impressed Henry that he resolved to have his own copy of anecdotes by the first-century rhetorician and historian. William the Englishman made the copy in Provins and inscribed his name and date of completion, 1167, in a colophon.[124] Henry's copy of *Memorable Deeds and Sayings* is distinctive in that it was made from the very ninth-century manuscript owned and annotated by Loup of Ferrières (ca. 805–62), an esteemed collector of ancient books, and includes Loup's marginal notations as if they were integral to the original text.[125] It is not coincidental that Henry had his tomb inscribed with allusions to himself as an Apollonian sun god.[126]

In that same year, 1167, Henry wrote to Herbert of Bosham, who had studied with Peter Lombard in Paris, asking him to explain the discrepancy between the gospels of John and Mark regarding the number of Marys present at the Crucifixion. Bosham replied that he was at the moment at St-Denis with Master William of London and another William (le Mire), a physician who became a monk (later abbot) at St-Denis and who had returned from Constantinople with Greek books.[127] Bosham said he had engaged the two Williams and John of Salisbury ("whom you know") in discussing the question of the three Marys. He concluded his letter by informing the count that "I do not have the book containing Aulus [Gellius]'s *Attic Nights*, which you have asked about many times; it belongs to Ste-Colombe."[128] Henry's repeated inquiries to Bosham suggest that he knew of *Attic Nights*, a second-century anthology of observations and anecdotes, perhaps from the extracts Nicholas had made in the *Florilegium Angelicum* or from John of Salisbury's *Policraticus*.[129] Again, it was William the Englishman who made a copy of *Attic Nights* for Henry, with a colophon identifying himself as the copyist and giving the date of completion, 1170.[130] The fact that William does not mention having made the copy in Provins suggests he worked from Ste-Colombe's exemplar in its library, and indeed may have made two copies concurrently, one for Henry, the other for Becket.[131] Henry must have appreciated *Attic Nights* for its exploration of etymology and correct word usage, which paralleled his own inquiries into the meaning of secular and sacred texts. *Memorable Deeds* and *Attic Nights* provided Henry with two canonical collections of easily digestible anecdotes regarding the customs and moral conundrums of the ancients, with examples of proper conduct.

Henry acquired at least three other books directly or indirectly through the English exiles. All three were made in multiple copies, with each bibliophile arranging for painting at his own expense. The exemplar of Livy's *Third Decade*, an account of the Second Punic War, was copied first at St-Denis, then passed successively to Herbert of Bosham for copying in Sens and to Nicholas of Montiéramey for making Count Henry's copy in Troyes, each book being locally produced and illustrated.[132] Three copies were made of Cyprian's letters as well, one for Henry, a second for Becket, and a third for Bishop Hugh (of Le Puiset) of Durham, the son of Henry's aunt Agnes and protégé of her brother Bishop William of Winchester.[133] Count Henry and Bishop Hugh had been in Rouen in May 1160, when the kings of France and England signed a marriage treaty for their children; later they acquired related copies of the poems of Claudian, again with Henry's copy likely being painted in Troyes.[134] Although Herbert of Bosham and Nicholas of Montiéramey are rarely visible in the extant records as procurers of books, they were the key facilitators in the great enterprise of exchanging, copying, and illuminating books, often in multiple copies, while the English exiles were in Pontigny and Sens. Kindred spirits, they were knowledgeable clerics who knew their books, both the classics and religious texts, and skilled secretaries who wrote for and "in the name of" distinguished personages, Bosham even writing a letter to the pope "in the name of" Count Henry.[135]

Count Henry knew another active bibliophile, Abbot Milo of St-Marien of Auxerre, the youngest of the Traînel brothers, his butler Anselm II and

Garnier, who were constantly in the count's company. Born in 1127 and thus the same age as Count Henry, Milo was placed in St-Marien (Premonstratensian) in 1136 on the advice of Abbot Hugh of Pontigny, and remained there for the rest of his life as monk and abbot (1155–1203). A fellow monk who knew Milo well later wrote a brief *vita* extolling Milo for his virtues and frugality, for shunning ostentation and public display, for being discreet and serious in counsel and a lover of truth who hated injustice, in effect, a perfect reformed abbot. Although his family was "among the wealthiest and most powerful in Champagne," Milo did not abuse his familial ties, and in fact he solicited financial support for his new abbey at "the courts of princes and bishops," no doubt including Count Henry.[136] But Milo also shared a deep love of books, wrote his biographer, so much so that "he spared no expense for the copying of books and, collecting volumes from wherever he could, he built a distinguished library collection," a fact also noted in his tomb epitaph.[137] It is not too far fetched to imagine Milo using his official visits to Troyes as occasions to meet his brothers and to discuss books with Count Henry at the very time when both were acquiring libraries.

The regional bibliomania of the 1160s relates entirely to the "old learning" in Latin, of classical, patristic, and sacred texts from the ancient world, and of current treatises, letters, and sermons by *literati* prelates and clerics. *Imitatio* of the ancients and *inventio* by contemporaries, both written in Latin, corresponded well to Henry's traditional education, his interest in history, and his relations with local *literati* prelates. Henry had no interest in the vernacular "romances of antiquity" circulating by the mid-1150s as adaptations of ancient Latin works directed to a lay audience.[138] It is curious, however, that he did not commission a dynastic foundation story of the Thibaudians or even a celebration of his own achievements. Beyond the *Ylias*, the only original work that he is known to have commissioned—and it is more a reworking than wholly original—there is not a single allusion to his patronage of contemporary writers. Chrétien de Troyes, who was writing his first Arthurian romance, *Erec et Enide*, about the time that William the Englishman was copying *Attic Nights* in 1170, proudly proclaims himself "of Troyes" in his prologue. But the story of Erec and Enide, its locales, and its personages belong rather to the world of King Henry II of England, and although Chrétien does not refer explicitly to either Henry II or Queen Eleanor, the guest list at Erec's coronation at Nantes on Christmas 1169 strongly suggests that Chrétien was quite familiar with the Plantagenet realm.[139] Nothing in the story relates to Champagne or to Henry or Marie. Henry's culture was resolutely Latin and, in a sense, "academic."

Chapter 7

Count Henry in Mid-Life, 1171–1175

Just days before the murder of Thomas Becket on 29 December 1170, Count Henry turned forty-three. He had ruled for nineteen years, during which his county had evolved into one of the more prosperous and influential principalities in northern France. After six years of marriage he and Marie, then twenty-five, had a four-year-old son Henry and soon would have a daughter, Marie. Shortly after her birth the count expressed his deep satisfaction with his family in making a gift to the priory of St-Jean-en-Châtel in Troyes, where his good friend Nicholas was prior, "for the salvation of my soul and the souls of my parents, and for my wife and my children so that God preserve them in well-being and good fortune."[1] One way to assure their well-being and good fortune was to arrange suitable marriages, and by August 1171 Henry was arranging matches with Count Philip of Flanders. It was Philip's father, Count Thierry, who in the fall of 1147 had joined Henry and Count William IV of Mâcon in crossing the Meander River with such verve that they saved the crusader army from Turkish archers on the opposite bank. Those overseas experiences forged lasting bonds among crusader veterans and led to marriage alliances between their children and grandchildren. Since Count Philip himself lacked children, he acted on behalf of his sister Margaret and her husband Baldwin V, the new count of Hainaut (1171–95), in contracting marriages between their infant children and Count Henry's children.[2]

Gislebert of Mons, Count Baldwin's chaplain and later chancellor, describes the terms of the double marriage contract, which he himself may have drafted. Count Henry's eldest son Henry, then five years old, was betrothed to Count Baldwin's year-old daughter Elizabeth, while the newly born Marie was betrothed to the infant Baldwin (VI) of Hainaut. Each couple would marry "when they both reach a marriageable age."[3] In the event of death before marriage, a younger sibling would substitute. Many oaths were taken to the agreement, reports Gislebert. Of course marriage negotiations could be problematic, even duplicitous affairs, as this one turned out to be, despite the oaths and good intentions at the time. Ultimately the marriage contract was only "partly" observed, as Gislebert put it discreetly: Marie and Baldwin VI were married in 1186 and had an exceptionally close marriage, but young Henry did not marry Elizabeth (she married King Philip II).[4] Still, the prospect of a double marriage held great promise for the comital family through the 1170s, and it seems to have prompted Guy of Bazoches, the canon at Châlons who had enjoyed Count Henry's financial support during his studies in Paris, to research the count's ancestry and produce an elaborate genealogy of his royal origins. Henry must have been delighted to learn that he descended from Clovis, the founder of the Frankish royal dynasty, as well as from the kings of England.[5]

Much more challenging than arranging marriages for his children were three other matters that arose in the early 1170s. The first related to the exemption of Henry's chapel from episcopal authority, an issue that rapidly became a cause célèbre and jeopardized the count's relations with the region's prelates. The second, initiated by the archbishop of Reims, involved borders and posed a serious threat to the integrity of the count's principality. Just as these two conflicts were quieted, Henry entered the fray on the side of the Plantagenet brothers in their revolt against King Henry II of England. Notwithstanding these pressing issues, Henry was fully engaged with the business of his court and the economic life of his county. He did not, however, attend the numerous tournaments taking place at the very borders of Champagne, which drew large contingents of northern French lords and knights, most prominently Count Baldwin V of Hainaut.[6] William Marshal was a regular participant at these regional tournaments, where he honed his jousting skills and entrepreneurial talents.[7] Marshal's biographer does not mention Count Henry at any of the tournaments that he describes at length, and indeed there is no mention of the count at any tournament after his succession in 1152, when he seems to have abandoned his youthful passion for the sport. It would appear that Henry, like the king of England, prohibited tournaments within his lands. The fortunes of Henry's county, and of Henry himself, depended on taxing peaceful commercial exchange rather than sponsoring violent sporting events.

New Prelate Troubles

The Count's Chapel

Count Henry's maternal uncle, Henry of Carinthia, died on 30 January 1169 after almost a quarter-century as the first Cistercian bishop of Troyes. He appears to have tolerated well a chapter of unreformed, that is, secular canons, who included luminaries like Gebuin of Troyes and Peter Comestor and pluralists who held positions in the count's chapel, notably Haice of Plancy, Manasses of Pougy, the provost of St-Étienne, and Manasses of Villemaur, archdeacon and dean of St-Étienne (see Table 2 in Appendix 1). Two years earlier, when Bishop Henry retired to the Cistercian monastery he refounded at Boulancourt, Count Henry remitted the ancient custom of despoliation of the bishop's residence and personal possessions during an episcopal vacancy.[8] The count promised that his provosts and agents would protect the bishop's possessions, houses, granaries, and animals until a new bishop was elected. After Bishop Henry's death, Count Henry and his brother William, by then archbishop of Sens, played a critical role in selecting Mathieu Burda of Provins as the next bishop of Troyes.[9] Mathieu was a well-known figure, as a canon in Sens and as leader of the secular canons of St-Quiriace in their campaign to regain control of the chapter from the regulars. As dean of the restored chapter of seculars since 1159, he had worked closely with William of Champagne, the chapter's provost, and Count Henry. The Burda family was a powerful and well-connected urban lineage in Provins, linked by marriage to the equally important Bristaud family: Mathieu's brother Walter was the count's marshal, and his brothers-in-law Peter Bristaud, viscount of Provins through marriage, and the knight Drogo Bristaud often attended the count's court. Henry could reasonably have expected Mathieu to be an accommodating bishop of Troyes.

It is not clear whether Archbishop William and Bishop Mathieu anticipated how explosive the issue of St-Étienne's exemption from episcopal authority would prove. Certainly William had discussed a range of subjects with Becket in Sens, including the "liberties" of the church, an issue on which Herbert of Bosham, Becket's theological adviser, was resolute. At issue was St-Étienne's anomalous status vis-à-vis the bishop of Troyes. Unlike the chapters of St-Quiriace of Provins and St-Maclou of Bar-sur-Aube, St-Étienne had been founded as an entirely new chapter without benefit of episcopal authority, and its canons were nominated by the count. The issue remained dormant through the episcopacy of Bishop Henry, only to emerge with the arrival of a new bishop with close ties to Sens, the exiled pope, and the archbishop of Canterbury. In submitting a traditional petition for papal confirmation of a new bishop's episcopal possessions, Bishop Mathieu inserted a clause relating to the count's chapel. Alexander III's confirmation of 6 September 1169 included "the church of St-Étienne newly constructed by the noble Count Henry next to the [old] city of Troyes, with the obedience and submission that the dean and men of the church ought to render to you [the bishop] and your successors."[10]

Faced with a fait accompli, Count Henry raised a vigorous, emotional protest at what he regarded as a provocation. He sent nuncios to Rome, where they argued "insistently" that his *capella palatina* had been exempt from the bishop's jurisdiction since the time of his father and grandfather, and "just like the chapels of kings and princes which are traditionally served by clerics of their household, it should be exempted by the pope from the jurisdiction of the bishop of Troyes." Moreover, Henry claimed, "the chapel of St-Étienne was built within his palace compound and therefore should not be subject to anyone." And, continued the pope in citing Henry's words, "if you [the pope] do not acquiesce in this matter, I will withdraw my sincere esteem for the bishop and his church, and will show neither devotion nor a pure heart toward the church of Rome; and further I will completely dismantle that chapel which I founded and endowed with a rich treasury, possessions, and ornaments, and will rebuild it elsewhere." The pope granted Henry a seven-year exemption.[11]

That compromise did not go down well within the church in France, especially with Becket close by in Sens presenting a model of principled resistance to secular rulers. In the spring of 1170 Becket sent the pope a rebuttal to the count's position, arguing that to diminish a bishop's authority would set a bad precedent.[12] After Becket's murder it was inconceivable that the king or any prelate would condone the count's brazen threats against the bishop of Troyes. And there was more: Archbishop William was consumed by Becket's murder, no doubt encouraged by Herbert of Bosham, who had sought refuge in Sens.[13] In January 1171 Archbishop William interdicted all King Henry II's Angevin lands. As to Count Henry and his chapel, the king, the archbishop of Sens (also papal legate in France), and "many other worthy men," said the pope, had sent letters protesting that such an exemption for St-Étienne would perturb the entire church and set a bad example for the clergy and laity alike. In May 1171 Alexander therefore quashed the seven-year exemption and restored his original confirmation by which St-Étienne came under episcopal

"jurisdiction, obedience, and subjugation." He explained his reversal in identical letters to the bishop of Troyes and the canons of St-Étienne.[14]

Henry's claim that the canons of St-Étienne were like the household clerics of his predecessors was disingenuous, to say the least. His "chapel" was
larger (36 x 68 meters) than the bishop's much older cathedral (20 x 73 meters).[15] And the canons, far from being his household clerics, were de facto
civil servants who regularly attended his court and staffed his full-service
chancery. Indeed, who could fail to see the twenty-five canons' houses poised
along the "Street of the Close" as anything but a powerful new presence in
Troyes, not retiring household chaplains and clerics but a chapter of active
canons who together with a number of nonresident canons rivaled the size of
the cathedral chapter.[16] There was another undercurrent; by its very magnificence, the count's chapel surpassed the cathedral in splendor. Henry continually added to St-Étienne's interior appointments and its budding collection of
relics, which he recently had augmented with the relics of Saints Altinus and
Potentianus, the third-century bishop of Sens who had evangelized Troyes and
its region. According to the Chronicle of St-Pierre-le-Vif of Sens, the bodies
of the two saints were discovered under the abbey's high altar on 7 June 1160,
and after a large public display were returned to their resting place.[17] Several
years later Count Henry asked the abbot about acquiring them for his chapel.
The abbot was amenable, but knowing that Henry was seeking relics for his
chapel in a tight market for relics of secure provenance, he drove a hard bar-
gain. Henry paid a princely sum: the church of St-Loup de Naud (the abbey
already owned Saint Loup's remains) with all his property there except fiefs,
and exemption of the abbey's two commercial houses in Provins from the
count's sales tax. Henry also swore that the relics never would be transferred
from his chapel. In the translation of the relics, Henry himself did the honors:
"I placed [the relics] with greatest veneration and reverence in the church of
the martyr Saint Stephen in Troyes."[18] That was not as laden an event as the
one he had witnessed at St-Denis in 1144, when King Louis carried the remains of Saint Denis in solemn liturgical procession to the new high altar, nor
as powerful an act as occurred in Aachen in 1165, when Emperor Frederick
lifted the bones of Charlemagne from his coffin and placed them in a gold
vase.[19] But it did carry special significance for Henry and his new chapel,
which he already might have imagined as a dynastic mausoleum.

St-Étienne's relic collection contributed to the allure of the count's chapel
as a pilgrimage site, which consequently diminished the central role of the
cathedral, to the displeasure of Bishop Mathieu. St-Étienne was in fact a

glittering jewel of a church built in the latest style. Philip of Harvengt, writing to Henry ca. 1160 as the recently elected abbot of Bonne-Espérance, captured the significance of St-Étienne for Henry and for his principality: you have chosen a gifted architect for your churches, he wrote, and have provided them with "generous interior decorations in gold, silver, and precious stones, as well as books, chalices, and fabrics."[20] Philip did not mention relics, which were acquired in the 1160s, nor St-Étienne's stained glass panels, which he surely would have noted if they had existed when he wrote. A decade later, however, at the time of Henry's clash with the bishop, those magnificent panels crafted by Mosan or Mosan-trained glaziers would have been in place. Suger had recuited Mosan and Italian glaziers to produce the sparkling windows at St-Denis, which Henry must have seen at the dedication of the new choir in 1144 and at the departure of the Second Crusade. In fact, Suger was so pleased with them that he mentioned them in his writings and even appointed a custodian to look after them.[21] Henry may well have seen, or at least heard about, the new Crusading Window at St-Denis commissioned ca. 1158 by Abbot Odo of Deuil, whom Henry knew from their crusading days.[22] A wealthy, assertive prince would have expected no less impressive stained glass windows in the chapel he had richly furnished, and it is likely that Mosan-styled glazing was installed in St-Étienne of Troyes in the decade of the 1160s, before Henry's bruising conflict with the bishop and the pope over the status of his chapel.

The chapel also was graced with portal column-sculptures. If the Corinthian capital that survives from St-Étienne's stonework is any indication, they were carved in the same style as the column-statues made for the rebuilt churches of St-Ayoul and St-Thibaut of Provins, both closely dated to ca. 1160 and identified with "the first generation of portal figures following in the Chartrain tradition."[23] St-Étienne's portal sculpture would have stood at the chapel's only public entrance, where the tympanum depicted Count Henry presenting a model of his chapel to its patron saint, an image repeated on Henry's tomb and a century later in the chapter's cartulary.[24] The count's chapel, connected to his residence and lavishly furnished by his endless benefactions, and staffed by canons who appeared as the count's functionaries, seemed an extension of Henry himself and his palace. No less galling to the bishop was the fact that regular canons of two local chapters, St-Martin-ès-Aires and St-Loup, were processing with the canons of St-Étienne on the feast days of their patron saints and at the death of their member canons.[25] And in 1170, perhaps piqued by the pope and the bishop, Henry induced the brothers of St-Jean-en-Châtel, where his chaplain and close friend Nicholas was prior, to process with his canons.[26] With its new liturgical music and its theatrical exterior processions, St-Étienne had acquired a public persona far beyond the traditional notion of a prince's "chapel."

Henry's reaction to the issue of episcopal exemption was not so much a miscalculation as an attempt to protect the independence of his administrative personnel ("my canons") and his private chapel. By 1170 St-Étienne was an exceptionally wealthy chapter. Within two decades it had amassed a portfolio of properties and revenues tied to the fairs that must have been the envy of the bishop.[27] Beyond the sheer opulence of St-Étienne, and the presumption of its canons in dominating the liturgical life of the city, another factor was at play in 1170–71: the count's campus had just been enclosed by a wall, making his glittering chapel a more commanding religious site than the bishop's cathedral within the ancient city walls.[28] The bishop and his episcopal palace were being eclipsed by the count's newly walled campus and his bustling commercial quarter with its fairs.

Ultimately it was Henry's belligerence toward the pope that stiffened the backs of the regional prelates in regard to his chapel, for the very next year his nephew Hugh III, duke of Burgundy, obtained papal exemption from episcopal jurisdiction for his newly founded chapter of Ste-Chapelle with twenty canons in Dijon, which he built in thanks for his safe return from pilgrimage to the Holy Land.[29] Henry had threatened to dismantle his chapel but of course did nothing of the sort. Sixty years later the chronicler Aubri of Trois-Fontaines cited this incident as having sullied Henry's reputation, despite his penance for it, but there is no evidence of any regret on Henry's part.[30] In fact, he remained unrepentant and undeterred, and no bishop of Troyes ever intruded in the chapel or in the affairs of Henry's canons. The principle of the bishop's jurisdiction was settled, but life went on as before. In 1175 Henry funded two chaplaincies in St-Étienne and in 1175 he enhanced the chapter's endowment with a substantial new revenue to support the construction of his tomb. [31] His achievement in creating a new site of religious and cultural life in Troyes, one tied to his principality and future dynasty, was secure.

Archbishop Henry of Reims

Shortly after Becket's murder, and with the status of St-Étienne still unresolved, Count Henry was drawn into a protracted conflict with his brother-in-law, Archbishop Henry of Reims.[32] The count already had experienced the archbishop's intransigence during the communal revolt in Reims in 1167, when Count Henry joined Philip of Flanders in mediating a peace between the townsmen and the archbishop. At the same time the count began to pay closer attention to the Marne valley and the broad swath of lands extending to the Meuse River. Perhaps as a result of events in Reims, Henry acquired from his butler and fast companion Anselm of Traînel the castle of Neuilly-St-Front and half the town of Oulchy, where he already held the fortress.[33] That announced his intention to extend his authority north of the Marne, in effect, to revive his father's attempt in the 1130s to penetrate the former county of Reims. In the next few years violence engulfed the entire province of Reims, as powerful lords like the counts of Rethel and Grandpré resisted the archbishop, whose strident attitude became more pronounced after Becket's murder.[34] By 1171 even Count Henry was at war with the archbishop.

The *casus belli* was the archbishop's routing a nest of brigands who, he claimed, took refuge in the fortress at Sampigny on the Vesle River after plundering episcopal villages along the road between Reims and Châlons and murdering their tenants.[35] The archbishop had the fortress dismantled, and after purchasing its village from the count's knight Boso, who held the fortress in fief, had a new tower erected on St-Remi's property at Sept-Saulx.[36] Count Henry initially expressed satisfaction with the archbishop's decisive action: "I have heard that you dismantled Sampigny, which much pleases me; but it also has come to my attention that you wish to harm Guermond of Châtillon [the count's castellan at Bussy], who is in my company and who I think and believe would never harm you; but if he ever does so in any way, I will make it right for you at your discretion."[37] Pope Alexander shed more light on these events in an accusatory letter to the archbishop regarding the collateral damage caused by the prelate's men: after expelling the monks from the church at Sept-Saulx, they built a tower from the stones intended for rebuilding the monastery; they caused 300*l.* in damage to the abbey's woods; they extracted 60*l.* from residents of Verzy and 40*l.* from another village; and to top it all, they seized the abbot on his way to Reims to complain, releasing him only after he paid a 100*l.* ransom.[38] But the monks had to make the best of it; forced to surrender the ban and justice of Sept-Saulx to the archbishop, they were fortunate in keeping their altars, tithes, and other revenues.[39]

At that point the archbishop's provosts and armed men strayed onto Count Henry's lands, killing several of his men. The count retaliated in kind, unleashing armed men and mercenaries who ravaged episcopal lands, with ensuing loss of life. The archbishop complained that Henry, not having renounced his ligeance, was still "my liegeman," saving fidelity to the king, and thus was responsible for killing the prelate's knights, taking others into captivity in chains, and causing the deaths of thirty-six men and women burned in the church where they had sought refuge. The count began to build towers on the archbishop's lands, for which the archbishop excommunicated him, without, however, making it public. The count proposed a truce, postponement of the excommunication, and the return of captured property, which he failed to observe, claimed the archbishop, who consequently pronounced the excommunication in Reims cathedral and directed his suffragan bishops to proclaim it each Sunday thereafter.[40] It may have been at this point that the count allowed his treasurer Artaud to build a new fortress at Nogent-sur-Marne, later dubbed Nogent-l'Artaud (Artaud's Nogent), as a way of strengthening his northern borders.[41] The violence unleashed by the two Henrys, especially the count's use of foreign mercenaries, threatened to spill over into neighboring provinces, leading Frederick Barbarossa and Louis VII to sign a treaty in the presence of a great number of barons prohibiting the use of Brabantine mercenaries in the area bounded by the Rhine, the Alps, and Paris. Count Henry was pledge for the king, while the duke of Lotharingia was pledge for the emperor.[42]

The count and the archbishop sent nuncios to Rome. The count's representatives claimed that Henry's excommunication was illegal because he had appealed it before it was published, to which the archbishop's legates replied that Henry had committed further hostilities. It was an awkward situation involving the king, his brother the archbishop, and their brother-in-law Count Henry. The pope reviewed the recent events and concluded that "since there is disagreement over this matter," the archbishop of Tours and bishop of Rouen would determine whether the count's provosts and armed men had acted on the count's authority in ravaging the prelate's lands (that is, after he had appealed the sentence but before it was published), and whether the count had refused to release his prisoners. Regarding the construction of castles, however, the pope suggested a compromise in consultation with the king.[43] On the same day Alexander sent two other letters. The first advised Archbishop Henry to reach an amicable settlement with Count Henry through the king's good offices.[44] In the second, to the king, the pope wrote that since the root cause of the conflict was the count's claim to have been injured by the archbishop's newly built castles, Louis should work out a settlement before the papal judges delegate did so.[45] The pope reminded Louis that his reputation was at stake and he should not allow "noble and powerful" individuals to disturb the peace of the realm. The outcome of the matter remains unknown, but within months the king and Count Henry were drawn into an even messier and more consequential affair involving the Plantagenets of England.

The Plantagenet Eruption

Becket's murder had lingering repercussions in France, for the archbishop and his household had developed an extensive network of relationships during their six years of exile. Archbishop William of Sens had been a staunch supporter of Becket, in part because of a friendship formed in England in the 1140s and strengthened in Sens in the 1160s. At Becket's last meeting with Henry II in the summer of 1170, it was William who acted as Becket's personal advisor and intermediary with the king.[46] After the murder William initiated a review process (February 1171) that led to Becket's canonization two years later (21 February 1173).[47] No doubt the archbishop was encouraged by Herbert of Bosham, who had returned to Sens and whose role as Becket's theological mentor was recognized by the pope's personal letter of condolence after Becket's death.[48] At Reims, too, an influential core of Becket supporters included the king's brother Archbishop Henry, Abbot Peter (of Celle) of St-Remi, and his guest-in-exile John of Salisbury, who had witnessed the murder in Canterbury cathedral and wrote a brief account of Becket's life soon after.[49] About the same time Prior Simon Aurea Capra of Mont-Dieu wrote a verse narrative of key moments in Becket's life.[50]

Becket's murder caused more than revulsion in northern France; it allowed Henry II's eldest son and crowned heir to conflate his personal grievances against his father with a promise to restore the liberties of the church in England, in effect to justify a revolt against the king. Although Henry II carried out his penance for Becket's death at Avranches cathedral on 21 May 1172, admitting that his anger had incited the deed but swearing that he neither ordered nor desired Becket's death, he failed to dispel the unsavory air that still hung over him. The most important princes of northern France, including the king and the entire house of Champagne, supported Young King Henry, while the disaffected Norman barons took the occasion to vent their own grievances. The Young King had been crowned in June 1170 and again in August 1172, this time with his wife Margaret of France, who had been staying with Queen Eleanor in Caen. But he lacked the resources to live regally, for despite being count of Anjou and Maine, he could take possession of those lands only at his father's death.[51] Yet in France, where he spent much of his time and resources on the tournament circuit, he cut a fine figure as King Louis's son-in-law. Gervase of Tilbury, perhaps the most effusive in praise, cited his tall stature, graceful manners, generosity, and skill at arms, while contemporary poets celebrated his largess, courtesy, and chivalry.[52] An audience listening to Chrétien de Troyes's romance *Erec et Enide* in the early 1170s might well have associated him with the "young king" Erec, who spent his youthful years at the court of King Arthur defending the honor of women in spectacular feats of arms while waiting to inherit his father's kingdom. But unlike Arthurian Erec, who came to value his conjugal state before inheriting his father's lands, Young Henry continued to pursue martial arts at tournaments without his wife.

King Louis stoked his son-in-law's discontent in Paris on 11 November 1172, and in Limoges the next March Young Henry, encouraged by Eleanor, challenged his father in public to grant him either England or Normandy.[53] A bill of particulars sent to the pope complained about his shame and dishonor at not being able to fulfill his responsibilities because his father had failed to provide the requisite resources; moreover, it added, Becket's murderers had not been punished, and the ancient liberties of the English church needed restoration.[54] Those charges resonated in France, coinciding as they did with Becket's canonization. The chronicler Ralph of Diceto justified the Young King's rebellion by citing several biblical, classical, and medieval examples of sons rebelling against their fathers.[55] Count Henry and his brothers Thibaut, Stephen, and William joined Louis VII and the other French princes in supporting the young king, whom they regarded as a brother-in-law. On Easter (8 April) 1173 the three Plantagenet brothers appeared at the French royal court, and in May a large assembly of French lords supported their revolt. According to the chronicler Roger of Howden, King Louis convoked an assembly of counts, barons, and prelates in Paris, where he swore on a Bible to support Henry II's son. The Champenois brother-counts Thibaut, Henry, and Stephen did likewise, as did the king's brother Robert of Dreux, Count Philip of Flanders, and many unnamed barons and prelates.[56] The chronicler noted that the Young King received the homage of Counts Philip of Flanders (for a 1,000*l.* rent), his brother Mathieu of Boulogne, and Thibaut V of Blois (for the castle of Amboise and a 50*l.* rent). Louis confirmed these acts by sealing letters with his new seal. Jordan of Fantosme, who was sympathetic to Henry II in that conflict, blamed Counts Thibaut of Blois and Philip of Flanders for convincing Louis to support the Young King against his father.[57]

In July 1173 Count Henry and his brothers, this time including Archbishop William of Sens, accompanied the king, his brother Robert, and the three Plantagenet brothers to Normandy, where they were joined by a contingent of disaffected Norman barons. According to Ralph of Diceto, the siege of Verneuil was a pivotal event. Counts Henry and Robert of Dreux swore in the name of the French king that if the townsmen surrendered within three days, they would be spared retribution. Roger of Howden's fuller account includes Archbishop William of Sens and Count Thibaut of Blois among those who swore to that on Louis's behalf.[58] The townsmen reported their dilemma to the English king, who was enraged. Howden adds that Louis proposed a meeting the next day but failed to appear or to send nuncios in his stead. The English king reacted with great force, and the French, violating their assurances, destroyed Verneuil and took captives. Count Henry, having been implicated in Louis's actions, soon returned home.

The next July, 1174, Count Henry reappeared with the French forces besieging Rouen, and again the English king outmaneuvered and defeated the French coalition. Henry and Louis withdrew for good, and on 11 October 1174 King Henry made peace with his sons.[59] At Westminster the next May, the Young King did homage and swore an oath on Scriptures to his father, and he promised to obtain King Louis and Counts Henry and Thibaut as pledges to his good conduct.[60] For Count Henry and his brothers the Plantagenet revolt had few lasting consequences, but it did reveal how the Champenois clan was drawn by ties of blood and marriage to the Young King, the half-brother of Countess Marie and husband of her half-sister Margaret of France. For one disruptive moment, a Capetian-Champenois-Plantagenet sibling alliance trumped the filial bonds between Henry II and his sons.

Armed confrontations between the French and English monarchs were not new, nor were the interminable failed negotiations or the seemingly capricious acts of the kings. But the revolt did expose a new aspect of the Plantagenet-Capetian rivalry: the participation of the new archbishop of Sens in the king's affairs and the solidification of a Champenois party at the royal court. Count Henry had been a loyal supporter of Louis's military and diplomatic ventures since 1147, as had Count Thibaut as royal seneschal since 1154, but only after William's consecration as archbishop of Sens in December 1168 did the three brothers act in concert with the king, soon joined by Count Stephen of Sancerre. Archbishop William brought a special force to the group in 1169 and 1170, as the cause of the archbishop of Canterbury became entangled with the king's interests. Having known Becket in Sens, and indeed since his days in England two decades earlier, William was involved personally as well as professionally in Becket's cause. He also remembered his uncle Bishop Henry of Winchester's self-imposed exile to Cluny in 1154, in a sense antici-pating Becket's own exile a decade later. Archbishop William and his brother the royal seneschal increasingly appeared together with Louis, even on the field of battle against the Plantagenet king. Roger of Howden, who was well informed about events in the 1170s, cites the brothers William and Thibaut as being with Louis on several important occasions, and includes the text of let-ters that Louis, Thibaut, and William wrote to the pope regarding Becket's murder.[61] Henry II's acts were pleasing to a tyrant, not to God, wrote Count Thibaut, and he should be punished by the church. Fulminating in biblical anger, William announced that he had interdicted Henry II's lands in France and had directed all prelates to observe his sanction. Thereafter, for the next three decades, William became indispensable to the French king.

At Court

Throughout his tribulations with prelates and Plantagenets, Count Henry heard and disposed of an array of cases at court, usually in Troyes or Provins. A remarkably stable core of trusted officials provided institutional memory for the count entering his third decade of rule. The butler Anselm II of Traînel, the seneschal Geoffroy III of Joinville, the marshal William Rex of Provins, and the chancellor William had served him for more than twenty-five years, as had the notary William, who inscribed himself in Henry's letters as the court's primary stenographer. Several barons and knights without portfolio, includ-ing Garnier of Traînel, Daimbert of Ternantes, and Drogo Bristaud of Provins, were regulars as well. By 1174 only two of Henry's old hands, constables Odo of Pougy and William of Dampierre, had died and were not replaced.[62] Most of Henry's other court officers and technicians, like the scribe Thibaut of Fis-mes, served into the 1170s, and the new bursar, Artaud, who entered the count's service by 1158, continued in that position to 1188. Increasingly Henry also relied on a small group of canons from St-Étienne and St-Quiriace who were conveniently available to witness and vet the count's acts in return for their generous prebends. Rarely did a baron attend court except in litigation. Nor did Countess Marie, although she did seal letters relating to her dower lands, both alone and jointly with Henry, and in one instance, as a personal favor to the bursar Artaud, she and Henry sealed separate letters confirming the dower that Artaud settled on his second wife.[63]

As earlier, the court dealt with the resolution of disputes, the registration of nonlitigious transactions, and various matters of feudal tenure. Henry continued to discipline misbehaving lords like Nicholas of Bazoches, who surrendered a fief "though my hand," said the count, for ravaging monastic lands, and Odo of Vendeuvre, who similarly surrendered the *mouvance* over two fiefs of his knights.[64] In ordinary disputes over property, privileges, and jurisdictions, Henry often appointed arbitrators to reach amicable settlements. When the monks of Trois-Fontaines challenged the knight (and future marshal) Erard of Aulnay over his claim to their grange, Henry directed the dean of Vitry and a monk, Odo, a former knight, to collect testimony and examine the monks' document presented in evidence. On hearing it read in court, Erard accepted the finding of fact, that his aunt had possessed the grange in dowry, that is, "by right of inheritance," and consequently could alienate it; the count directed the chancery to seal a letter so declaring.[65]

Not all conflicts were resolved as easily. One intractable case involved lands and benefactions disputed by Larrivour and Montiéramey, two prominent monasteries near Troyes. Henry delegated the butler's brother, Garnier of Traînel, who frequented the court without portfolio, to resolve it. Garnier conducted a fact-finding inquest, then presented it to the court along with a document describing "what I [Garnier] saw and heard and what was done through my hand," in effect a compromise accepted by the two parties.[66] On review at court by Thibaut the scribe, William the marshal, and Artaud the treasurer, the count approved it and had the chancery recopy Garnier's report verbatim in his own letters patent.[67] In this and similar cases the court served as a clearinghouse for the registration of disputes settled in Henry's presence or under his auspices. Henry's reputation for mediation even led his nephew Hugh III of Burgundy and cousin Guy of Nevers to accept him as the final arbiter of their dispute, as to whether Guy owed homage to Hugh, in the event that the two barons and two Cistercian abbots charged with resolving the issue failed to do so.[68]

Of course feudal matters continued to appear on the court's docket.[69] Occasionally Henry participated in a ceremonial transfer at court, accepting a fiefholder's divestiture of a fief before personally investing the recipient. "First they divested themselves and then I invested the church," said Henry of two brothers, one a canon at Château-Thierry, who sold their inherited fief to the monks of Valsecret.[70] The usual practice, as before, was for a donor/seller to seek the count's consent only after making the transaction and to present the recipient with Henry's letter of confirmation as a title deed. The knight Milo of Evry did that in 1173 when he appeared at court in Troyes with his wife and two sons seeking the count's confirmation of his sale of a fief (a water right) to the monks of Pontigny; Henry ordered a letter of confirmation drafted for Milo to give to the monks.[71] But not every transfer required the count's explicit consent. Ever since his accession Henry had authorized a number of monasteries to acquire his fiefs freely, without having to seek permission for each acquisition, in recognition of the unstoppable flow of feudal property to monastic institutions.[72] He seems to have been untroubled by the loss of his fiefs, no doubt because the commercial success of the trade fairs and the substantial revenues produced by his tolls, sales taxes, and rental income far surpassed the value of his alienated fiefs.

Henry also granted new fiefs at court, just as Count Baldwin did in Hainaut, and had the chancery draft letters describing them, a practice that was becoming routine for even minor transactions regarding fiefs.[73] We know about these new and augmented fiefs because several of Henry's letters later were returned to the count's chancery or passed as title deeds with the fiefs to ecclesiastical institutions, which preserved them.[74] But one new practice becomes visible in the 1170s: the count often promised a fief in terms of its annual revenue without designating its source, pending consultation with his treasurers to determine where it would be assigned.[75] Only when reminded that he failed to assign a promised 25*l.* fief revenue to Count Mathieu I of Beaumont-sur-Oise, did Henry encumber the tolls at Rebais, where Mathieu or his agent could collect the money on presentation of the count's letter at the Fair of May in Provins.[76] Walter of Combault encountered a more complex process. The count authorized a 50*l.* cash disbursement for Walter to purchase property to be held as a comital fief, but it was contingent. As the count said, "I make notice that Walter of Combault has from me 50*l.* to be placed in my fief, of which he has received 25*l.*; the remaining 25*l.* will be given to him by order of my lord Anselm of Traînel [the butler], on condition that he has placed the initial 25*l.* in my fief."[77] Since only the revenue, not the actual property, was at issue, Walter was free to acquire or to designate any property as the count's fief so long as it was worth 50*l.* or about 5*l.* annually. Like Matthew of Beaumont's fief rent, Walter's landed fief was identified primarily by its annual revenue.[78] That practice of evaluating fiefs in terms of annual revenue became a characteristic feature of fiefs in Champagne.[79]

The 1170s saw Henry respond to powerful demographic movements within his lands. He already had developed what might fairly be called an immigration policy, encouraging immigration from beyond the county and

channeling in-migration within the county by ameliorating tenurial conditions in his own and in monastic villages. We know that immigrants were
settling in Champagne before 1150 and that by the 1160s both lay and ecclesiastical lords were offering advantageous tenures to attract tenants to their
lands.[80] Henry authorized monastic communities and lay lords to accept newcomers, essentially lordless men, within existing communities so that they
would establish residency and come under a lord's jurisdiction. The canons of
Vertus, for example, were allowed to receive in their lands immigrants "from
"beyond Sens, Paris, and Soissons and beyond the borders dividing the kingdoms of France and Germany," and the knight Thibaud Revelard was licensed
to accept "foreign men" in his village, that is, "men coming from beyond the
Marne," but not men from the count's own villages.[81] In Henry's own towns,
especially in the fair towns of Troyes, Provins, and Bar-sur-Aube, he allowed
newcomers to choose their lords—whether the count, the viscount, or a religious community—within one year and one day of establishing residency.[82]
But he changed that policy in 1170 in response to heavy immigration to
Provins, reserving to himself the jurisdiction over immigrants "from the
French kingdom" and from his own lands, while leaving jurisdiction over immigrants "from beyond the kingdom" to the chapter of St-Quiriace.[83]

Henry followed an ad hoc approach to his rural communities, commut-
ing traditional obligations in a few villages to a single annual payment and
granting franchises to several others.[84] He also entered into co-lordships with
monasteries, and in a few cases even founded new villages on monastic lands,
with their respective provosts sharing the administration and revenues of
those communities. But his most novel act in the 1170s was to create eleven
"new villages," meaning either entirely new settlements or reconstituted older
ones with liberalized written "customs." Those made Champagne a region par
excellence of new villages.[85] By the 1170s Henry was as attentive to the rural
economy of his county as he had been earlier to the urban economy of his fair
towns.

It is not known whether Henry made his famous remark about Jewish
law at court, but it reflects the spirit of Henry's performances as recorded by
the court stenographer. Just before Easter 1171, thirty-one Jews were said to
have been burned in his brother Thibaut's lands in Blois after one was accused
of murdering a Christian.[86] According to Salomo bar Simeon, it was reported
to Henry that Jewish law justified the murder of Christians, to which Henry
replied: "We find nothing in the teaching of the Jews that permits the killing
of a Christian. Yesterday, on the eve of Easter, such a rumor was heard in

Épernay, but I do not believe it."[87] Except for that reference, we have no surviving evidence for Henry's interactions with the many Jewish communities
in Champagne at that time, and cannot determine whether he granted them
charters of privilege or franchises as he did to other rural communities.[88] His
keen interest in biblical history and practices must have been influenced by
the presence of a Jewish community in the old city of Troyes, and especially of
Hebrew scholars, descendants of the famous school of Rashi. To Rashi's
grandson, Rabbenu Tam, Henry posed questions like the ones he asked Master Alberic of Reims: Why did God take Enoch at a relatively young age despite his exemplary life, especially as compared to others who lived longer?
Why did God place leprosy in a house of the promised land? And why was
Saul deprived of his throne whereas David, who committed a greater offense,
was allowed to pass his kingdom to his son?[89] Henry had his own Latin version of Josephus's *Jewish Antiquities* and *The Jewish War Against the Romans*,
and he certainly knew of Herbert of Bosham's interest in Hebrew learning and
Peter Comestor's reliance on Josephus for "the truth of history" in preparation
for his *Scholastic History*. Henry knew enough about the history of the Jews
and Judaism that he could dismiss the rumors from Épernay regarding Jewish
law as simply lacking credibility.

Henry's Tomb

In the aftermath of his bruising conflicts with the prelates of Troyes and
Reims, Henry enhanced his chapel with an array of liturgical objects, relics,
and splendid furnishings, for which St-Étienne was noted.[90] In addition to the
relics purchased in 1161 and the relics of saints Potentianus and Altinus acquired in 1167, he obtained Thomas Becket's iron ring and several pieces of
Becket's clothing, including one stained with the martyr's blood.[91] St-Étienne's treasury later held a sizable collection of relics encased in sumptuous
reliquaries, and although their dates of acquisition cannot be determined, it is
highly likely that Henry, given his taste for relics and his desire to burnish his
chapel, acquired a good number of them, including the skull and bones and
two teeth of Saint Anthony.[92] He also subsidized an exquisite glazing program
at St-Étienne that is known for its striking coloring and painting techniques
produced or influenced by Mosan enamelists.[93] The count's chapel would be
larger, richer, and more luxurious than the old cathedral in Troyes; indeed, as
a gem of a princely chapel, it anticipated Louis IX's Ste-Chapelle in Paris. The

canons, too, delighted in St-Étienne. When Master André, the stonemason who may have been the primary contractor of the building, sold his substantial revenue from two of the count's mills in Troyes, the event was attended by a large number of canons, including all the chapter's officers, as if the beneficiaries of his great work were honoring him on the occasion of his retirement.[94] But the chapel lacked one thing: a princely tomb. The grandiose size of St-Étienne and its lavish furnishings suggest that Henry intended from the start to establish a dynastic necropolis, to house a collection of comital tombs to rival the royal tombs at St-Remi and St-Denis. Unlike contemporary monarchs and princes, however, who chose to be buried in monastic churches under the eternal custody of monks, Henry located his tomb within his private chapel, where his own secular canons would watch over it just as cathedral canons cared for a bishop's tomb. The fullest analysis of the extant evidence suggests that he commissioned his tomb in the mid-1170s, perhaps as early as 1173, and that it was most likely completed before his departure on crusade in May 1179.[95]

Planning for a tomb coincided with several unrelated events in the early 1170s. The canonization of Becket was followed by the canonization of Bernard of Clairvaux, whom Henry had known since his earliest childhood.[96] In 1174 Henry's "dearest sister" Marie, widowed duchess of Burgundy, entered Fontevraud, where her never married sister Margaret was a nun.[97] About the same time the choir of Canterbury cathedral burned down (5 September 1174), whether by accident or by arson is not certain.[98] Since Becket earlier had approached the mason-builder William of Sens about building a new French-style cathedral at Canterbury, the monks of Christ Church Canterbury agreed, according to Gervase of Canterbury, that William, "a workman most skillful both in wood and stone," should supervise the rebuilding of the choir. Gervase's *On the Conflagration and Rebuilding of Canterbury Cathedral* reports that the choir was not simply restored; rather it was rebuilt with the new Becket chapel as a mausoleum for the archbishops of Canterbury.[99] Henry would have known about the redoing of Canterbury cathedral in the Gothic mode of Sens, which had inspired his own chapels in Troyes and Provins, from the English canons in Sens, notably Herbert of Bosham, who received a continual flow of news from Canterbury.

Whatever inspired Henry to plan his own tomb, it resulted in an exceptional undertaking. He may have remembered what he had seen in Sicily, the two porphyry sarcophagi that Roger II acquired in the 1140s, one for his body, the other to serve as his memorial, as he himself explained.[100] The Frankish

royal tombs at St-Denis and St-Remi of Reims also might have prompted
Henry to think about his chapel as a dynastic mausoleum. He knew of the
rivalry between Abbots Odo of St-Remi and Suger of St-Denis, who used the
ancient royal tombs in their possession to claim an exclusive right to bury future kings. After Abbot Odo obtained a papal privilege to crown the kings of
France (1129), he undertook an ambitious sculptural program in the 1130s to
craft tombs for the Carolingian kings Lothair and Louis IV, the so-called
Hincmar monument, as well as the effigy statues, of which the magnificent
head of "King Lothair" survives.[101] Henry saw the sculptural program at
St-Remi during his visit in the spring of 1152, and surely was apprised of Peter
of Celle's later rebuilding of the abbey church, where the saint's relics made it
a pilgrimage destination.[102] And the count was familiar with Suger's work at
St-Denis, which he visited in 1144, then at the launch of the Second Crusade
in 1147, and no doubt during his several expeditions with the king since the
early 1150s. Whatever the specific influence on Henry's thinking, St-Remi and
St-Denis were well-known models for a princely mausoleum.

    Henry enlisted Mosan or Mosan-trained artisans and enamelists to craft a
sumptuous metalwork tomb rather than a traditional stone one used for royal
burials. It would sit prominently within the chapel's choir, not far from the
altar and clearly visible to all, where it could be attended by his canons. Henry's gambit was an unheard of audacity, and a sharp riposte to the bishop of
Troyes for having troubled him over the chapel's exemption from episcopal
authority. Henry would lie in a spectacular reliquary tomb, the likes of which
the bishop had never imagined. That both Walter of Châtillon and Chrétien
de Troyes added tomb scenes to the narratives they were writing in those years
strengthens the suspicion that talk about tombs was in the air while work on
Henry's tomb was proceeding.

    Walter of Châtillon composed the *Alexandreis*, a Latin verse rendition of
the fourth-century *History of Alexander* by Quintus Curtius Rufus, over the
course of five years following Becket's murder.[103] It was immediately recognized as one of the finest Latin poems of the twelfth century and survives in
more than 200 manuscripts. In 1176 Walter added an eighteen-line dedication
to Archbishop William on the occasion of his transfer from Sens to Reims; his
love of learning, the poet hopes, will calm the strife-torn see of Reims.[104]
Count Henry knew the story of Alexander from his copy of Rufus's *Alexander*,
which was illustrated by the same hand that painted his copies of Freculf and
Josephus. Rufus briefly describes Alexander's visit to the tomb of the Persian
king Cyrus, which was said to be unremarkable. But in retelling Alexander's

life, Walter dwells on four other tombs, none of which is mentioned by Rufus: the tomb of Achilles, which young Alexander visits; the tombs of Darius and his wife; and Alexander's own tomb.[105] Most interesting are the tombs of Darius and his wife, which Walter describes in ekphrasis: Darius's tomb contains a map of the world and an inscription, while his wife's tomb is inscribed with a history of the world since Adam.[106] It is striking that Walter, who was closely associated with Archbishop William, invented those tomb scenes at the very moment that Henry's tomb was taking shape.

Chrétien de Troyes penned two dramatic tomb scenes in those same years. In *Cligés* (ca. 1176) the artisan John, "who paints and sculpts marvelously" and whose work is said to be imitated by artists in Rome and Antioch, is commissioned to construct a tomb for Fenice, who had staged a fake death in order to escape an unconsummated marriage with the emperor of Constantinople so she could join Cligés, the emperor's nephew and her true love.[107] The tomb was to be "so beautiful and artfully made" as to be without rival. In fact, John already had made such a tomb with the intention of placing relics in it, but since Fenice was a saintly creature, said John, she could well occupy the (reliquary) tomb.[108] Soon after Fenice was buried in it, she was rescued (resurrected) by Cligés. A reliquary tomb was exactly what Count Henry was having constructed, perhaps to the same effect. In the *Knight of the Cart* (*Lancelot*), composed perhaps in 1177, Chrétien depicts another unique tomb.[109] On his way to rescue the queen, Lancelot passes a cemetery with prebuilt tombs inscribed with the names of the knights from King Arthur's court who will occupy them. But one tomb, carved from marble and the finest of all, and even more beautiful within, lacked a name, reported a local hermit, because it was reserved for the person who freed all those trapped in a kingdom from which none could escape. According to the tomb's inscription, whoever lifted the tomb's lid would free the trapped prisoners and thereby earn a place within it, which Lancelot easily did.[110] We can only surmise that Count Henry would have been delighted in hearing about Chrétien's and Walter's imagined tombs as singular as his own.[111]

Henry's tomb was unique in its form and materials.[112] Arnaud's engraving (1837), based on the architect Mouillefarine's drawing made before the tomb was dismantled, captures its originality (see Figure 7).[113] It was a metalwork tomb, the earliest known from northern France. Crafted of gilt and enameled bronze, silver, and gold, it was covered with brightly colored Mosan enamel plaques, which are remarkably similar to those commissioned by Bishop Henry of Winchester and perhaps acquired in Troyes during a trip to Cluny or Rome.[114] Count Henry's recumbent, gilded bronze effigy placed within the tomb was fully visible through four bisected open arches on either side and at each end. It was quite literally a reliquary tomb, with Henry as its relic fully visible in its jeweled casing. Dressed in a belted tunic and mantle, the count wears a skullcap rather than a helmet. His eyes are open, and his hands clasped in prayer. He sports a beard and long, curly hair.

The lid of the tomb, not visible to visitors, was filled with the imagery of death, resurrection, and the afterlife. A large gilded bronze and enamel cross dominated the central space. An enamel medallion depicting an allegorized prophet Isaiah in the form of a tree producing a flower announces the coming of Christ. At the base of the cross, in a low relief sculpture, Christ with a book in hand exits a cloud across from two angels. In the top quadrant next to the cross was a statue of Henry offering a model of his chapel to Stephen, traditionally regarded as the first Christian to die for his faith and the first to have been promised a resurrection. The very same scene appears in the chapter's cartulary a century later, with the count offering the saint a model of his chapel in the presence of the chapter's canons.[115] Placed within the orbit of Stephen, the count enjoyed the same exaltation and, by extension, the same sanctification.[116] The rest of the tomb was covered with enamel plaques of various sizes and forms, perhaps one hundred in all, of which sixty-one survive today.[117] A single craftsman or workshop used similar colors, composi

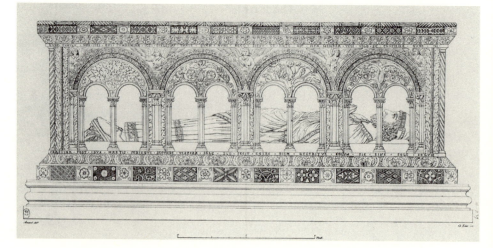

Figure 7. Count Henry's tomb, from Arnaud, *Voyage archéologique*, 28.

tional style, and related subject matter for two sets of enamels: seventeen extant rectangular plaques depict the Old Testament prophets, the four evangelists, and virtues, while nineteen semicircular plaques represent the crucifixion and resurrection, all in reference to Count Henry.[118] Set implicitly within a dynastic necropolis in the manner of the royal ones at St-Denis and St-Remi of Reims, Henry's prebuilt tomb, like Lancelot's, awaited its occupant and inscriptions before the count, in his fifty-second year, departed on crusade in May 1179. [119]

Cultural Patronage

Count Henry's book collecting, at least of historians and classical authors, ended with Becket's departure from Sens. The latest securely dated book in his collection, a copy of Aulus Gellius's *Attic Nights*, was completed by William the Englishman in 1170. About that time the scribe and priest Daniel made a two-volume copy of Jerome's *Commentary* on Ezekiel, ostensibly for Henry.[120] Like William the Englishman, Daniel was not a native of Champagne, and to judge from his handwriting, dating, and self-identification, he was probably English. As archdeacon of Provins and canon at St-Quiriace, he occasionally drafted the count's letters, notably Henry's renunciation of his *regalia* in Troyes in 1167.[121] The fact that Daniel appended a table of contents to an anthology of sermons that Henry had inherited from his father suggests that Daniel might have served as the count's librarian until he left for St-Victor of Paris.[122] If Daniel's copy of Jerome's *Commentary* was in fact intended for Count Henry, it might have been part of a larger project to acquire commentaries on the Old Testament, reflecting Henry's interest in ancient and biblical history, especially after Peter Comestor had finished his *Scholastic History.* Henry had copies of Jerome's commentaries on Jeremiah and Isaiah and *Against Jovian*, as well as Peter Lombard's *Commentary* on the Psalms and Jerome's *Commentary* on the letters of Paul, which were copied at the same time in the 1170s and painted by Mosan artists.[123] It would be interesting to know how those copies were related to Henry's tomb at a time when Mosan or Mosan-trained metalworkers and enamelists were working on it, and when painters were illuminating books in the Mosan style and glassmakers were crafting the stained glass panels in the same style for St-Étienne. The similarity of style and technique in glass, enamel, and book illustration points to a substantial number of craftsmen working at the count's expense through the

1160s and 1170s. The glazing program and style of composition, in particular, are related to similar works in Sens, while in Reims glaziers were doing the same in the renovated abbey church of St-Remi.[124]

Sens continued to be an intellectual and artistic center in the 1170s, at least until Archbishop William left for Reims. It was there that Herbert of Bosham completed his massive, four-volume annotated edition of Peter Lombard's *Great Gloss*, originally dedicated to Becket but then rededicated to the archbishop.[125] Peter Comestor, chancellor of the cathedral school in Paris, dedicated his *Historia Scholastica* to Archbishop William in memory of their days together in the cathedral chapter in Troyes.[126] Peter of Blois, who spent several years in Sens in the archbishop's company, later dedicated his *Speculum iuris canonici* to William, by then archbishop of Reims.[127] Walter of Châtillon, who was in Reims at that time, dedicated his *Alexandreis* to William on the occasion of the archbishop's arrival in Reims in 1176.[128] That four authors dedicated their innovative works—an edition of the *Great Gloss*, a manual of biblical history, a book on canon law, and a popular verse biography of Alexander the Great—to Archbishop William in the 1170s is a measure of his role as cultural patron. Count Henry, who continued to fund substantial prebends in his several towns, received not a single dedication.

Compared to Sens and Reims, with their long traditions of episcopal and monastic schools, Troyes was a less stimulating intellectual environment after the departure of its chief luminaries. Peter Comestor left for Paris before 1160, Gebuin the chancellor and sermonizer died in 1161, and Peter of Celle transferred to St-Remi of Reims in 1162. The count's chaplain Nicholas was still prior of St-Jean-en-Châtel, but after the murder of Becket and the scattering of the English, he seems to have lost his drive for finding books to copy, as he had been doing for the past twenty-five years, and is not known to have made additional books for Count Henry. In a letter to Archbishop William written between 1176 and 1179, Nicholas captured the subdued spirit of the time. After due platitudes in praise of the archbishop, he excused himself for not writing or visiting William because of the distance between Troyes and Reims and the difficulty of the journey (he was in his sixties), nonetheless announcing his arrival in Reims after Easter. "But," he reflected, "the journey is brief and the road smooth in the company of my many friends."[129] Perhaps Nicholas, too, was thinking about last things while reworking his collection of letters, the only work he is known to have written or compiled after 1170.[130]

There is but one reference to Countess Marie as patron of writers in the 1170s. Chrétien de Troyes announces at the beginning of *The Knight of the*

Cart (*Lancelot*) that "my lady of Champagne wishes me to begin a romance." She provided the book's subject matter (*matiere*) and its meaning (*san*), said Chrétien.[131] That single mention has established Marie's reputation as patron of the arts and, by extension, the repute of a "court of Champagne." What Marie actually gave Chrétien, if anything, remains a mystery, for his claim that he brought to the tale only his labor and skill of writing might be read as a disclaimer in the matter of the queen's adultery, or an ironic comment by an author in full control of his narrative.[132] It is likely that Countess Marie had a copy of *Lancelot*, although there is no record of it, nor is there mention of any other work in her possession before Henry left on crusade in 1179. It is thought that Chrétien wrote *Yvain* (*The Knight with the Lion*) concurrently with *Lancelot* in the late 1170s, but the story lacks any conceivable link to Marie or to Champagne. Nor is Marie cited elsewhere as a patron of vernacular literature in the 1170s. With the exception of *Lancelot*, not a single original work written in the 1170s, in either Latin or French, can be attributed to the patronage of Henry or Marie.

Chapter 8

The Last Years, 1176–1181

By the spring of 1176 Henry had ruled his county for a quarter century. He was forty-nine. He had been married to Marie, then thirty-one, for more than a decade and had three children—ten-year-old Henry (II), five-year-old Marie, and Scholastique.[1] The year began with the death or resignation of his chancellor William, who had served him since 1149 and his father even before then, and the appointment of a new chancellor and adoption of a new seal. In those same months his brother William capped a meteoric rise in the church with his election as archbishop of Reims, and the pope called for a new crusade. Preparations for the expedition began in 1177 and would consume all of 1178 and the first half of 1179. Henry would spend almost two years abroad before returning home in March 1181.

The new chancellor, Stephen of Provins, was an old friend of the family, most likely Henry's tutor in the 1130s. He had studied with Gilbert de la Porrée and Abelard, and was "skilled in both French and Latin," according to Helinand of Froidmond, but "avaricious."[2] As a cathedral canon in Troyes in the early 1150s, he witnessed "on the count's behalf," and in 1160 he joined Henry and his brother William at Countess Mathilda's deathbed. Master Stephen was also a canon of St-Étienne, and in 1169 he succeeded William of Champagne as provost of St-Quiriace of Provins.[3] A highly literate cleric and pluralist, an experienced ecclesiastical administrator in the confidence of both Archbishop William and Count Henry for at least a quarter century, Stephen brilliantly fused personal and institutional loyalties in Henry's employ. The fact that Thomas Becket, while chancellor of Henry II, inquired about Stephen suggests that he was a person of consequence long before becoming the count's chancellor.[4] His appointment in 1176 continued what was by then a tradition in Champagne, of the chancellor being an intimate of the count but not a prelate, unlike the royal chancellors of France, England, and Germany, who held episcopal office while serving as chancellor. A new chancellor and new seal in 1176 marked the most important symbolic change in the chancery since the beginning of Henry's rule.[5] The chancellor not only supervised the production of documents in anticipation of the count's journey overseas; he would also accompany Henry and draft his letters in the course of the expedition.

The death of Archbishop Henry of Reims (13 November 1175) ended a particularly contentious episcopacy that had alienated the townsmen and knights of Reims, the cathedral canons, the castle lords in the archiepiscopal domain, and even Count Henry. The poet Walter of Châtillon alluded to that troubled state of affairs in his dedication of the *Alexandreis* to the new archbishop, William of Champagne, under whose hand, he prophesied, "the warlike land" of Reims would lose "its name for harshness."[6] William's election in fact ushered in a quarter century of remarkably peaceful and prosperous conditions in Reims and its surrounding countryside.[7] His election was unusual, however, in that a sitting archbishop rarely transferred his see, and then only by special papal authorization. The well-informed English historian Ralph of Diceto felt that he had to justify William's transfer from Sens to Reims with examples from the earliest years of Christianity.[8] In this case Pope Alexander III allowed it as a personal favor to one of his staunchest supporters during the schism and after.

William's election at forty years of age to the see of Reims was a remarkable achievement. It was generally agreed that he was exceptionally well qualified. "Brother of the queen, esteemed for his wisdom, and an exemplar of the religious life," commented Gervase of Canterbury, and "almost lord of the king and the kingdom," which indeed he was by the time Gervase was writing in the 1190s.[9] Even so, the actual election played out against the background of his predecessor's troubled years in Reims and in consideration of the interests of King Louis, Queen Adele and her brothers, and Pope Alexander, who needed a reliable primate in Reims. There were other factors at work, too, in particular the presence of an influential contingent of Englishmen within the cathedral chapter of Reims sympathetic to an archbishop raised in the household of Bishop Henry of Winchester. And Peter of Celle, who had known William earlier as cathedral provost in Troyes and who, as abbot of St-Remi, was alter ego of the archbishop of Reims since 1162, surely had a say in William's election. Count Henry joined William in Sens in February 1176 and perhaps accompanied him to Reims in late March or early April.[10] Four months later, on 8 August, William was ceremoniously installed as archbishop of Reims, no doubt in the presence of his sister Queen Adele and brothers Henry, Thibaut, and Stephen. Through the next quarter century Archbishop William would play a major role in the political and ecclesiastical history of France.

A Call to Crusade

In January 1176 Pope Alexander III, apprised of the dire condition of Westerners in the Levant, directed his legate Peter of Pavia, cardinal-priest of S. Crisogono and former bishop of Meaux, to invite Louis VII and the French barons to undertake an expedition to Jerusalem.[11] The pope's letter was only the latest attempt to rouse Western leaders to aid their compatriots in the Levant, whose fortunes were becoming increasingly problematic in the wake of Nur ad-Din's conquests. A number of French princes had undertaken pilgrimages and small armed expeditions in aid of the overseas Franks—Count Thierry of Flanders went in 1157–58 and 1164–65—but they failed to halt the deteriorating conditions of the Western settlements, and a steady stream of disturbing reports prompted the pope to renew the call to crusade. In 1165 Alexander had appealed to the "princes, counts, barons, and all Christians" in language adopted from Eugenius's bull *Quantum praedecessores*, calling for an expedition to rescue the Holy Land from the grip of the infidel, to liberate the Eastern Church, and to recover the castles lost to the Saracens. Recalling the great expedition summoned by Pope Urban II, he lamented the recent loss of life among Westerners, especially in defense of Antioch, and warned of the threat to Jerusalem and its holy places. For the remission of your sins, he promised, you should gird the sword for this mission: you, your family, and your lands will come under the church's protection the moment you take the cross, and you will be exempt from repaying any debts. It was permitted to mortgage fiefs to the church and to religious persons, he added, with the permission of one's family and the lord from whom the fief is held. But, he cautioned, do not go in fancy dress and weapons; take only the arms, horses, and items necessary to expunge the infidel.[12] Count Henry certainly knew of the bull, for his cousins Count William IV and Guy of Nevers did respond, but it had no visible effect at the time on the recently married Henry or on King Louis, who had just seen the birth of his son.[13]

With conditions in the East becoming desperate by 1169, the archbishops

of Caesarea and Tyre (William of Tyre) solicited aid in the West. Bearing letters from King Amalric of Jerusalem, they appealed to the monarchs of
France, England, Germany, and Sicily, and to the counts of Flanders, Champagne, and Chartres, among others.[14] They reached Rome by July and Paris by
September 1169, perhaps bearing the pope's own appeal, *Inter omnia*, dated 29
July 1169 and addressed to all "princes, knights, and Christians." The pope
reiterated that crusaders were exempted from all legal obligations, including
debts, from the moment the taking of the cross was announced to one's family
"or the lord to whom the fief belongs."[15] On 16 November the kings of France
and England met at St-Denis to discuss a new crusade, among other outstanding issues.[16]

The pope's call failed to resonate with Count Henry, however, who was
occupied with defending his chapel from episcopal jurisdiction. But his
younger and recently widowed brother Stephen accepted King Amalric's proposal to marry his widowed daughter Sibyl, and left after Easter 1170, bearing
the monies Louis VII had collected for the Christians in Jerusalem.[17] Traveling with him were his nephew Hugh III, duke of Burgundy; their cousin Odo
the Champenois of Champlitte, seneschal of Burgundy; Count Stephen of
Burgundy; several castle lords from the two Burgundies; and a number of
Cistercians, including the bishop of Verdun.[18] On his return early in 1173,
Stephen gave a first-hand report on conditions in the East, no doubt with
good information from Milo of Plancy, seneschal of Jerusalem (1167–74) and
younger brother of Count Henry's chancellor Haice.[19] But again the timing
was wrong for Count Henry. Any thought about returning to the Levant was
overshadowed by the revolt of Henry Plantagenet's sons, which the Champenois brothers supported. Yet the steady stream of great lords and knights traveling to Jerusalem and the Levantine coastal cities in the 1170s, and the stories
of their hardships, were a constant reminder of the eroding position of the
Franks in the East, especially with Saladin's successes after 1174.

The crescendo of appeals for aid culminated in the pope's letter of 29
January 1176. The Turks are burning down cities and castles, and conditions
are dire, he wrote. It was time to exhort the king, the princes, counts, barons,
and other faithful men in the kingdom of France to aid the Western Christians. The first task of the papal legate Peter was to reconcile the kings of
France and England, a process requiring almost two years of difficult negotiations. Louis VII would not leave his kingdom as long as his daughter Alice
remained in King Henry II's custody, promised but not yet married to Prince
Richard as provided by the Treaty of Montmirail. In May the pope warned

Henry II to arrange the marriage or to return the girl to her father, and in August the legate threatened to interdict the English king's lands unless he allowed the marriage and also made peace with the French king. The legate succeeded in arranging a temporary peace (the Treaty of Nonancourt) between Louis and Henry II, who promised to take the cross and lead an expedition to the East (21 September 1177). The two kings would travel together after providing for the governance of their kingdoms by "custodians or governors" who would swear to keep good faith; the kings also affirmed that merchants and all others, lay and cleric, would come under royal protection in their respective realms.[20] It is not known whether Count Henry witnessed the king's cross-taking, but his brother Thibaut and the king's brothers Robert of Dreux and Peter of Courtenay did.[21] Yet distrust between the two monarchs ran too deep, and neither carried through. In fact Louis already was in ill health.

Count Philip of Flanders and a few French barons recently had left for Jerusalem (11 April 1177), but many were slow to follow.[22] Behind the scenes, the pope was bringing the moral force of the Cistercians to bear on reluctant princes. Aubri of Trois-Fontaines, writing a half century later, reported that Abbot Henry of Clairvaux "induced" the English king to make peace with King Louis and then convinced "Count Henry, who was well known for his liberalities, that he should, for his sins, take the cross and go to Jerusalem." Which the count did, noted Aubri, accompanied by some nobles, including Count Henry of Grandpré.[23] Abbot Henry wrote to the pope that he witnessed Count Henry take the cross from the hand of the papal legate in a public assembly shortly before Christmas (1177). Henry promised to lead the expedition, said the abbot, and placed his lands under the pope's protection.[24]

It was exactly thirty years since Henry had embarked on the Second Crusade, and just before he turned fifty. King Louis expected to accompany him in what would have been a memory trip of two aging veterans of the Second Crusade. It is interesting to speculate whether Chrétien de Troyes's romance *Cligés*, completed by 1176, just as the pope was pressuring Western leaders to aid their coreligionists in the Levant, rekindled Henry's memory of his earlier exploits overseas. Chrétien's narrative cleverly crosses a response to the Tristan story of adultery with a Byzantine imperial family drama, as in the romances of antiquity but within the frame of an Arthurian adventure. In Chrétien's story the emperor's eldest son and heir, Alexander, seeks to prove his worth in arms by traveling to King Arthur's court to be knighted by none other than Arthur, for "he was so courageous and bold that he would not consider becoming a knight in his own land," an obvious play on Count Henry's receiving arms from Emperor Manuel Komnenos in Constantinople in 1147.[25] In case anyone missed the allusion, Chrétien has the emperor give good advice to Alexander on setting out to Britain: "largess is the lady and queen who brightens all other virtues."[26] Henry must have been delighted to recognize himself as a new Alexander in the business of *translatio* of chivalry and learning, which Chrétien mentions in his introduction as having come from Greece to Rome and then to France, where, the poet wishes, it may never leave. Since the king was seriously ill by 1177 and clearly unable to undertake the journey, Count Henry would revisit Jerusalem alone. As he announced to the monks of Premontré while visiting their monastery, he had "assumed the sign of the Lord's cross."[27]

Preparing for the Expedition

Henry spent 1178 putting his affairs in order, raising money and materiel for a trip expected to last several years, and arranging for Marie to rule in his absence. It is unlikely that he appeared at the tournament held at Pleurs near Sézanne, where William Marshal excelled and Count Thibaut was said to have put in a stellar performance.[28] Henry was concerned about the conduct of the fairs during his absence: he did not want bellicose young men traversing his county, disrupting commerce, and intimidating merchants and marketplaces. There is no record of any tournament held near his most commercially developed towns of Troyes, Provins, or Bar-sur-Aube, unlike the rest of northern France and Germany, where tournaments often were held near large towns.[29] For Henry, the peace of his realm was of critical importance, not only for the viability of his fairs but also because in 1178 his only son was a minor of twelve and Countess Marie would rule the county until he returned. She wrote to the pope announcing Henry's planned expedition and seeking papal protection during his absence. Alexander readily conceded it, placing Henry and all his possessions under papal protection until his return.[30]

Realigning Castle Mouvances

In the summer of 1178 Archbishop William made a highly visible visit to Canterbury in honor of Thomas Becket. It was more than a pilgrimage for William, who had been instrumental in obtaining Becket's canonization; it was a

triumphal homecoming for the archbishop of Reims who had spent his formative years in England. Before crossing the channel, he dined with gusto at
Ardres castle as the guest of Count Baldwin of Guines, causing a scene when
he demanded water to dilute the many servings of wine.[31] On 27 July he met
with King Henry II and many English bishops and barons, and stayed for
three days at the royal palace in London, where he was lavishly entertained.[32]
Shortly after returning to Reims, William traveled to Besançon to attend the
court of Frederick Barbarossa, who was returning from Italy. William may
well have stopped in Troyes, where Count Henry joined him for the final leg
of the trip to Besançon. Their nephews, Count Henry I of Bar-le-Duc and
Duke Hugh of Burgundy, and their cousin Odo the Champenois also attended, as did a large number of castle lords from southern and eastern Champagne. Sitting at court with Frederick Barbarossa on 13 September, they heard
the abbess of Remiremont accuse her advocate, Rainer of Bourbonne, of seizing one of her villages; the emperor confiscated the advocacy.[33] Two days later,
on 15 September, Henry and William witnessed Henry of Bar-le-Duc feudal-
ize his most important fortress and town of Amance and his castle at Mousson
to the emperor's wife, Countess Beatrice of Burgundy, in return for which she
gave him Briey as a fief.[34] That realignment of feudal *mouvance* in a small but
important principality on the eastern border of Champagne was one of several
in those years.

   Soon thereafter, most likely in the fall of 1178, Henry and William realigned the *mouvance* of four castles and castellanies in the archiepiscopal
lands of Reims. The archbishop transferred the lordship of Braine, Roucy,
Rethel, and Château-Porcien to the count of Champagne, so that the four
castle lords would hold those castles in fief directly from Henry (see Map 3).
That was William's way of calming the troubled countryside he inherited from
his predecessor. According to the pope's confirmation of the realigned *mouvances* in Reims, "the noble count of Champagne is held to do liege homage
to you [the archbishop], saving fidelity to the king, for the [named] fiefs that
he holds from your church," although there is no evidence that Henry actually
did the prescribed homage to his brother.[35] The transfer of feudal *mouvance*
was the same solution that Archbishop Guichard of Lyon and Count Guy II
of Forez had arranged five years earlier in 1173, when Guy acquired the *mouvance* of five castle lordships on archiepiscopal lands west of the Loire River in
exchange for all of his lands east of the river, ending years of baronial discontent within the archbishop's lands.[36] It is highly likely that Henry and William
knew about that realignment, since Archbishop Guichard was well known in

Champagne as the former abbot of Pontigny (1136–65), and the motives in each case were the same: troublesome castle barons, chafing under the hand of their episcopal lords, preferred a secular overlord. Henry consequently held nine castle-towns with their castellanies from the archbishop of Reims, the four new ones being added to the five—Vitry, Vertus, Châtillon-sur-Marne, Épernay, Fismes—already in the count's hand. Whether the brothers drew up a formal record of the feudal realignment is not known, but the archbishop took a copy of their understanding with him to the Third Lateran Council, where the pope confirmed it in April 1179.[37] It was the most significant expansion of Henry's overlordship since 1162, when he acquired the *mouvance* of nine castles on his eastern borders from Frederick Barbarossa.

The realignment of *mouvance* was a win-win arrangement all around. In the north, Henry's *mouvance* reached beyond his towns on the Marne to the Aisne River. In the south, it extended below his castle-towns at Isle-Aumont, Ervy, and St-Florentin into the Auxerrois, where his maternal cousin Count Guy of Nevers had transferred to Henry the *mouvance* of four castles that he held from the bishop of Auxerre, with the bishop's tacit assent.[38] Prelates no longer had to deal with troublesome barons, and the barons escaped the increasingly unpalatable appearance of holding what they regarded as family property from an ecclesiastical lord and being liable, like the count of Nevers, to render their castles at the bishop's will.[39] In all cases the realignment of *mouvance* was a peaceful affair, reflecting the right of feudal lords to transfer the *mouvance* of their castles.[40] The chief beneficiary was Count Henry, who extended his overlordship beyond his inherited lands, in the process stabilizing his ill-defined border zones in the north, south, and east before his impending trip overseas.

It is not known whether the formalization of *mouvances* in the southern borderlands led Henry himself to do homage, as his father had done to the duke of Burgundy in 1143. Duke Odo III later claimed that he did, but failed to mention the time and place of Henry's homage, for which there is no concurring evidence.[41] If it did occur, and it may well have, no one thought to record it at a time when homage among lay lords in Champagne was still an oral affair and even Henry's chancery did not record the homages done for his fiefs. There is nothing comparable in Champagne to the chronicles from the Plantagenet realm, which frequently mention homage, or the narratives of Robert of Torigni (ca. 1186) and Gislebert of Hainaut (1195/96), who furnish numerous examples of routine homages among laymen at that time.[42] In Champagne only prelates and their chanceries deemed homage worthy of recording. By an interesting coincidence, the Arthurian world depicted by Chrétien de Troyes in this very decade of the 1170s is resolutely secular, with prelates like the archbishop of Canterbury in *Erec and Enide* limited to solemnizing weddings and crownings. Episcopal lords are notably absent from Arthur's realm, at least in their capacity as overlords of the barons.

The Fiefs of Champagne

After Henry returned from Besançon in the fall of 1178, his chancellor supervised an inquest of his fiefholders.[43] The marshal, William of Provins, knew about the disposition of the count's castles and military forces, but since he expected to accompany Henry overseas, it was important to leave an accurate record for Countess Marie.[44] The inquest differed from the contemporary survey in Normandy, in that at Caen in 1172 the barons swore before the king's justices to the number of knights they had enfeoffed and the amount of service owed to the king; each baron had two letters drawn up, a sealed one in which he certified the number of knights he owed in service to the king, and an unsealed letter providing the names of the knights. Both letters were deposited in the royal treasury and later copied into the Red Book of the Exchequer.[45] The process was simpler in Champagne, where oral testimony was taken by the count's provosts in each of his thirty castellanies and written on "field returns," which were recopied at the chancery on strips of parchment, one per castellany, and then rolled up like the English Exchequer pipe rolls and the Flemish financial accounts.[46] The rolls of fiefs were not administrative registers per se, that is, current working records, but rather documents of record for the benefit of Countess Marie in the absence of the count and his chief officers—the chancellor, the marshal, and the treasurer—who would accompany Henry overseas. And as commemorative records the rolls, unlike the transactional letters patent, were deposited in St-Étienne's treasury for safekeeping.[47]

A quarter century later the marshal Geoffroy of Villehardouin referred to the rolls as "records of fiefs" (*scripta feodorum*).[48] They were, in essence, a form of institutional memory, the earliest written representation of Henry's principality organized by castellany. The importance of the rolls as foundational records was indicated a half century later (ca. 1230), when chancery scribes copied them into codices as security copies, and at midcentury (1249–50), when the original rolls were cited as *antiqua scripta* of the principality.[49] They encoded Henry's principality just as his palace-chapel complex embedded the political center of his county and his tomb would enshrine Henry himself.

Departure

Henry may have planned to leave for the East in the early spring of 1179, but by February Marie was six months pregnant, and he decided to postpone his departure until the birth of their fourth child. As the count's chief officers and entourage were making their final preparations, so, too, did a large contingent of Champenois barons and knights. Coincidentally, the regional prelates, including Archbishops William of Reims and Guy of Sens, and Bishops Mathieu of Troyes and Simon of Meaux, were preparing to attend the Third Lateran Council (5–19 March).[50] In the early weeks of 1179 bishops and abbots from northern Europe passed through Troyes on the way to Rome. So, too, did Walter Map, a secular cleric in the service of Henry II, who left a lively recollection of his stopover in Troyes:

> The count of Champagne, Henry son of Thibaut, received me hospitably. He was the most generous (*largissimus*) of men, so much so that to many he seemed prodigal, for to all who asked, he gave. While in conversation he praised his nephew Renaud of Mouzon [of Bar-le-Duc, canon of Tours] in all things except that he was immoderately generous (*largus*).[51] I, however, who knew that the count himself was so generous as to seem prodigal, asked with a smile whether he himself knew the limits of generosity. He replied: "Where there remains no more to give, that is the limit, for it is not generous to give away what you have acquired through base means." To me this seemed wittily said, for if you seek to give ill-begotten gains, you become miserly in order to seem generous.[52]

More than three hundred bishops attended the conclave in Rome, according to Bishop William of Tyre, the official secretary of the Lateran Council, who had just completed his history of the Latins in the Holy Land.[53] He was part of a delegation sent by Sybil, the recently widowed sister of King Baldwin IV of Jerusalem, who was seeking marriage with Count Henry's divorced nephew, Duke Hugh III of Burgundy. In Rome, William of Tyre and Walter Map witnessed the elevation of Archbishop William of Reims as cardinal-priest of Santa Sabina (14 March). The pope also promoted Abbot Henry of Clairvaux over several other distinguished prelates listed as worthy candidates, including Peter of Celle (abbot of St-Remi of Reims), Simon Aurea Capra (prior of Mt-Dieu), and John of Salisbury (bishop of Chartres).[54]

William became a "residential cardinal" and primary papal legate in France. It was a fitting reward for one of Alexander's closest supporters and a luminary prelate in France. Before returning home, the new cardinal obtained papal confirmation of his archiepiscopal rights and possessions in Reims, including the nine castle lordships whose *mouvance* he had transferred to Count Henry.

About the same time, just before Henry's departure, his old friend Peter of Celle sent him a copy of his treatise *On the Discipline of the Cloister*, dedicated "to his lord and friend Henry, illustrious count palatine of Troyes, [from] Peter, humble abbot of St-Remi, greetings and all prosperity."[55] Written while Peter was ill, too ill in fact to attend the Lateran Council ("I am waiting the judgment of God"), it was a meditation on the monastic life and death.[56] He asked the count, in reading the treatise, to look for "what you might become rather than what you are." Peter had developed a close relationship with Henry during his seventeen years as abbot of Montier-la-Celle near Troyes at the time when Henry was building his new capital. "On what grounds, most noble prince, do I send a crude and unenlightened treatise to be read by someone of so subtle and vivacious intelligence (*ingenium*)?"[57] He asked indulgence for placing Henry's name in the dedication and hoped that readers would overlook the faults of a work associated with the renown "of such a great prince." All that fell within the province of rhetoric, as did Peter's references to the Tabernacle and the Temple, which surely must have reminded Henry of his earlier visit to Jerusalem. What was unusual, however, was Peter's wish for Henry's good fortune or prosperity (*prosperitas*). Perhaps it was a gentle critique of Henry's extravagance in furnishing St-Étienne or in constructing such a lavish tomb, but it also alluded to the fact that much of Henry's achievement, and sense of accomplishment, rested on the economic prosperity of his county.[58] The treatise itself was a curious gift, a defense of regular canons in the face of Henry's programmatic installation of secular canons in his largest and most prosperous fair towns, canons who by 1179 had become a major presence in his lands. Ultimately, Peter's dedication was a token of friendship, a parting gift from an ill abbot "to my lord and dearest friend" (of four decades) who was undertaking an arduous and dangerous journey to Jerusalem.[59]

In the eight weeks preceding his departure (1 April through May 1179) Henry confirmed a number of small transactions for local religious houses and sealed several acts on his own account.[60] He endowed a chapter of canons in his chapel in Provins, and considerably enlarged the endowment of St-Nicolas of Sézanne.[61] He exempted the Hospitallers from taxes in all his land, except from his tolls and sales taxes on their commercial transactions, and from the jurisdiction of his provosts except in cases of theft, murder, and rape.[62] His most unusual act was to grant a communal charter to the residents of Meaux, the first of its kind in Champagne.[63] It was a radical act in that it applied to all the residents of Meaux, including the bishop's men, and was granted while Bishop Simon of Lizy was still in Rome at the Third Lateran Council. Henry and the townsmen of Meaux apparently negotiated the terms of the commune after the bishop left for Rome in late January, with the intent of establishing the count's direct lordship over the entire city of Meaux, where Henry had shared lordship with the bishop. The charter's first clause required all "men of Meaux" to swear faithful service to Henry, his wife Marie, their eldest son Henry (II), and their successors "in perpetuity." The townsmen owed the count military service, essentially as a communal militia, and received a number of liberties typical of other franchised communities, including the freedom to marry at will, freedom from seizure except by the mayor, and exemption from the *taille* and taxes, all in return for a 140*l.* annual payment. Henry took under his protection all foreign merchants doing business in Meaux and installed a notary public (*scriptor*), to be appointed by his chancellor, who would swear fidelity to both the chancellor and the commune, thus providing an alternative to the bishop's chancery for drawing up legal documents and commercial transactions.

Since the establishment of a commune in Meaux constituted a coup d'état against the bishop, the townsmen, mindful of Henry's refusal in 1167 to support the commune of Reims in the absence of their archbishop, asked for assurances that Henry would not abandon them after the bishop returned. And so the knight Daimbert of Ternantes, one of Henry's intimates, swore on his behalf that the count would abide by all the provisions of the charter in perpetuity. Countess Marie and thirteen-year-old Henry gave their consent in the presence of the count's officers and closest advisers, most of whom would accompany him overseas. Henry finally had outmaneuvered the bishop and his powerful Cornillon lineage in Meaux, where the count had few baronial allies. But Henry did have one important enabler in Meaux, his steadfast friend Archdeacon Roric, one of the original canons of St-Étienne of Troyes and brother of Countess Marie's escort Nevel of Ramerupt. Whether it was Henry or the townsmen of Meaux who initiated the commune is unknown, but it played to Henry's interests by bringing under his hand a large episcopal city at the border of the royal domain. We can only speculate as to whether he hoped to make Meaux another fair town at the expense of Lagny, whose fairs were being dwarfed by the fairs in his three southern towns. In one respect, however, it was Henry's payback to Bishop Simon, the treasurer of the cathedral of Meaux in 1165 when Henry was called to account for counterfeiting the bishop's coins. Whatever Henry's intent, the bishop of Meaux, faced with a fait accompli on his return, could do nothing to counteract the commune before Henry's imminent departure as a crusader, whose person and lands fell under papal protection.[64]

In May Count Baldwin V of Hainaut arrived in Troyes to confirm the marriage contract that his brother-in-law, Count Philip of Flanders, had negotiated with Henry in 1171.[65] Baldwin had been a habitué of tournaments since his knighting at eighteen (1168), and perambulated with a large team of experienced knights, much like Prince Henry of England.[66] Baldwin's chancellor, Gislebert of Mons, recorded the event in Troyes. On the Sunday after Ascension (13 May), he wrote, Baldwin reaffirmed the contract for the double marriage of their children, his nine-year-old daughter Elizabeth/Isabelle with thirteen-year-old Henry of Champagne, and his son Baldwin with Marie of Champagne, both eight years old. On that very day, reports Gislebert, Countess Marie (then thirty-four) gave birth to a son, Thibaut.[67] Shortly afterward, at the end of May, Count Henry left for Jerusalem. He was fifty-two.

The Journey

As a young man thirty-two years earlier Henry had joined the king's expedition at St-Denis to travel across central Europe to Constantinople. This time he took a southern route, down the Rhône River to Marseille (see Map 2). From Troyes he headed to Châtillon-sur-Seine, where he made a benefaction to the nuns of Jully in the presence of his closest councillors: his marshal William, treasurer Artaud, scribe Thibaut of Fismes, chancellor Stephen, notary William, and Peter of Langres.[68] At Dijon the count's party was joined by Master Philip of Sézanne, Duke Hugh III of Burgundy, and Odo the Champenois (of Champlitte) who witnessed Henry make amends with the abbot of St-Bénigne regarding the misconduct of his bailiffs in the abbey's parishes in Champagne. The abbot also complained about the conduct of Wiard, lord of Reynel, who exercised custody over the priory of St-Blin, contrary to the promise of Count Hugh of Troyes, whose charter of at least a half century earlier the abbot presented to Henry. After "carefully examining" the charter, Henry said that he was unable to rectify the situation at the moment but, he is quoted as saying, "I promised them in good faith that on my return [from overseas] I will retrieve that custody into my own hand and will not allow anyone in the future to contravene it, and if by chance I do not return from my journey, I direct my heir to do it."[69] The scribe, perhaps Chancellor Stephen, captured the moment by concluding the letter with "Done at Dijon, on my way to Jerusalem." The duke of Burgundy accompanied Henry to Beaune, where they were joined by Count Henry of Grandpré and his brother Geoffroy, who witnessed the count's benefaction to the monks at Cîteaux in support of the General Chapter meeting of abbots. "Done at Beaune on my way to Jerusalem," wrote the chancellor in presenting the letter to the monks, who took it to Countess Marie in Troyes for her confirmation.[70]

From Marseille, Henry sailed to Sicily and reached Brindisi by July. There he met Bishop William of Tyre, chancellor of the king of Jerusalem, who was returning from the Lateran Council in Rome on his way to Constantinople on an unspecified mission for Pope Alexander III.[71] From Brindisi Henry sailed directly to Acre. The king's brother Peter of Courtenay and his nephew Philip, bishop-elect of Beauvais, came in the same July crossing.[72] As soon as they landed they were summoned to the defense of Tiberias, where the Templars were besieged at Le Chestellet. But the relief expedition arrived after the fortress had fallen to Saladin (30 August), and Henry is not known to have participated in any military engagement thereafter.[73] He seems rather to have spent the fall months of 1179 and spring of 1180 touring the sites he had visited three decades earlier—Jerusalem, Hebron, Sebastia, and Nazareth— making suitable benefactions at each. In Jerusalem he sealed two grants. The first was for a 10l. annual payment to Notre-Dame of Josaphat, which he promised to assign on the understanding that if he did not return home, his wife or son or guardians of his lands, that is, his bailiffs and provosts, would assign the revenue, and he further licensed acquisitions from his fiefs and rents by gift or purchase.[74] The second grant was for Amalric, the first Latin bishop of Hebron: a 15l. annual revenue, a house or plot of land for building a house for canons in Troyes exempt from taxes and tolls, and license to acquire property from his fiefs in Champagne. He had been moved by his visit to "the holy sites of the patriarch Abraham, Isaac, and Jacob" at Hebron, he said, and so he made this gift "for the souls of my father and mother, and my wife and sons, and all my predecessors." He ended by proclaiming himself "I, Henry, count palatine of France." Virtually the entire court from Champagne witnessed.[75]

Henry visited the cathedral of St. John the Baptist at Sebastia, second in size to the Church of the Holy Sepulcher in Jerusalem and a pilgrimage site for both Christians and Muslims after the remains of John the Baptist were discovered there in 1145.[76] In 1168 his sister Elizabeth made a donation for the soul of her second husband, William IV of Montmirail and Perche-Gouët, who was buried at Sebastia after he died on a pilgrimage to expiate his misdeeds.[77] Henry's brother Archbishop William, too, had made donations to the church and perhaps was involved in the design of its rebuilding after the model of Sens cathedral.[78] Sebastia was a "must see" for Henry, who could report to his brother on the state of the church building. After his visit he gave a 10*l*. revenue to the church, to be collected at the gate of St-Jean in Provins during the May Fair.[79]

In the spring of 1180 Count Henry left Jerusalem for Constantinople. His motive is unknown. The political situation in Jerusalem might have been far too complicated and dangerous for someone of his disposition, and he may have thought it prudent to exit an impossible scene.[80] He also may have been troubled by a letter from his nephew Philip II of France, who was crowned king on 1 November 1179. The fourteen-year-old king, who held Henry in high regard from seeing him in Paris in the 1170s, appealed for his intervention in a dispute with the queen mother, Adele.[81] Henry did not sail directly home but instead traveled to Constantinople, perhaps to attend the wedding of Agnes of France and Alexius Komnenos. As the daughter of King Louis and Queen Adele, Agnes was Henry's niece and Countess Marie's half sister. Her marriage to the future emperor of Byzantium would certainly have been of interest to Henry, especially since Emperor Manuel Komnenos had dubbed Henry in Constantinople three decades earlier. Pope Alexander III had suggested the alliance after Agnes's birth in an attempt to dissuade King Louis from betrothing her to a son of Frederick I of Germany, the pope's bitter enemy.[82] Count Philip of Flanders returned from Constantinople in 1178 with a letter from Manuel agreeing to the marriage, but since Agnes was at that time "not yet nubile," Louis agreed to send her when the time was right.[83]

On 11 March 1180 eight-year-old Agnes was married in great splendor to ten-year-old Alexius II.[84] A special illustrated book was prepared for the young foreign-born empress, now renamed Anne, to ease her acculturation into the Greek-speaking imperial court.[85] William of Tyre, who had sailed from Brindisi directly to Constantinople in August 1179, witnessed the wedding and stayed on to conduct some unspecified business for the pope, while at the same time acting in his capacity as royal chancellor of King Baldwin IV of Jerusalem. He took his leave the next month (23 April 1180), still carrying his transcript (*scriptum*) of the Third Lateran Council's proceedings, which he later deposited, together with his personal collection of books, in his church's archive in Tyre.[86]

Count Henry missed the wedding. "Returning from Jerusalem [to Constantinople]," reported André of Marchiennes, "Henry fell into the hands of the Saracens," who killed or captured almost all his companions.[87] Henry's two treasurers who were with him, Artaud and Milo I Breban of Provins, later testified that Henry "vowed to Saint Mammes [who was martyred nearby] that if he was liberated, he would grant 30*l.* annually to the church of St-Mammès of Langres."[88] Ultimately Henry was ransomed by Emperor Manuel Komnenos and arrived in Constantinople in August 1180, just one month before Manuel died (24 September 1180), and probably witnessed the accession of Alexius II as emperor and Agnes/Anne as empress of Constantinople.[89] He left at the end of the month, proceeded across Illyricum and probably stopped in Rome, where the pope gave him a tooth of Saint Peter, which he later deposited in his chapel in a reliquary containing the skull of Saint Philip.[90] From Rome he took the French Road, crossed the Italian passes to Burgundy, and arrived in Sens in time for Philip II's Christmas court, where the king and the great men of the realm were considering war against the German emperor. Since Frederick had dispossessed Henry the Lion, duke of Saxony, King Philip and Count Philip of Flanders invited the king of England to join them in a punitive expedition against the emperor.[91] King Philip and the great barons received Count Henry "with great favor," reported André of Marchiennes, and solicited his advice. Henry, "a wise man," counseled against a military response because it was "neither useful to the king nor just."[92] That advice, to avoid war if possible, reflected Henry's experiences on two crusades and several campaigns with Louis VII, but it was also a good reading of his Vegetius, just as John of Salisbury had recommended. The young king, more confident than his years might warrant, listened to his experienced and esteemed uncle.

Death and Remembrance

After an arduous, nineteen-month journey, Henry arrived in Troyes in ill health on 8 March 1181. According to Aubri of Trois-Fontaines, Henry was struck by a malady as soon as he entered his lands and made his confession on reaching Troyes.[93] He had lost several of his most experienced officials, who had helped him administer his principality from the start of his rule. Those who did not return included his longtime marshal William Rex of Provins, his intellectual mentor Nicholas of Montiéramey, Master Philip of Sézanne (who had become close to Henry in the 1170s), Viscount Peter (Bristaud) of Provins, the knight Daimbert of Ternantes, and Thibaut the Scribe, who had drafted many of the count's letters. Whether they remained in Jerusalem or died in Asia Minor is unknown, but Henry must have felt an acute sense of loss when confirming several acts in the week following his return to Troyes. He sealed letters of non-prejudice for the residents of Chablis, who had raised 300*l.* to support his journey, reaffirming that their contribution for his recent expedition did not set a precedent; he had no right, he declared, nor was it customary for him to collect any such tax in the future.[94] He exempted from all taxes the sixteen houses owned by the priory of Foissy, six in Troyes and ten in Bar-sur-Aube.[95] Then, sensing that he was "gravely ill" and would not survive, he made a deathbed grant to the cathedral chapter of Troyes with the consent of his brother William and "my dearest wife Marie and my devoted son Henry." Since he had abused his right to collect *tailles* and taxes from the bishop's tenants during an episcopal vacancy, he said, he (and his heirs implicitly) promised to collect only 200*l.* in *tailles* and other taxes from them during a vacancy, as provided by his earlier privilege, and he further allowed the dean and cathedral chapter rather than his agents to collect the tax. The new chancellor, Haice of Plancy, had a formal letter drawn up, to which he added at the bottom, "Given by the hand of the chancellor Haice." That was Henry's last letter.[96] But he made one last act before dying, fulfilling a vow he made to Saint Mammes after he fell captive to the Turks: he invested Bishop Manasses with the promised revenue and directed the chancellor to draft a letter recording it.[97]

Henry died in the night of 16 March 1181, eight days after returning to Troyes.[98] He was fifty-four. We do not have a record of his funeral, but it may have resembled the two-day funeral liturgy for Count Thibaut III in May 1201, an event known from an anonymous, retrospective, and perhaps invented account based on later practices.[99] The entire chapel would have been draped in black cloth, with 120 candles lit amid banners and pennons bearing the coat of arms of Champagne. The count's crown, breastplate, and sword were placed on his tomb. The chapel's towers were hung with flags, and while the chapel bells rang continuously, the canons of St-Loup recited the Psalms throughout the day. At 8:00 in the evening the entire town stopped for a moment of silence—even prayers were suspended. Then the dean of St-Étienne pronounced the funeral oration and distributed a princely sum of 4,000*l.* to the poor, as if to seal Henry's reputation for generosity. A thirteenth-century obituary notice states that Henry's anniversary was observed by "reading the Psalms after Prime for two days beginning with the day before his death, after which the bells will be rung just as on the Saturday before Lent."[100]

Henry was remembered in many monastic obituaries. For the nuns of Faremoutiers he was a "venerable count," and for the canons at Chartres he was "Henry called the Liberal (*Largus*)"[101] For the monks of Notre-Dame de Châge in the suburb of Meaux he was "a most illustrious and pious count who was most generous (*liberalissimi*) to all."[102] The canons of St-Loup noted his "many benefactions," not the least being the exquisite gospel book he gave in commemoration of his son's birth in 1166.[103] The monks of Montiéramey likewise noted "the many good things (*multa bona*) he gave," alluding to the books Henry had funded or donated to their priory of St-Jean-en-Châtel, where the recently deceased Nicholas had been prior.[104] The cathedral canons of Troyes, too, celebrated his anniversary, but perhaps mindful of the bishop's recent clash with the count, they distributed bread and food during Lent rather than on his anniversary itself.[105] The canons of his chapel of St-Étienne recalled him simply as the "illustrious Count Henry of Champagne" who bequeathed 5s. for each canon and 20s. for bread for the poor on his anniversary.[106]

Guy of Bazoches, the canon at Châlons who had written two praise letters to Count Henry, wrote what amounts to a funeral eulogy, the only commemoration comparable to Arnold of Bonneval's tribute to Count Thibaut thirty years earlier. The two portraits diverge profoundly in tone and content. Most notable in Thibaut, according to Arnold, was the count's material support of the Cistercians, his attention to the poor, his admirable conduct while his lands were being savaged by King Louis VII, and his extraordinary gift of precious stones from his treasury. For Guy of Bazoches, it was Henry's character that was remarkable: "a man of whom there certainly was no one nobler of character (*animo*)," and who "displayed a novel and delightful kind of appearance." Unlike his father, who suffered at the hands of Louis VII, Henry was intimately connected to the king: "Henry's sister was queen of France and his wife a daughter of the king," wrote Guy, and his innate virtues and largess (*largitas*) strengthened the kingdom. Guy ended his encomium with Henry's great project, the church dedicated to the martyr Stephen built next to his palace. Guy surely had seen the church and knew canons from St-Étienne. He noted that Henry enriched the church with property, furnished it with silk hangings, and endowed its treasury. "I must admit," concluded Guy, "that I have not seen nor do I remember having read of a prince exhibiting such liberality (*liberalitas*)." Unlike his father, however, who unburdened himself of his fortune to the benefit of monasteries, Count Henry invested his resources in a magnificent jewel of a church to serve as his mausoleum. In sum, according to Guy, "Henry, count palatine of Champagne, flourished in France, or it might better be said that France flourished in him."[107]

The Speaking Tomb

Henry in death remained a powerful material presence in Troyes. He left not only a stunning chapel, comital residence, and campus of canons' houses but even his body encased in a spectacular tomb and placed centrally in the choir of St-Étienne, facing the altar (see Figure 7).[108] Although lacking the quasi-sacral attributes of a monarch, Henry succeeded in his own way in breaching the lay-sacral divide. Just as the tribune of his residence projected his presence, while living, into the chapel itself, so his tomb intruded into, indeed dominated, the chapel's liturgical space after death. The tomb itself must have been dazzling, with glistening metals and bright enamel plaques. Closer inspection reveals a complex iconographical program that drew a double parallel, between Henry and the sun and between Henry and Christ, all linked to the theme of resurrection.[109] Carved on the lid was a large cross divided into five parts, with a central enamel figure of Isaiah and with Christ emerging from a cloud flanked by the sun, moon, and stars. Henry himself presents a model of his chapel to Saint Stephen, the same image painted in the chapter's cartulary a century later.[110]

Even more unusual than the tomb's iconographic program is the set of inscriptions wrapped around it. On the inner ring of the tomb's cover frame, not visible to most viewers and perhaps addressed to the heavens, an inscription on a gilt bronze band announces:

Here lies Henry, the courtly count of Troyes who also founded this place and still remains its protector. You, Christ, had completed one thousand one hundred and twenty-seven years when this donor was given (*datus est dator iste*). It was twenty years short of one thousand two hundred years in Christ when the mediator Mars silenced him with death.[111]

Two other inscriptions written on gilt bronze and enamel bands encircled the tomb. Probably commissioned by Marie after Henry's death, they clearly were the work of Simon Aurea Capra, one of best Latin poets of his time and known for his pithy verse.[112] Henry had long esteemed Simon. Three decades earlier, while the poet was prior of St-Ayoul of Provins, Henry had commissioned a set of epitaphs and a Latin condensation of the *Aeneid* from him, and so it was natural for Countess Marie to call on Simon to compose an appropriate epitaph for Henry. Simon became abbot of St-Rémi of Reims shortly after Henry's death, a position he doubtlessly acquired through the good offices of his predecessor, Peter of Celle, who succeeded John of Salisbury as bishop of Chartres (1181–83), and of Archbishop William of Reims.[113] Simon's task in 1181 was to fit his verses on an already completed or almost completed tomb, and at that he proved supremely adept, being a master of the concise phrase. On the upper fillet, running around the chest at eye level, the inscription's voice shifts to Henry, who speaks to the viewers of his tomb:

My death summoned me here from my pilgrimage so that my ashes may remain here forever.[114] God himself made this funeral bed for me so that the heart of those whose affairs I rule, whose chapter I serve, may remember me. I made this tomb for me, who laid the foundation of such a great church, which I govern now just as before. Here I wish my remains to be sheltered, thus to confirm what I have done.[115]

On the lower fillet, clearly visible to visitors, the voice shifts again to celebrate Henry:

He was of strong faith, of certain hope, fervent in devotion, possessed of a pious mind, a generous hand, an eloquent tongue. In dying, he offered more than his possessions, but his very self. This gift, after so many benefactions, the author (*author*) provided. At vespers on Monday, the day after the Ides of March, he deprived the day of his sun; thus it is, abandoned by the sun, [the land is] alone without the sun (*sic sine sole solum*).[116]

That lapidary phrase was Simon Aurea Capra's, but the sun imagery was not his alone. John of Salisbury had given it currency in the 1160s through his description of the virtues of a prince: "The sun shines over the whole world so that it may be seen and discerned all at once; I believe the prince to be another sun."[117] The prince, like the sun, shines over his whole realm, as he acts properly, advances religion, checks the powerful, protects the weak, and walks with justice and prudence. But it was Guy of Bazoches who developed the imagery most fully in a letter addressed to Henry, "magnificent prince and count palatine of Champagne," that plays directly to the tomb's sun imagery. "It is not without merit that I refer to you, not by a celestial sign but by the sun itself," explains Guy, because the sun illuminates the earth and "you therefore are another true sun, illuminating the land."[118] Guy's obsequious letter, with repeated references to the sun, is more than a thanks for the count's financial support, which may have funded Guy's studies at St-Martin in Paris. It is not difficult to imagine that a well educated and adept wordsmith like Guy had read the *Policraticus* (John of Salisbury was at St-Remi of Reims in the 1160s while Guy was a canon at nearby Châlons), and it is highly likely that he had seen or been informed of the programmatic scenes being crafted for Henry's tomb in the mid-1170s.

Walter of Châtillon, too, invented a powerful tomb scene in the *Alexandreis*, in which Alexander encounters the tomb of Achilles:

And thus the Macedonian slowly wandered
among so many tombs of Argive warriors,
their buried shades and ashes, whom inscriptions
still gave their titles clearly carved, behold!
He saw Achilles' tomb, of lesser breadth
than fame, adorned with verses such as these . . .
            . . . when the broad earth
contents itself with but a single prince (*sic solo principe*)
as with a single sun (*ut solo sole*), one thing alone
I dread will fail my buried dust—lapsed fame,
which I would set before Elysian bliss.[119]

Henry's tomb was unusual in being so egocentric in death. As the earliest example of a metalwork tomb, it was the most sumptuous celebration of Henry in its materials (gold, silver, gemstones, enamels), in its visual program (placing Henry with Christ and Saint Stephen), and in its representation of Henry (as the beneficent sun). Henry in effigy appears in civil dress, clothed in a simple tunic and mantle, with his feet in slippers resting on a support. He lacks all accoutrements and symbols of the warrior. His eyes are open, his face sports a full beard, and he wears a cap over his curly hair. With his hands joined in prayer on his breast, he was depicted in the position of eternal rest according to the Requiem Prayer of the Office of the Dead.[120] His effigy was as understated as his tomb was resplendent. But if the tomb qualified as a reliquary tomb, its location right in the center of the count's own chapel made it a unique example of a secular ruler being buried in his own chapel, like a prince of the church, rather than in some quiet monastery where monks could attend to his soul. Louis VII, who predeceased Henry by only six months, chose to be buried in the rural Cistercian monastery of Barbeau, which he founded for that purpose.[121] Henry preferred to remain ever present in his capital city, amid the bustle of a secular chapter in service to him and his successors, and easily accessible to passersby on the great international route between northern Europe and the Mediterranean. If Henry began his rule thirty years earlier with the brilliant performance of his cap in the cathedral of Troyes, he ended it with an ultimate performative act, placing his monumental tomb for all to see within his jewel of a chapel in the capital city of his principality.

Chapter 9

Legacy and Afterlife

France was still a realm of principalities at the death of Count Henry, with the king's lands being no more than a "royal principality" among several wealthier and better-ordered principalities of northern France.[1] The county of Champagne was somewhat of an anomaly, however, in that it coalesced as a viable territorial state only during Count Henry's rule and took its characteristic shape from his initiatives. The county was distinctive in several other respects as well. Its economic "take-off" under Henry, driven largely by commercial exchange at its trade fairs and the adoption of the *provinois* as an international currency, provided a major source of the count's revenues through tolls, rents, and sales taxes, creating in effect a new financial base for his polity. In those same years Count Henry was Louis VII's most constant ally in military and diplomatic affairs, despite their strikingly different personalities, and became a major player in dealing with the pope and in mediating between the monarchs of England and Germany. The Angevin expansion in western France certainly played a role in the rapprochement between Capetians and Champenois, but the core of that new relationship was the personal bond (Louis called it *amor*) formed between Louis and Henry on the Second Crusade. By the late 1160s Henry and his siblings—the royal seneschal Thibaut of Blois, Queen Adele, and Archbishop William of Sens—formed a veritable Champenois party around the king.

The County of Champagne in 1181

The county of Champagne as a political entity was barely three decades old at Henry's death. For his generation the comital quarter constructed in the suburb of St-Denis of Troyes was still of recent vintage. Visually striking, the buildings announced an energetic new prince and a new order, as did his unique and newly minted title, "count palatine of Troyes." The count's campus not only transformed the topography of Troyes; it made Troyes the chief city of his principality, the place where he most often held court and where the chancery drafted most of his letters patent. His resplendent tomb, in what was intended as the centerpiece of a family mausoleum in his lavishly provisioned chapel, embedded his lineage in the capital city of his principality. St-Étienne with Henry's tomb became the symbol of both Henry and his works, and a destination thereafter for visitors to Troyes.

Less visible than the newly constructed campus but just as transformative was the administrative reorganization of Henry's lands. From his residence and chancery in Troyes, he and his chancellor viewed his lands not as a collection of counties and lordships held from a handful of overlords—the duke of Burgundy, the king, the bishop of Langres, and the archbishops of Sens and Reims—but rather as a set of thirty castle-towns linked by an internal network of protected roads. The template of castle-towns with their surrounding districts created a new administrative structure divorced from the *mouvance* of the count's nominal overlords. The count's castellanies centered on those castle-towns subsumed his domain lands, rural communities, knights' fiefs, and even allodial castle lordships. Although Henry retained "count palatine of Troyes" as his exclusive title, neither he nor his chancery ever mentioned the county of Troyes or the counties of Vitry and Bar-sur-Aube, which he had ruled for three years, or any of the other constituent lordships of his principality. Within a decade of his accession, Henry had reimagined Champagne as a territorial state anchored on thirty walled towns and fortifications with their geographically defined districts administered by his provosts, bailiffs, and toll collectors.

The inquest of Henry's fiefholders undertaken two years before his death embodied that new administrative structure and reveals several important features of his principality.[2] Unlike contemporary inquests in Normandy and England, which asked the barons to name their knights and knight service, Henry's inquest surveyed only his direct fiefholders, mostly knights, according to the castellanies in which they held their fiefs. About half of his 1,900 fiefholders (49 percent) held their primary fiefs in liege homage from him, which is to say that just as many held their primary fiefs from other lords.[3] In effect, multiple fief tenures were the norm. That was a customary practice, as the barons on the Second Crusade agreed, in rationalizing their homages to

Emperor Manuel Komnenos: "after the king, we can—by custom—possess fiefs from several lords."[4] Certainly the castle lords held mixed portfolios of landed assets. Bartholomew of Vignory, for example, held the town of Vignory as an allod, his castle and towers of Vignory as a fief from the count of Burgundy, and only an unspecified fief from Count Henry, for which he was "liege after the count of Burgundy."[5] For a border lord like Bartholomew, a contingent ligeance was a hedge against domination by any single overlord.[6] But what was significant about Count Henry's inquest is that castle lords were listed in the rolls of fiefs whether or not they held their castles from him in fief. Bartholomew of Vignory was among two dozen castle lords named along with almost one hundred knights in the count's castellany of Bar-sur-Aube.[7] Count Henry thus began the process of envisioning baronial properties, whatever their tenurial status, as being located within his own administrative districts. That quiet imposition of a new administrative organization over the castle lords was not completed by 1181; it was left to Henry's successors in the thirteenth century to compel the barons to hold their castles in liege homage within "the county of Champagne and Brie."[8]

The inquest of 1178 also reveals that in the event of war all "knights of the castellany" (*milites castellarie*), whether or not they owed annual castle-guard in the count's towns, were obligated to serve in a defensive capacity for as long as needed.[9] Only 40 percent of the count's fiefholders owed annual castle-guard duty, ranging from six to twelve weeks of service.[10] Indirect evidence suggests that castle-guard, which required temporary residence in one of the count's towns, was as much a social as a military event, and the occasion for bringing wives and families to share a brief urban experience. The bishop of Troyes, for example, authorized monks from the priory of St-Flavit to celebrate Mass in the town of Villemaur and to "administer to the knights staying in that castle with their wives and households."[11] On that occasion the seven resident garrison knights in Villemaur were joined by six knights who came annually to perform their castle-guard.[12] Those fortunate enough to serve in Provins, Troyes, or Bar-sur-Aube during the fairs could shop for goods at the many commercial halls and socialize with other knight families and castle lords who likewise rendered castle-guard in the count's towns. That shared experience contributed far more to regional and social cohesion than would have been possible through a forty-day service in the field, of which there is no evidence in Champagne under Count Henry. By all accounts the county was a peaceful realm. Henry corrected the abuses of his officials and castle lords who mistreated villagers, but neither in his towns nor in the countryside is there evidence of disorder requiring his military intervention. Nor is there any mention of the count's towns being threatened by external forces. All of Henry's military adventures occurred beyond his lands.

If a fixed residence and chancery in Troyes and a new conception of Champagne as a set of linked castle-towns were fundamental to the constitution of the county, it was Henry's performances at court that animated his principality. He was fortunate in having been mentored in the art of governance since the age of seven, in commanding the Champenois contingent on the Second Crusade as a young man of twenty, and in acquiring on-the-job experience in ruling two counties after returning from overseas. The crusade, in fact, was a critical experience for Henry, both for what he saw and did and for his bonding with a cohort of young Champenois aristocrats who would serve him loyally through his three decades of rule. That stability in court personnel and officers, with even brothers and brothers-in-laws attending court without portfolio, was a hallmark of Henry's rule. In addition to those men from lordly families around Troyes, Henry relied on several of his father's old hands from substantial Provinois families for their technical expertise, and on the canons from his chapters in Troyes and Provins, especially the prominent pluralists he recruited from the cathedral in Troyes. Whether he held court in Troyes or in one of his secondary residences, a varying representation of those three groups—veterans, technicians, and canons—vetted most of his acts before the chancery drafted and the chancellor sealed his letters patent.

There is no evidence that Henry convened assemblies of barons or sought their collective advice in governance. His "barons," like those who swore on his behalf that he would do nothing "without their assent or counsel" regarding the counterfeiting of the bishop of Meaux's coin, were his court officers, none other than his three closest crusade companions—his butler Anselm of Traînel, his constable Odo of Pougy, and lord Hugh of Plancy.[13] When Henry wrote to the king that he had summoned his *barones*, who were not with him at the moment, to meet at Easter to take their counsel, he was referring to those who routinely sat at his court, not to the castle lords as a body.[14] But if he did not routinely consult with the castle lords in matters of governance or policy—the case of the mortaged castle of Possesse being a notable exception—neither did he intrude in their lordships, either to summon them with their enfeoffed knights to military service or to require the rendition of their castles for his use.[15]

Henry was exceedingly fortunate that his father laid the foundations of the Fairs of Champagne, and that Italian merchants after the Second Crusade found Champagne a convenient venue for doing business north of the Alps. But it was Henry's achievement to make the fairs an integral part of his county's economy, indeed, the engine of his principality's prosperity and the primary source of his own revenues. The three fairs in Provins would have remained limited events had he not established his primary residence and chancery in Troyes, which as a princely capital stimulated the growth of the three fairs in Troyes. The cluster of six alternating fairs in Provins and Troyes, supplemented by the one in Bar-sur-Aube, made possible year-round commercial transactions within a relatively limited zone. Even the Templars, who like their Cistercian counterparts located their earliest commanderies in the countryside, acquired urban compounds in Provins and Troyes by the 1170s.[16] In Provins a Templar brother, Bernard, was a money changer and de facto banker who handled the transfers of funds overseas as well as loans to crusaders.[17] In Troyes the Templar house was located next to the money changers in the commercial quarter.[18] By then, merchants from Reims, Paris, Rouen, Étampes, and Limoges were coming to the fairs at a time when Italian merchants had become a fixture at the fairs.[19] Genoese notarial registers from 1190 testify to the existence of nascent textile industries within the fair towns, especially of woolens in Provins and linens in Troyes, which were exported to Italy along with northern French cloth.[20] Although local cloth production was still modest in the 1170s, it spawned a range of subsidiary industries and spurred the production of wool, especially by the numerous Cistercian communities in southern Champagne, thus creating a symbiotic economic relationship between town and countryside.[21]

Count Henry's quiescent towns remained untouched by the urban violence that afflicted Orléans, Poitiers, Reims, and Sens before the Second Crusade, and then Vézelay, Châlons, and again Reims, where the king intervened to suppress communal movements, in several instances after recognizing them. Henry saw no need to grant communal charters, the exception being his charter to the townsmen of Meaux on the eve of his departure on crusade in 1179; but that seems to have resulted from his own economic policies rather than the demands of the townsmen, and might have been an attempt to displace nearby Lagny as a fair town.[22] While his provosts and bailiffs directly controlled the conduct of the fairs and protected the roadways on which merchandise moved, Henry was exceptionally generous in sharing the fruits of commercial exchange. Early in his rule he exempted most monasteries from tolls on the roads leading to his fairs and from gate taxes at his fair towns. As the fairs became more profitable, he granted more lucrative rights, including rents from merchant halls and exemption from the sales taxes he collected from all commercial transactions within his fairgrounds. Those tax-free halls, in fact, were coveted assets. By the 1170s most monastic communities had commercial interests and halls in at least one of the fair towns. The Fontevrist priory of Foissy, not far from Troyes, had six houses in the market of Troyes and nine and a half houses in Bar-sur-Aube, altogether a substantial exposure by an aristocratic convent to the commercial economy.[23]

Like his father, Henry was exceptionally generous in his benefactions and justly celebrated for them. But whereas Thibaut distributed huge sums of money to support monastic endowments and their building programs, Henry's generosity was more practical. By granting commercial benefits to monasteries and financial privileges to his rural tenants, he was practicing a new form of lordship, one that stimulated agrarian production and generated taxable commercial exchange. The increase in liquid revenues funded not only his ambitious construction projects and charitable endowments but also prebends for his canons and fief rents for his knights in addition to the numerous benefactions for which he was known. The fact that fiefs, even landed fiefs, came to be valued in terms of their annual revenue (*libratus terre*) testifies to the pervasiveness of the monetized economy in Champagne by the 1170s. Within two decades of Henry's accession, the county had been transformed from an undeveloped hinterland of the more urbanized episcopal lordships of Reims, Châlons, and Sens into one of the more dynamic regions of the realm. With a commercial economy that rivaled even the highly urbanized and industrialized Flanders, Champagne under Henry became part of the "new France" of the late twelfth century.[24]

The commercial activities of the fair towns involved more than commerce in goods. Merchants depended on written records for their transactions just as much as the count's toll and tax collectors and bursar depended on financial records. Although none of the latter survive from Henry's rule, their existence can be deduced from the procedures described in his letters patent for the assignment of revenues and fief rents, and for receiving, encumbering, and disbursing monies by his tax and toll collectors. At the same time, the count's chancery vastly expanded the production of letters patent, which the chancellor presented not only to religious houses with the count's benefactions, but also to knights with their fiefs and even to urban and rural communities with their privileges. Many of those documents were retained by laymen until the property or revenue at issue was transferred or, in the case of rural communities, the documents were copied several centuries later. Merchants, knights, townsmen, and village communities all needed authenticated written records to substantiate their rights, privileges, and revenues.

Another source of written records emerged in those same decades after 1150, as aristocratic men and women acquired personal seals, which allowed them to authenticate letters patent drawn up by their household clerics.[25] Those privately generated letters added to the increasing volume of documents flowing from the comital and episcopal chanceries and monastic scriptoria. Beyond drafting those practical documents, scribes were busy copying books for both institutional and personal collections in what became a charged moment for the production of manuscript books in southern Champagne. The new Cistercian foundations and urban chapters, the presence in Sens of the highly literate entourages of the pope and the archbishops of Sens and Canterbury, and the probing intellectual interests of Henry the Liberal all contributed to the quest for books of both ancient and recent provenance. It was precisely during Henry the Liberal's rule that written materials in all forms passed beyond the bounds of monasteries and cathedral schools to become an integral part of life in Champagne.

Modern histories of twelfth-century France place a fundamental break with the accession of King Philip II in 1180. But for Count Henry and his generation of veterans it was the Second Crusade, three decades earlier, that marked the end of one age and the opening of another—what might be called, at least in Champagne, the age of Henry the Liberal. The county would evolve after his death, but Henry had fixed its fundamental institutions, infrastructure, practices, and identity.

The Afterlife of Henry the Liberal

Countess Marie was thirty-six when Henry died, with four children ranging in age from two to fifteen. She was an experienced countess, having ruled alone in Henry's absence overseas for almost two years. She continued to rule as regent countess through the minority of Henry II (1181–87), during his absence on the Third Crusade and residence overseas (1190–97), and for several months as regent for her younger son, Thibaut, until she died in March 1198. In all, she ruled the county for almost sixteen years. Her primary achievement was to preserve Henry the Liberal's principality for her sons, which she did with vigor. Evrat, a canon in St-Étienne who knew Marie personally from having translated Genesis into vernacular verse for her, said it best: "well did she protect and govern the land."[26]

If Henry's principality endured, memory of Henry himself faded quickly. None of the *literati* prelates or canons with whom he associated penned a personal remembrance of Henry. Even Evrat, writing in the 1190s, recalled Henry simply as "the good count who did so much good," and in a brief epilogue (ca. 1200) remembered him only in terms of having built and richly provisioning his chapel, which "has enriched the entire land."[27] Evrat was intimately familiar with the chapel and its contents, noting for example that Henry's body lay entombed within the chapel, but he apparently had not known Henry personally.[28] Nor did Jean le Nevelon, who wrote a verse continuation of the Alexander romance, *La venjance Alixandre* (ca. 1190), which begins with a brief encomium of Count Henry. Wise, courteous, and *preus*, Henry loved the church and honored the clergy, observed the poet, and gave rents, lands, and fiefs to poor *gentils homes*. Not since the time of Alexander had there been his equal.[29] Those were clichés circulating in the decades after Henry's death; there is no evidence that Jean had personal knowledge of Henry. The old count would have appreciated the comparison with Alexander, and surely his tomb in St-Étienne was worthy of comparison with Alexander's, but Henry already had passed beyond the realm of living memory. By the time Countess Marie died, all of Henry's companions, prelate friends, and siblings had died except for his youngest brother William, archbishop of Reims, who died in 1202 at sixty-seven, and his youngest sister Adele, the queen mother, who died in 1206 at sixty-one. At about that time Guiot of Provins, a poet-turned-Cluniac monk after witnessing the terrible losses on the Third Crusade, remembered Henry only as "the most generous man of his time."[30]

Visitors to St-Étienne encountered two representations of Count Henry, the effigy on his tomb and the statuette on Thibaut III's similar metalwork "tomb of kinship" placed next to it (ca. 1205–9), which featured a gallery of statuettes of Thibaut's powerful relatives. Henry's statuette represents him holding a model of St-Étienne inscribed "Here is Henry, Thibaut, your father who had this church built."[31]A third image of Henry was created ca. 1228 in the rebuilt cathedral in Troyes: high above the choir, within a four-panel procession of relics, a bearded youthful Henry, wearing his cap, offers Bishop Manasses of Troyes the tooth of Saint Peter, which he had received from Pope Alexander III, perhaps in 1180.[32] The canons of St-Étienne harbored another, private image of Henry painted ca. 1270 in the chapter's cartulary: next to a copy of the count's endowment charter of 1157 is a scene depicting Henry on a horse, presenting a model of his chapel dedicated to Saint Stephen.[33]

Anecdotes and Exempla

For those who neither visited Henry's chapel and tomb nor read the Latin encomia to him, memory of the count circulated in anecdotes. The story of Anne Musnier was among the most popular. Rendered in multiple versions from the thirteenth century, it was recounted in schoolrooms as late as the eighteenth century. In one version, a Latin canticle composed of bits of Old Testament verses, three knights plot to kill the count. Anne Musnier, wife of Girard of Langres, overheard the conspirators, killed one with her knife, and called for help when attacked by the two others. Captured and tortured, they confessed and were condemned by Henry to be hanged. In thanks, Henry ennobled Anne.[34] That last detail suggests that the written version of the tale was composed after 1290, when royal grants of nobility were first enacted. A letter of 1175 refers to Henry's commutation of the servile obligations of Girard of Langres and his wife and heirs, but not to an ennoblement, which was unknown in Henry's time.[35] The story may have been an elaboration of a fraudulent attempt by Girard's heirs in the fourteenth century to acquire noble status, a not uncommon quest at the time.

There were two less flattering versions of the Anne Musnier story.[36] According to one, Anne was the most beautiful woman of the time, and Henry's mistress. While in the palace, the story goes, she heard three men enter, armed with knives under their cloaks. She killed one and disarmed the two others before calling for aid; the two were duly drawn and quartered. More challenging in terms of Henry's image was the third version, in which Henry accosted Anne in the streets of Troyes. After rejecting his advances, she was abducted by Henry's men as she left her parents' house, then forcibly undressed and placed in his bed. This time, in bed, she fought back and cut Henry on the cheek. But the count pardoned her, praised her virtue, and arranged her marriage with a dowry to Girard of Langres. Neither the authors nor the dates of these stories impugning Henry's moral character are known.

Aubri of Trois-Fontaines, the Cistercian chronicler writing in the 1230s, adds to the thirteenth-century interest in Henry's sexual life. Aubri reports under the year 1163 that Henry contracted a contagious malady (*lues pestifera*), which has long been taken to mean the plague. But, adds Aubri cryptically, the count repented and was cured, unlike many others who failed to follow his example. Aubri links Henry's repentance to his taking the cross (in 1177), perhaps alluding to the report that Abbot Henry of Clairvaux had persuaded the count to go to the Holy Land in order to expunge his sins.[37] Repentance and healing suggest that Henry had somehow caused his malady, which might be read as syphilis.[38] Aubri is deliberately vague here, leaving much to the reader's imagination. More troubling for Aubri was Henry's clash with Bishop Mathieu of Troyes. The bishop appealed to the pope, says Aubri without explanation but obviously referring to Henry's resistance to episcopal jurisdiction over his chapel in 1170. It is not clear why that event, without apparent consequence at the time, troubled Aubri, or whether he even knew the details of the conflict. It seems that he inserted the two incidents, Henry's malady and his clash with the bishop, in order to balance Guy of Bazoches's florid encomium to Henry, which Aubri had just quoted at length, as if the chronicler were attempting to offer a balanced assessment of the count. If Aubri was reticent about Henry's syphilis and his clash with the bishop, which he knew only from hearsay, he was more comfortable in copying earlier praises of the count, lifting Guy of Bazoches's characterization of Henry as "famous for his largess and liberalities" and paraphrasing Robert of Auxerre's report that Henry "built the church in honor of Saint Stephen next to his palace, endowed it with properties, decorated it with silk [hangings], and enriched its treasury."[39]

Aubri relates another, apparently well-known tale about Henry's love of relics.[40] The count had a vision one night, says Aubri, in which he fell into a well but was saved by a young woman named Hilda. Seeking to discover her identity, he was told that she was Saint Hilda, a servant of Constantine's mother, Helen. Shortly afterward the count happened upon a noble squire carrying Hilda's remains in a sack, which he immediately acquired and deposited in St-Étienne, where they were placed, says Aubri, not in a gold or silver case but in an ivory vase. Here Aubri was conflating Henry's interest in relics with the cult of Saint Helen, which developed after Bishop Garnier of Troyes sent back Helen's remains following the sack of Constantinople in 1204. The rebuilding of the cathedral during the next two decades included a glazing program devoted to the life of Saint Helen, which seems to account for the crossing of the older stories of Henry's quest for relics with the new interest in Saint Helen.[41]

Stories about Henry and Anne Musnier, Henry's clash with the bishop of Troyes, and his quest for relics resonated primarily within Champagne. Beyond the county Henry's reputation circulated through the exempla of

popular preachers. Perhaps the most pointed story was told by Jacques of
Vitry, who compiled his sermon anecdotes ca. 1228. It involved a poor knight
in search of dowry money for his two daughters, who accosted the count at
the entrance to St-Étienne. Before the count could react, his treasurer Artaud
upbraided the knight for his audacity: the count had already been so generous, said Artaud, that he had nothing more to give. To which Henry replied
that he still possessed Artaud and forthwith handed him over to the knight.
Artaud managed to ransom himself for 500*l*., equivalent to twice the value of
an average fief yielding about 25*l*. annually.[42] It was such a good story that the
Dominican Stephen of Bourbon later borrowed it for his own collection of
sermon anecdotes. But for Stephen, Artaud was a "certain rich townsman"
and Henry a "certain" count of Champagne. In several other anecdotes regarding a count of Champagne and the poor, Stephen failed to distinguish
between Henry I and his father Thibaut, as if by the time his sermons were
compiled in the 1250s the two twelfth-century counts were confounded in the
popular imagination.[43]

The story of the count, his treasurer, and a poor knight improved with
retelling. Jean of Joinville, the seneschal of Champagne, embellished it with a
particular spin in the early years of the fourteenth century while dictating his
earliest memories of King Louis IX. In describing the relationship between
the counts of Champagne and the kings, Joinville explains that Count Henry
was known as "li Larges" because he was generous to God—witness St-Étienne in Troyes and the other beautiful churches he founded in Champagne—
and generous to the world—witness Artaud of Nogent.[44] What troubled the
seneschal was the fact that Artaud, whom "the count trusted more than any
other in the world," had become so wealthy in the count's service that he
could afford to build a castle at Nogent on the Marne that was named "Artaud's Nogent" (Nogent-l'Artaud) in his own lifetime. Unlike Jacques of Vitry
and Stephen of Bourbon, whose out-of-context anecdotes served for moral
edification, the seneschal connected his story to the construction of St-Étienne of Troyes, whose glazing and two tombs survived as powerful monuments in Joinville's time. Jean expanded the count's retort to his treasurer as
"lord villein, you do not tell the truth when you say that I have nothing left to
give, for I have *you*—take him lord knight." Joinville was illustrating not the
count's generosity but the comeuppance delivered to an upstart who, by the
time Joinville was writing, had succeeded in establishing one of the very few
new baronial lineages within Champagne. Jean may have heard the story from
his father, Simon, the count's seneschal from 1204, that is, within living

memory of Artaud, but his retelling had more to do with his own sense of caste-like nobleness and of Artaud's transgressing the social divide by building his own castle. Jean could not have imagined that within a few years of his telling the tale, for all purposes an exemplum, his youngest daughter Alix would become, through her second husband, lady of Nogent-l'Artaud.[45]

Liturgical Remembrances

While Count Henry's foibles were being spread through oral anecdotes and exempla sermons, a poet and musician, perhaps Philip the Chancellor of the cathedral of Paris (1218–36), composed a lament, *Omnis in lacrimis*, a monophonic Latin song on Henry's death.[46] The author must have visited Henry's tomb in St-Étienne, for he plays on the tomb's inscription by calling Henry "the light (sun) of Champagne who was snatched from us."

A man bright with largess,
full of the gifts of grace,
a count, flower of counts,
not unequal to kings,
to the cruel fates
has discharged his debt.

Champagne is deprived
of its protector.
Let the church mourn,
deprived of his protection,
the clergy of his patronage,
the knights of his fiefs,
the poor of his support,
France of his counsel.[47]

If Philip was referencing Henry's tomb inscriptions and oral tradition, it was because memory of the count as a person had become increasingly elusive compared to the remains of his works, which stood as powerful visual monuments: not so much the comital residence and great chapel facing the suburban canons' quarter, whose originality no longer resonated in the thirteenth-century cityscape as it had in the mid-twelfth, but rather Henry's own tomb in St-Étienne, still a striking monument after half a century. And

Philip would have heard the canons celebrate Henry's anniversary in St-Étienne, just as they would for the next six hundred years, until 1790.

According to an eighteenth-century memoir, Henry's anniversary celebration lasted two days.[48] On 16 March, with the altar adorned in red cloth,
officiating canons dressed in red chanted the Office of the Dead after Com-
pline. At the fifth Psalm, two canons censed the tomb during the singing of
the Magnificat, and during the third response of each nocturn, two members
of the choir accompanied the chanter and subchanter in censing the altar and
the two tombs. The next day, matins began at 3:00 a.m., followed by the rec-
itation of the entire Psalter. A Mass in music followed, then the seven psalms
of penance were recited, during which two choir boys continually censed the
tombs of Henry and Thibaut III. As the daily Mass was sung, 6*l.* was distributed to those who attended both the vigils and the Mass.

What made the ceremony especially poignant was the presence of the second tomb, commissioned by Countess Blanche and placed directly behind
Henry's, which faced the altar.[49] Thibaut's tomb was a metalwork tomb like
Henry's, with the same outer dimensions and decorated with similar enamel
plaques of bronze, silver, and gold made most likely by Mosan craftsmen. But
its spirit was different. Whereas Henry's tomb celebrated himself, his benefactions, and his foundation of St-Étienne, with his effigy visible through the
tomb's arches, Thibaut's effigy reclined on the top of his tomb whose closed
arches contained statuettes of his closest relatives. It was the earliest example of
a "tomb of kinship," and its iconographical program asserted both Thibaut's
lineages and his legitimacy.[50] Each reliquary tomb was magnificent, wholly
unique, and, as a contemporary guidebook might say, worth a visit. There was
nothing comparable to the chapel with its tombs before the construction of
Ste-Chapelle in Paris in the 1240s. But even then, the royal tombs lay in monasteries, whereas the tombs of Henry and Thibaut were cared for by their own
canons, under Henry's beneficent gaze, as his tomb inscription proclaimed.

What St-Étienne lacked was the tombs of successor counts. Henry II died
and was buried in Acre (1197), and both Thibaut IV (1253) and Henry III
(1274) were buried in the cathedral at Pamplona, where they died as kings of
Navarre. The heart of Thibaut V, who died in Sicily (1270), was sent to Provins
for burial.[51] Instead of being continually replenished as a living memorial to a
line of princely rulers, St-Étienne became a time capsule from the twelfth
century. The symbolism of Henry's residence in Troyes also changed, as it no
longer served as the primary comital residence. After Count Thibaut IV as-
cended the throne of Navarre (1234), he spent the rest of his life traveling

between his two lands, and remained for long periods in Navarre. Thibaut V (1253–70) spent even less time in Troyes after his marriage to Isabelle of France, preferring the pleasures of Paris, where the couple had a sumptuous residence and enjoyed the company of her father, Louis IX, and the royal court. With the early death of Count Henry III (1270–74) and the remarriage of his widow, Blanche of Artois, to Edmund of Lancaster, brother of King Edward III of England, the comital residence in Troyes became superfluous.[52] As soon as the heiress of Champagne, Countess Jeanne, was betrothed to a son of Philip III (May 1275), she was sent to the royal household in Paris until her marriage to Prince Philip (16 August 1284).[53] As queen of France (1285–April 1305) she rarely, and only briefly, visited her ancestral lands in Champagne. Although she styled herself countess of Champagne and sealed documents involving her lordly rights, Philip IV effectively ruled the county on her behalf, directing the bailiffs, wardens of the fairs, and tax collectors of Champagne, and appointing members of the High Court, the Grand Jours of Troyes. By 1314 the royal hand had become so heavy that the nobles of Champagne, acting in the long absence of a resident count, formed a league to protest royal taxation.[54]

King Philip V (1316–22) calmed the regional aristocracy but effectively completed the subordination of the county under royal administration. In 1319 all items in the count's chapel—relics, clothing, liturgical objects, books, even the count's cap—were inventoried according to whether they were located in the large treasury, the small treasury, or in various cases, in anticipation of their transfer.[55] Count Henry's library was noted as being stored at the top of the "old treasury."[56] On 10 March 1321 a royal ordinance ordered an examination of all titles to fiefs, domain, and jurisdictions in Champagne, and within a year the king's bailiffs conducted inquests and drew up detailed rolls enumerating all property alienated since 1285, that is, from the beginning of Philip IV's assumption of control over the county.[57] Soon thereafter the entire chancery archive was transferred to Paris: thousands of incoming letters patent, the original rolls of fiefs and homages, the registers of domanial properties and financial accounts, and the codex copies of the fief rolls and archived letters patent.[58] In effect, the entire documentary basis of the principality created by Henry was removed to Paris.[59] Nevertheless, the canons of St-Étienne continued to celebrate annual Masses for Henry and Thibaut III through the fourteenth and fifteenth centuries, long after the comital dynasty ceased to exist. The count's palace was renamed the Royal Palace and the Palace of Justice, since the building served as the administrative center of the royal *bailliage* of Troyes and as the seat of the High Court. The count's chapel of St-Étienne, with its tombs in situ, had become a museum of the lost world of Count Henry the Liberal.

Final Dispositions

Henry's tomb survived intact to the sixteenth century, until the night of 30/31 March 1582, when unknown malefactors stole seven silver plaques from it and vandalized much of the rest.[60] The custodian and four canons in charge of St-Étienne's treasury were reprimanded and ordered to repair the tomb, which was then closed to the public except on special occasions.[61] Still located at the center of the choir, with the head facing the altar, the tomb remained in a state of disrepair through the next century, until a partial restoration was undertaken in 1711 or 1712. Edmund Martène saw it there in 1717 during his "literary voyage" through Champagne and pronounced it "an admirable piece of work."[62] Curiously, Martène does not mention the even more dramatic and sparkling tomb of Thibaut III, the first tomb a visitor would see on entering the choir, according to a slightly later engraving.[63]

Martène was more interested in St-Étienne's library and treasury. It was not especially large, he noted:

> but for its riches, there are few that can surpass it, or even equal it, in France. There are gold and precious stones—agate, rubies, and topazes of wondrous sizes and worked with indescribable skill. There are Bibles bound with gold covers and enhanced with precious stones of various colors so well placed that one would say that the colors were put there expressly to decorate the works. There are crosses of gold decorated in the same manner, and the Psalter of Count Henry is written in letters of gold in a style more than eight hundred years old.[64]

Martène goes on to describe the porphyry altar of Saint Martin and a gold chalice, which might have come to Troyes from Marmoutier or Tours because, he reminds us, the counts had been counts of Blois and Tours. He concludes by noting St-Étienne's rich collection of manuscript books, which for him was equal in riches to the relics and precious stones. He saw copies of Augustine's sermons, *The City of God*, and *On the Trinity*; the letters of Bernard of

Clairvaux; Jerome's works on Isaiah, Jeremiah, Ezekiel, and Daniel; and works by Alcuin, Isidore, Eusebius, and Freculf, among many others.[65]

Some of the books survived the French Revolution, but the comital buildings were soon disassembled and their objects dispersed, all part of the general dismantling of the material remains of the ancien régime. The National Assembly ordered the secularization of ecclesiastical property on 2 November 1789, and the suppression of religious communities in February 1790. When the count's chapel was inventoried on 26 February 1790, there were found twenty-eight reliquaries of various types as well as Count Henry's cap, a sort of profane relic, described earlier as "the cap that Count Henry, founder of this church, made of a cloth of gold, sprinkled with pearls, in a purse also of gold cloth with flowers."[66] On 6 December 1790, several days after the cathedral chapter was suppressed, the chapter of St-Étienne with its forty-four canons was dissolved. On Sunday, 26 February 1791, the relics in St-Étienne were carried in solemn procession to the cathedral and deposited in the treasury.[67] Whatever remained in St-Étienne—sculpture, altars, stained glass windows—was later taken to be stored in the cathedral pending future disposition.[68]

An arrêt of 17 February 1792 ordered the exhumation of the remains of Henry and Thibaut III and their transfer from St-Étienne. At 3:00 p.m. on 23 February, the physician François-Joseph Bouquot and the surgeon Nicolas-Simon Bergerat conducted the exhumation in the presence of the Directory of the Département of the Aube.[69] As the stones were lifted from Henry's tomb, still located in the middle of the choir, the audience saw a skeleton with its face turned eastward toward the altar. The body had not been embalmed. Parts of the skull were missing, but the lower jaw still contained several teeth, an incisor, a canine, and four molars. There were no remains of vertebrae from the neck and only fragments of the clavicles. The rest of the skeleton was in various stages of decomposition. Louis-Joseph Rondot, a professor at the local school of design, painted a watercolor depicting the position of the skeleton and two antique vases, containing perhaps an aromatic liquid, placed near it.[70] After the examination, Henry's remains were placed in an oak coffin, on which the count's initial "H" was carved, and returned to the tomb. Rondot, being a goldsmith and engraver, was asked to inventory and appraise the gold, silver, and enamel of the tombs as well as the items in St-Étienne's treasury.[71]

Four days later, on 27 February 1792, the remains of the two counts were formally transferred to the cathedral.[72] At 10:00 a.m. the bishop and clergy, preceded by several companies of military bands, formed a solemn procession of local dignitaries at St-Étienne. The two sarcophagi were followed by their tombs, each on a carriage led by three horses decked in funerary drapes. On their arrival at the cathedral, the bishop celebrated Mass. The sarcophagi were placed in the sites excavated for them behind the choir in the chapel of Notre-Dame, and the tombs were placed on each side of the chapel. The next year, 1793, the revolutionary fervor that caused the systematic destruction of the royal tombs at St-Denis carried over into Champagne.[73] On 12 November 1793, Rondot prepared a detailed list of the precious objects from the count's chapel and the cathedral treasury to be destroyed. All were to be melted down, except for the eight items he identified as "gothic" and worthy of preservation for their historical interest. On 18 November an arrêt ordered the destruction of the tombs and the dispersal of the ashes of the two counts. But the deputies of the Société Populaire, charged with the task of digging up the remains of the two counts and mixing them with those of other citizens, refused to do so, and the coffins of the two counts remained in the ground. On 6 January 1794 Rondot was ordered to strip the tombs and the treasuries of their valuable objects, and on 22 and 23 January those items—vases, ornaments, reliquar-ies—were systematically smashed and melted down, and the metal sent to Paris.[74]

On 29 July 1796 the count's residence and chapel, which had survived for more than six hundred years, were sold for 15,300 francs and soon dismantled, as were the churches of Notre-Dame-aux-Nonnains and St-Jacques just oppo-site. The materials from the buildings were used to build a grain hall on the site of the two churches, but after that structure in turn was demolished in 1804, the stone was reused to build the Hôtel de Ville.[75] Within a decade of the French Revolution the monuments Henry built to his own glory—his residence, chapel, and tomb—had been thoroughly razed. The administrative and financial registers that formed the written basis of Henry's principality had perished even earlier, and the rolls of fiefs, the most distinctive records from his rule, are known only from later copies.[76] Of the 552 letters patent known to have been sealed in his name, 209 (39 percent) survive as originals, but only a handful still carry intact seals. Some of the books from Henry's personal library survive, as well as some enamel plaques from his tomb. But the only other intact memento of his life is his cap, which acquired a mystique in his own lifetime, a sort of relic encapsulating perfectly the mixture of the sacred and the profane that Henry had inscribed on his tomb.[77] The tomb, the chapel of St-Étienne, and the comital palace, all constructed as central fixtures of his new principality, survive only in eighteenth-century sketches, almost as shadows of Henry and his world.

Appendix 1: Tables

Table 1: Count Henry's Officers

Office	Dates	Relationships
Chancellor		
William	1152–76	Cleric to Count Thibaut (1136–52)
Stephen	1176–81	Brother of marshal William *Rex* of Provins
Haice of Plancy	1181–87	Brother of Hugh II, lord of Plancy (1138–89), and Milo, sensechal of Jerusalem (1167–74)
		Brother-in-law of butler Anselm II of Traînel (1152–84) and Milo of Traînel, abbot of St-Marien of Auxerre (1155–1203)
Seneschal		
Geoffroy III of Joinville	1152–88	Brother of Alice, abbess of Avenay (1150–64), and Guy, bishop of Châlons (1164–90)
Constable		
Odo I of Pougy	1152–69	Brother of Manasses, provost of St-Étienne (1160–79), bishop of Troyes (1181–90)
William I of Dampierre	1171–74	Brother of Guy, bishop-elect of Châlons (1162–63), and Heloise, wife of Geoffroy IV of Joinville
?Guy II of Dampierre	1174–1216	Son of William I of Dampierre
Butler		
Anselm II of Traînel	1152–84	Brother of Garnier of Traînel, lord of Marigny, and Milo, abbot of St-Marien of Auxerre (1155–1202), and Isabelle (wife of Hugh II of Plancy)
		Brother-in-law of Haice of Plancy, provost of St-Quiriace and chancellor (1168–86), and Milo, seneschal of Jerusalem (1167–74)

Office	Dates	Relationships
Marshal		
Geoffrey of Chartres	1152–58	
Walter (Burda) of Provins	1152–58	Brother of Mathieu, precentor of Sens (1142), dean of St-Quiriace (1160–69), bishop of Troyes (1169–80)
		Brother-in-law of Peter Bristaud, viscount of Provins
William Rex Breban of Provins	1158–79	?Half brother of Abraham of Provins
		Brother of Stephen (?tutor of Count Henry), canon of St-Étienne and chancellor (1176–79)
		Father of Milo I Breban of Provins, treasurer
Treasurer (*camerarius*)		
Peter the Bursar	1138/1152–66	
Rainald of Provins	1158–?68	Treasurer of St-Quentin
Robert of Milly	1161–85	
Milo I Breban of Provins	1165–86	Son of marshal William Rex of Provins
		Husband of Helie (daughter of Manasses, viscount of Villemaur)
Abraham of Provins	1169–79	Son of Peter the Bursar
		?Half brother of marshal William Rex of Provins
Artaud of Nogent	1163–90	
Without Portfolio		
Hugh II of Plancy	1138–89	Brother of Haice, provost of St-Quiriace, chancellor (1181–87), bishop of Troyes (1191–93)
		Brother of Milo, seneschal of Jerusalem (1167–74)
Garnier of (Traînel) Marigny	1152–95	Brother of butler Anselm II of Traînel
		Brother of Milo, abbot of St-Marien of . Auxerre (1155–1202), and Isabelle (wife of Hugh II of Plancy)
		Brother-in-law of Haice of Plancy, provost of St-Quiriace, chancellor (1168–86), and Milo, seneschal of Jerusalem (1167–74)
Peter Bristaud, viscount of Provins	1156–79	Brother-in-law of Walter of Provins, marshal (1152–80), and Mathieu, precentor of Sens, dean of St-Quiriace (1160–69), bishop of Troyes (1169–80)
		Brother of Drogo Bristaud

Office	Dates	Relationships
Drogo Bristaud	1152–77	Brother of Peter Bristaud, viscount of Provins Brother-in-law of Walter and Mathieu of Provins
Nevel of Aulnay, knight	1153–86	Brother of Roric, archdeacon of Meaux, canon of St-Étienne (1159–88)
Daimbert of Ternantes, knight	1155–79	
Girard Eventat of Bray, knight	1158–97	Brother of Geoffroy Eventat, knight

Table 2: Count Henry's Pluralist Canons

Canon	Troyes cathedral	Troyes St-Étienne	Provins St-Quiriace	Meaux cathedral	Sens cathedral
Manasses of .Villemaur	canon	dean			
Manasses of Pougy	canon	provost			
Guirric Boceps,	treasurer	canon			
*Peter Comestor	dean	canon			
Bernard of Langres	canon	canon			
*Haice of Plancy	canon	dean	canon		
*Stephen of Provins	canon	canon	provost		
Alexander of Provins	chaplain	canon	canon		
Wm of Champagne	provost		provost	dean	
Odo	canon				dean
Rainald of Provins		canon	treasurer	canon	
Roric of Ramerupt		canon		canon	
Clarembaud of Broyes		canon		canon	
Mathieu of Provins			dean		precentor

*Master

Table 3: Regional Bishops

See		Dates	Relatives
Autun	Henry of Burgundy	1148–70	Brother-in-law of Count Henry
	Stephen	1170–89	
Auxerre	Hugh of Mâcon	1137–51	First Cistercian abbot of Pontigny, 1114–36
	Alan of Auxerre	1152–67	Cistercian abbot of Larrivour, 1140–52
	William of Toucy	1167–82	Brother of Archbishop Hugh of Sens
Châlons	Haimo of Bazoches	1152–53	Uncle of Canon Guy of Bazoches
	Bozo	1153–62	
	Guy of Joinville	1164–90	Brother of seneschal Geoffroy III of Joinville
Langres	Geoffrey de la Roche	1139–63	Cistercian
	Walter of Burgundy	1163–79	Brother-in-law of Count Henry
	Manasses of Bar-sur-Seine	1179–93	Brother of Count Milo III of Bar-sur-Seine
Meaux	Manasses II of Cornillon	1134–58	
	Renaud	1158–61	
	Hugh	1161	
	Stephen de la Chapelle	1162–71	Brother of king's treasurers
	Peter of Pavia	1171–74	Cardinal legate, 1173–79
	Simon of Lizy	1176–95	Treasurer of Meaux, archdeacon of Sens, nephew of Bishop Manasses II
Reims	Samson of Mauvoisin	1140–61	
	Henry of France	1162–75	Cistercian; brother-in-law of Count Henry
	William of Champagne	1176–1202	Brother of Count Henry
Sens	Hugh of Toucy	1142–68	
	William of Champagne	1168–75	Brother of Count Henry
	Guy of Noyers	1175–93	
Troyes	Hato	1122–45	Former archdeacon of Sens
	Henry of Carinthia	1145–69	Cistercian; uncle of Count Henry
	Mathieu of Provins	1169–80	Brother of marshal Walter of Provins
	Manasses of Pougy	1181–90	Brother of constable Odo of Pougy

Appendix 2. Chronology

1140s	Count Thibaut formalizes fairs in Troyes
1141	May 25–26. Council of Sens: Peter Abelard condemned
1142	April 21. Death of Peter Abelard
	Summer and fall. Louis VII attacks and destroys Vitry
1143	Count Thibaut does homage to duke of Burgundy for county of Troyes
	Byzantine Emperor Manuel Komnenos (1143–80)
1144	Count Geoffroy of Anjou conquers Normandy
	June 11. Dedication of St-Denis
1145	March/April. Marie of France born to King Louis and Queen Eleanor
	Abbot Peter of Montier-la-Celle (1145–62)
	Pope Eugenius III (1145–53)
	December 1. Crusade bull *Quantum praedecessores*
	December. Louis VII's Christmas Council at Bourges
1146	March 31. Bernard of Clairvaux preaches crusade at Vézelay
	Henry of Carinthia (maternal uncle), bishop of Troyes (1146–68)
	Nicholas of Montiéramey at Clairvaux (1146–51)
1147	April 11. Pope Eugenius III preaches crusade in Troyes
	June 11. Henry (twenty years old) departs on Second Crusade
	October 4. Henry arrives in Constantinople
	December 28. Henry at Meander River skirmish
	Earliest mention of Fair of St-Remi in Troyes
1148	January. Crusader army at Mt. Cadmus
	March. Council of Reims
	June 24. Henry at Council of Palmarea
	Simon Aurea Capra, prior of St-Ayoul of Provins (1148–54)
1149	Spring. Henry returns from crusade, becomes count of Bar-sur-Aube and Vitry
1150s	Italian merchants at Fairs of Provins
	The *provinois* as standard coin of international currency
1151	January 13. Death of Abbot Suger of St-Denis
	Nicholas of Montiéramey as Henry's chaplain (1151–60)
	Roman de Thèbes (1150/55)
1152	January 10. Count Thibaut dies
	Henry (twenty-five years old), count palatine of Troyes
	Thibaut V, count of Blois (and Chartres)
	Stephen, count of Sancerre

Construction of comital compound, residence, and chapel of
    St-Étienne in Troyes
Foundation of chapter of secular canons of St-Étienne
February 15. Death of Emperor Conrad of Germany
    Frederick I Barbarossa succeeds (1152–90)
March 21. Divorce of Louis VII and Eleanor of Aquitaine

1152–54	Simon Aurea Capra composes *Ylias* for Count Henry
1153	April 23. Death of Bernard of Clairvaux
	July 8. Death of Pope Eugenius III
	Earliest mention of hot and cold fairs of Troyes
1154	Henry confirms Fair of St-Ayoul of Provins
	Betrothal of Henry and Marie of France
	Count Thibaut V of Blois is royal seneschal (1154–90)
	October 25. Death of King Stephen of England.
	December 19. King Henry II Plantagenet of England (1154–89)
	December. Pope Adrian IV (1154–59)
1155	June 10. Peace of Soissons
	June/July. Henry travels to Rome; audience with Pope Adrian IV
	June 18. Coronation of Emperor Frederick I
c. 1156	*Roman d'Enéas*
1157	Henry confirms endowment of St-Étienne of Troyes
	Regular canons leave St-Quiriace of Provins for St-Jacques
	Hospital of St-Jacques of Provins transferred to residence of countess
	Fire destroys St-Ayoul of Provins
1158	June. Chancellor Thomas Becket negotiates royal marriages in Paris
1159	John of Salisbury sends *Policraticus* to Peter of Celle
	September 7. Pope Alexander III (1159–81)
	September. Secular canons formally restored at St-Quiriace of Provins; reconstruction of the church (1159–64)
1160	Henry founds chapter of secular canons at St-Maclou in Bar-sur-Aube
	Nicholas of Montiéramey, prior of St-Jean-en-Châtel in Troyes (1160–79), undertakes Count Henry's "History Project"
	May. Henry witnesses kings of France and England sign marriage treaty for their children
	July. Council of Beauvais. Henry likely present as kings of

France and England make peace and recognize Pope Alexander III

October 2. Queen Constance dies.

November 2. Marriage of Margaret of France and Young Henry of England

November 13. Louis VII marries Henry's sister Adele

December 11. Henry's mother Countess Mathilda dies

1160–65   Benoît of Ste-Maur writes *Roman de Troie*

1161   Henry buys relics for St-Étienne

Count William IV of Nevers reopens conflict with abbot of Vézelay

First mention of bailiffs at Fairs of Champagne

1162   May. Henry and Bishop Manasses of Orléans meet Frederick I in Pavia regarding papal schism

September 19/22. Aborted meeting between Louis VII and Frederick I at St-Jean-de-Losne

Henry accepts *mouvance* of nine borderland castles from Frederick I

Henry of France, archbishop of Reims (1162–75)

Peter of Celle, abbot of St-Remi of Reims (1162–81)

1163   Hugh (Henry's half brother), abbot of Lagny (1163–71)

May 19. Council of Tours: recognition of Pope Alexander III

September 30. Pope Alexander III resides in Sens (30 September 1163–April 1165)

Year-long cycle of Fairs of Champagne in operation

1164.   Henry expands Fairs of May in Provins

April 22. Anti-Pope Victor IV dies; end of papal schism

May 16. Death of Abbess Heloise at the Paraclete

September. Henry's brother William elected bishop of Chartres in disputed election

September/October. Count Thibaut V of Blois marries Alice of France

October. Council of Northampton. Condemnation of Thomas Becket

November 29. Becket arrives in Sens

Dec. Becket in residence at Pontigny (December 1164–November 1166)

1164/5   Marie of France arrives in Troyes as countess of Troyes

1165	January 13. Second election of William of Champagne as bishop of Chartres (13 January 1165–1175)
	July 14. Papal call to crusade
	August 21. Birth of Philip II of France
	December 29. Charlemagne sanctified
1166	June 12. Becket excommunicates Henry II's appointees
	July 29. Birth of Henry II of Champagne on feast of Saint Loup
	November 10. Peace at Vézelay
	November 11. Becket at Ste-Columbe of Sens (11 November 1166–December 1170)
1167	William the Englishman copies Valerius Maximus, *Memorable Doings and Sayings*, for Henry
	William Gap (physician, monk, Greek translator) brings books from Constantinople to St-Denis
	Henry purchases relics of Saints Potentinus and Altinus for St-Étienne of Troyes
	Bishop Henry of Troyes retires to Boulancourt abbey
	Townsmen of Reims revolt against Archbishop Henry of France
	Fire in count's castle-town of Vertus
1168	Count Philip of Flanders (1168–91)
	October. William of Champagne elected archbishop of Sens
	December 22. William of Champagne consecrated archbishop of Sens (1168–76)
1169	January 6. Conference at Montmirail
	Mathieu (Burda of Provins) elected bishop of Troyes (1169–18 September 1180)
	December 25. King Henry II and Queen Eleanor celebrate Christmas at Nantes
1170	William the Englishman copies Aulus Gellius, *Attic Nights*, for Count Henry
	December 29. Archbishop Thomas Becket murdered in Canterbury cathedral
c. 1170	Chrétien de Troyes completes *Erec and Enide*
	Walter of Châtillon writes *Alexandreis* (completed by 1176)
	Chrétien de Troyes writes *Cligés* (completed by September 1176)
1171	January 25. Archbishop William of Sens interdicts King Henry II's lands in France
	July. Double marriage contract for Henry (II) of Champagne

with Isabelle of Hainaut, and Marie of Champagne with Baldwin (VI) of Hainaut

August 8. Death of Bishop Henry of Winchester

1172   William the physician, abbot of St-Denis (1172–86)

Merchants from Milan at Fairs of Provins

1173   February 21. Thomas Becket canonized

Louis VII's Easter court in Paris supports Plantagenet revolt

1173/74   Begin construction of Henry's tomb

1174   January 18. Bernard of Clairvaux canonized

Nur ed-Din dies. Saladin captures Damascus

First mention of wardens of Fairs of Champagne

1176   January. Pope Alexander III invites kings of France and England to undertake a crusade

Henry appoints Stephen of Provins as chancellor (1176–81), adopts a new seal

August 8. William of Champagne consecrated archbishop of Reims (1176–7 September 1202)

         John of Salisbury consecrated bishop of Chartres (1176–25 October 1180)

After August. Walter of Châtillon dedicates *Alexandreis* to Archbishop William of Reims

Before September. Chrétien de Troyes completes *Cligés*

Henry confirms St-Quiriace's endowment

1177   Henry mediates between Henry Plantagenet and Louis VII

Saladin invades kingdom of Jerusalem

Before Christmas. Henry takes the cross, plans a crusade with Louis VII

c. 1177   Chrétien de Troyes completes *The Knight of the Cart* (*Lancelot*)

c. 1177/81   Chrétien de Troyes completes *The Knight with the Lion* (*Yvain*)

1178   September. Henry and Archbishop William attend Frederick I's court in Besançon.

After September. Archbishop William transfers *mouvance* of four episcopal castle-fiefs to Henry

Fall? Inquest on Count Henry's fiefs (*Feoda Campanie*)

1179   January 6. Treaty of Montmirail between kings of France and England

February/March. Walter Map visits Henry in Troyes

March 5–19. Third Lateran Council. William of Tyre as official
recorder of the proceedings
April/May. Henry grants a communal charter to townsmen of
Meaux
Peter of Celle dedicates *On the Discipline of the Cloister* to Henry
May 13. Birth of Thibaut III. Reaffirmation of double marriage
contract of 1171
Late May. Henry departs on crusade. Marie governs county
(May 1179–March 1181)
June 10. Saladin invades Galilee
November 1. Coronation of King Philip II of France (1179–1223)
by Archbishop William of Reims

c. 1179/91   Chrétien de Troyes writes *The Story of the Grail* (*Perceval*)
1180   Henry captured by Turks, ransomed by Emperor Manuel
Komnenos
March 1. Agnes of France marries Alexius II Komnenos in
Constantinople
April 28. King Philip II marries Isabelle of Hainaut (betrothed
to Count Henry II)
May 14. New marriage contract for children of Baldwin V of
Hainaut and Countess Marie
June 28. Gisors. Kings Philip and Henry II meet; Queen Adele
reconciles with Philip
September. Henry in Constantinople
September 18. King Louis VII dies
September 24. Emperor Manuel Komnenos dies
December. Henry arrives in Sens for King Philip II's Christmas
court
Merchants from Piacenza at Fairs of Champagne

1181   March 8. Henry arrives in Troyes
March 16. Death of Count Henry

Abbreviations

Actes	*Recueil des actes d'Henri le Libéral, comte de Champagne (1152–1181)*; documents cited by edition number and date
AD	Archives Départementales
AN	Archives Nationales (Paris)
BEC	*Bibliothèque de l'École des Chartes*
BM	Bibliothèque Municipale
BnF	Bibliothèque nationale de France (Paris)
Feoda	*Feoda* 1 (ca. 1178), *Feoda* 2 (ca. 1190). Surveys of comital fief-holders, in Longnon, *Documents*, 1
GC	*Gallia Christiana in provincias ecclesiasticas distributa*
MGH SS	*Monumenta Germaniae Historica. Scriptores*
MSA	*Mémoires de la Société d'Agriculture, Commerce, Sciences et Art du Département de l'Aube*
MSM	*Mémoires de la Société d'Agriculture, Commerce, Sciences et Art du Département de la Marne*
n.s.	new style. Scribal practice in Champagne was to begin the year at Easter; thus a date given between 1 January and Easter is converted here to the next year, n.s.
PL	*Patrologiae cursus completus. Series Latina*
RHF	*Recueil des Historiens des Gaules et de la France*

Notes

PREFACE

1. Pierre Pithou, *Le premier livre des mémoires des comtes héréditaires de Champagne et de Brie* (1572).

2. Henry d'Arbois de Jubainville, *Histoire des ducs et des comtes de Champagne*, 7 vols. (1859–69). For the local and regional historians who collected documents and wrote unpublished histories after Pithou and before Arbois de Jubainville, see Michel Bur's introduction to *Recueil des actes d'Henri le Libéral, comte de Champagne*, 1: xvi–xviii.

3. John Frederic Benton, "The Court of Champagne Under Henry the Liberal and Countess Marie," Ph.D. dissertation, Princeton University, 1959.

4. *Recueil des actes d'Henri le Libéral (1152–1181)*, 2 vols. (2009, 2013), begun by John F. Benton (based on his 1988 unpublished "pre-edition," "Recueil des actes des comtes de Champagne, 1152–1197") and completed by Michel Bur and his collaborators (cited hereafter as *Actes*). A total of 552 acts are included in vol. 1 (539 acts) and vol. 2 (13 acts).

5. Benton summarized his findings in "The Court of Champagne as a Literary Center."

6. See Stirnemann's articles cited in the bibliography.

CHAPTER I. THE YOUNG COUNT, 1127–1145

1. Barthélemy, *Châlons-sur-Marne*, 2: 378, at Vitry, dated December 1127, without provenance. If this letter was given to the franchised family, it would be the earliest known letter of personal franchise in Champagne. How it survived until Barthélemy copied it is unknown.

2. Brouillon, *Recherches sur Vitry-en-Perthois*. See also Bur, *Vestiges*, 130–34.

3. Robert of Torigni, *Chronicle*, 143: *castellum optimum*.

4. Orderic Vitalis, *The Ecclesiastical History*, 6: 42. For Thibaut and his condominium lordship with his widowed mother, see LoPrete, *Adela of Blois*.

5. Count Hugh joined the Templars in 1125; he is last attested in 1130 as witness to an act in Jerusalem (*St-Sépulcre de Jerusalem*, 347–48, appendix no. 1). For the vexed issue of the transfer of his lands to Thibaut, see LoPrete, *Adela of Blois*, 570–74.

6. *La chronique de Morigny*, 21–22. The chronicler adds that Thibaut, "swollen with pride because of his wealth and nobility," had attacked the king since his youth, forcing the magnates to choose sides in his wars with the king. For Thibaut's earlier armed conflicts with Louis VI, see Bournazel, *Louis VI*, esp. 111–16 and 199–203.

7. Orderic Vitalis, *The Ecclesiastical History*, 6: 294–307, describes the sinking of the White Ship and lists Thibaut's sister Mathilda and her husband Richard, earl of Chester, among the dead.

8. For Thibaut's marriage, see LoPrete, *Adela of Blois*, 560–69, and Jaksch, *Geschichte Kärntens*, 1: 257–58. Grill, "Heinrich von Kärnten," 37, suggests that Henry of Carinthia, while a Cistercian monk at Morimond (1123–32), proposed that Thibaut marry his sister Mathilda.

9. Clairvaux founded 57 of the 352 Cistercian monasteries in existence by 1152. See Bredero, *Bernard of Clairvaux*, 249–56, and Locatelli, "L'expansion de l'ordre cistercien," 107, 114, 122.

10. Arnold of Bonneval's additions to the *Vita prima sancti Bernardi*, 299, cap. 8.

11. See Leroy, *Hugues de Payns*, the only complete biography of Hugh, and West, "Count Hugh of Troyes." The foundation of the Templars is best told by Barber in *The New Knighthood*, 1–37, and "The Origins of the Order of the Temple."

12. *Temple*, 6, no. 9, enacted in Provins (= *Templiers de Provins*, III, no. 93): Thibaut also allowed the Templars to receive fiefs from his knights but did not remit their service (*servicium*).

13. For Hugh's recruiting tour, see Barber, *The New Knighthood*, 8–14. King Henry I of England received Hugh with honor and gave much treasure, reports the Peterborough Chronicle; Hugh was so successful, it was said, that more people followed him to Jerusalem than had gone on the First Crusade (*The Peterborough Chronicle*, 50–51).

14. Cerrini, *La révolution des Templiers*, 109–10, lists the named participants. André of Baudement, seneschal of Count Hugh of Troyes (1103–8) then of Count Thibaut (1108–33), joined the Cistercians and became abbot of Chaalis, 1137–42 (Evergates, *Aristocracy*, 270 n. 28, and Peyrafort-Huin, *La bibliothèque médiévale de Pontigny*, 26). Count William II of Nevers (ca. 1101–46) entered La Grande Chartreuse in 1147 and died there in 1149 (Lespinasse, *Le Nivernais*, 1: 310).

15. Hugh's *sermo* to the Council was followed by a *conversatio* in which the three laymen participated *intentissima cura*. See Cerrini, "Le fondateur de l'ordre du Temple" and *La révolution des Templiers*, 102–4, 128–29. The seneschal André of Baudement, moved by Hugh's speech, gave the Templars all his possessions and revenues at Baudement except his tower and his knights' fiefs; he did this, he said, primarily for the soul of his son William, who had joined the Templars, with the consent of Count Thibaut from whom the property moved (*Templiers de Provins*, 101–2, no. 81, 1133).

16. Hugh of Payns died in the mid-1130s, perhaps in 1136 (Barber, *The New Knighthood*, 36). His widow Elizabeth was still alive in 1170 (*Actes*, no. 308), when she and her brother, Laurent of Vendeuvre, shared property held in fief from Clarembaud IV of Chappes (Leroy, *Hugues de Payns*, 100–102). For Bernard's role in recruiting Templars, see Schenk, *Templar Families*, 91–92, 207–14.

17. Champollion-Figeac, *Documents*, 2: 14–17, no. 8, 1132, act of Count Thibaut. Henry is said to have placed his *signum* on the document (*Signum Henrici filii comitis Theobaldi*). Henry confirmed this act in his first year as count (*Actes*, no. 14, 1152). See also LoPrete, *Adela of Blois*, 119–21, 152–55, 478–80 (no. 67, 1197).

18. See ch. 3 at n. 74.

19. In a letter to Henry, Peter complained that he had repaid a 60*l.* debt, and although the "court session for taking counsel about a certain matter was fixed," Count Henry conveniently forgot about it (Peter of Celle, *Letters*, 326–27, no. 71, 1152x54).

20. Vallet de Viriville, *Les archives historiques*, 395–96, no. 2, 1134 (= AD Aube, 5bis H 127), done in Troyes, with the consent and approval "of my son Henry, who *scripta hoc signum + hic*

impressit." The count's chaplain Ralph sealed the document. Witnesses included the abbot of Montier-la Celle (Walter), the archdeacons of Meaux (Thibaut) and Troyes (Manasses of Villemaur), the archdeacon and cathedral cantor of Troyes (Gebuin), and several local barons: Hulduin of Vendeuvre, Count Guy of Bar-sur-Seine, Odo of Villemaur, André of La Ferté-Gaucher (later of Montmirail), Jean of Isle-Aumont, Walter of Bernon, and the provost of Troyes (Guiard of Pont). See also Baudin, *Les sceaux*, 72. For twelfth-century autograph crosses, see Parisse, "Croix autographes."

    21. Helmerichs, "The Defense of Normandy," 135–38.

    22. *Gesta Stephani*, 4–5. The author was probably Robert of Lewes, bishop of Bath (1136–66), a staunch supporter of Bishop Henry. William of Malmesbury (*Historia novella*, 28–29) delivered a more reserved judgment in light of later events: "He was a man of energy but lacking in judgment, active in war, of extraordinary spirit in undertaking difficult tasks, lenient to his enemies and easily appeased, courteous to all: though you admired his kindness in promising, still you felt his words lacked truth and his promises fulfillment."

    23. King, *King Stephen*, 8–9. Biographical studies are Voss, *Heinrich von Blois*, and Riall, *Henry of Blois*.

    24. *Gesta Stephani*, 8–9.

    25. King, *King Stephen*, 316–20, decribes Bishop Henry's role in Stephen's reign. Bishop Roger of Salisbury made much of the fact that his oath had been conditional and that Matilda was not to marry outside the realm without consulting the magnates, which she failed to do (William of Malmesbury, *Historia novella*, 10–11, 40–41).

    26. Orderic Vitalis. *The Ecclesiastical History*, 5: 454, 458. Robert of Torigni also reported Thibaut's resentment; see King, "Stephen of Blois," 294–96.

    27. That is also the conclusion of LoPrete, *Adela of Blois*, 390–98.

    28. *Notre-Dame de Chartres*, 1: 131–34, no. 43, 1136. Thibaut's charter of 1128 confirmed Adela's transfer of the church of St-Martin-au-Val in Chartres to Marmoutier ca. 1107; see Lo-Prete, *Adela of Blois*, 250–51, 497–500, no. 98. In that same year Henry had a new tutor, Master Ebrard (AN, K 22, no. 9, 1136, done in Vertus).

    29. Thibaut compensated the canons of St-Martin of Épernay for their loss of the sales tax after he transferred the fair of Épernay to Troyes (*Épernay*, 2: 128, no. 9, 1136). He heard a second case at Épernay, involving a knight who gave one-half of his property to St-Faron of Meaux on taking the habit there, for which the monks paid him 24*l*. But since the property was a fief moving from Walter II of Châtillon, the latter insisted on receiving 100*s*. for consenting to the alienation (Duchesne, *Chastillon, preuves*, 2: 24, 1137).

    30. King, *King Stephen*, 71–73.

    31. Thibaut's traveling party included his chaplain Ralph, Anselm I of Traînel, Hulduin of Vendeuvre, and Galeran, count of Meulan (*Calendar of Documents Preserved in France*, 1: 373–74, no. 1055, 1137).

    32. *Recueil des actes de Louis VI*, 2: 331, no. 396, between 1 May and August 1137. Stephen, future count of Boulogne (1147–53), had just married the king's sister Constance (Pacaut, *Louis VII et son royaume*, 42).

    33. Luchaire, *Études sur les actes de Louis VII*, 266, no. 584.

    34. Suger, *Vie de Louis VI*, 278–84, cap. 34, describes the royal procession with "five hundred or more knights" to Bordeaux and their return to Paris. See also the *Chronique de Morigny*, 67–68, bk. 2, cap. 2, and Turner, *Eleanor of Aquitaine*, 39–49. Louis had anticipated his death two years earlier, when he reconciled Thibaut and Ralph so that they would act as joint guardians of young Louis (Orderic Vitalis, *The Ecclesiastical History*, 6: 446–47).

35. Baudin, *Les sceaux*, 515–16, no. 1, 1137 after 1 August (death of Louis VI), done in Provins (= Provins, BM, ms. 86, no. 2 = Bourquelot, *Histoire de Provins*, 2: 379–80 = Mesqui, *Provins*, 187, no. 1); see also Baudin, *Les sceaux*, 72 and illustration no. 4 (photograph of Henry's *signum*). It is not known when Thibaut dowered Mathilda with property in and around Provins, which later was given to Countess Marie (Bur, *Formation*, 321). In 1199 Countess Blanche's dower of seven entire castellanies did not include Provins, perhaps because the fair revenues had made it too valuable. This document of 1137 is the earliest known to have been sealed by a countess of Champagne, but Mathilda's seal on it disappeared before 1850, replaced by a seal of Alice of Courtenay (Baudin, *Les sceaux*, 137–38).

36. As in 1136 (AN, K 22, no. 9, done at Vertus), when Thibaut ordered that his seal be attached to a document presented by the abbot of Prémontré. In 1145 Thibaut sealed a letter of donation drawn up by the monks of Pontigny in the name of Garnier, lord of Vénisy, his wife Petronilla, and their son Anselm; each placed a cross on the document. The scribe states that Garin, a monk at Pontigny, took the document for sealing to the archbishop of Sens, then to Count Thibaut (*Pontigny*, 130–31, no. 58).

37. That was made explicit in two documents drafted by the monks of Montiéramey. The first was drawn up in the chapter hall before being confirmed by the count *per manum* in Troyes and authenticated by his seal (*Montiéramey*, 54–56, no. 31, 1138). The second was drafted in Montiéramey's priory of St-Jean-en-Châtel of Troyes; the count's cleric William affixed Thibaut's seal after thirteen-year-old Henry and his mother Mathilda drew their *signa* on the document to indicate their consent (*Montiéramey*, 56–58, no. 32, 1140).

38. Thibaut's cleric William drafted the count's documents occasionally from 1126 and routinely from 1136, while his chaplain Ralph (1137–51), archdeacon of Meaux, affixed the count's seal (Baudin, *Les sceaux*, 187–88). At Isle-Aumont in 1138 Henry heard his father decide that the monks of Montier-en-Der could collect a death tax and one-third of the property of their tenants who died without heirs in the count's lands; Henry and his mother indicated their consent by drawing crosses next to their names on the document prepared and sealed by the count's chaplain (AD Haute-Marne, 7 H 13, 1139: each cross seems to be a personal one [= *Montiérender*, 201–2, no. 77, 1139 = Arbois de Jubainville, *Histoire*, 3: 426, no. 94]).

39. Suger, *De glorioso rege Ludovico*, in *Oeuvres*, 1: 164–66. Suger claims that he "directed" Thibaut to meet Louis at Auxerre because the young king needed the guidance of, and needed to be seen with, a mature leader like Thibaut. There is no evidence that Thibaut did homage to Louis at Auxerre (as claimed by Pacaut, *Louis VII et son royaume*, 40–41). For the bishop of Langres, see Constable, "The Disputed Election at Langres in 1138," and Wurm, *Gottfried, Bischof von Langres*.

40. Suger, *De glorioso rege Ludovico*, in *Oeuvres*, 1: 164.

41. Suger, *De glorioso rege Ludovico*, in *Oeuvres*, 1: 166–72.

42. Louis granted the townsmen in Reims a charter of liberties based on his 1128 charter for Laon; he confirmed it in 1139 but withdrew it on 30 April 1139 while the see was vacant. After the election of Archbishop Samson of Mauvoison (19 November 1140), Louis and Thibaut proceeded to quash the commune; see Pacaut, *Louis VII et les élections épiscopales*, 93–94. Mews, "The Council of Sens," 350–51, and 360–64, cites the threat of communal social disorder in the years 1138–41 as an important backdrop to the theological issues vetted at the Council of Sens.

43. Mews, "The Council of Sens," 345–54.

44. Archbishop Henry Sanglier began the rebuilding of the cathedral in the mid-1120s, but it was still unfinished in 1141. It is debated whether the original plan of construction was followed consistently through the four decades required for its completion. See Henriet, "La cathédrale Saint-Étienne de Sens," and Mews, "The Council of Sens," 354–58.

45. Ida of Carinthia, the younger sister of Countess Mathilda, married William III of Nevers ca. 1142. She would be regent of Nevers during William III's absence on the Second Crusade and later (1161–68) for the underaged William IV, when she was demonized by the monks of Vézelay; she died in 1179. For her life, see Lespinasse, *Le Nivernais*, 1: 311–38. For a genealogical table of the counts of Nevers, Auxerre, and Tonnerre, see Bouchard, *Sword, Miter, and Cloister*, 342.

46. Bernard of Clairvaux, *Epistolae*, in *Opera*, 8: 424, no. 447 (*Letters*, 351, no. 279): a letter to the abbot of Hautecombe explaining that King Roger asked for two Cistercian brothers to evaluate the grounds he offered for founding a Cistercian monastery. The ships Roger sent to Montpellier to bring the girl probably carried the "exquisite vase" as a gift for Thibaut, who later presented it to Suger at the dedication of St-Denis (see n. 89 below). Gouet and Le Hête, *Les comtes de Blois et de Champagne*, 45–46, place Elizabeth's birth in ca. 1130 and her marriage in 1142. Houben, *Roger II of Sicily*, 86–88, suggests that the marriage might have been delayed to 1143, until Roger II could explore marriage possibilities with a daughter of the Byzantine emperor; that would make Elizabeth about thirteen when she married Roger of Apulia. After Roger died, on 2 May 1149, she returned home to marry William IV of Perche-Gouet ca. 1150/55. She was widowed again in 1169 and entered Fontevraud in 1180 (Thompson, "The Formation of the County of Perche," 306–7). She was remembered by the nuns of Fontaines-les-Nonnes as *Domina Elisabeth, venerabilis monacha, ducissa, soror domine Marie ducissa* (*Obituaires*, 4: 192, 13 August).

47. See Pacaut, *Louis VII et les élections épiscopales*, 94–97, and Devailly, *Le Berry*, 390–404.

48. *Chronique de Morigny*, 81.

49. William of Nangis, *Chronique*, 1: 34. See also the *Chronique de Morigny*, 81.

50. William of Nangis, *Chronique*, 1: 34.

51. Sigebert of Gembloux, *Continuatio Premonstratensis*, 451–52. See Mews, "The Council of Sens," 348–49. The anonymous (mid-twelfth-century) *Historia Francorum*, 116, also cites Thibaut's refusal to accompany Louis on the expedition to Aquitaine as the beginning of a conflict that continued with the Bourges affair.

52. Robert of Auxerre, *Chronicon*, 235.

53. Peter the Venerable, *Letters*, 1: 256–57, no. 96, September 1141, and 2: 163. The bishop noted that Bernard of Clairvaux, the papal legate Bishop Geoffroy of Chartres, and Hato's secretary Nicholas of Montiéramey were with him in Troyes. Nicholas, who had observed the condemnation of Abelard at the Council of Sens, had just returned from Rome; see Mews, "The Council of Sens," 372–74.

54. Crouch, *King Stephen*, 135–43, and King, *King Stephen*, 145–74.

55. Eleanor was probably the daughter of Thibaut's older brother William, lord of Sully by marriage to Agnes of Sully (LoPrete, *Adela of Blois*, 389 n. 41 and appendix 3 n. 24). John of Salisbury, *Historia Pontificalis*, 12–13, states that Ralph later returned Eleanor's dowry to Thibaut, indicating that Thibaut had provided his niece a dowry worthy of marriage to a royal like Ralph of Vermandois.

56. The bishops were Simon of Noyon (Ralph's brother), Bartholomew of Laon (Ralph's cousin), and Peter of Senlis; see Pacaut, *Louis VII et les élections épiscopales*, 97–100. The royal apologist William of Nangis later blamed all this on Count Thibaut (*Chronique*, 35). See also *Historia Francorum*, 116.

57. Sassier, *Louis VII*, 112–13, places the destruction of Vitry in mid-1142 rather than the generally accepted date of late fall 1142 or early months of 1143. See also Pacaut, *Louis VII et son royaume*, 39–46.

58. Robert of Torigni, *Chronicle*, 143.

59. Sigebert of Gembloux, *Continuatio Praemonstatensis*, 387–88, also notes that Louis gave Vitry to Odo, the son of Count Hugh of Troyes, because "his patrimony was stolen from him," and that the king wished on this occasion to recover it for him. Anonymous of Laon (*RHF* 13: 678n) repeats that assertion. William of Nangis, a royal sympathizer writing in the 1290s, reports that Louis captured the castle of Vitry, that 1,300 people died there in the church fire, and that Louis gave Vitry to Count Hugh's son Odo ("the Champenois"), whose inheritance Thibaut had "stolen" in 1125 (*Chronique*, 35, under the year 1143). The *Historia Francorum*, 116, states that Louis, repentant for the deaths of 1,300 souls, went on crusade to liberate the Holy Land from the Turks and that he gave Vitry to Odo because "his patrimony was stolen from him." The "dispossession" of Vitry seems to have been floated as a justification for the king's invasion of Thibaut's lands; Vitry was in fact held as a fief from the archbishop of Reims (see ch. 8 at n. 37). LoPrete, *Adela*, 393–95, 570–74, concludes that Odo "Champenois" might have been raised in Thibaut's household and that he in fact had good relations with Thibaut.

60. *Vita prima sancti Bernardi* (297, bk. 2, cap. 8). The Annales of Ste-Colombe of Sens, where Hugh of Payns's son Thibaut was abbot (1137–48), echoes that assessment: "The king captured by arms and fire the count's finest fortresses" ("Annales sanctae Colombae Senonensis," 209).

61. Oury, "Recherches," 104–5.

62. *Vita B. Petri Julieacenesis*, 1266; Bur, *Formation*, 29–92.

63. Cowdrey, "Peter, Monk of Molesme and Prior of Jully."

64. In his charter for Val-Chrétien, Thibaut is quoted as saying, "My wife Mathilda conceded this, as did my son Henry and my other two sons Thibaut and Stephen, who conceded and even confirmed it by their crosses" (Collection Moreau, vol. 60, fol. 60r–61r, 1142, in Sézanne). All three sons marked a cross. In another act of about the same time Countess Mathilda and her three oldest sons confirmed in the hand of Abbess Petronilla of Fontevraud (died 1149) all the gifts, in all places, that Count Thibaut had granted to the nuns. Odo "Campanus" was among the witnesses (*Fontevraud*, 1: 409–10, no. 416, undated act done in the chapter hall of La Charme). The absence of William (born 1135 and therefore of an age to witness) from both letters suggests that he had been sent to England.

65. Gouet and Le Hête, *Les comtes de Blois et de Champagne*, 45, place Marie's birth ca. 1128, one year after Henry's. She would have been about fourteen when she married Odo II, duke of Burgundy, between 1142 and 1144; she witnessed Odo's act of 1145 (Petit, *Histoire*, 2: 236–37, no. 293). Her eldest son, Hugh III (born ca. 1148), attained his majority in April 1165 (Petit, *Histoire*, 2: 89–90). Marie was regent of Burgundy from September 1162 to April 1165 while in her mid-thirties. She entered Fontevraud in 1174 (see ch. 7 n. 97) and was still there in 1187 (Benton, "Recueil," 1187e-add 1). She died ca. 1190 (Petit, *Histoire*, 2: 134).

66. Longnon, *Documents*, 1: 466, no. 1 (= Quantin, *Yonne*, 1: 369–70, no. 226). See Evergates, *Aristocracy*, 11 n. 46. Since Duke Hugh II of Burgundy died ca. 6 February 1143 (Petit, *Histoire*, 2: 42), Thibaut probably did homage (*fecit homagium*) to the new duke in the spring of 1143 for the lands he held in fief (*de feudo*). Lemarignier, *Hommage en marche*, 155–65, discusses this and other homages at the borders of Champagne. Benham, *Peacemaking in the Middle Ages*, 21–43, underscores the significance of meeting places at borders in western France.

67. Richard, *Les ducs de Bourgogne*, 30, 42, interprets this as a homage owed to a new lord, but Bur, *Formation*, 290–91, suggests that it was Thibaut who sought out the new duke in order to do homage as a way of confirming his possessions. That accords with what Gillingham, "Doing Homage," finds was a similar practice by twelfth-century kings of England, who as heirs-apparent did homage to the king of France as a way of legitimizing their successions before

their crowning, at least until 1183, when Henry II felt compelled to do homage to Philip II. Count Thibaut seems to have referred to that practice in 1149 when he reminded Suger and Count Ralph of Vermandois, the king's regents, that he held the *regalia* of the bishop of Chartres *in feodo* from the king, *cum alio feodo* (*RHF* 15: 507–8, no. 65). Suger, *Vie de Louis VI*, 272, cap. 33, refers to Château-Renaud as a *feudum* that Count Thibaut held from the king in 1132–33, but does not mention homage.

68. Evergates, *Aristocracy*, 11.

69. In 1115 Thibaut (as count of Blois and Chartres) claimed that the king, as his lord (*dominus*), should hear a case in his court, which the king refused to do (Graboïs, "De la trêve de Dieu," 589 n. 34). At the Council of Reims (20 October 1119), Louis VI claimed Thibaut as "my vassal" (*RHF* 12: 726–27, letter to Pope Calixtus II). Bernard of Clairvaux urged Thibaut to "do the homage you owed for the fief you hold from the bishop of Langres" (*Epistolae*, in *Opera*, 7: 97–98, no. 39 [*Letters*, 73–74, no. 41], ca. 1127). None of these references state that Thibaut actually had done homage.

70. *Clairvaux*, 19–20, no. 10, 1143. Photograph of the original document, with the pendant seal of Count Thibaut still attached and Henry's hand-drawn cross (AD Aube, 3 H 101), in *The Knights Templar*, 118, illustration 88.

71. Sigebert of Gembloux, *Continuatio Gemblacensis*, 388.

72. A close reading of the letters exchanged by the prelates on each side reveals the concerted attempts to resolve a very complicated situation (Grant, *Abbot Suger*, 148–52).

73. Bernard of Clairvaux, *Epistolae*, in *Opera*, 8: 86–89, no. 222, August 1143 (*Letters*, 366–68, no. 298, dated by the editor to September).

74. The proposal involved a double marriage, in that one of Thibaut's daughters would marry Ivo of Nesle, who had just become count of Soissons (Newman, *Nesle*, 1: 25–26).

75. *RHF* 15: 409, no. 2, 6 November 1143.

76. Pacaut, *Louis VII et les élections épiscopales*, 99–100. See also Oury, "Recherches," 107–8, and Vacandard, *Vie de Saint Bernard*, 2: 189. Ralph of Vermandois died on 14 October 1152.

77. *Vita prima sancti Bernardi* (by Arnold of Bonneval), 301–2. See also Buc, "Conversion of Objects," 127.

78. Suger, *De administratione* [*Gesta*], in *Oeuvres*, 1: 128.

79. Grant, "Suger and the Anglo-Norman World," 61.

80. Buc, "Conversion of Objects," 143.

81. See Cothren, "Suger's Stained Glass Masters."

82. Suger, *De administratione* [*Gesta*], in *Oeuvres*, 1: 130.

83. Grant, *Abbot Suger*, 265–70, and Snyder, *Early Gothic Column-Figure Sculpture*. Dectot, *Sculptures*, 62–69, reproduces Montfauçon's engravings of the portal statues and photographs of the recently (1986–92) recovered heads of those statues, which join the one in Cambridge, Massachusetts, and the two in Baltimore—all six were carved between 1137 and 1140.

84. Rudolph, "Inventing the Exegetical Stained-Glass Window."

85. It is highly likely that the entire compex of buildings was Suger's work in the 1140s (Grant, *Abbot Suger*, 251–52).

86. Maines, "Good Works, Social Ties, and the Hope for Salvation."

87. Suger, *De consecratione*, in *Oeuvres*, 1: 34. See also Buc, "Conversion of Objects," 114–17.

88. Suger, *De administratione* [*Gesta*], in *Oeuvres*, 1: 152. Suger later had a metal base crafted for it, with the inscription "As a bride, Eleanor gave this vase to King Louis, Mitadolus [the last Muslim king of Saragossa, 1110–30, gave it] to her grandfather, the king [Louis, gave it] to me

[Suger], and Suger [gave it] to the saints." For the significance of the Eleanor Vase, see Beech, "The Eleanor of Aquitaine Vase," and *La France romane*, 166–67, fig. 113.

89. Suger, *De administratione* [*Gesta*], in *Oeuvres*, 1: 154. Suger called it a *lagena preclara*, which accords with its clear crystal appearance, despite the editor's opinion that *lagena* refers to a much larger (lost) object (Suger, *Oeuvres*, 1: 241 n. 284). Gaborit-Chopin accepts this crystal vase, known as "the Ewer of St-Denis," as the one that Thibaut gave to Suger; see her "Suger's Liturgical Vessels," 284–85 and fig. 3, and *La France romane*, 167, fig. 114.

90. *Vita tercia sancti Bernardi* (by Geoffroy of Auxerre), 527, cap. 8, which purports to quote Eleanor's complaint to Bernard that, although she had become pregnant in her first year of marriage (while in her mid-teens), she miscarried and since then had been barren, to which the abbot "promised" her a successful birth if she reconciled Louis to Thibaut, which she promised to do. Sigebert of Gembloux, *Continuatio Praemonstratensis*, 452, repeats the story, which is accepted by most modern historians.

91. The *Continuatio* of Sigebert of Gembloux, 388, states that Louis VII, realizing how the disturbances were threatening his realm, made peace with Count Thibaut.

92. *RHF* 15: 416, no. 14, 27 December 1144. The pope directed the king's adviser, Bishop Alvisius of Arras, to monitor the accord.

93. King, *King Stephen*, 181–202, ascribes Stephen's "loss of Normandy" in 1142–44 to Geoffroy of Anjou's artful detachment of the Norman church, barons, and mercantile class from the king.

94. Baudin, *Les sceaux*, 101–3, and Corpus (CD-ROM), no. 3: Thibaut's right hand holds a lance with a banner resting on his shoulder. Baudin finds no evident reason for the change from the leftward direction of the figure in the seals of Counts Hugh and Thibaut to the rightward direction in Henry's seal.

95. + *Sigillum Henrici filii comitis Teobaldi* +. The fact that Henry does not carry a sword suggests that he might not have been knighted in 1145. Bony, *Un siècle de sceaux figurés*, 25, points out that the lance with standard is modeled on Louis VII's seal.

96. Peter was born ca. 1115 and probably spent his early years as a monk at Montier-la-Celle before studying at St-Martin-les-Champs in Paris, where he probably met John of Salisbury. For Peter's biography, see ch. 5 n. 28.

97. *Actes*, no. 2, 1145.

98. Neither the original document nor the seal survives. But an early example of Henry's preaccession seal survives on an undated document (AD Marne, 22 H 105, no. 3 = *Actes*, no. 8) by which Henry, "son of Count Thibaut," announces that he witnessed a certain Beroard and his son William give part of their fiefs and allods at Villiers-en-Lieu to Trois-Fontaines. Henry does not approve, but simply confirms what he witnessed; he appears with six knights but without his chancellor. Ralph, dean of the cathedral chapter of St-Étienne of Châlons, sealed a similar document for the same act, *mutatis mutandis*, dated 1146 (AD Marne, 22 H 105, no. 1). Since both documents were drawn up concurrently by the episcopal chancery of Châlons, Henry's extant seal can be dated to 1146. See Baudin, *Les sceaux*, Corpus (CD-ROM), no. 4 (color photograph); Bony, *Un siècle de sceaux figurés*, plate IX, no. 47, and Arbois de Jubainville, "Sigillographie," 44, plates 1–4.

99. For William, see ch. 4 at n. 28. For Hugh, see Cline, "Abbot Hugh."

100. Biographical details of Henry's siblings are in Gouet and Le Hête, *Les comtes de Blois et de Champagne*, 45–48. Margaret's obituary at Fontaines-les-Nonnes remembers her as an exemplary nun (Pavillon, *Le vie du bienheureux Robert d'Arbrissel*, 563–64).

101. Dufour, "Adèle de Champagne," 35, dates her birth to 1142/45.

CHAPTER 2. THE SECOND CRUSADE, 1146–1151

1. Grosse, "Überlegungen zum Kreuzzugsaufruf Eugens III," 90–92 (= *PL* 180: 1064–66, no. 48); trans. in Phillips, *The Second Crusade*, 281–82. For an analysis of the bull and its reissue of 31 March 1146, see Phillips, *The Second Crusade*, ch. 3.

2. Phillips, *The Second Crusade*, 38, concludes that Edessa's fate was known in Rome only by May 1145, when an experienced group of ecclesiastics vetted the issue, and that the decision to call a crusade was more than a Cistercian project.

3. William of Nangis, *Chronique*, 35; *La chronique de Morigny*, 85. The Annals of St-Denis state that the occupation of Edessa was the primary reason for Louis's expedition to Jerusalem ("Annales de Saint-Denis," 19). Otto of Freising reports that Louis was carrying out a wish of his older brother Philip, who died in 1131 (*Gesta*, 57; *Deeds*, 70). Otto may have heard that story while on the crusade (Graboïs, "The Crusade of King Louis VII," 95).

4. Phillips, *The Second Crusade*, 64–65, reviews the possible motives.

5. Odo of Deuil, *De profectione Ludovici VII*, 6. There is no evidence that Bishop Geoffroy had been to the Levant (Wurm, *Gottfried, Bischof von Langres*, 18 n. 3).

6. Kienzle, *Cistercians, Heresy and Crusade in Occitania*, 78–108.

7. Geoffroy (of La Roche-Vaneau) was born ca. 1090, entered Cîteaux (1112), then followed Bernard to Clairvaux (1115), where he served as Bernard's assistant (*vices*) before becoming the first abbot of Fontenay (1119–30). He returned to Clairvaux as prior (1131–38) and conducted diplomatic activities for Bernard before becoming bishop of Langres (1138–62/63) after a contentious election (Constable, "The Disputed Election at Langres in 1138"). Geoffroy was a powerful proponent of the Second Crusade and developed violent anti-Greek feelings. He retired to Clairvaux and died there in 1166. See Wurm, *Gottfried, Bischof von Langres*, chs. 1–2, and Veyssière, "Le personnel de l'abbaye de Clairvaux," 57–58.

8. Phillips, *The Second Crusade*, 62–65.

9. Graboïs, "The Crusade of King Louis VII," 97–98, argues that Louis had agreed at the dedication of St-Denis to go on pilgrimage to expiate his sin of swearing an oath against the archbishop of Bourges, and that Bernard was primarily responsible for converting the king's pilgrimage into a formal crusade to protect Jerusalem. Although Louis kept to his original vision of a personal pilgrimage, the barons and knights, stirred by Cistercian preachers, understood the expedition as primarily a military affair.

10. For an account of the king's crusade, see Sassier, *Louis VII*, 152–200.

11. *La chronique de Morigny*, 84–86 (perhaps an invented speech).

12. *Historia gloriosi regis Ludovici VII*, 126.

13. *Historia gloriosi regis Ludovici VII*, 126.

14. Otto of Freising, *Gesta*, 58 (*Deeds*, 71–72).

15. *La chronique de Morigny*, 86, lists the notable participants (Henry is "count of Meaux"). Phillips, *The Second Crusade*, ch. 6, lists all known participants at Vézelay. For the Champenois contingent, see Evergates, *Aristocracy*, 221–22 (Walter II of Châtillon), 219 (Jacques I of Chacenay), 242–43 (Anselm II of Traînel); Roserot, *Dictionnaire*, 2: 863 (Garnier II of Traînel, lord of Marigny). See also Lespinasse, *Le Nivernais*, 1: 311–38; Bouchard, *Sword, Miter, and Cloister*, 347–47; Hugh of Poitiers, *Chronique*, 423–24 (*Vézelay Chronicle*, 164–65).

16. Bourquelot, *Histoire de Provins*, 1: 89–98.

17. Petit, *Histoire*, 2: 94–100 (list of Burgundian crusaders). Josbert made his gift to Bernard of Clairvaux at Laferté-sur-Aube in the presence of Count Thibaut and young Henry, who consented because the property was a fief held from the count; Josbert retained a lifetime right

over some the property in the event that he returned from overseas (*Clairvaux*, 20–21, no. 11, 1146, before 31 March; trans. in Evergates, *Documents*, 109, no. 86).

18. Brunn, *Des contestaires aux "Cathares"*, 126–31. For a detailed itinerary of Bernard's trip to Germany, see Parisse, "Les relations (de Saint Bernard) avec l'empire," 419–23. See also Willems, "Cîteaux et la seconde croisade."

19. Phillips, *The Second Crusade*, 80–97.

20. Constable, "The Second Crusade," 244–65. Bernard's secretary, Nicholas of Montiéramey, drafted letters to various French and German political leaders promoting the crusade (Willems, "Cîteaux et la seconde croisade," 127–29).

21. Martène and Duran, *Thesaurus*, 1: 399–400, August 1146.

22. The "Annales de Saint-Denis," 277–78, state that the counts of Anjou, Blois, Flanders, and Nevers attended the council.

23. *La chronique de Morigny*, 86. Odo of Deuil, *De profectione Ludovici VII*, 14–15.

24. John of Salisbury, *Historia Pontificalis*, 14–15. See also Pontal, *Les conciles*, 328–33.

25. For a reading of his bull *Divina dispensatione* in Troyes as "mission creep," see Constable, "The Second Crusade," 270–71.

26. *Clairvaux*, 22–23, no. 13, 1147. Clairvaux received so many donations (no doubt partial sales) that it asked Bishop Geoffroy of Langres to seal six long *pancartes* listing its recent acquisitions (*Clairvaux*, 23–48, nos. 14–19, 1147). For the drafting of *pancartes* related to crusade transactions, see Veyssière's remarks in *Clairvaux*, lxxvii–lxxix.

27. *Paraclet*, 70–71, no. 52, 1146.

28. Arbois de Jubainville, "Les premiers seigneurs de Ramerupt," 456–57, no. 3, done on the eve of their departure (between 8 and 15 June 1147), and "Catalogue d'actes des comtes de Brienne," 152 n. 46, done on the day of departure, the same act but with an additional clause on fiefs.

29. Evergates, *Aristocracy*, ch. 3. Odo of Deuil, who furnishes most of our information about the crusade, fails to mention the bull's explicit approval of mortgaging fiefs (Odo refers only to "certain other provisions") or the actual mortgaging and selling of properties in 1146 and 1147 preparatory to the expedition. Helias-Baron, "Ferveur des laïcs," concludes that the *pancartes* from Clairvaux and Morimond in 1147–48 are recapitulative; that is, they do not reflect a sudden increase in the transfer of property to monasteries in preparation for the crusade, despite the provision in *Quantum praedecessores* specifically permitting (for the first time) the mortgaging of fiefs in order to fund the journey. But we can say that the drawing up of *pancartes* was directly related to the imminent departure of so many property holders and of the bishop of Langres, who sealed the *pancartes*; not all crusaders would return, and Clairvaux needed written records of its acquisitions.

30. Hugh III of Broyes and Étiennette of Bar-le-Duc were married shortly after 22 October 1144 (Poull, *La maison souveraine et ducale de Bar*, 106). Hugh became lord of Broyes while still very young (ca. 1120) and was in his mid-thirties in 1144; see Evergates, *Aristocracy*, 218. See also Bouchard, *Sword, Miter, and Cloister*, 338–40 (Anseric of Montréal, 1129–ca. 1170); Roserot, *Dictionnaire*, 1: 109 (Milo III of Bar-sur-Seine), 1: 330 (Clarembaud III of Chappes); Flammarion, "Le sceau de silence" (Bartholomew of Vignory); and Evergates, *Aristocracy*, 274 n. 80 (Pougy), 359 n. 34 (Geoffroy III of Joinville).

31. Phillips, *The Second Crusade*, 126–27.

32. Phillips, *The Second Crusade*, ch. 10, provides an overview of the expedition.

33. A chronicler at Sens reported that King Louis brought with him to Jerusalem his wife (Eleanor) and "Henry, the eldest son of Count Thibaut, later count of Champagne," who

together led a force of two hundred noble lords, *proceres nobiles* (*Chronique de Saint-Pierre-le-Vif de Sens*, 313–14, brief additions made ca. 1184). Writing more than thirty-five years after the event, the chronicler added that Louis and Henry comported themselves "with much arrogance."

34. See at n. 44.

35. *Vita Adalberonis Trevirensis archiepiscopi*, 357.

36. Odo of Deuil, *De profectione Ludovici VII*, 20–24, mentions only a few incidents.

37. *RHF* 15: 487, no. 12.

38. *RHF* 15: 488, no. 4, letter to Suger. Phillips, *The Second Crusade*, 188–89, concludes that the 110-day journey from Metz to Constantinople was relatively easy because the French were better disciplined than the Germans who preceded them.

39. *RHF* 15: 495–96, no. 36, written in Antioch after 19 March 1148.

40. Odo of Deuil, *De profectione Ludovici VII*, 58–61.

41. William of Tyre, *Chronique*, 747 (*History*, 2: 172), bk. 16, cap. 23, reports that Louis had several *colloquia* with Manuel, who received the king's *principes* with great honor.

42. Odo of Deuil, *De profectione Ludovici VII*, 64–67.

43. Odo of Deuil, *De profectione Ludovici VII*, 62–63, 66–67. Kalavrezou, "Helping Hand for the Empire," discusses the history and contents of the imperial chapel, which contained "the most important relics of Christendom, those of Christ's passion" (55).

44. *RHF* 15: 607–8, no. 81 (= *PL* 182: 672–73, no. 478); trans. in Evergates, *Documents*, 103–4, no. 81. The letter was written by Nicholas of Montiéramey and survives in his collection of letters written "in the name of" Bernard. It does not appear in Bernard's letter collections and therefore is not included in the modern edition of his letters by Leclercq and Rochais.

45. Flori, *L'essor de la chevalerie*, 211, interprets this as a "giving of arms" to someone defending the church rather than as a dubbing into knighthood.

46. Odo of Deuil, *De profectione Ludovici VII*, 78–83.

47. The relics may have come from the chapel of Constantine's palace (Odo of Deuil, *De profectione Ludovici VII*, 63 n. 4). Henry gave his piece of the "true cross" to his chaplain in 1153 (see ch. 3 at n. 88).

48. Odo of Deuil, *De profectione Ludovici VII*, 108–11. See also Phillips, *The Second Crusade*, 197–98.

49. William of Tyre, *Chronique*, 749–50 (*History*, 2: 174–75), bk. 16, cap. 24, regards the crossing of the Meander as a great victory, as does Niketas Choniates, *O City of Byzantium*, 28–42, who magnifies its significance by including a long, invented exhortation by Louis to the troops. Neither account mentions Count Henry.

50. Odo of Deuil, *De profectione Ludovici VII*, 112–13. See Evergates, *Aristocracy*, 13, 69, 93, 94, 239.

51. Odo of Deuil, *De profectione Ludovici VII*, 114–21, and John of Salisbury, *Historia Pontificalis*, 54–55, who ascribes the disaster to Louis's failure as commander.

52. *RHF* 15: 495–96, no. 36, written from Antioch after 19 March 1148.

53. Leroy, "The Organization of the Champagne Templar Network."

54. Odo of Deuil ends his account of the French expedition with its arrival at Antioch in March 1148. Although Odo remained with the king for another year, until Easter 1149, before returning to France, he failed to leave any account of that period, no doubt in the absence of anything favorable to report.

55. John of Salisbury, *Historia Pontificalis*, 52–53, relates what must have been commonly known about the royal couple in Antioch.

56. William of Tyre, *Chronique*, 2: 760 (*History*, 2: 184–86), bk. 17, cap. 1. William was writing in the 1170s of events that transpired two decades earlier while he was a student in France. Although his statement has been challenged as a later insertion (Fourrier, "Retour au *Terminus*," 301), it does seem accurate for the 1140s, when Henry was only a prospective son-in-law. If William was inserting into the 1140s what he knew in the 1170s, he would have called Henry instead the brother-in-law of Louis (who married Henry's youngest sister, Adele, in 1160). For Henry's betrothal to Marie during the crusade, see Evergates, "Louis VII and the Counts of Champagne."

57. Bernard of Clairvaux, *Epistolae*, in *Opera*, 8: 330–31, no. 371 (*Letters*, 473–74, no. 401, dated to mid-1146).

58. That decision is no longer seen as being entirely ill conceived (Phillips, *The Second Crusade*, 217–26).

59. Kenaan-Kedar, "The Cathedral of Sebaste," 101–3.

60. *RHF* 15: 502, no. 53, undated, in which Louis speaks of his *amor* for Henry. If Henry carried the letter with him, it was most likely drawn up between 24 July and Henry's departure in August or September 1148 (Luchaire, *Études sur les actes de Louis VII*, 175, no. 237, dates it from 24 July 1148 to 3 April 1149). It is also possible that Louis sent the letter directly to Suger (it is one of five letters in Suger's collection of 188 letters that is not addressed to Suger), in the expectation that he would forward it to Count Thibaut (Nortier, "Étude sur un recueil de lettres," 57, no. 77).

61. See Haseldine, "Friendship, Intimacy and Corporate Networking," for how the epistolatory language of friendship could serve multiple purposes.

62. Bishop Henry of Troyes related the circumstances of that event in his confirmation of the count's endowment for three canons: a 10*l.* revenue from the two (unnamed) fairs in Troyes, 100*s.* from the land tax at Donnement, and 3 *modii* of grain from the count's mills in Troyes. At the same time the brothers Odo, Renaud, and Manasses of Pougy endowed two additional prebends that Manasses (a cleric) would award during his lifetime, after which that right reverted to the bishop of Troyes. Since Manasses ultimately became bishop of Troyes, he continued to appoint canons to the chapter at Pougy until his death in 1190. Bishop Henry, who sealed the document in 1154, states that Count Henry also would seal it (AD Aube 8 G 1, 8 April 1154 = Camuzat, *Promptuarium*, fols. 30v–31r). Henry recalled that event in 1169, when he confirmed his endowment to Pougy (*Actes*, no. 290).

63. The origin of the Pougy is obscure. It is not clear whether they were of knightly or baronial background, or even distantly related to the counts (Roserot, *Dictionnaire*, 2: 1183–84; Evergates, *Bailliage of Troyes*, 193–95), but the brothers formed a strong bond with Count Henry.

64. Hugh of Poitiers, *Chronique*, 423–24 (*Vézelay Chronicle*, 164–67).

65. *RHF* 15: 513, no. 81, between 21 August and 10 October: Louis wrote to Suger that he landed at Calabria on 29 July. John of Salisbury reports that Roger then escorted the royal couple to Rome to meet with Pope Eugenius III (*Historia Pontificalis*, 60–62).

66. See ch. 1 at n. 46.

67. See ch. 1 at n. 89.

68. Magdalino, *The Empire of Manuel Komnenos*, 46–55.

69. See Tronzo, *The Cultures of His Kingdom.*

70. Suger, *Epistolae*, in *Oeuvres*, 2: 33–37, no. 6, before 3 April 1149.

71. The "Annals de Saint-Denis," 278, intimating an attempted coup d'état, credit Suger with having prevented turbulence and saving the kingdom from Robert. Lewis, *Royal Succession*, 61, discounts that possibility.

72. *Decrees of the Ecumenical Councils*, 200, canon 14.

73. Bernard does not specifically mention tournaments, but his depiction of "secular knights" in his "Liber ad milites Templi de laude novae militiae" implicitly places them at tournaments (*Opera*, 3: 213–39; "In Praise of the New Knighthood," 132–33).

74. Bernard of Clairvaux, *Epistolae*, in *Opera*, 8: 339–40, no. 376 (*Letters*, 476–77, no. 405, dated to January–March 1149); trans. in Evergates, *Documents*, 106–7, no. 83.

75. Tournaments usually took place after Easter; they were prohibited during Lent, from Ash Wednesday to Good Friday, a prohibition that extended through the duration of the crusade (Crouch, *Tournament*, 34).

76. *RHF* 15: 511, no. 72; trans. in Evergates, *Documents*, 107, no. 84.

77. *Les vers de Thibaut de Marly*, line 320 (*poème moral* written ca. 1173/89), cited by Civel, *La fleur de France*, 396.

78. Suger, *Epistolae*, in *Oeuvres*, 2: 41–43, no. 7: letter addressed to Archbishop Samson of Reims, in which Suger states that he convoked archbishops, bishops, and the great men (*optimates*) of the realm to provide for the kingdom and the church. It is not certain that the meeting was held; Pontal, *Les conciles de la France*, does not mention it.

79. *PL* 180: 1394–95, no. 355, 8 July 1149, and a similar letter on the same day to Suger (*PL* 180: 1395–96, no. 356).

80. Bernard of Clairvaux, *Epistolae*, in *Opera*, 8: 216–17, no. 300 (*Letters*, 436–37, no. 365, dated 1152); trans. in Evergates, *Documents*, 107–8, no. 85. Arbois de Jubainville, *Histoire*, 3: 36–37, and Faugeras, *Étienne de Champagne*, 49–50, identify the son as Stephen, then in his late teens, in view of Stephen's later behavior (as in taking the bride of Anselm II of Traînel). But there is no corroborating evidence for Stephen's conduct during Bernard's lifetime. Henry seems the more likely person here, as Thibaut's eldest son would have encountered Bernard more frequently, which would explain Bernard's favorable mention of the son's past behavior toward him.

81. Indirect evidence (the tower of Ste-Germaine in Bar-sur-Aube was called "the old castle" in 1149 and 1151) suggests that Henry had begun to construct a new residence there (Rubaud, "Bar-sur-Aube," 96). Vitry, even rebuilt after 1142, was less attractive to the young count than the more commercially active Bar-sur-Aube.

82. Arbois de Jubainville, *Histoire*, 3: 440–41, no. 111, 1151: the mayor claimed a hereditary right to his uncle's oven at Damery. Provosts from Thibaut's castle-towns of Provins, Épernay, Châtillon, Dormans, and Château-Thierry witnessed.

83. *Clairvaux*, 51–52, no. 23, 1151. Countess Mathilda and Henry's brothers Thibaut and Stephen marked their *signa*. A notice (perhaps a a preliminary draft) of the same act (*Clairvaux*, 52, no. 24) lacks a date and seal.

84. *Actes*, no. 6, 1151.

85. William Godel, an English monk living in Sens who was well informed about the count and his sons, states that Thibaut died in Lagny on 10 January 1152 (*Chronicon*, 13: 676).

86. "Annales de Lagny," 480. The translation occurred between 1073 and 1078.

87. Hill, *Two Old French Poems*, 75–108, and *Vie de Saint Thibaut de Provins*, 141–50, based on an eleventh-century Latin *vita*.

88. *Actes*, no. 15, 1152.

89. An extract from Dom Changy's manuscript history, published as "L'abbaye royale de Saint-Pierre de Lagny," 246–47, describes the tomb. In his manuscript (BnF, Collection de Champagne, t. 18, fol. 28) Dom Chagny provides a sketch of the tomb; he also reports that a silver box recently discovered beneath the tomb contained what seemed to be the bones of the eleventh-century saint. The porphyry might have come from Rome, where Abbot Suger, Bishop Henry of Winchester, and King Roger II of Sicily obtained stone in the 1140s (Deér, *The*

Dynastic Porphyry Tombs, 118–19). It is possible that Thibaut, like Roger, acquired the stone for his own tomb, and that Thibaut's daughter Isabelle/Elizabeth, who married Roger's son ca. 1140, facilitated its acquisition and transport to Champagne.

90. *Actes*, no. 13, 1152. The money came from the count's tolls collected at Coulommiers (*Obituaires*, 4: 21).

91. *Obituaires*, 4: 291 (10 January).

92. *Sugeri vita*, in *Oeuvres*, 2: 312.

93. Arnold devotes most of the last chapter (chapter 8) in his biography of Bernard to the character and deeds of Count Thibaut (*Vita prima sancti Bernardi*, 297–302). It appears that Arnold added those four long paragraphs after completing his biography in 1153. In paying tribute to Thibaut, Arnold also was acknowledging the count's special relationship with Bonneval abbey, where Thibaut had been the king's advocate (*vice*) since 1110 (*Recueil des actes de Louis VI*, 1: 86–90, no. 46). Oury, "Recherches," who gathers all that is known about Arnold, argues convincingly that Arnold knew Bernard reasonably well since their earliest encounter, especially since the Council of Étampes (summer 1130) and from later visits to Clairvaux. Moreover, Arnold was close to his diocesan bishop Geoffroy (of Lèves) of Chartres, who knew Bernard and must have related many anecdotes to Arnold, as evidenced by the detail that Arnold brings to Book 2 of the *Vita prima*. It was Arnold's personal knowledge as well as his esteem for Bernard, Oury claims, that led the monks at Clairvaux to invite him to contribute to Bernard's official biography. Oury has Arnold writing Book 2 after Bernard's death, that is, in 1153 (against Bredero, *Bernard of Clairvaux*, 38, who prefers a date from 1148, that is, five years before Bernard's death).

94. See ch. 1 at n. 78.

95. Baudin, *Les sceaux*, 110–12 and illustration no. 8 (color photo): *hec cedrus fuit comes Teubaldus*.

96. Robert of Torigni, *Chronicle*, 164, was one of many who noted that Thibaut's eldest son inherited "the county of Troyes and Champagne and what his father had beyond the Seine," whereas "Thibaut the second son took the county of Chartres, Blois and the land of Dun."

97. Ralph of Diceto, *Ymagines*, 1: 291; Robert of Torigni, *Chronicle*, 160.

98. See ch. 4 ("The Fairs").

99. John of Salisbury, *Historia Pontificalis*, 14; Robert of Torigni, *Chronicle*, 163.

100. Gerald of Wales, *De principis instructione liber*, 135–37. See Bartlett, *Gerald of Wales*, 62–68.

101. Robert of Auxerre, *Chronicon*, 233. For Robert's methods as a historian, see Chazan, "L'usage de la compilation," esp. 278–83.

CHAPTER 3. COUNT PALATINE OF TROYES, 1152–1158

1. See ch. 1 at n. 17.

2. *Actes*, no. 15, 1152.

3. *Versus magisteri Symonis cognomento Capra Aurea, canonici Sancti Victoris Parisiensis summi et celerrimi versificatoris, quos composuit precibus comitis Henrici* (*PL* 185: 1251–54) The identification of Simon as canon of St-Victor places the composition in the period 1155–60, although he might have composed the epitaphs earlier while at St-Ayoul. The epitaphs for Hugh of Mâcon and Pope Eugenius III might have been commissioned by the monks of Pontigny (Stohlmann, "Magister Simon Aurea Capra," 348–51).

4. *Actes*, no. 17, 1152: *scriptsit et recognovit*. The suit was brought to Count Thibaut's court, with Henry present, after the death of Anselm I of Traînel (probably late in 1151). Thibaut decided that the brothers should pay the canons 120*l*. but died before the chancery drafted the letter recording his judgment. Both the comital and royal chanceries used the Carolingian validation clause *recognovi et subscripsi* (McKitterick, *Charlemagne*, 199–204). Since *recognoscere* also was used in the twelfth century by those who made public, hence oral, admissions or statements of fact in court, it is highly likely that the new chancellor read the letter out loud in court.

5. King Lothair (954–86) granted the palatine title to Herbert of Vermandois, whose lands in Champagne the counts of Blois inherited; Count Odo II of Blois carried the palatine honorific in 1021 (Bur, *Formation*, 156–57, 191, 230).

6. *Actes*, no. 26, 1152. The original document (BnF, Lat. n.a. 2567, no. 4), with a well-preserved seal of brown wax on red threads, is like the equestrian seals of Guy II of Châtillon and William I of Dampierre (Baudin, *Les sceaux*, 336); see also Chassel, "L'usage du sceau," and Bony, *Un siècle de sceaux figurés*. Henry's brother Thibaut V, count of Blois, adopted a similar seal, with an inscription reading "Seal of Thibaut, count of Blois," but their younger brother Stephen, count of Sancerre, adopted a variant of their father's seal, with his horse galloping to the left; see Baudin, *Les sceaux*, Corpus (CD-ROM), nos. 44–46.

7. Chassel, *Sceaux*, 43, fig. 33 (color photograph of Henry's seal of 1168): *Sigillum Henrici Trecensium Palatini Comitis*. See also Bony, *Un siècle de sceaux figurés*, 28, plate XII, fig. 63 (of 1163), and Baudin, *Les sceaux*, illustration 7, and Corpus (CD-ROM), no. 5 (color photo of undated seal).

8. The colored threads were bundled in several combinations of red, green, yellow, blue, and white (Arbois de Jubainville, "Sigillographie," 15–18). Baudin, *Les sceaux*, 220, finds no pattern in the color of the wax seals, except for the increase in green wax after 1170.

9. Baudin, *Les sceaux*, Corpus (CD-Rom), no. 6. Baudin, "Les sceaux du comte Henri Ier," 96–109, catalogues all of Henry's known seals, which became the model for all subsequent comital seals in Champagne (Baudin, *Les sceaux*, 102, table 4).

10. *Actes*, no. 18, 1152 (a photograph of the original letter in *Splendeurs*, 57, fig. 15). I take the chancellor's quote as being a verbatim record of Henry's words.

11. The canons still had a papal confirmation of Count Hugh's gift and Count Thibaut's confirmation of their possession of the church of St-Denis with its immunities (*Acta Pontificum Romanorum inedita*, 1: 147–48, no. 169, 28 April 1132). Count Thibaut initially refused to recognize the exemption of the bishop's agents from his officials but agreed to contact Count Hugh, who was in Palestine at the time (1125–30). Hugh's deposition states that the bishop's agents were exempt from all "secular lordship" except if caught committing a crime (AD Aube, G 465, seventeenth-century copy of a notice). My thanks to Charles West for pointing out the reference and its significance.

12. Bernard already may have been afflicted with the serious ailments he described in a letter to Arnold (Bredero, *Bernard of Clairvaux*, 102–18).

13. The cathedral canons obtained a papal confirmation of Henry's letter reaffirming their claim, that Count Hugh had exempted them from his jurisdiction and taxes in the suburb of St-Denis (*St-Pierre*, 23–27, no. 17, 31 December 1152). An inventory of 1319/20 lists the "*capellus* of Count Henry*"* in the "large treasury" (Lalore, *Inventaires*, 2: 7, no. 43).

14. Renoux, "Espaces et lieux de pouvoirs," 30–33; Héliot, "Sur les résidences princières," 37; and Roserot, *Dictionnaire*, 3: 1655. The donjon was later called the Tower of Homages (photograph in *Splendeurs*, 8).

15. Arbois de Jubainville, *Histoire*, 2: 76, and Roserot, *Dictionnaire*, 3: 1654–55.

16. Count Hugh held court there "in the hall of the count" (*Montiéramey*, 29–22, no. 16, 1100). Renoux, "Espaces et lieux de pouvoirs," discusses the Carolingian precedents of the "palace" as consisting of an *aula, camerae,* and a *capella*

17. Hubert, "La vie commune des clercs," 150–51, compares the campus in Troyes with those of other chapters.

18. William of St-Denis, *Sugerii vita,* in Suger, *Oeuvres,* 2: 337 (restoration of the royal residence and rebuilding of the walls and towers).

19. Biddle, "Wolvesey."

20. *Actes,* nos. 22–23, both April 1152.

21. *Actes,* no. 21, ca. 13 March 1152.

22. *Actes,* no. 24, 30 March–18 April 1152: *pro mea prosperitate et salute.*

23. Nees, "The *Fastigum* of Saint-Remi."

24. Turner, *Eleanor of Aquitaine,* 104–12, recounts Eleanor's divorce and remarriage. Sassier, *Louis VII,* 232–33, accepts the possibility of Eleanor's infidelities. For Louis, the risk of her bearing an illegitimate royal heir and the incessant rumors that besmirched the king's dignity outweighed the loss of her vast inheritance.

25. Robert of Torigni, *Chronicle,* 165–66.

26. *Cartulary of Countess Blanche,* 104–6, no. 84 (9 July) 1217 and 372–74, no. 416, 9 July 1217 (two virtually identical copies of Guy's deposition); no. 416 is trans. in Evergates, *Documents,* 38–39, no. 25. See Sassier, *Recherches,* 84–90, and Evergates, *Aristocracy,* 102.

27. *Actes,* no. 42, 1153: *anno illo quo filiam ipsius regis affiduciavi.* That phrase was repeated in a second letter (*Actes,* no. 37, 19 April 1153–3 April 1154).

28. Adelaide died there in 1154 after commissioning her own tomb, the earliest surviving effigy tomb of a French queen (Nolan, *Queens in Stone and Silver,* 47–64).

29. See ch. 6 at n. 3.

30. King, *King Stephen,* 270–300.

31. Thibaut became seneschal between 1 August and 24 November 1154 (Luchaire, *Études,* 47).

32. Graboïs, "De la trêve de Dieu à la paix du roi," 592–93, 594–95 n. 3 (text).

33. See ch. 4 at n. 103.

34. Bishop Anscoul of Soissons excommunicated the cathedral canons and the entire town because the canons claimed the right to interdict; the king heard the case and decided for the canons (*RHF* 15: 681 note a). Sassier, *Louis VII,* 269, notes the irony of the king notifying the pope of the council's decision to confirm the chapter's right to interdict.

35. Dufour, *Le strade cristiane per Roma,* provides excellent maps of the several stages of the *via francigena* and photographs of what travelers would have seen along the way.

36. *Actes,* no. 51, 1154.

37. LoPrete, *Adela of Blois,* 457, no. 27

38. See Demouy, *Genèse d'une cathédrale,* 624–28, for a brief biography of Samson.

39. *Actes,* no. 51, 1154.

40. Quantin, *Yonne,* 1: 537–40, no. 377, 11 April 1156, papal confirmation of the possessions of the archbishop of Sens.

41. Gillingham, "Doing Homage," describes the twelfth-century practice of the kings of England, who had their minor heirs do homage to the king of France in order to confirm their Continental inheritances.

42. *Actes,* no. 95, 1157, without witnesses, presented in Troyes by Chancellor William. This document has been taken as a "foundation charter," that is, marking the beginning of the

chapel's construction next to an already built residence; in fact, it speaks of the church as if it already existed and itemizes the chapter's substantial possessions acquired by that date. Chapin, *Les villes de foires*, 18, reads the text in the same way.

43. *Actes*, no. 107, 1158, known through two eighteenth-century copies: one with the date of 1159, the other with 1158 (which I have adopted, following Lalore and the *Actes*). In either case, 1158 or 1159, the chapel must have been roofed by that date.

44. *Actes*, no. 125, 1159: *ex parte mea*.

45. Brühl, *Palatium und Civitas*, 1: 149–50, reaches the same conclusion, that the new residence and chapel were built concurrently and were essentially completed by 1157. The rapidity of construction was due to Count Henry's substantial resources and to the easy access to quarries nearby at Bar-sur-Seine, from which stone was transported by water directly to the gate of Croncels in Troyes, and at Tonnerre, from which stone was carted to Troyes; see Piétresson de Saint-Aubin, "La fourniture de la pierre," 570–73, 591–92.

46. *Langres*, no. 17, 1157.

47. Grant, *Abbot Suger of St-Denis*, 238–74.

48. See ch. 1 at n. 46.

49. Biddle, "Wolvesey," 32, notes the similarity to Wolvesey, the episcopal residence built in the early 1130s by Bishop Henry in Winchester, except that it lacked a fortified tower. See King, *King Stephen*, plate 8 (a reconstruction of Wolvesey as it was in 1171).

50. In 1188 Count Henry II stated that his father had given six *modii* of wine from the storeroom on the ground floor of the comital residence (*in cellario meo Trecensi*); see Arbois de Jubainville, *Histoire*, 3: 474–75, no. 156, 1188.

51. It was in Count Henry's bedroom (*in thalamis comitis*) that Henry licensed Geoffroy of Bar-le-Duc to mortgage his fief worth 100*l.* to the Templars, that is, the 10*l.* he collected annually from the market at Ramerupt (*Actes*, no. 458, 1176). Since that was an entirely private matter between Henry and Geoffroy, the document lacks any mention of witnesses.

52. See ch. 9 n. 27.

53. Pastan, "Realpolitik and Artistic Patronage," 536, and "Fit for a Count," 368–70, who notes the similarity of the architecture and glazing to those of St-Étienne of Sens. Dectot, "Les tombeaux," 31, gives the length as 40 meters, excluding the tribune and radiating chapels, and the width as 13 meters (3 meters for each aisle and 7 meters for the nave). The twelfth-century chapel lacked the spire and top of the tower depicted in the later anonymous sketch. The construction of St-Étienne of Sens was begun by Archbishop Henry Sanglier (1122–42) and continued by his successor Hugh of Toucy (1142–68). Its large central nave, built to accommodate crowds of pilgrims—"the conquest of space in width" (Bony, *French Gothic Architecture*, 72)—required ogival vaulting (Henriet, "La cathédrale Saint-Étienne de Sens"). It has been characterized as "utterly simple" in plan and detail (Severens, "The Early Campaign at Sens" and "The Continuous Plan"), and unique in medieval Europe, a reprise of the earliest Constantinian basilicas and "the first Gothic cathedral" (Erlande-Brandenburg, "La cathédrale Saint-Étienne de Sens," 35–38). Von Simson, *The Gothic Cathedral*, 142, concurs. William of Sens, the architect of St-Étienne of Sens, may have had a hand in the derivative design of Count Henry's chapel. The cathedral of Sens was the architectural model for St-Germain-des-Prés in Paris and St-Quiriace of Provins.

54. Some sense of the chapel's interior can be seen in the surviving church of St-Quiriace of Provins, whose earlier frame was modified in the 1160s according to the same Gothic architectural model; see Timbert, "Le chevet de la collégiale Saint-Quiriace de Provins." St-Étienne was unusual in having a room built off the nave, which may have served initially as Henry's treasury/

archive and perhaps library; Pastan, "Fit for a Count," 370–71, notes that the treasury's location off the choir was more common in Rhineland churches.

55. Pastan, "*Realpoltik* and Artistic Patronage," 538–39 and photograph (29.4). See also *Splendeurs*, 57, fig. 16.

56. *Actes*, no. 76, 26 February 1156: the monks were exempted from feeding his traveling officials, except on presentation of his sealed letter.

57. Philip of Harvengt, *Ad Henricum*, 154–55; trans. adapted from Benton, "Court" (1959), 143.

58. *Actes*, no. 95, item 22, 1157.

59. *Actes*, no. 95, items 32–36, 1157.

60. *Actes*, no. 195, 2 September 1163: Henry promised Abbot Guitier of St-Loup the fifth vacant prebend.

61. The plan of the quarter, which may reflect the site at a later date, locates some canons' houses beyond the compound. The canons of St-Quiriace likewise had houses in Provins beyond the cloister (*Actes*, no. 166, item 1, 1166).

62. It is possible that chancery personnel moved there only after Stephen became chancellor in 1176. He was a canon of St-Étienne by 1167 and succeeded the count's brother William as provost of St-Quiriace in 1169 before becoming chancellor (1176–79). He bequeathed St-Étienne a 20*s.* rent from his stone house located between the hospital of St-Étienne and the chancellor's house (*Obituaires*, 4: 417, 28 November: *Obiit Stephanus cancellarius et canonicus hujus ecclesie, qui dedit nobis xx s. annui redditus in domo sua lapidea, que est inter Domus Dei et domum cancellarii*). If the chancery was transferred to the "house of the chancellor" under Stephen, its new location might explain the destruction of the chancery archives in the fire of 1188, which devastated much of the old city within the walls, including the cathedral. If so, the room off the nave of St-Étienne might have functioned not as a chancery/archive but as a library and treasury, where Henry II deposited his fief rolls in 1190 before leaving on crusade; see the letter from Geoffroy of Villehardouin and Milo II Breban (*Cartulary of Countess Blanche*, 294–95, no. 333, ca. 1209).

63. Roserot, *Dictionnaire*, 3: 1563, reasonably concludes that the hospital was founded and built concurrently with St-Étienne. The earliest mention is in 1174 (*Actes*, no. 371: *domus Dei que est ante ecclesiam Beati Stephani*). After the fire of 1188, which destroyed the hospital and its records, Count Henry II confirmed its substantial portfolio of properties and rents acquired in the preceding three decades (Benton, "Recueil," 1189j). In his testament of ca. 1190 Hagan of Ervy left 20*s.* revenue to "the count's hospital in Troyes" for an anniversary Mass (Quantin, *Yonne*, 2: 424–25, no. 420), but it was still known as the "Hospital of St-Étienne" in 1207 (*Cartulary of Countess Blanche*, 82–83, no. 54).

64. Herbert (of Villemaur) was deacon of St-Étienne (*Actes*, no. 125, 1 February 1159; no. 195, 2 September, 1163) and chanter (*Actes*, no. 310, 1170). He was probably the same as Master Herbert, a physician, who resigned his prebend at St-Étienne (Arbois de Jubainville, *Histoire*, 4.2, no. 490, August 1199) after Countess Marie appointed him *procurator pauperum* of the hospital. He resigned that office in February 1223, n.s. (BnF, Lat. 5993A = Chancery Cartulary 8, fol. 551r).

65. The leper house founded by Count Hugh in 1123, Les Deux-Eaux of Troyes, was the earliest and largest of its kind (Touati, *Maladie et société*, 261–62). See also Roserot, *Dictionnaire*, 3: 1563–64.

66. Henry II gave the *annualia* as an enhancement of his father's endowment for the hospital (Benton, "Recueil," 1189j).

67. In 1169 St-Martin-ès-Aires was identified as being located *juxta urbem* (*St-Pierre*, 81–85,

no. 73), which I take as a reference to the wall surrounding "the suburb of the bishop." In 1173 Count Henry franchised the oven that his agent Mathieu of Troyes had built "at the Gate of the Bears," that is, just inside the new wall (*Actes*, no. 359).

68. In 1163 the count affirmed his right to grant the sixth available prebend "in consultation with the chapter" (*Actes*, no. 195).

69. Otto of Freising, *Gesta*, 180–81 (*Deeds*, 186–87), bk. 3, cap. 12.

70. Hubert, "La vie commune," 129, likens the canons' quarter in Troyes to a "cité-jardin."

71. *Chronicon Universale Anonyme Laudunensis*, 18–19, undated comment added after the writer remarks that Louis VII, having replaced the secular canons at Compiègne with monks, asked the pope to confirm that institutional reformation, which the writer dates to 1173. He then remarks: "About that time" Count Henry assigned sixty "most excellent" prebends to "secular clerics" in St-Étienne. The writer is reporting hearsay and obviously is unsure of the date, but the only time that Louis VII is known to have visited Troyes was in 1157.

72. *PL* 196: 1651–52, no. 56 (= *RHF* 16: 700–701, no. 3), an undated letter in the collection of his letters presented to Henry ca. 1160; modified trans. of Benton, "Court" (1959), 137–38.

73. Philip of Harvengt (born ca. 1100), prior (1130) then abbot of Bonne-Espérance (1158–December 1182, died 11 April 1183). His various works are in *PL* 203. For his life, see Robertson, "Correspondence and Hagiographical Works of Philip of Harvengt."

74. *Ad Henricum*, *PL* 203: 151–56, no. 17 (= *RHF* 16: 703–6, no. 16), partial trans. as "Letter to Henry, Count of Champagne," in Nederman and Forhan, *Medieval Political Theory*, 64–66. Philip's collection of twenty-four letters includes two addressed to laymen, Counts Henry of Champagne and Philip of Flanders; they are compared in Robertson, "Correspondence and Hagiographical Works of Philip of Harvengt," 40–65. Philip's precise personal references were intended to be seen by (or read to) Henry, and the substance of the letter—praise of the count's father and of Henry's own intellectual proclivities, and mention of Henry's lavish decoration of his churches (thinking no doubt about St-Étienne) and generous prebends for secular canons—points to a date of ca. 1160, shortly after Philip became abbot.

75. Nederman, *John of Salisbury*, 23–24, gives the date of completion.

76. Lachaud, *L'éthique du pouvoir*, 125–216.

77. For an analysis of his acts by date and beneficiary, see Bur, in *Actes* 1: x–xi, and *Actes* 2: 71–78.

78. André admitted that he did not have any other customary right or jurisdiction at Villiers-Templon, a village of Marmoutier's priory of Celle-en-Brie, and that the tenants there who owed him two *modii* of oats paid it directly to two knights who held the revenue from him in fief (*Actes*, no. 104, 1158, unspecified place of the session). The count's scribe identified André as lord of La-Ferté-Gaucher because his mother Adelaide resided in her dower castle at Montmirail (1158–66); see Evergates, *Aristocracy*, 175.

79. *Actes*, no. 48, 1154.

80. For a brief biography of Anselm II of Traînel, see Evergates, *Aristocracy*, 242–43. Guy Gasteblé recalled in his testimony in 1217 that Count Henry *tantum diligebat* Anselm (*Cartulary of Countess Blanche*, 104–6, no. 84, 1217). Henry had known Anselm since at least 1145, when Anselm *père* and his son came to Troyes regarding a dispute with the monks of St-Loup over the intermarriage of their respective tenants. The notice drawn up by the monks describes the settlement they reached with Anselm's father, with the consent of his sons Anselm and Garnier and their mother Helisende. Anselm *père* requested that it be confirmed "by the seals of Count Thibaut of good memory and his son Lord Henry, at that time a young man." The document is dated 1145, but since it is known only from a copy, it is impossible to know whether the last

clause was added after Henry's accession (*St-Loup*, 30–31, no. 13 = Arbois de Jubainville, *Histoire*, 3: 432–33, no. 101).

81. Odo of Pougy was in Henry's retinue before 1152 (*Actes*, no. 12). He was remembered in the cathedral's obituary (*Obituaires*, 4: 225, 22 January). At least one brother, and possibly all three, accompanied Henry on his perilous return voyage from the Levant. For the Pougy, see ch. 2 at n. 63.

82. William of Dampierre was very young in 1133 when he and his father witnessed Count Thibaut's act. He was a regular at Henry's court from 1152 and succeeded Odo of Pougy (his wife's stepfather) as constable in 1171/72 (Mathieu, "Recherches," 45–48).

83. Geoffroy III, lord of Joinville from 1137/41, was still a *puer* in 1127, when he witnessed Count Thibaut's act. For his life, see Lusse, "D'Étienne à Jean de Joinville," 12–14.

84. Arbois de Jubainville, *Histoire*, 3: 125–26. Peter the Bursar of Provins witnessed Count Thibaut's acts since 1138 and usually appears in witness lists directly after the barons. In 1140 his name appears under *De curia comitis sunt testes* immediately after Stephen of Garlande and Hulduin of Vendeuvre (Arbois de Jubainville, *Histoire*, 3: 427, no. 95). In Henry's letters he is occasionally called *camerarius*, but he usually appears without title (*Actes*, no. 167, 1161). His first wife Halbide/Havide died ca. 1160 and was buried in St-Quiriace (Benton, "Recueil," 1166d, letter of Countess Marie), where his brother Mathieu was dean of the chapter. An entire quarter of Provins near the new market was named after Peter the Bursar (Mesqui, "Notes," 48 and map 1).

85. Benton, "The Court" (1959), 162–63, calls them "court knights." The Bristaud were a well-to-do knight family from Provins. The brothers Drogo and Peter were regular witnesses to the count's acts, often without title: Drogo, the elder and a knight (1152–77), never held office; Peter (1156–79), who became viscount of Provins through his second marriage (ca. 1161) to its heiress, Heloise of Nangis, witnessed the count's acts (1156–77) and held several comital fiefs (*Feoda* 1, 56, no. 1533; 57, no. 1598 [liege for two fiefs]), but did not return from Henry's crusade in 1179. Their half-brothers were Walter, one of the count's marshals (1152–59), and Mathieu, dean of St-Quiriace of Provins and later bishop of Troyes. See also Verdier, *Saint-Ayoul*, 88–94. Daimbert of Ternantes witnessed forty acts between 1155 and 1179; he may have died on Henry's pilgrimage. He and his two sons owed all-year castle-guard at Bray (*Feoda* 1, 52, no. 1359).

The Le Plessis-Eventat of Bray had comital fiefs in several castellanies and other properties near Preuilly. Hugh Eventat accompanied Count Henry on the Second Crusade and witnessed the count's acts between 1159 and 1176. Geoffroy Eventat witnessed the count's first act in 1145 (*Actes*, no. 2), then in 1158 (*Actes*, no. 121) and thereafter to 1197; he held comital fiefs in Provins and Bray, for which he owed castle-guard (*Feoda* 1, 52, no. 1360; 55, no. 1464, ca. 1178). Girard Eventat, who accompanied Henry to St-Jean-de-Losne in 1162, was the "youngest brother" of Geoffroy Eventat and owed castle-guard at Bray (*Feoda* 1, 53, no. 1361). In 1201, after Countess Blanche surrendered her castles at Bray and Montereau to the king (*Cartulary of Blanche of Champagne*, 405–7, no. 449), Girard drew up a list of the count's knights in the castellany of Bray (Longnon, *Documents*, 1: 99–101, nos. 2608–90). Perhaps it was at that time that he recalled the agreement between Henry and Frederick Barbarossa forty years earlier regarding the *mouvance* of several castles (see ch. 4 at n. 77). The hospital of Provins remembered him in an obituary as *dominus* Girard Eventat, knight, who gave 10 *setiers* of wine annually at Sézanne (*Obituaires*, 4: 965); see also Bur, *Formation*, 405, and Benton, "The Court" (1959), 161–62.

86. For Garnier (of Marigny-le-Châtel) of Traînel, see Roserot, *Dictionnaire*, 2: 862, and Lalore, "Anciens seigneurs de Traînel," 194–95. For Hugh II of Plancy, who witnessed more than forty acts between 1152 and 1179 and two under Countess Marie in 1181–82, see Roserot, *Dictionnaire*, 3: 1131.

87. For a biography of Peter of Blois, see Cotts, *The Clerical Dilemma*, 7–48. If Peter was born ca. 1130, he would have been in his early twenties when he witnessed Count's Henry's first act given "in Troyes in the church of St-Étienne" in the presence of the chapter's fourteen named canons (*Actes*, no. 125, 1 February 1159). He witnessed acts involving monasteries near Troyes in 1154, 1158, 1161, and 1169 (*Actes*, nos. 44, 116, 161, 176, 284).

Peter acquired his early education at Chartres and Tours, but little is known about him before he went to Palermo in 1166 (Türk, *Pierre de Blois*, 13–26). His periodic presence in Troyes suggests a connection with someone of stature there, either Master Girard, archdeacon of Troyes (Williams, "William of the White Hands," 377–78), or perhaps William of Champagne, provost of the cathedral chapter, who after being elected bishop of Chartres on 13 January 1165 promised Peter a prebend at Chartres. In 1167, in his mid-thirties, Peter reappeared in Troyes as "master Peter" witnessing the act by which William, bishop-elect of Sens, claimed a lifetime right to the provostship of the cathedral chapter of Troyes (*St-Pierre*, 27–31, no. 20, 1167). Peter apparently remained in the archbishop's household (1168–70), for he later wrote that he had been forced to give up teaching after returning from Sicily (1168) in order to accept a prebend from Archbishop William (Türk, *Pierre de Blois*, 136–39, no. 24, where Peter's letter appears in approximate chronological order). In 1170/71 Peter left for England, where he became archdeacon of Bath and frequented the royal court. In 1180, in Amiens, he witnessed an act of Archbishop William of Reims under *De sociis domini archiepiscopi* (Williams, "William of the White Hands," 386 n. 20). He must have retained fond memories of his days in Sens with Archbishop William, for he dedicated his *Speculum iuris canonici* (dated 1175–91) to *Domino Remensi*, that is, William of Champagne, who was by then archbishop of Reims (1176–1202).

88. *Actes*, no. 30, 1153, 19 April–28 November. The canons paid Peter 40*s.* to quitclaim his right to mill grain at Frignicourt without charge, and 30*s.* to Peter's lord to guarantee that no layman would ever claim that right again.

89. *Actes*, no. 57, 1154. For Hulduin, lord of half of Vendeuvre castle since 1121, see Roserot, *Dictionnaire*, 2: 1721, and Evergates, *Aristocracy*, 120–21.

90. Henry sealed two letters, one for Guy of Bar-sur-Seine and one for the monks of Quincy, confirming the settlement they had reached earlier (*Actes*, no. 259, 1167).

91. *Actes*, no. 106, 1158, perhaps done at Igny abbey where he stayed with a small traveling party, including his notary William, who probably drafted the letter on the spot. The surrendering lords were Geoffroy, count of Château-Porcien, and his brother Renaud of Rozoy. In another case Henry elicited the testimony of local men to ascertain whether the village of Oyes belonged to the monks there; finding that it did, he declared the lord of Pleurs "never had any right or lordship or custody" (*Actes*, no. 64, April 1155).

92. *Actes*, no. 217, 1164.

93. AD Haute-Marne, 5 H 10, no. 491, 1160, a dispute involving land and granaries.

94. Henry facilitated peace between the monks of LaCrête and Witter of Aubonville by warranting the abbey's adherence to the agreement, while his seneschal Geoffroy of Joinville and Arnold of Reynel warranted Witter (*Actes*, no. 124, 1158). When Henry's companion Hugh of Romilly and his wife Elizabeth were excommunicated for pestering the priory of St-Sépulcre (today Villacerf), which was in the count's custody, Henry convinced the couple to make peace in order to have the sanction lifted (*Actes*, no. 205, 1163).

95. *Actes*, no. 83, 1156. Either the count's provost at Wassy or the community itself (later called La Neuville-à-Remy) retained the count's charter, which is known only from a royal *vidimus* of 1377.

96. *Actes*, no. 31, 1153; he quit his claim only in those villages, not elsewhere in his domain.

97. St-Remi's men at Courtisols paid 10*l.* annually for the count's protection, which he promised never to alienate (*Actes*, nos. 34, 35, 1153). The villagers of Sogny-en-l'Angle paid one *mine* of oats per household, delivered to the count's granary at Vitry (*Actes*, no. 78, 13 August 1156). For lordly violence as a consequence of lordship, see Bisson, *The Crisis of the Twelfth Century.*

98. In one case Count Thibaut reduced a protection tax because the monastic land no longer produced the customary amount of wine; henceforth, the count directed, his advocate could collect only 36 (instead of 100) *modii* of wine and could exercise his right of hospitality only once annually, limited to eight days and a maximum expense of 23*s.* (Tardif, *Monuments,* 245–47, no. 446, 1146, done in Provins).

99. *Actes*, no. 78, 1156.

100. *Actes*, no. 19, between 10 January and 24 March (Easter) 1152, beneficiary-redacted letter in which Henry declared his promise in the presence of his brother Count Thibaut of Blois, his brother-in-law Count William III of Nevers, and his two closest companions, his constable Odo of Pougy and his butler Anselm II of Trâinel. The next year Henry remitted the taxes he had collected there after hearing the villagers from Chablis testify that they, rather than the canons, paid for his procuration of Chablis (*Actes*, no. 43, 1153).

101. Provosts generally received one-third of any fine they imposed. That was implicit in Henry's grant to St-Remi of Reims, whose own provost collected two-thirds of any fine imposed at Condé-sur-Marne, while the count's provost collected one-third, *sicut jus est advocati* (*Actes*, no. 24, 1152).

102. *Actes*, no. 15, 1152.

103. *Actes*, no. 76, 28 February 1156 (n.s).

104. *Actes*, no. 153, 1160. Similarly for the priory of Ventelay, no provost, sergeant, or anyone of the count's household was permitted to receive hospitality in the count's absence (*Actes*, no. 212, 1164).

105. *Actes*, no. 59, 1154: Henry ordered a letter to be written and sealed; the notary William presented it in Troyes.

106. *Actes*, no. 26, 1152. This was Havidis's dowry or the dower from her first marriage.

107. *Actes*, no. 111, 1158.

108. *Actes*, no. 25, 1152. The chancellor wrote at the bottom of the letter that he presented it, probably to the abbot.

109. *Actes*, no. 33, 1153.

110. *Actes*, no. 75, 1156, done in Meaux.

111. *Actes*, no. 56, 1154: the nuns included Thibaut's endowment of 1133 as well as more recent donations, including fiefs, made by local barons and knights. In 1162 they brought another *pancarte* for confirmation, of property acquired during the intervening eight years: the count sealed that prewritten document without vetting by the court after adding two final clauses to it, granting the nuns permission to use his woods (*Actes*, no. 192).

112. Evergates, *Aristocracy*, 17–21.

113. Evergates, *Aristocracy*, ch. 3.

114. Evergates, *Aristocracy*, 68–69.

115. Even Count Thibaut purchased a fief in order to donate it to the Cistercians at Preuilly (*Preuilly*, 24–25, no. 24, between 1139 and 1152).

116. The prior of Coincy, for example, asked for his confirmation of gifts from his ancestors and his barons and knights; the count also allowed them to "have any fief (*beneficium*) conceded as an allod" (*Actes*, no. 42, 1153).

117. *Actes*, no. 168, 1161.

118. *Actes*, no. 98, 1157: Olivier of Drosnay and his son "divested themselves [of the fief] and invested me with it, and I, through my hand, invested the abbot [of La Chapelle-aux-Planches]."

119. *Actes*, no. 90, 1157. In a similar case, Henry confiscated the fief (a tithe) that Oleard of Baslieux had given to the priory of Belval without the count's license, but on complaint by the monks, he allowed it (*Actes*, no. 255, 1167).

120. After confirming the sale of property by Garnier of Bussy-en-Othe and his wife to Dilo, Henry licensed the monks to acquire property from his men "by gift or purchase," that is, without his prior license (*Actes*, no. 86, 1156). In 1156 he confirmed the alienation of his fiefs by the lords of Braine, Bazoches, Montmirail, Simon of Oisy, "or by others" to the monks of Igny "up to the day" of his confirmation (*Actes*, no. 112). To the nuns of Fontaines-les-Nonnes he confirmed "whatever will be given from my fiefs" (*Actes*, no. 76, 1156). To the new chapter of St-Maclou of Bar-sur-Aube he allowed the acquisition of his fiefs "by gift or purchase," provided that he not lose the ligeance or castle-guard of the fief (*Actes*, no. 142, item 6, 1160). Similarly for St-Quiriace, permission to acquire his fiefs "by gift, purchase, or exchange," provided that he not lose their ligeance (*Actes*, no. 166, item 11, 1161).

121. *Actes*, no. 16, sealed but undated (and seriously damaged) letter from the first few months of his rule, after 10 January 1152; a late thirteenth-century dorsal note suggests that Hugh or his descendants transferred the woods together with the count's letter to the nuns of Foissy. Hugh may have been Henry's mentor in the knightly arts whose son Geoffroy witnessed Henry's first sealed act (*Actes*, no. 2, 1145). Hugh died by 1158 (*Actes*, no. 114).

122. *Actes*, no. 116, 1158. See also Chapin, *Les villes de foires*, 79 n. 110.

123. In 1158 the count took the 120*l*. rent that Archambaud held *in feudum* as collateral for a loan of 550*l*. (*Actes*, no. 110 = *Littere Baronum*, 86–87, no. 46). The count explained that he was renewing the fief that his father had granted to Archambaud. Since the loan was not redeemed, Archambaud's grandson, Archambaud II of Sully, returned the letter in 1202 (*Littere Baronum*, 75, no. 34). Odo of Sully, bishop of Paris, sealed a renunciation in that same year (*Littere Baronum*, 121, no. 86, 1202).

124. The count sealed a two-part chirograph (known from the surviving one-half containing the words CLAVIS CYROGRAPHI written on the right side). It describes the settlement that Count Thibaut reached regarding Neuville-au-Temple: the Templars retained jurisdiction over themselves and occupants of the Templar house, while Gorman of Marueil retained his jurisdiction and banal right beyond the village (*Actes*, no. 22, April 1152). Each party needed a copy of the accord reached earlier in the presence of both Thibaut and Henry and witnessed by the old count's court, perhaps in the last months of his life. This document is interesting as well for the motivation Henry ascribes to the settlement: "since my father Thibaut, count of Blois, wished to preserve the right of each, he forcefully urged them to reach a settlement."

125. *Actes*, no. 63, 27 November 1155, done in the abbey's chapter hall (this is the abbey's half-part chirograph). The monks gave property at Dormans to the count, who in turn gave it to Gervais; Gervais paid the monks 50*l*., in effect purchasing the property he held from the count.

126. *Actes*, no. 32, 1153 (*vidimus* of 1382): the count commuted their obligations for an 18*l*. rent.

127. *Actes*, no. 83, 1156. See also Higounet, *Défrichements*, 177–78.

128. The same is true with Henry II of England; see Everard, "Lay Charters and the *Acta* of Henry II."

129. *Acts*, 1: x–xi. The same rate, 1.5 letters per month, holds for the 552 letters from his entire rule, 1152–81.

CHAPTER 4. THE LATE BACHELOR YEARS, 1159–1164

1. *Actes*, no. 141, 1159, presented at Vertus by the chancellor William.

2. If Henry promised Marie her dower on this occasion, the notary may have been entirely correct in regarding her as de facto countess. Fourrier, "Retour au *Terminus*," proves Marie was still betrothed in 1159, not yet married, despite Robert of Torigni's remark that Henry "took back the daughter of King Louis whom he earlier had sent away." Torigni might have referred to the fact that Marie did not cohabit with Henry for another five years after giving her consent to marriage.

3. Dereine, "Chanoines," provides a succinct history of secular canons.

4. Boureau, "Hypothèses sur l'émergence lexicale et théoretique de la catégorie de séculier."

5. *Libellus de diversis ordinibus et professionibus* [ca. 1130–40s], 50–51, 87–107. The issue was acute at Liège, where the movement to impose regular canons was conflated with fighting "heretics" (Brunn, *Des contestaires aux "Cathares"*, esp. 112–24). For contemporary discussions on the nature and variety of religious orders, see Constable, *The Reformation of the Twelfth Century*, 44–87.

6. Forced conversions also occurred in Paris (Pacaut, *Louis VII et son royaume*, 79–80), in Flanders (Meijns, "L'ordre canonial dans le comté de Flandre," esp. 42–44), and in Hainaut (Nazet, *Les chapitres de chanoines séculiers*).

7. See Corbet, "Les collégiales comtales."

8. For Thibaut's attempt to convert St-Quiriace, sometime between 1132 and 1143, and subsequent developments at St-Quiriace, see Vessière, in *St-Quiriace*, 39–41.

9. AN, K 22, no. 1, 1122, act of the bishop of Soissons announcing it; witnesses include his seneschal André of Baudement and Walter I of Montmirail (castellan of Château-Thierry).

10. Conflicts over the status of chapters continued in the 1150s. Abbot Peter of Montier-le-Celle reported that after seculars had taken over the priory of St-Flavit in Villemaur the count's uncle Henry, the (Cistercian) bishop of Troyes, restored the priory (with regular status) to Montier-la-Celle (Peter of Celle, *Letters*, 17–19, no. 7, May 1153x1154: letter to the papal chancellor Cardinal Bandinelli, reporting that the bishop of Paris would explain this case to him in person). Peter also apprised the pope of a lingering issue at his abbey's priory of La Celle-sous-Chantemerle, where regulars had recently replaced seculars, as to whether it still was permissible for laymen to be buried in the priory's cemetery (Peter of Celle, *Letters*, 8–10, no. 3, 1153x1156, and 696–98).

11. In his 1176 confirmation of St-Quiriace's posssssions, Count Henry stated that the restoration of the seculars occurred in September 1157 (*Actes*, no. 425, item 40). Archbishop Hugh reported that Pope Adrian directed him and the two bishops to resolve the dispute (*St-Quiriace*, 236–40, no. 11, 1160). At about the same time Henry exempted St-Quiriace's chapel of St-Laurent (and its grounds within the Fair of May) from all his taxes; see Vessière's analysis in *St-Quiriace*, 46–61.

12. Two years earlier Archdeacon William had helped to resolve the dispute between Henry and the canons of St-Martin of Tours over Henry's rights at Chablis (*Actes*, no. 19, 1157).

13. *Actes*, no. 128, 27 September 1159 (= *St-Quiriace*, 231–32, no. 8), done in Provins: Henry confirms his recent grants to St-Jacques. Henry's seneschal, butler, constable, and treasurer witnessed, as did Mathieu Burda of Provins, precenter of the cathedral of Sens and brother of the count's marshal Walter. Counts Stephen of Sancerre and Thibaut V of Blois sealed separate confirmations (*St-Quiriace*, 231, no. 8).

14. Abbot Renaud of St-Jacques confirmed his acceptance of the terms and listed the

properties and revenues that the regulars took with them, including 100*l.* in annual revenue and 300*l.* cash for building their new quarters (*St-Quiriace*, 233–34, no. 9, 1160). Renaud's letter addressed to Mathieu, dean of the seculars at St-Quiriace, is interesting in that it addresses him with the familiar *tu*. Mathieu sealed a corresponding letter on behalf of the seculars of St-Quiriace (*St-Quiriace*, 235, no. 10, 1160), and Archbishop Hugh of Sens sealed letters confirming the endowments of both chapters (*St-Quiriace*, 236–40, nos. 11–12, 1160). Alexander III confirmed the separation of the canons (*St-Quiriace*, 245–48, no. 17, 15 July 1164, done in Sens), then confirmed St-Quiriace's possessions (*St-Quiriace*, 248–51, no. 18, 16 July 1164, done in Sens).

15. *St-Quiriace*, 244, no. 15, 1163.

16. Mathieu, son of Herbert Senex of Provins, had been a canon of Sens cathedral since 1134, and precentor since 1142, the year that Hugh of Toucy became archbishop. In 1148 he appeared with Simon Aurea Capra, prior of St-Ayoul of Provins, at Count Thibaut's court at Jouy to confirm his gift to the priory (*Montier-la-Celle*, 30–31, no. 24). He became dean of St-Quiriace by 1160 (*St-Quiriace*, 235, no. 10), then bishop of Troyes (1169–80). His brothers (or half-brothers) were Peter Bristaud, viscount of Provins (1156–79); the knight Drogo Bristaud, who witnessed a number of the count's acts (1152–77); and the marshal Walter of Provins (1152–60). John of Salisbury described Mathieu to Pope Adrian IV as a learned scholar (*Letters*, 1: 30, no. 18, autumn 1156). See Benton, "The Court" (1959), 158–60, and Verdier, *Saint-Ayoul de Provins*, 88–94.

17. The regulars at St-Jacques reopened the case in 1164 while Alexander III was at Sens; he chose to ratify the earlier arrangement but artfully increased by 40*l.* the annual revenue owed to the regulars (*St-Quiriace*, 245–48, no. 17, 15 July 1164). The next day the pope confirmed St-Quiriace's possessions (*St-Quiriace*, 248–51, no. 18, 16 July 1164) as listed in Count Henry's letter of confirmation (1161), together with acquisitions made since 1161.

18. *Actes*, no. 166, items 3, 7, 10, 1161: I read *duas partes decimi omnium redditum* as two-tenths, or 20 percent of the fair revenues.

19. The revenue came from the tithe at Quincy, which Henry had granted in fief to Hugh of Cornillon but then repurchased from Hugh in 1164 for 160*l.* cash, representing about 16*l.* in annual revenue (*Actes*, no. 238, 1166, reporting the transfer of two years earlier).

20. Timbert, "Le chêvet de la collégiale Saint-Quiriace de Provins," 243–44, and "Le déambulatoire de la collégiale Saint-Quiriace." Timbert concludes that the footprint for St-Quiriace was set in the 1140s and that the lower walls of a new church were already built up to the portals when Henry succeeded in 1152. A "master of St-Quiriace" undertook to finish the structure in the new Gothic style, but that work apparently stopped in the 1170s, not to resume until 1238. St-Quiriace lacked a tribune like the one in St-Étienne of Troyes, perhaps because constraints in the existing fabric allowed only a narrow stairway leading to an upper elevation. Maillé, *Provins*, 1: 5–173, analyzes the church and its setting.

21. Mesqui, "Le palais des comtes," 350–53, finds the two residences similar in conception.

22. Mesqui, *Provins*, 49–52, concludes that the tower was built under Henry in the 1150s or 1160s on the site of an older tower.

23. *Actes*, no. 136, 1159: Henry paid the abbot of St-Oyend a 10*l.* rent for his consent. He already had good relations with the monks, having confirmed their possessions at Sermaise in 1149 while still an apprentice count (Blampignon, *Bar-sur-Aube*, 399–402, no. 21).

24. *Actes*, no. 147, 1160; Henry also gave 300*s.* from the *taille* paid by his men there. He reissued the charter with few changes in 1170 (*Actes*, no. 301).

25. The endowment grew appreciably between 1161 (*Actes*, no. 166) and 1176 (*Actes*, no. 425), but in 1165 the bishop of Langres removed the canons to Ste-Madeleine "until they are able to have houses" (Arbois de Jubainville, *Histoire de Bar-sur-Aube*, 144, no. 9).

26. Manasses of Villemaur, son of the viscount of Villemaur, was archdeacon of Troyes and dean of St-Étienne in 1160 (*Actes*, no. 154).

27. Roric was archdeacon of Meaux (*Actes*, no. 147, 1160) and one of the original canons of St-Étienne (*Actes*, no. 125, 1159). In 1153 he gave the fief he held from the count of Brienne to the monks of La Chapelle-aux-Planches, with the consent of his wife and his brother Nevel's children (*Actes*, no. 41). Nevel of Ramerupt-Aulnay was close to the count in the 1150s before becoming Countess Marie's personal knight-escort (see ch. 6 at n. 6). Roric left his prebend to the cathedral of Meaux in the count's memory (Benton, "Recueil," 1188x). His fief in Meaux (*Feoda* 1, no. 1147) reverted to the count after his death ca. 1190.

28. There are three references to young William of Champagne in England: (1) Herbert of Bosham's letter (*Epistolae*, 229–33, no. 5) to Archbishop William of Sens recalled him as a *parvulus* in England; (2) William was reported to have seen the holy man Gilbert while a *juvenus* in England (Foreville and Keir, *The Book of St Gilbert*, 176–78); (3) Becket's cleric wrote to William while archbishop of Sens: "You were in England with your uncle the bishop of Winchester when this occurred" (a reference to Roger of Pont l'Évêque, at the time archdeacon of Canterbury, 1148/49–54, then of York); see John of Salisbury, *Letters*, 2: 746, no. 307. I thank Ruth R. Cline for pointing out the significance of these references.

29. Bernard of Clairvaux, *Epistolae*, in *Opera*, 8: 181–82, no. 271, 1151 (*Letters*, 419–20, no. 341, with a date of 1147; and 548 [table of dates]). A date of 1151 accords better with the sequence proposed here.

30. Peter of Celle, *Letters*, 10–13, no. 4, 1154x56 (probably 1155 or 1156), to Adrian IV.

31. William replaced Bishop Hato's nephew Odo, provost of the cathedral chapter since 1133 (*St-Pierre*, 10–12, no. 8). Odo might have accompanied his sister Mathilda to Champagne in 1126 for her marriage to Count Thibaut. William appears as provost of St-Quiriace in 1163, listed as the first witness to an act of Mathieu, dean of St-Quiriace (*St-Quiriace*, 244, no. 15). In renewing the fairs of Provins in 1164, Count Henry named William ("my brother") first among the witnesses, then the four most important canons of St-Quiriace: the dean Mathieu, the treasurer Rainard, Haice of Plancy, and Master Stephen (*Actes*, no. 214, 1164). After his election as archbishop of Sens, William passed the office of provost of St-Quiriace to Master Stephen (*St-Quiriace*, 255–56, no. 23, ca. 1169). As archbishop of Reims in 1199, William still collected revenues in Provins acquired from his father (*Littere Baronum*, 127, no. 93 = *Cartulary of Countess Blanche*, 272–73, no. 304).

32. Mathorez, *Guillaume aux Blanche-Mains*, 196–97.

33. *Actes*, no. 174, 1161: Henry called the obligation *servitium pro feodo*.

34. *Actes*, no. 195, 1163. The canons of St-Loup had approached Henry regarding a local lord who was harassing one of their villages. Since the canons of St-Étienne had access to "noble and more powerful persons," said the count, they could take care of the matter.

35. André of Baudement was the count's seneschal (1111–33), a Cistercian monk (1133–37), then abbot of Chaalis (1137–42); see Evergates, *Aristocracy*, 270 n. 28, and Peyrafort-Huin, *La bibliothèque médiévale de Pontigny*, 26.

36. In 1170 Henry extended that institutional association to the monks of St-Jean-en-Châtel, where his friend Nicholas of Montiéramey was prior (*Actes*, no. 307).

37. *Actes*, no. 163, 23 October 1161: the relics were sold to furnish lighting in the monks' church.

38. *Actes*, no. 173, 1161: Arnulf, *aurifaber comitis*. Nothing is known about him or the goldsmith Guibert (*Actes*, no. 211, 1163).

39. An inventory of St-Étienne's relics in 1319/20 describes them; see Lalore, *Inventaires*, 2: 5 (no. 24), 13 (no. 111), 20 (no. 164), 24 (no. 202).

40. Hany-Longuespé, "Les vestiges de Saint-Étienne," 31.

41. The count's act promising Peter of Montier-la-Celle the fifth available prebend at St-Étienne, with a 50s. revenue annually until the prebend became vacant, was witnessed by twenty-three named canons of St-Étienne: the provost, dean, chanter, succentor, schoolmaster, seven priests, four deacons, and seven subdeacons (*Actes*, no. 195, 2 September 1163). The anonymous Chronicle of Laon states that Henry funded sixty canons at St-Étienne, an exceptionally large number that must have included prebends for nonresident canons (see ch. 3 at n. 71).

42. For St-Quiriace, see *Actes*, no. 425, item 43, 1176, where Count Henry noted that its foundation charter allowed up to one hundred prebends but that he was reducing that number to forty-four; in addition, following the customs of the church of Sens, nonresident canons were allowed to collect only 20s. annually, a token 1l. For St-Maclou, see Corbet, "Les collégiales comtales," 204–6.

43. A foundation act does not survive, but Henry's transfer of the fairs at Rebais to Sézanne in 1161 suggests that he intended the fair revenues to support the new chapter of St-Nicolas of Sézanne (*Actes*, no. 163). In 1164 Henry prohibited the canons there from selling or mortgaging any property they received from him (as a prebend); all prebends reverted to the chapter after their deaths (*Actes*, no. 219). Compare the chapter's endowment fifteen years later (*Actes*, no. 495, 1 April–mid-May 1179).

44. *Actes*, no. 430, 1176: the count promised not to appoint additional canons at Sézanne until the seven promised prebends were received and the total number of prebends was reduced to thirty-four (*Actes*, no. 416, undated but between 1164 and 1175).

45. *Actes*, no. 350, 1173: Count Stephen of Sancerre had asked Henry to promise a local priory a prebend there. In 1175 Henry increased the chapter's endowment with his own revenues in Bray (20 percent of the tolls collected by his provost there) and authorized an unspecified increase in the number of prebends (*Actes*, no. 395). He acknowledged that Milo, viscount of Bray, had founded the chapter but spoke as if he were funding the prebends.

46. The fifth available prebend at St-Étienne, which Count Henry promised in 1163 to Abbot Guitier of St-Loup (*Actes*, no. 195), was still outstanding in 1173, when Henry promised the third available prebend to the abbot of St-Martin-ès-Aires of Troyes, that is, after St-Loup and the priory at Traînel received their promised prebends (*Actes*, no. 365).

47. Advice of Bishop John of Poitiers, one of Becket's oldest friends (*Thomas Becket, Correspondence*, 1: 214–19, no. 51, early August 1165, after Becket had settled in Pontigny). By a curious coincidence in that very year, Henry asked the abbot of Cluny to return its prebend in the cathedral of Troyes, which the abbot did (*St-Pierre*, 27–28, no. 18, 1164: letter of Abbot Stephen of Cluny to Bishop Henry of Troyes, accepting a 12l. annual revenue from Count Henry in lieu of the prebend). In a separate letter, the prior of Cluny confirmed the resignation of that prebend to the bishop: it was "against the practice of our church," he said, "but for the love of the count, I have confirmed it with my seal" (*St-Pierre*, 28–29, no. 19, 1165). Bishop Hato gave that prebend to Cluny in 1140/42 (*St-Pierre*, 12–14, no. 9). It would be interesting to know whether that recovered prebend was intended for Becket in exile.

48. Philip of Harvengt, *Ad Henricum*, 154. See also Putter, "Knights and Clerics," 252–53.

49. The 150 canons do not include nonresident canons. If St-Étienne did in fact have 60 canons in ca. 1160 (see ch. 3 at n. 71), Henry would have created a total of at least 170 canons (Arbois de Jubainville, *Histoire*, 3: 178–79, counted 190 canons). Earlier 23 cathedral canons witnessed an act of Bishop Hato of Troyes: the provost, 4 archdeacons, 5 priests, 2 deacons, 10 subdeacons, and the chancellor (*St-Pierre*, 16–17, no. 13, ca. 1146). The chapter of St-Loup of

Troyes had 16 regular canons: an abbot, a prior, 5 priests, 3 deacons, and 6 subdeacons, not counting pluralists (*Actes*, no. 195, 2 September 1163).

50. See ch. 6 at n. 23.

51. Diggelmann, "Marriage as Tactical Response," accepts the date of May rather than October 1160 for the marriage agreement (text in *Recueil des actes de Henri II*, 251–53, no. 141, in Rouen = *RHF* 16: 21–23, no. 80). Among those present besides Count Henry were his nephew Hugh, bishop of Durham (son of Henry's paternal aunt Agnes), Count Thierry of Flanders, the counts of Beaumont and Soissons, and the bishops of Lisieux, Bayeux, and Evreux.

52. *Historia gloriosi regis Ludovici VII*, 129. Dufour, "Adèle de Champagne," provides a biographical sketch.

53. Ralph of Diceto, *Ymagines*, 1: 303.

54. Canon Stephen (of La Chapelle-en-Brie) was brother of the royal treasurers Adam and Gautier; see Falkenstein, "Étienne de la Chapelle."

55. *Historia gloriosi regis Ludovici VII*, 129.

56. Diggelmann, "Marriage as a Tactical Response," 957–59 and 962–63.

57. Dunbabin, "Henry II and Louis VII," 53–54.

58. Date of death is given by the obituary of Collinance priory near Meaux, which she and Thibaut founded ca. 1135 (*Obituaires*, 4: 203).

59. In 1154 she sealed a letter for the Paraclete confirming the bequest of her cleric William, who probably drafted the letter, of a tithe revenue he had purchased earlier with Count Thibaut's approval (*Paraclet*, 74–75, no. 55, 1154, done at La Celle-sous-Chantemerle). Her baker, treasurer, two knights, and two squires witnessed.

60. *Actes*, no. 152, 1160: her bequest of three mills and 35*l.* annually from the tolls in Provins. Stephen, "canon of Troyes" and close associate of Henry since 1153 (*Actes*, no. 27, 22 May), became provost of St-Quiriace after William of Champagne's election as bishop of Chartres (1169), and then Count Henry's chancellor (1176–80). Most likely he was the same Stephen who was Henry's tutor in 1134 (as suggested by Bezzola, *Les origines et la formation de la littérature courtoise*, 3.2: 370 n. 3); that is, he was an old friend of the family.

61. *Actes*, no. 149, 1160.

62. For a recent summary of Alexander III's life, see Duggan, "Alexander *ille meus.*"

63. Falkenstein, "Alexandre III et Henri de France," provides the most detailed account of the archbishop's relations with the pope. See also Demouy, *Genèse d'une cathédrale*, 419, and "Henri de France et Louis VII."

64. Cheney, "The Recognition of Pope Alexander III."

65. Sassier, *Louis VII*, 307–30, provides a clear summary of events. Detailed accounts are in Schmale, "Friedrich I. und Ludwig VII"; Pacaut, "Louis VII et Alexandre III"; and Laudage, *Alexander III. und Friedrich Barbarossa*, 101–49, and esp. 129–41 for Count Henry. See also an analysis of Henry's dealings in Heinemeyer, "Die Verhandlungen an der Saône," 156–71.

66. *MGH Constitutiones*, 1: 289, no. 207, 31 May 1162. For the notion of *amicitia* as used by prelates in difficult negotiations, see Haseldine, "Friends, Friendship and Networks."

67. Demouy, "Henri de France et Louis VII," 53–54.

68. Hugh of Poitiers, *Chronique*, 525 (*Vézelay Chronicle*, 241–42). Hugh of Poitiers (died 1167), secretary to Abbot Pons of Vézelay, provides an engaging, if selective, account of the events.

69. Laudage, *Alexander III. und Friedrich Barbarossa*, 133, concludes that Louis had been duped by a "cunning intrigue" between Count Henry and Frederick Barbarossa. Such an interpretation ignores Henry's very close ties forged with Louis since the Second Crusade, and the

fact that Henry was betrothed to Louis's eldest daughter and Henry's youngest sister was Louis's new queen.

70. *RHF* 16: 690–91, no. 14, Frederick's letter to the archbishop of Lyons, in which he depicted Count Henry as the king's "legate" rather than as an independent mediator, and suggested that the archbishop attend with his suffragans "so that we definitively confirm Victor as pope." Frederick sent a similar letter to the king's brother, Archbishop Henry of Reims, in effect inviting him to come to St-Jean-de-Losne in order to consecrate Victor IV (*RHF* 16: 30–31); the archbishop forwarded a copy of the letter to the king, perhaps to expose Count Henry's apparent duplicity (*RHF* 16: 31).

71. Hugh of Poitiers, *Chronique*, 524–28 (*Vézelay Chronicle*, 240–45). That Henry was dealing independently with Frederick emerges from his letter to Louis: he was forwarding one of two identical letters from the emperor, he said, without stating their content (*RHF* 16: 68, no. 215, dated by the editor to 1163).

72. *Actes*, no. 184, September 1162, done in Châtillon-sur-Seine.

73. Jaksch, *Geschichte Kärntens*, 1: 295–97.

74. Hugh of Poitiers, *Chronique*, 526 (*Vézelay Chronicle*, 243).

75. Helmold of Bosau, *Helmoldi presbyteri bozoviensis Chronica Slavorum*, 178 (*Chronicle of the Slavs*, 238–39).

76. Jaksch, *Monumenta historica ducatus Carinthiae*, 3: nos. 1053–54, 7 and 8 September 1162.

77. Two entries regarding this affair were added to the chancery's roll of fiefs (1178) for Châtillon (Longnon, *Documents*, 1: 83, no. 2283). One records Girard Eventat's recollection (ca. 1201?) of Count Henry's pledge to place himself in captivity if the king did not abide by the negotiated *conventiones* with the emperor; Girard said that he could remember the names of only four of the castles at issue: Bourmont, Raucourt, Is-en-Bassigny, and Monthureaux-en-Vosges. The second entry is an abstract of a letter from imperial chancellor Conrad, bishop of Metz and Speyer (1212–24), perhaps written after Count Thibaut IV's marriage to Gertrude of Dagsburg ca. 1220, in which he names the nine castles, no doubt copied from a written memorandum: Belrain, Bourmont, Cornay, Dampierre-le-Château, Gondrecourt, Lafauche, Possesse, Raucourt, and Reynel. The last two castles named by Girard Eventat are not in Conrad's list, suggesting that Girard may have misremembered events in 1162, forty years earlier, although Bur, "Recherches sur la frontière," 167–68, accepts Girard's testimony as essentially correct. See the analyses in Arbois de Jubainville, *Histoire*, 4: 47–65; Heinemeyer, "Die Verhandlungen an der Saône"; and Bur, *Formation*, 405–8, and "La frontière entre la Champagne et la Lorraine," 147 (map), 154–56.

78. Bur, "Recherches sur la frontière,"164–71, and Parisse, "La frontière de la Meuse," who maps the shifting location of meetings between the French and German monarchs.

79. At Moret (Luchaire, *Études sur les actes de Louis VII*, 420, no. 479, *in colloquio*) and at Châlons (*Actes*, no. 202, 1163: "done in the church of St-Memmie, when the lord king and I were at Châlons").

80. Somerville, *Pope Alexander III and the Council of Tours (1163)*, 19–32.

81. For Alexander's stay in Sens, see Soria, "Alexander III and France."

82. Thomas Becket, *Correspondence*, 1: 116–25, no. 33, July 1164, report to Becket from an unnamed messenger.

83. *Actes*, no. 134, 1159, given in Provins, Henry's confirmation of the abbey's liberties and his earlier privileges. Trouble had been brewing since ca. 1140, according to Innocent II's letter to Abbot Ralph, which states that the abbot was accused of giving monastic property to his relatives and imprisoning the monks, which he denied, and worse still, of tearing up a papal letter

of rebuke, which he also denied, displaying the intact letter with its seal to the papal legate (*RHF* 15: 399, no. 50).

84. Chagny, "L'abbaye royale de Saint-Pierre de Lagny," 248, relates the following story, without citation. Abbot Geoffroy, elected on the advice of Bernard of Clairvaux and Count Thibaut of Blois, led an irregular monastic life after the fire of 1157. A provincial ecclesiastical assembly denounced him to Pope Adrian IV, who delegated the bishops of Auxerre and Paris to investigate; but before they could report, the abbot convinced the pope to suspend their commission. After new accusations were made to Pope Alexander III in 1160, judges delegate deposed Geoffroy in 1162.

85. Robert of Torigni, *Chronicle*, 218–19.

86. See Cline, "Abbot Hugh."

87. Count Henry granted Hugh 60 *arpents* of land and 60 *arpents* of woods near Dormans (*Tiron*, 2: 83–84, no. 310, 1155).

88. *Actes*, no. 198, 1163, Henry's gift of land to Lagny, done in Lagny, letter presented in Meaux. I infer Hugh's installation from the presence of Hugh's three half brothers, which can be explained only by some singular event, in this case Hugh's installation as abbot.

89. For the Lèves family and its allies who dominated the chapter, see Fassler, *The Virgin of Chartres*, 181–93.

90. See ch. 6 at n. 17.

91. *RHF* 15: 823.

92. *RHF* 16: 103, no. 318, 1164. According to Fourrier, "Retour au *Terminus*," 301–3, the marriage occurred between 23 September and 9 October. For a biography of Alice of France, see Armstrong-Partida, "Mothers and Daughters," 81–89.

93. Bur, *Formation*, 292–307.

94. Two factors were at play. Demouy, "Les archevêques de Reims," 85–86, attributes the decline of the old commercial route (Langres-Châlons-Reims) to the continuing conflict between the townsmen of Reims and Archbishops Samson (1141–61) and Henry of France (1162–75). Desportes, *Reims et les Rémois*, 103–16, stresses Thibaut's concerted policy of attracting cloth exporters from Arras to his markets via the road passing through Soissons rather than the old Roman road from Arras and St-Omer to Reims, Châlons, Bar-sur-Aube, and Langres.

95. Dubois, "Les institutions des foires médiévales," emphasizes the critical importance of roadway security (*conductus*) to the success of the fairs. Mesqui, "Les ponts sur la Seine et ses affluents," tracks the secondary road system between Troyes and the royal domain. See also Chapin, *Les villes de foires*, planche 1 (map of roads), and Richard, "Le 'conduit' des routes," who emphasizes the importance of toll stations as frontier posts marking the traveler's entry into the count's protected domain.

96. Bautier, "Provins and les foires de Champagne," 157, concludes that the merchants from Arras and St-Omer who paid tolls at Bapaume in 1127 were exporting cloth by that date and most likely to Provins. See also Chapin, *Les villes de foires*, 35–48.

97. Mesqui, *Provins*, 187, no. 1, after 1 August 1137 (= Provins, BM, ms. 86, no. 2). The count did not explicitly mention the "new market" centered on the church of St-Laurent in the upper town, which he described in 1164 (see n. 100 below). Mesqui provides a thorough topographical study of medieval Provins.

98. Mesqui, *Provins*, 13–18 (and plate 7) describes the locations.

99. Bautier, "Provins et les foires," 157–58, proposes a date of ca. 1141 for Thibaut's lost charter for the Fair of May. Thibaut's reference in 1137 to the "old" market suggests the existence of the "new" market by that time. Mesqui, *Provins*, 16–17, dates the walls to this period.

100. *Actes*, no. 214, 1164, done in Provins in the count's residence (= Mesqui, *Provins*, 189, no. 5 = Chapin, *Les villes de foires*, 282–84); trans. in Evergates, *Documents*, 28–30, no. 20.

101. The fair of St-Ayoul commenced on 3 September in the mid-twelfth century but later began on 14 September (Verdier, *Saint-Ayoul*, 129). The Merovingian priory developed a cult of Saint Ayoul after the discovery ca. 1020 of unidentified remains that were attributed to Ayoul. In 1048 the priory was attached to the Benedictine house of Montier-la-Celle. Count Stephen and Countess Adela of Blois, who witnessed the translation of relics in the 1090s, collected one-half of the revenues generated by the priory's market (*feriae*) as well as their protection tax (LoPrete, *Adela of Blois*, 456, no. 25, ca. 1099/1100), revenues that Count Henry continued to collect.

102. *RHF* 15: 503, no. 56, dated by Gasparri to 11 June 1147–early November 1149 (Suger, *Oeuvres*, 2: 132, no. 93). Thibaut accused the son of Salo, viscount of Sens, of being responsible.

103. About the same time Thibaut sought the release of the king's merchants and their property seized near Sens; they had paid the toll at Orléans (and thus came under the king's protection), said the count, and if Suger could not obtain their release, "I will send my own forces to help you do it" (*RHF* 15: 511, no. 73, before November 1149). Thibaut sent a follow-up letter asking that Suger confirm by return letter with his messenger that Renaud of Cortenay, who seized the merchants, had rendered satisfaction to them (*RHF* 15: 511, no. 74).

104. Robert of Auxerre, *Chronicon*, 235–36.

105. The Fair of St-Remi is first mentioned in 1147 (*St-Loup*, 33–36, no. 16, 14 April 1147, a papal confirmation of Loup's possessions and revenues, including 2*d.* collected from each house where merchandise was sold during "the Fair of St-Remi"). The Fairs of St-Remi and St-Jean were named in 1153 (*Montier-la-Celle*, 207–11, no. 195, 10 December 1153, papal confirmation of Montier-la-Celle's possessions) and 1154 (Camuzat, *Promptuarium*, fols. 30v–31r, 8 April 1154, confirmation of the count's foundation of St-Nicolas of Pougy by the bishop of Troyes). The location of the Fair of the Close, which Count Thibaut transferred to Troyes from Épernay in 1136, is not known before 1157, when Henry confirmed that he had given all its revenues to the new chapter of St-Étienne (*Actes*, no. 95, item 32). Chapin, *Les villes de foires*, 30–34, describes the fairgrounds.

106. The monks resisted, however, forcing Henry to reverse himself. Mindful that they cared for his father's tomb, he allowed merchants to trade there "whenever they wish" and without tax on their transactions, and further guaranteed their safe coming and going in all his lands (*Actes*, no. 55, 1154). For what little that is known about the fairs at Lagny, see Chapin, *Les villes de foires*, 48–52.

107. Bautier, "Provins et les foires," 161, and Spufford, *Handbook*, 164–67. By 1154 the *provinois* was circulating in Italy, and in 1184 the Roman senate authorized the minting of an imitation "penny of Provins"; see Toubert, "Une des premières vérifications de la loi de Gresham."

108. Thomas, "Die Champagnemessen," 20.

109. *PL* 180: 1550–51, no. 528 (*Vézelay Chronicle*, 121–22). One year later Pope Anastasius IV reissued the letter (*Monumenta Vizeliancensis*, 368–69, no. 59, 25 December 1153, given at Rome). See Berlow, "The Rebels of Vézelay (1152–55)."

110. *Actes*, no. 55, 1154 (Lagny); no. 54, item 13 (St-Ayoul).

111. Graboïs, "De la trêve de Dieu à la paix du roi."

112. Thomas, "Die Champagnemessen," 18, 32 (map), notes that it excluded the Plantagenet realm of western France.

113. Thomas Becket, *Correspondence*, 1: 52, no. 20, November 1163.

114. *St-Loup*, 14–16, no. 4, 2 April 1104, n.s., renewed by Henry in 1152 (*Actes*, no. 27).

Montier-la-Celle, 284–87, no. 233, 1114 (= Arbois de Jubainville, *Histoire*, 3: 415–17, no. 83), renewed by Henry in 1154 (*Actes*, no. 53).

115. *Actes*, no. 165, 1161. Here he confirms the abbey's *dominium*, that is, its lordship within
the old town of Troyes, by exempting its administrative personnel (mayors, submayors, sergeants) from all tolls, gate taxes, the weighing tax, the sales tax, and all other "customary taxes,"
"whatever they are called," on its commercial transactions (*mercatura*) within all the count's
lands, for which the abbey owed two pounds of wax annually. But to the men of St-Pierre-aux-
Monts living in its suburb at Châlons (beyond the count's lands), Henry granted only safe conduct to and from his "fairs and markets," not exemptions from his tolls and taxes (*Actes*, no. 248,
1166).

116. Identical letters of exemption, with different witnesses, presented at Château-Thierry
to the monks of Igny (*Actes*, no. 88, 1159) and Vauclair (*Actes*, no. 89, 1159).

117. *Actes*, no. 46, 1154 (= *Clairvaux*, 55–56, no. 28). The Cistercians at Vauluisant received
similar privileges (*Actes*, no. 197, 1163). In 1135 Louis VI exempted the monks at Pontigny, Clairvaux, and the other Cistercian houses from tolls, wagon taxes, and sales taxes in all the king's
lands, and allowed them peaceful travel by water and by road without payment of any tax (*Clairvaux*, 10–11, no. 6). In 1142 Count Thierry of Flanders exempted Clairvaux and all its associated
abbeys from tolls and road taxes while in transit through his lands (*Clairvaux*, 18–19, no. 9).

118. *Actes*, no. 154, 1160. That exempted house was described in 1164 as the place where
merchants from Hesdin and Eu were required to sell their cloths; the prior enjoyed the sales
taxes collected on their transactions at the Fairs of St-Jean and St-Remi of Troyes (*Actes*, no. 210).

119. *Actes*, no. 201, 1163. Sellers of fustian were not allowed to do business elsewhere until
Habran's hall was full.

120. The date of the fire cannot be determined with certainty, since nothing remains of the
original mid-eleventh-century priory (Verdier, *Saint-Ayoul*, 63, 219). Peter of Celle wrote to John
of Salisbury that the entire (wooden) church was reduced to ashes (Peter of Celle, *Letters*, 320–
21, no. 69, probably late 1159), and in a letter to Bishop John of St-Malo he states that only books
and relics were saved from destruction (48–51, no. 18, 1157). For the portal column-sculptures of
the new church, see Snyder, *Early Gothic Column-Figure Sculpture*, esp. illustrations 1.50, 1.57,
B.7. See also Verdier, *Saint-Ayoul*, 225–36.

121. *Actes*, no. 127, 1159.

122. *Actes*, no. 199, 1163 (Vitry); no. 115, 1158 (Ramerupt).

123. *Actes*, no. 163, 1161. At Coulommiers, where the count had a provost, the toll station
had both a duty collector (*telonearius*) and a toll collector (*pedagerius*) (*Actes*, no. 14, 1152).

124. *Actes*, no. 54, item 14 (St-Ayoul). *Obituaires*, 1.2: 933, 17 March (Hôtel-Dieu): an entry
of ca. 1270 states that Count Henry gave a 10*l.* annual revenue from the tolls at Provins in addition to 5*s.* from each money-changing table at the Fair of May.

125. *Actes*, no. 75, item 11, 1156.

126. *Actes*, no. 147, 1160.

127. *Actes*, no. 166, item 10, 1161 (St-Quiriace), and *Actes*, no. 54, item 13, 1154 (St-Ayoul).
An undated mandate ordered the toll collectors at Vitry to give 10 percent of all they collected to
the canons (Benton, "Recueil," sdh H-12, done without witnesses and probably sent by the
chancellor at the count's oral direction).

128. *Actes*, no. 133, 1159, presented in Provins. Photograph of the document (AN, S. 4955,
no. 7) is in *The Knights Templar*, 53, illustration 34, and 221 (catalogue no. 8). In effect, the count
shifted the cash payment, made directly from his treasury in Provins, to the sales tax collected in
in Troyes. Five years later, in 1164, he reassigned that revenue to the sales tax on woolen cloth

sold in Provins (*Actes*, no. 223), which was more convenient for the Templars, who had a house in the new market (which they exchanged in 1171 for a stone house with outbuildings in the old market [*Actes*, no. 318]).

129. *Actes*, no. 152, 1160: Countess Mathilda's bequest of 15*l*. each at the Fairs of May and St-Ayoul and 5*l*. at the Fair of St-Martin.

130. *Epistolae Pontificum Romanorum ineditae*, 122, no. 225, 17 October 1155. The pope authorized the archbishops of Reims and Sens to interdict Henry's lands, but that seems not to have been done. Abbot Hugh of Lagny complained to the pope that the knight Simon refused to hand over half of the rents from his houses in the fairs (139–40, no. 250, 1168).

131. Henry recognized St-Loup's "liberties" in its properties in Troyes, exempt from his bailiffs and other agents except in cases of rape, burglary, murder, and melée, that is, exemption from payment of tolls, sales taxes, and all customary payments for commercial activities (*Actes*, no. 165, 1161). Bailiffs appeared in Flanders about the same time (1160s) as comital agents in urban areas (De Gryse, "Some Observations," esp. 270–85). Royal bailiffs in the city of Paris sat at the royal court in 1173 (Bautier, "Quant et comment Paris devint capitale," 42). Henry's letter of 1158 exempting the nuns of Longueau from payments to his "bailiffs and sergeants" (*Actes*, no. 105) is suspect because of its reference to "Champagne and Brie" and its dating by kalends, neither of which was followed by Henry's chancery.

132. Bur, *Formation*, 450–51, posits the creation of viscounts in the towns of Champagne from the late eleventh century as protectors of markets and roadways. See also nn. 102–3 above regarding the viscount of Sens.

133. Wardens of the fairs (*custodes nundinorum*) are first mentioned in 1174, specifically regarding their crying out the opening of the fairs (*Actes*, no. 382). In 1190 they paid out revenues to the monks of Pontigny at each fair of St–Jean and St-Remi (*Pontigny*, 245–46, no. 200). Bur, *Formation*, 451, suggests that the delegated functions of the viscounts were taken over by the wardens of the fairs, who were part of Count Henry's direct administration.

134. Benton, "The Court" (1959), 86 (in charge of household finances) vs. Arbois de Jubainville, *Histoire*, 3: 125 (minister of finance). The comital chancery referred only to the count's *camerarius*, not to a *thesaurarius*, a term used only for treasurers of religious communities.

135. That was the case in Flanders as well; see Verhulst, "Flemish Financial Institutions."

136. Artaud (of Reims) was in the count's service before 1152 (*Actes*, no. 12); he was identified as *camerarius* in 1158 (*Actes*, no. 118), and continued to witness at court through 1188; see Evergates, *Aristocracy*, 182–84, 260, and Benton, "Court" (1959), 87–92. He was remembered by the nuns of Notre-Dame-aux-Nonnaines (*Obituaires*, 4: 352, 20 January) and the monks of St-Germain-des-Prés (*Obituaires*, 1.1: 281, 21 January, and 287, 20 January). The sisters of the hospital of Provins later recalled that Artaud had funded the building of their new refectory and dormitory ca. 1160 (*Obituaires*, 1.2: 925, 20 January).

137. Bishop Thierry of Amiens asked Suger to expunge his promised contribution for the king's expedition from the account because the royal and papal obligations weighed too heavily on him (*RHF* 15: 496–97, after 11 June 1147): *Obsecro, mi domine, dele me de libro tuo quam scripsisti.*

138. Verhulst, "Flemish Financial Institutions," 28.

139. Bisson, *The Crisis of the Twelfth Century*, 340–43, gathers references to Flemish accounts in 1089, 1117, 1118, 1127, that is, at least a half-century before the *Grote Brief* of 1187. For the English exchequer, see Hagger, "Theory and Practice in the Making of the Twelfth-Century Pipe Rolls."

140. Rainald was archdeacon of Provins (*Pontigny*, no. 58, 1141), canon of Meaux with his

brother Girard (*Actes*, no. 81, 1156), treasurer of St-Quiriace (*Actes*, no. 107, 1158), and canon of St-Étienne (*Actes*, no. 174, 1161). See Table 2 in Appendix 1.

141. Maillé, *Provins*, 1: 143, 147, fig. 78.

142. In confirming St-Quiriace's possession (*Actes*, no. 166, item 7, 1161), Henry declared that his mint (*moneta mea*) should always be located on St-Quiriace's property, and that by custom the canons should receive a tax (*census*) for each coin struck.

143. *Actes*, no. 166, item 12, 1161.

144. For the fragmentary evidence of financial accountancy from the early twelfth century, with examples from monastic estates as well as from princely and royal bureaus, see Bisson, *The Crisis of the Twelfth Century*, 328–48.

145. With one possible exception: in a letter drawn up by a scribe from Vauluisant (*Actes*, no. 197, 1163), Henry exempted the monks from tolls and sales taxes on their sales and purchases "in all the lands of my principality" (*tribui libertatem in omni loco mei principatus vivendi et emendi*). It is doubtful whether that was the language of the chancery. The phrase appears to have been copied from a document drawn up by the monks of Valsecret in 1140, in which Count Thibaut is said to have referred to *principatus meus*, a unique occurrence (Bur, *Formation*, 465–66) and of course meaning something quite different from Henry's polity in 1160.

146. Leyser, "Frederick Barbarossa and the Hohenstaufen Polity," 156–57, argues that Frederick I's main challenge was the lack of administrative uniformity within the German empire.

147. Bur, *Formation*, 282 n. 4, lists earlier mentions of "castellany" for several towns before 1152. Henry spoke of "the right to pasture pigs throughout the castellany of Ervy" (*Actes*, no. 102, 1152/58), and of "land taxes within the castellany of Jouy" (*Actes*, no. 75, item 3, 1156).

148. The rolls of fiefs for Provins and Montereau state that, according to the "custom" of those castellanies, knights owing castle-guard were obligated to remain on duty (*stare*) during any crisis (*Feoda* 1, nos. 1285, 1643). For castellanies as districts of "customs," see Hubert, "*Consuetudo*."

149. *Actes*, no. 199, 1163. Cash was involved at each stage: the abbot paid the count 2s. in recognition of the property's status as the count's fief; the count later paid the abbot a 20s. revenue, payable by the toll collector at Vitry, to recover the fief. In 1178 Adam Bridaine still owed six weeks castle-guard (*custodie*) at Vitry for that fief (*Feoda* 1, 17, no. 512) in addition to unspecified castle-guard (*estagium*) at Épernay for another fief (*Feoda* 1, 21. no. 654).

CHAPTER 5. THE CULTURE OF COUNT HENRY

1. *Actes*, no. 79, 1156.

2. Jordan, "*Quando fuit natus*," 188.

3. *Walter of Châtillon: The Shorter Poems*, 156–57, poem 49, stanza 5: *Sed, o comes largitatis, propagator equitatis*. The poet addresses the "men of Troyes" (*o Trecensite*, 162–63, stanza 19) either in Troyes, as the editor suggests, or elsewhere, when the poet may have turned to address the count and his traveling companions.

4. John of Salisbury, *Letters*, 2: 314–39, no. 209, undated treatise (ca. 1166/67) in the form of a letter to Count Henry responding to the count's questions.

5. Peter of Celle, *Letters*, 326–27, no. 71, 1152x54, to Henry.

6. Leclercq, "Gébuin de Troyes," and Tibber, "The Origins of the Scholastic Sermon," ch. 4.

7. John of Salisbury, *Letters*, 1: 48–51, no. 31, 1–8 April 1157; Peter of Celle, *Letters*, 328–31, no. 72, 1155x1162, probably spring of 1157, following John of Salisbury's request.

8. *St-Pierre*, 102–4, no. 98, January 1201, n.s., Bishop Garnier of Troyes describes Henry's endowment for the chanter.

9. For Nicholas's life before 1151, see Constable, in Peter the Venerable, *Letters* 2: 316–30, and Benton, "Court" (1961) in his *Culture*, 7–9.

10. Writing to the abbot of Cluny, Bishop Hato of Troyes appended Nicholas's personal greeting to Peter (Peter the Vernerable, *Letters*, 1: 203–6, no. 71, March/April 1138).

11. Bishop Hato said he gave a church to Montiéramey "for the love of God and especially for my dear Nicholas, your brother, who served me faithfully and effectively in Rome and in many other places" (*Montiéramey*, 60–62, no. 36, ca. 1143). Nicholas was described as *monachus, capellanus episcopi* (*Montiéramey*, 64–65, no. 39, 1144). About the same time, if not on the same occasion, Abbot Peter the Venerable entrusted Nicholas with Cluny's *negotia* in Rome (Peter the Venerable, *Letters*, 1: 222, no. 85).

12. Nicholas apparently went through a spiritual crisis before entering Clairvaux; it is described in the *Vita prima sancti Bernardi*, 263–64, cap. 68. He wrote that his private writing room (*scriptoriolum*) faced the hall for novices (*Epistolae*, 1626–27, no. 35).

13. Nicholas's letter to Archbishop Henry, ca. 1174 (*PL* 196 [*Epistolae* of Archbishop Henry]: 1575–76, no. 20) recalls his conversion at Clairvaux and their conversations there almost three decades earlier.

14. It is now known that Henry of France's books were produced at St-Victor (Stirnemann, "La production manuscrite," 140, and "Gilbert de la Porrée," 86–87). They included a glossed Psalter made in 1137 (with an autographed ex libris: *Henricus regis filius*) and a gloss of Luke (Vernet and Genest, *La bibliothèque de l'abbaye de Clairvaux*, 131–32, 173). It is not clear whether he left his personal collection of books to Clairvaux when elected bishop of Beauvais in 1149 or at his death as archbishop of Reims in 1175. For his library, see De Hamel, *Glossed Books*, 5–7, and Stirnemann, "Quelques bibliothèques," 12–21, and "Où ont été fabriqués les livres de la glose ordinaire," 264–66.

15. *PL* 202: 475. See also Barker, "A Lost Lactantius," 33–34.

16. In a letter to Peter, Bernard wrote that he retreated to a quiet place with Nicholas ("of whom you are so fond") to read Peter's letter; Nicholas added in his own hand: "And I, Nicholas, add my undying affection for you and all your household" (Bernard of Clairvaux, *Epistolae*, in *Opera*, 8: 356–57, no. 389 [*Letters*, 379–80, no. 309, redated to November 1149]).

17. Freculf, *Opera omnia*, 1: 54, 411 and plate X, between 1145 and 1151.

18. Peter the Venerable, *Letters*, 1: 417, no. 176, autumn 1150, to Nicholas, and *Letters*, 2: 217. Nicholas did return them; they are listed among Cluny's books in 1158/61 (the *History of Alexander* was lost later). After making Clairvaux's copy of *Contra Julian* from the Cluny exemplar, Nicholas made marginal corrections (Vernet and Genest, *La bibliothèque de l'abbaye de Clairvaux*, 53–54, 411–12, plate X).

19. While at Clairvaux, Nicholas gathered a sample of his letters which he later polished as a collection of fifty-three letters; see Wahlgren-Smith, "Editing a Medieval Text."

20. Nicholas of Montiéramey, *Epistolae*, 1600–1601, no. 6. Nicholas reiterates his request in a second letter (*Epistolae*, 1613–16, no. 17), in which he makes a play on Peter's name *Manducator*.

21. Bernard of Clairvaux, *Epistolae*, in *Opera*, 8: 214, no. 298 (*Letters*, 435–36, no. 363, redated to 1152, after May).

22. Peter the Venerable, *Letters*, 1: 432–25, no. 181, autumn 1150/March 1151, to Bernard.

23. Nicholas is first identified as Henry's chaplain while Henry was still count of Bar-sur-Aube in 1151 (*Actes*, no. 6).

238 Notes to Pages 88–90

24. *Actes*, no. 27, 22 April 1153: Nicholas appears as *capellanus (comitis)* under *Ex parte comitis*.

25. *Actes*, no. 345, 1172: Count Henry remits his right to hospitality at Montiéramey's village of Fravaux *ad preces dilecti et familiaris mei magistri Nicholai*.

26. Philip of Harvengt, *Ad Henricum* (*PL* 203: 151–56, no. 17).

27. Alexander III, *Epistolae*, 109–10, no. 38, 6 March 1161. In that same year the pope granted "Master Nicholas, prior" of St-Jean-en-Châtel, a special license to bury laymen in the priory's cemetery (*Acta Pontificum Romanorum inedita*, 1: 231, no. 247, 21 December 1161).

28. Peter's family took its name from Aulnoy near Provins; see Verdier, *Saint-Ayoul*, 75–82, esp. 81 (genealogical table). Peter was the nephew of Count Thibaut's seneschal André of Baudement, and cousin of William of Dampierre, the companion and later constable of Count Henry. In 1152 André of Baudement's daughter Agnes married as her second husband Robert of Dreux, brother of Louis VII, thus connecting Peter with the king; her sister Helvide took as her second husband Guy I of Dampierre, whose son was William of Dampierre (Evergates, *Aristocracy*, 216). For biographies of Peter, see Haseldine's introduction to Peter of Celle, *Letters*, xix–xxxiv, and Prache, *Saint-Remi de Reims*, 31–57.

29. John of Salisbury, *Letters*, 183–84, no. 112, provisionally dated to 1159. As abbot of Montier-la-Celle from 1145, Peter was the superior of Simon Aurea Capra, prior of St-Ayoul from 1148, when John of Salisbury most likely spent time there after finishing his studies in Paris; see Nederman, *John of Salisbury*, 11. John remembered Count Thibaut's patronage, which had allowed him to "flourish in France" (John of Salisbury, *Letters*, 2: 315–39, no. 209, of uncertain date). John's statement has been taken to mean that Thibaut subsidized his studies in Paris, which might be true, but John might have referred rather to the count's support in Provins.

30. Abelard, *Letter Collection*, 76–77, cap. 49 (Letter 1, *Historia calamitatum*). Abelard says that he lived in the *castrum* (upper town) of Provins, but St-Ayoul was actually located in the suburb that later became the lower town. Abelard recalled Thibaut's largess in his *Carmen* to his son Astrolabe, where in a poem of advice on moral conduct, Thibaut was the only living person worthy of mention along with Abraham, Solomon, and Achilles; see Abelard, *Carmen*, lines 921–34. Nothing is known about Ralph, prior of St-Ayoul until 1122 (Godefroy, "L'histoire du prieuré Saint-Ayoul," 30).

31. Cotts, "Monks and Clerks," gives a close reading of the letters exchanged between Peter of Celle and John of Salisbury (eighteen from Peter, eleven from John). Nederman, "Textual Communities of Learning," argues convincingly that John's letters display a conception of friendship based on Cicero's *De amicitia*, as developed in the *Policraticus* (ca. 1159) and revealed in his second collection of letters (from 1168). Peter was one of John's closest friends in that respect, and probably the reason that John later settled in Reims, where Peter was abbot of St-Remi, rather than following Becket to Sens.

32. John of Salisbury, *Letters*, 1: 48–51, no. 31, 1–8 April 1157. John also promised that he or his messenger would visit Peter (in Troyes) before the end of autumn.

33. John refers to Thomas as Anglicus (John of Salisbury, *Letters*, 1: 55–58, no. 33, autumn 1157).

34. Peter of Celle, *Letters*, 328–71, no. 72, 1155x1162, probably in the spring of 1157, to Thomas Becket.

35. John of Salisbury, *Letters*, 1: 55–58, no. 33, autumn 1157. Text of *De panibus* in *PL* 202: 927–1046.

36. Peter of Celle, *Letters*, 48–51, no. 18, 1157, to Bishop John of St-Malo. In a letter to John of Salisbury about the same time, Peter wrote that the church's "panelled ceilings, beams, posts, and strong timbers" were but dust and ashes (*Letters*, 320–21, no. 69)

37. John of Salisbury, *Letters*, 1: 59–62, no. 34, October/November 1157 or later. It would be interesting to know whether John left his copy of Boethius at St-Ayoul out of prudence before attending the Council of Reims in the spring of 1148, where Gilbert de la Porrée, bishop of Poitiers, was condemned for his commentary on Boethius' *On the Trinity*. In recalling the Council's discussions of Boethius in his *Historia Pontificalis*, written ca. 1164 while he was in Reims, John mounted an extended defense of Gilbert (John of Salisbury, *Historia Pontificalis*, 14–42).

38. John of Salisbury, *Letters*, 1: 59–62, no. 34, October–November 1157 or later. John also asked for a copy of an unspecified commentary of Hugh of St-Victor that, John recalled, Peter possessed.

39. John of Salisbury, *Letters*, 1: 52–54, no. 32, July–August 1157, letter of thanks.

40. Peter of Celle, *Letters*, 318–21, no. 68, 1157, and John of Salisbury, *Letters*, 1: 52–54, no. 32, 1157. The head and body of Ayoul were later placed in a new reliquary in the rebuilt church (Peter of Celle, *Letters*, 326–27, no. 70, after 1157).

41. In the twelfth century only the cathedral of Laon is known to have sent relics on tour in England (in 1112 and in 1113) to support its rebuilding campaign (Héliot and Chastang, "Quêtes et voyages de reliques"). Seven canons and six laymen went on the first tour; nine clerics went on the second (Sigal, "Les voyages de reliques," 77–78, and 102, a map of the second itinerary).

42. John of Salisbury, *Letters*, 1: 180–82, no. 111, autumn 1159. It would be interesting to know whether Peter of Celle shared that draft of the *Policraticus* with Count Henry.

43. Peter of Celle, *Letters*, 323–27, no. 70, 1161x62.

44. McGuire, *Friendship and Community*, esp. 231–95, terms the mid-twelfth century the "age of friendship" for the extensive writings, primarily letters, on *amicitia*. For specific friendship networks, see Haseldine's studies on the letter collections of Bernard of Clairvaux and Peter of Celle.

45. Bibolet, "La biliothèque des chanoines de Troyes," can identify only a handful of surviving books made before 1200.

46. For a biography, see Grill, "Heinrich von Kärnten," and Jaksch, *Geschichte Kärntens*, 1: 257.

47. Bishop Hato of Troyes (1122–45/46, died 30 September) had been dean and archdeacon of Sens (Prévost, *Histoire du diocèse de Troyes*, 1: 77–85). He resigned his office in late 1145 or early 1146 (Peter the Venerable, *Letters*, 2: 97–98). Bernard of Clairvaux, *Epistolae*, in *Opera*, 8: 137–38, no. 246 (*Letters*, 396–97, no. 322, dated early 1146) complained to Eugenius about the lack of bishops in Troyes and Nevers. The episcopal election may have been delayed by the canons' unease at having a Cistercian bishop. Aubri of Trois-Fontaines (*Chronicon*, 840), writing ca. 1240, states on the authority of Guy of Bazoches that Countess Mathilda asked Pope Eugenius III at the Council of Reims (March 1148) to consecrate her brother Henry as bishop of Troyes. Aubri may have confused events a century earlier, but his remark suggests a delayed or disputed election.

48. Nothing is known about Peter Comestor before his appearance as dean of the cathedral chapter of Troyes in 1140, when he was pledge to two Romans for a debt owed by the nuns of the Paraclete (Gandil, "Pierre le Mangeur," 18–21). Peter appears with Nicholas of Montiéramey in two acts of Bishop Hato in 1144 and 1145, with Peter as dean and Nicholas as the bishop's chaplain (*Montiéramey*, 64–65, no. 39, and 60–62, no. 36). Peter and Nicholas thus were well acquainted, since at least 1140 and perhaps since 1138, when Nicholas became the bishop's chaplain.

49. Peter Comestor was probably the canon Peter of St-Loup who witnessed in 1145

(*St-Loup*, 32–33, no. 15) and remained a canon there for the rest of his life. One of the first acts of Bishop Henry of Troyes was to give "Master Peter Manducator, my cleric," the church at Laubressel with the right to appoint its priest; he did that at the request of Alan, first Cistercian abbot of Larrivour (*St-Pierre*, 17–18, no. 13, 1147). For Peter's prebend in St-Étienne, see n. 100 below.

50. The earliest (ca. 1170) versions are entitled *Historia scolastica*. Two related copies made in Troyes, perhaps from Peter Comestor's original drafts left in the cathedral, are dated to the mid-1180s on the basis of painting style; see Stirnemann, in *Splendeurs*, 65, fig. 31. For Peter's influence at the time, see Luscombe, "The Place of Peter Comestor in the History of Medieval Theology," and Mory, "Peter Comestor." Peter may have been in Paris from the early 1150s, although the earliest certain reference to him there is 1168; see Daly, "Peter Comestor," 65–66. In 1159 Peter witnessed Count Henry's act, *ex parte* of the count in his new chapel of St-Étienne (*Actes*, no. 125). Peter was still dean of the cathedral in 1167, when he and the entire chapter witnessed William of Champagne resign his prebend and provostship after being elected archbishop of Sens (*St-Pierre*, 29–31, no. 20). Peter retired to St-Victor of Paris, where he died in 1179.

51. Peter Comestor, *Scolastica historia*, 3. A copy of the *Historia scolastica* dated 1229 (Yale, Beinecke Library, 214, fol. 2v) contains an illustration of Peter Comestor presenting his book to Archbishop William of Sens, both appearing as idealized, clean-shaven young men. Below them the copyist, an otherwise unknown Peter of Mont-Saint-Quentin, is depicted at work (Clark, "Art and Historiography," 38, fig. 2). Aubri of Trois-Fontaines, writing in the 1240s, likewise recognized Peter's dedication to William as a noteworthy cultural fact (*Chronicon*, 841).

52. I have freely identified *magister* Stephen, Henry's tutor in 1132, with Stephen Alinerra, the master later described by Helinand of Froidmont as a "cleric" of Count Henry, a canon of Beauvais and St-Quiriace of Provins, and "skilled in both Latin and French, but avaricious"; see Benton, "Court" (1961), in Benton, *Culture*, 10–12.

53. *Actes*, no. 27, 1153: *ex parte comitis*; *Actes*, no. 152, 1160.

54. See McGuire, *Friendship and Community*, 251–95 ("A Mid-Century Network of friends: Troyes, Cluny and Clairvaux").

55. John of Salisbury, *Letters*, 1: 55–58, no. 33, autumn 1157 or later, thanks to Peter of Celle for his help during those early years and for making possible the esteem and career John enjoyed after returning to England. John may have left his books in Champagne as a token of gratitude.

56. John of Salisbury, who died bishop of Chartres, bequeathed his library to the cathedral chapter (inventory printed in *Notre-Dame de Chartres*, 3: 20); see also Barker, "A Lost Lactantius." For Archbishop Henry's library, see above, n. 14.

57. Gasparri, "Bibliothèque et archives," 275–76.

58. Gullick, "How Fast Did Scribes Write?," notes the importance of book copying in the early years of a monastery's foundation.

59. Pouzet, "La vie de Guichard," 130–38.

60. Peyrafort-Huin, *La bibliothèque médiévale de Pontigny*, 30–53.

61. Bougard and Petitmengin, *La bibliothèque de Vauluisant*, 37–68, note the similarity of the early collections of Pontigny and Vauluisant. Abbot Peter of Vauluisant was "a friend and familiar" of Thomas Becket, according to Herbert of Bosham, and probably was English.

62. Stirnemann, "En quête de Sens."

63. *Actes*, no. 72, 1155. Witnesses include Helisend's sons Anselm and Garnier, Hugh of Lisy, and an otherwise unknown *magister* Henry, perhaps an English colleague who copied

books with William. This William Anglicus might have been the same person as William Agne-lius, who witnessed with Count Thibaut, Countess Mathilda, and young Henry in 1140/45 (Quantin, *Yonne*, 1: 349–51, no. 210).

64. A William *scriba* witnessed the count's acts in 1161, 1164, 1169, and 1171 (*Actes*, nos. 164, 215, 285, 316); in each case he is listed just ahead of Thibaut (the Scribe) of Fismes, canon of St-Étienne. In 1174 William is identified as *scriba Provenienesis* (*Actes*, nos. 371, 380bis). His obit-uary states that Guillelmus Anglicus gave 20*s.* to St-Étienne (where he had held a prebend) for his anniversary, to be collected from the house of Hugh the Goldsmith in the Magnus Vicus of Troyes (*Obituaires*, 4: 453, 14 February).

65. Arbois de Jubainville, "Quatre petits hôpitaux," 104–5, no. 13, ca. 1150.

66. The chapter's endowment charter of 1157 (*Actes*, no. 95, item 22) lists his business part-ners. Thibaut died in 1175, one year before William the chancellor left office. His obituary reads: *Obiit Theobaldus Scriba, qui dedit nobis domum suam lapideam et alta multa bona fecit nobis* (*Obituaires*, 4: 466, 2 August).

67. Philip of Harvengt, *Ad Henricum*, 154, lists the "interior furnishings" that Henry pro-vided to his churches: "gold, silver, stones, <u>books</u>, chalices, cloth hangings" (*interioribus orna-menta, aurum, argentum, lapides, <u>libros</u>, calices, indumenta*).

68. Troyes, BM, ms. 2391. See Stirnemann, in *Splendeurs*, 61, fig. 23. The two volumes were later kept in the choir of St-Étienne (Lalore, *Inventaires*, 2: 41, no. 400).

69. Troyes, BM, ms. 458, vols. 1–2, ca. 1145–51; see Vernet and Genest, *La bibliothèque de l'abbaye Clairvaux*, 77–79. For the production of these volumes in Chartres, see Stirnemann, "Gilbert de la Porée," 88–91.

70. Troyes, BM, ms. 1484. It is listed in the 1320/21 inventory of St-Étienne's books (Lalore, *Inventaires*, 2: 271, no. 2308: *Sermones sancti Bernardi abbatis Clarevallensis*). Stirnemann (*Splen-deurs*, 56, fig. 14, photograph) dates the manuscript to the early 1150s and regards it as the only volume besides the "Bible of the Counts" that was made for Count Thibaut. The manuscript includes a letter to Abbot Guy of Montiéramey and two of Bernard's sermons in honor of Vic-tor, the patron saint of Montiéramey. If the copy was made before 1151, Nicholas of Montiéramey may have had a hand in copying it.

71. Stirnemann, *Splendeurs*, 60, fig. 21. See also Eschapasse, "Le trésor de la cathédrale de Troyes," 36–37, and van der Horst, *The Utrecht Psalter*, 186–87. The *Psalterium Comitis* was kept in the "small treasury" of St-Étienne in 1319/20 (Lalore, *Inventaires*, 2: 26, no. 218). It is possible that Count Thibaut received the Psalter in 1127 as a gift of appreciation from the abbot of Haut-villers, who found the count at Épernay and asked for permission to rebuild a destroyed village next to the walls of Vertus. Thibaut granted permission, exempted the monastery's tenants from his jurisdiction and taxes, and further prohibited his own men from settling there, in what was de facto a "new" or franchised village (Martène, *Thesaurus novus anecdotorum*, 1: 367–68, 1127, Thibaut's sealed letter for the abbot).

72. Stohlmann, "Magister Simon Aurea Capra," adds to the basic biography in Godefroy, "L'histoire du prieuré St Ayoul," 30–32. Simon first appeared in Champagne as prior of St-Ayoul in 1148, when at Count Thibaut's court at Jouy he purchased a tithe rent from Mathieu, precen-tor of the chapter of Sens (*Montier-la-Celle*, 30–31, no. 24, 1148). After Simon left St-Ayoul, Peter of Celle asked Count Henry to confirm the priory's possessions (*Actes*, no. 54, 1154). Simon's years as abbot of St-Remi of Reims are described in Prache, *Saint-Remi de Reims*, 41–42. See also Verdier, *Saint-Ayoul*, catalogue A-II-005.

73. Peter of Celle, *Letters*, 262–69, no. 57, letter of recommendation, ca. 1160, to the prior and monks of Mont-Dieu, which Simon entered after a stint as canon at St-Victor. Simon

sported the name Aurea Capra as a tribute to his own poetic brilliance; the name is perhaps a pun on "the golden goat" but more likely means "golden star in the constellation of Auriga" (Stohlmann, "Magister Simon Aurea Capra," 347 n. 1). Abbot Peter later played on the name in a letter recommending Simon as "certainly not gold (*aurum*) but a man after my own heart, and certainly not silver but rather my one son" (Peter of Celle, *Letters*, 270–75, no. 58, letter to the prior and monks of Mont-Dieu, ca. 1160).

74. See ch. 3 at n. 3.

75. Boutemy, "La Geste d'Enée par Simon Chèvre d'Or," 254–55. There are two complete but unpublished editions: Parrott, "The *Ylias* of Simon Aurea Capra" (1975), and Peyrard, "L'*Il-ias* de Simon Chèvre d'Or" (2007). The *Anonymi Historia Troyana Daretis Frigii*, ca. 1150, has few explicit similarities to the *Ylias* (Parrot, "The *Ylias* of Simon Aurea Capra," 69, who places the *Ylias* in the "Troyes-Rome" tradition of stories that include the *Excidium Troiae*).

76. Oxford, Bodleian, Rawlinson, G 109: *Explicit Aurea Capra super Yliade rogatu comitis Henrici* (Boutemy, "La Geste d'Enée par Simon Chèvre d'Or," 254–55, and Parrot, "The *Ylias*," 43). The manuscript also contains epitaphs Simon wrote as prior of Mont-Dieu (1160–82) for Peter Lombard (died 21 July 1160), Queen Constance (died 4 October 1160), and Prince Philip of France (brother of Louis VII and archdeacon of Paris, who died 3 September 1161); see Boutemy, "Quatre poèmes."

77. The base copy of the longer version of the *Ylias* may be BnF, Lat. 8430 the only copy to state that Simon had expanded the original, that is, while he was at St-Victor (1155–60). It would be interesting to know if Simon left Provins for the regular canons of St-Victor because of the conflict between regulars and seculars in Provins. Simon's successor, Prior Joscelin (1155–59), obtained a papal confirmation of the priory's possessions before 19 December 1155 (*Montier-la-Celle*, 211–13, no. 196). See Godefroy, "L'histoire du prieuré Saint-Ayoul," 34–35.

78. Bishop Philip's copy, now lost, was listed among his books in 1163; he might have obtained it directly from Simon between 1155 and 1160 (Rouse and Rouse, "Philip, Bishop of Bayeux, and His Books," 53–54). An organized system of book production under the supervision of the librarian at St-Victor may have facilitated the "publication" of multiple copies of *Ylias*, which survives in sixteen copies.

79. Rouse and Rouse, "Philip, Bishop of Bayeux, and His Books," 52.

80. See ch. 6 at n. 118.

81. Blumenfeld-Kosinski, *Reading Myth*, 13–51.

82. Friend, "Chaucer's Version of the *Aeneid*," argues persuasively that Chaucer later transformed Simon's set-piece exempla in ethics into dramatic narratives.

83. British Library, ms. Harley 3073. Leclercq, "Les collections de sermons de Nicolas de Clairvaux," 271–72, prints the dedication and provides an analysis. A photograph of the first few lines is in *Splendeurs*, 62, fig. 25 (*singulari domini et benefactori suo, Henrico Trecensium comiti palatino*), where Stirnemann dates the manuscript on stylistic grounds to the 1160s or 1170s. Benton, "Nicolas of Clairvaux," 49, 59 and n. 44, notes that the manuscript was written with great care and therefore might have been the presentation copy, which he dates to the 1150s or 1160s. I prefer a date of ca. 1160, that is, after Nicholas became prior of St-Jean-en-Châtel and when St-Étienne was roofed. Benton, 60–75, publishes the texts and sources of the sequences.

84. Leclercq, "Les collections de sermons," 282–300. The pope has traditionally been identified as Adrian IV, who died in 1159.

85. For Andrew of St-Victor, see Fassler, *Gothic Song*, esp. 137–38, 206–10. If Nicholas's collection of sequences, letters, and sermons was compiled in the late 1150s, during the pontificate of Adrian IV, it would coincide with Simon Aurea Capra's residence at St-Victor of Paris,

where Simon was expanding Count Henry's *Ylias*. It is possible that Simon sent copies of Andrew of St-Victor's sequences to Nicholas.

86. Rouse and Rouse, "The *Florilegium Angelicum*," provide a detailed analysis of the contents and the extant manuscripts. They conclude that Count Henry's volume (Vatican, Reg. Lat. 1575) was the exemplar for the copy presented to the pope (Rome, Bibl. Angelica 1895).

87. Stirnemann and Poirel, "Nicolas de Montiéramey," 175, opt for Adrian IV and suggest a date of 1158 or 1159.

88. Adrian IV, *Epistolae*, 1596–97, no. 219, to Bishop Henry of Beauvais, and 1597–98, no. 220, to Archbishop S[amson] of Reims, identical letters, done at the Lateran on 8 March.

89. Stirnemann and Poirel, "Nicolas de Montiéramey," 181.

90. Stirnemann, in *Une Renaissance*, 98–99, catalogue no. 33, dates the "Bible of Montiéramey" to 1160–65, that is, after Nicholas became prior of St-Jean-en-Châtel in 1160 and before Becket's arrival at Pontigny in November 1166.

91. Stirnemann, "Reconstitution des bibliothèques," 44, speaks of "un projet d'histoire."

92. *Actes*, no. 154, 1160, grant to Montiéramey, but with Nicholas enjoying the revenues.

93. *Actes*, no. 159, Easter (16 April) 1161, sealed on yellow and red silk threads (photograph in *Splendeurs*, 62, fig. 26): *ad facienda negocia sua*. William the chancellor and several canons of St-Étienne witnessed.

94. *Actes*, no. 160, 1161, April 16, with the same language and witnesses as the letter addressed to the abbot of Montiéramey (see n. 93 above).

95. *Actes*, no. 148, 1160: *Drogo subcapellanus*. He may have been Drogo Bristaud, brother of Peter, viscount of Provins, and later Countess Marie's chaplain (*Actes*, no. 285, 1169).

96. Stirnemann, "Private Libraries Privately Made," 189.

97. Henry's Josephus (BnF, Lat. 8959, copied from an unidentified exemplar) is listed in the inventory of his library (Lalore, *Inventaires*, 2: 271, no. 2292: *Item liber Josephi*). The exemplar may have been at Pontigny, which possessed a copy made by a Chartrain hand in the 1140s; see Peyrafort-Huin, *La bibliothèque médiévale de Pontigny*, 57, 76. Henry's copy was made in the 1160s (Stirnemann, *Splendeurs*, 37, 39, 63, fig. 27, dating on the basis of the painting style). For the construction and illumination of the copy, which was supplemented during the residence of Alexander III at Sens (30 September 1163–April 1165) by two quires of books missing from the *Antiquities*, see Stirnemann, "Reconstitution des bibliothèques," 40.

98. Geiger, "*Historia Judaica*: Petrus Comestor and His Jewish Sources," 132.

99. Peter Comestor, *Scolastica historia*, 3. See also Luscombe, "The Place of Peter Comestor in the History of Medieval Theology," 36–37.

100. The chronology of Peter Comestor's life is uncertain (see n. 48). He continued to hold at least two prebends in Troyes after leaving for Paris sometime between 1159 and 1164, and as chancellor of the cathdral school of Notre-Dame of Paris (1168–78). Count Henry apparently gave Peter a prebend in St-Étienne, where a subdeacon Peter appeared in 1159 witnessing *ex parte* of Count Henry (*Actes*, no. 125). The chapter's necrology lists *Magister Petrus Manducator* (*Obituaires*, 4: 474, 23 October).

101. It is listed in the inventory of Henry's library (Lalore, *Inventaires*, 2: 270, no. 2273: *Item Quintus Curtius Ruffi, Hystoriarum Alexandri Magni Macedonii liber tertius*). Photograph in Stirnemann, *Splendeurs*, 63, fig. 28. See Rolfe's comments on the author in Quintus Curtius Rufus, *History of Alexander*, xxi.

102. It is listed in the inventory of Henry's library (Lalore, *Inventaires*, 2: 270, no. 2281: *Item historia Freculphi hytoriographi et Luxoviensis episcopi*). Stirnemann, *Splendeurs*, 64, fig. 29, dates Henry's copy (Montpellier, BISM, H 41) on stylistic grounds to 1165–70 (the illuminations are

by the same painter of Henry's copies of Josephus and Quintus Curtius Rufus). A slightly early dating, to ca. 1160, after Nicholas became prior of St-Jean-en-Châtel of Troyes, fits the chronology here just as well, and places the beginning of Henry's history collection before the arrival of Becket in Sens in late 1164. Michael Allen, the modern editor of Freculf, suggests that Nicholas made Henry's copy from the same exemplar at Cluny that he had used earlier to make Clairvaux's copy (which appears in Clairvaux's inventory of books); see Freculf, *Opera omnia*: 145–46. Nicholas's hand is one of two that made Henry's volume; see Vernet and Genest, *La bibliothèque de l'abbaye de Clairvaux*, 1: 54, 411, plate X.1. A later hand copied John of Salisbury's letter of 1166/67 to Henry (see ch. 6 at n. 122) in the completed Freculf volume (fols. 187–89). Montier-la-Celle also had a copy of Freculf, which appears to have been the exemplar for the copies at Pontigny and Vauluisant; see Bougard and Petitmengin, *La bibliothèque de Vauluisant*, 159–60.

103. Depreux, "L'actualité de Fréculf de Lisieux."

104. Stirnemann, "Reconstitution des bibliothèques," 43, suggests that this copy of Hugh of Fleury's *History* (British Library, ms. Harley 3974) may have been made for Count Henry, since its illumination was produced by the same Troyes workshop that painted Henry's other histories. Bougard and Petitmengin, *La bibliothèque de Vauluisant*, 39, 51, 207–8, note that both Paris, Bibliothèque de l'Arsenal 1161, fols. 1–48 (which they suggest was Henry's copy) and Paris, BnF, Lat. n.a. 1791, fols. 140–95 (which belonged to Vauluisant) are unique copies of Baudri's *History* in that Baudri's text is followed by brief descriptions of the holy sites. Vauluisant's own volume most likely was copied from Pontigny's exemplar, which was a composite volume (Bougard and Petitmengin, *La bibliothèque de Vauluisant*, 208). Arsenal 1161, by contrast, is a single-authored volume consistent with Count Henry's interests; see Baudri of Bourgueil, *The Historia Ierosolomitana*, xcii.

105. Stirnemann and Poirel, "Nicolas de Montiéramey," 174, 177. In addition, the two-volume "Bible of Montiéramey" (dated to 1155–65 by Stirnemann, *Splendeurs*, 67, fig. 35) may have been commissioned by Abbot Guy III (1137–63).

106. The archbishop's copy of Sigebert contains continuations to 1162, and therefore was sent for painting after that date; see Stirnemann, "Quelques bibliothèques," 12–14, and Chazan, *L'empire et l'histoire universelle*, 324–26.

107. Philip of Harvengt, *Ad Henricum*, 151–56, which praises Henry for, among other things, his *Latinam linguam litteralemque scientiam*.

108. Nicholas produced only one anthology after 1160, a collection of his own letters sent to "the pope [Adrian IV], to the papal chancellor [Roland Bandinelli], and to certain others," which he dedicated to "his most serene prince and dearest lord Henry, count of Troyes." Only the dedication and four letters survive from this second collection of Nicholas's letters; see Wahlgren-Smith, "Editing a Medieval Text," 176–77.

109. John of Salisbury, *Letters*, 2: 314–39, no. 209, to Henry, undated but ca. 1164–66.

CHAPTER 6. PESKY PRELATES AND ENGLISH EXILES, 1165–1170

1. Louis married Constance of Castile at Orléans in the second half of 1154 (Sassier, *Louis VII*, 253).

2. *Avenay*, 1: 58–59.

3. *Actes*, no. 141, 1159, presented in Vertus. Alice of Mareuil is identified as Marie's *magistra*, which I take as governess or guardian. She was Elizabeth of Mareuil, heiress of the viscounty of Mareuil (3 km from Avenay), who first married Robert of Montaigu (died before 1154), then

Robert, count of Roucy (died 1178/80). The viscounty of Mareuil passed to her daughter Eusta-chia, who later inherited the county of Roucy after the deaths of her two brothers, Ralph (died 1196) and Jean (died 1200). See Bur, *Formation*, 250, 268–69.

4. *Actes*, no. 215, dated between 12 April 1164 and 3 April 1165: *Laurentius clericus comitisse*.

5. Laurent's prebend in Marie's service was at St-Quiriace (Provins, BM, ms. 85, no. 6, 1169 = Benton, "Recueil," 1169f). He is last mentioned as her cleric in 1176 (*St-Quiriace*, 259–60, no. 27).

6. Nevel "of Aulnay" and "of Ramerupt" appeared as *miles comitisse* in Marie's first act (Benton, "Recueil," 1166d). He held a fief from the count of Brienne and was married but with-out children when he named his brother Roric and Roric's sons and daughters as his "co-heirs" (*Actes*, no. 41, 1153). He witnessed Henry's acts from 1154, is listed in the roll of fiefs for Rosnay (*Feoda* 1, 7, no. 194), and is last mentioned in 1186 (*Paraclet*, 92–93, no. 75).

7. Benton, "Recueil," 1175g.

8. Troyes, BM, ms. 2275, copied between 1166 and 1174, most likely in 1166 or 1167 (photo in *Splendeurs*, 51, fig. 3). The canons had a close relationship with the count's father ever since Thibaut, with the help of Bernard of Clairvaux, reformed the chapter as regular canons (*St-Loup*, 18–22, no. 6, 19 March 1136). Henry continued making benefactions to St-Loup and in 1163 as-sociated its canons with his secular canons of St-Étienne (*Actes,* no. 195).

9. *St-Loup*, 7–8. In 1181 Abbot Guitier noted that Countess Marie, after Henry's death, gave her signet ring, which was attached to the volume's cover, as compensation for an infraction against the abbey (*St-Loup*, 8).

10. An inventory of St-Loup's treasury in 1544 describes the cover as being encased in silver and precious stones (Lalore, *Inventaires*, 2: 106, no. 836). It survived to 1637 (Desguerrois, *La saincteté chrestienne*, 289, 291) but was lost after 1789.

11. *Actes*, no. 404, 1175: Henry here gives the nuns a house in the market of Troyes next to the house of Manasses of Pougy, provost of St-Étienne, in exchange for the revenue he had given the nuns at the time of his son's birth.

12. Benton, "Recueil," 1166d, act of Countess Marie, done in Sézanne in the presence of Henry, his court officers, and Marie's escort Nevel of Ramerupt. She exchanged her two mills on the Vanne River for the grain revenue the canons had received from Peter Bristaud, viscount of Provins, for the burial of his first wife, Halvide, in St-Quiriace (where Halvide's brother Mathieu was dean).

13. *Sigill[um] Marie Reg[is] Francor[um] filie, Trecens[sis] comitisse*. See Chassel, *Sceaux*, 129, fig. 134 (seal of ca. 1184); and *Splendeurs*, 52, fig. 5. Baudin, *Les sceaux*, 140, and Corpus (CD-ROM), no. 29 (color photo of an undated seal), concludes that Marie used only one seal matrix except perhaps after 1192, when she may have lost her original matrix. Bony, *Un siècle de sceaux figurés*, Plate XXXI, no. 201, depicts a seal from 1197.

14. *Actes*, no. 243, 1166, done in Provins: Marie witnessed (since the matter pertained to her dower lands) as Henry exempted the monks of Jouy from all taxes on their sales and purchases for their own use at his fairs and markets. Henry later gave St-Quiriace use of the woods at Jouy, which were in Marie's dower, as he said, with her consent (*Actes*, no. 297, 1170, original letter in Provins, BM, ms. 85, no. 3, with slits for two pendant seals; over the left slit, intended for Marie's seal, is written *dote*).

15. The residence of the countess was taken over by the sisters of the hospital of Provins, who gave up their previous buildings to the regular canons of St-Jacques as part of the settlement between the regular and secular canons of St-Quiriace (*St-Quiriace*, 45 n. 10).

16. *RHF* 16: 115–16, no. 355, undated. Marie addressed two other letters to Louis about the

same time. In one, she asks him to accept back Peter of Melun, his former porter, writing that she had no knowledge of accusations against him (*RHF* 16: 115, no. 354). In the other, she wrote on behalf of Hugh of Sens, her husband's *hospes*, who had served him well but who had committed some undisclosed infraction for which the king, in anger, demanded a fine (*RHF* 16: 115, no. 353). Henry sent a similar but less personal letter on the same matter (*RHF* 16: 115, no. 352). The editors of the *RHF* date all three letters, without justification, to ca. 1164.

17. *RHF* 16: 103, no. 318, Thibaut's letter to Louis, dated between 23 September (death of Bishop Robert) and 8 October (letter of Alexander III); see Falkenstein, "Wilhelm von Champagne," 113–22.

18. As noted in Bishop Henry of Winchester's obituary (*Notre-Dame de Chartres*, 3: 151). This might have been the gold cross that Thomas Becket referred to in his letter upbraiding Bishop Henry for having alienated it from his own church (Thomas Becket, *Correspondence*, 1: 16–19, no. 5, undated).

19. Alexander III, *Epistolae*, 313–14, no. 276, in Sens, to Louis.

20. Alexander III's letter of 13 January 1165 (*RHF* 15: 823).

21. Alexander III, *Epistolae*, 402–3, no. 379, 18 December 1165 (= *Materials*, 5: 241–42, no. 132) to the bishop of Troyes. Bosham congratulated William on his election to Chartres (*Epistolae*, 260–62, no. 18).

22. For Becket's conflict with the king, see Barlow, *Thomas Becket*, 88–116.

23. William Fitzstephen recounts that event in his *Vita Sancti Thomae*, 29–31; trans. in Staunton, *The Lives of Thomas Becket*, 55–57. Barlow, *Thomas Becket*, 55–57, provides a summary.

24. Herbert of Bosham gives a discreet summary of Becket's reception in Sens, passing over the heated debate preceding it (*Vita Sancti Thomae*, 340–43). Alan of Tewkesbury provides an ample account (*Materials*, 2: 336–45; trans. in Staunton, *The Lives of Thomas Becket*, 128–34).

25. Falkenstein, "Wilhelm von Champagne," 138–57.

26. Herbert of Bosham, *Epistolae*, 229–33, no. 5, to Archbishop William of Sens.

27. Thomas Becket, *Correspondence*, 1: 214–19, no. 51, early August 1165.

28. Abbot Guichard (1135–65) left Pontigny later that year to become archbishop of Lyons (1165–81). For Becket's time at Pontigny, see below n. 101.

29. Barlow, *Thomas Becket*, 20–22.

30. *RHF* 16: 119, no. 366.

31. *RHF* 16: 119, no. 365, addressed to Louis, "king of the Franks, his lord and dearest father [-in-law]."

32. Bishop Stephen (de la Chapelle), brother of the royal chamberlains Adam and Walter, had been a canon in Paris and Sens before becoming bishop of Meaux (1162–71); see Falkenstein, "Étienne de la Chapelle."

33. That is the conclusion of Bur, "Meaux," who notes that Count Thibaut III finally succeeded in eliminating the coin of Meaux in 1201. Since the coin of the bishop of Châlons had ceased to circulate ca. 1185, the *provinois* became the exclusive coin of Champagne.

34. *Actes*, no. 226, 1165, done in Provins. The reference to "the counties of Provins and Troyes" was to the old districts in which their respective coins were minted and circulated; the bishop was simply equating his coin of Meaux with the count's two traditional coins. By 1165, however, the *provinois* had effectively displaced the coin of Troyes as the count's only coin.

35. Bisson, *Conservation of Coinage*, 130–35. Count Stephen of Sancerre gave the bishop a separate letter confirming Henry's letter (Bisson, 132 n. 1)

36. Vézelay had been a problem since 1148, when the new bishop of Autun, Henry of Burgundy, tried to impose his authority over Abbot Ponce (of Montboissier), who claimed

obedience only to the pope (Petit, *Histoire*, 2: 105–7). We know the details of these events primarily from Hugh of Poitiers, the abbot's secretary, who compiled a dossier of written records, oral testimony, and eyewitness accounts in support of the abbot's position (Hugh of Poitiers, *Chronique* [*Vézelay Chronicle*], bks. 1–3). See also Jacob, "Le pape, l'enquête et la coutume," and Berlow, "The Rebels of Vézelay (1152–55)."

37. Bernard of Clairvaux, *Epistolae*, in *Opera*, 8: 338, no. 375 (*Letters*, no. 418, dated to March/April 1148). See also Petit, *Histoire*, 2: 104–12.

38. Thomas Becket, *Correspondence*, 1: 308–17, no. 78, Becket's letter to all bishops in the province of Canterbury announcing his excommunications. He sent a summary to the pope (1: 316–21, no. 79, 12 June 1166).

39. Hugh of Poitiers, *Chronique*, 603–4 (*Vézelay Chronicle*, 311–13), contains what purports to be his direct observations. Two years later the young count took the cross and left for Acre, where he died of the plague on 24 October 1168 (Lespinasse, *Le Nivernais*, 1: 341–43).

40. Ralph of Diceto, *Ymagines*, 1: 329.

41. Quantin, *Yonne*, 2: 286–89, no. 81, 15 November 1157, papal confirmation of the abbey's possessions under papal protection, with permission to conduct services behind closed doors in the event of an interdict and to prohibit religious services without the abbot's permission.

42. See at n. 112.

43. Guyotjeannin, *Episcopus*, 125–32, reviews Henry's career in Beauvais.

44. Falkenstein, "Alexandre III et Henri de France," 116–18.

45. Guy of Dampierre died on 16 February 1163. See Falkenstein, "Alexander III. und der Streit um die Doppelwahl," and Ulrich, "Guy de Joinville, évêque de Châlons."

46. John of Salisbury, *Letters*, 2: 28–31, no. 143.

47. John of Salisbury, *Historia Pontificalis*, 69–70, written shortly after his arrival in Reims. John also noted the archbishop's softer side: he loved his brother Robert, count of Dreux, and delighted in Robert's children (John of Salisbury, *Letters*, 1: 77, no. 42, January 1165, to Thomas Becket).

48. John of Salisbury, *Letters*, 2: 2–15, no. 136, early 1164, to Thomas Becket.

49. Alexander III, *Epistolae*, 466–67, no. 419 (reprimand of the archbishop), 467–68, no. 420 (letter to the king), both in 1167.

50. A summary of events in Demouy, *Genèse d'une cathédrale*, 495–98, and Desportes, *Reims et les Rémois*, 82–85.

51. John of Salisbury, *Letters*, 2: 382–87, no. 223, ca. October 1167, to Bishop John of Poitiers, describing the following events.

52. Peter of Celle, *Letters*, 392–95, no. 93.

53. Lambert of Wattrelos, *Annales Cameracensis*, 540.

54. John of Salisbury, *Letters*, 2: 382–87, no. 223, ca. October 1167.

55. *Actes*, no. 257, 1167.

56. John of Salisbury, *Letters*, 2: 438–47, no. 236, December 1167, to Bishop John of Poitiers, and perhaps an earlier letter addressed to "a friend" (2: 405–15, no. 230, late November 1167). An internal report of the meeting was delivered to both John (*Letters*, 2: 416–23, no. 231, ca. 19 November) and Becket (*Correspondence*, 1: 664–75, no. 144). For these events in 1167–68, see Warren, *Henry II*, 103–8.

57. *Layettes*, 1: 94, no. 208, 1167, Louis VII announces what was done at Mantes in the presence of his seneschal Thibaut.

58. John of Salisbury, *Letters*, 2: 552–71 (esp. 562–71), no. 272, April/May 1168 (Soissons), and 2: 590–99 (esp. 596–99), no. 277, May 1168 (Mantes).

59. John of Salisbury, *Letters*, 2: 566–69, no. 272, April/May, 1168.

60. *Actes*, no. 262, 1168 (before late October), in Chartres: Henry gave the nuns of Hautes-Bruyères a 10*l.* annual revenue from the sales tax at the Fair of May in Provins for purchasing linen, in memory of his relative Mathilda, countess of Evreux. Witnesses included "my brother William, bishop-elect of Chartres," Daimbert of Ternantes, the treasurer Artaud, and Drogo and Peter of Provins.

61. Hugh of Poiters, *Chronique*, 579 (*Vézelay Chronicle*, 298).

62. For William's years in Sens, see Falkenstein, "Wilhelm von Champagne," 122–71.

63. Thomas Becket, *Correspondence*, 2: 812–15, no. 180, after 28 December 1168, report of the consecration to the pope.

64. John of Salisbury, *Letters*, 2: 574–70, no. 274, ca. April–May 1168, to Bishop John of Poitiers.

65. William Godel, *Chronicon*, 677. For his life, see Bougard and Petitmengin, *La bibliothèque de Vauluisant*, 67–68.

66. *St-Quiriace*, 255–26, no. 23, undated: William's letter addressed to Stephen, in which William states that he selected Stephen to succeed him as provost of St-Quiriace, with the right to sit in the choir next to the dean and to speak first in the election of the next dean. See Falkenstein, "Wilhelm von Champagne," 127–38.

67. *St-Pierre*, 29–31, no. 20, 31 March 1167/68, William to Bishop Henry and the cathedral canons of Troyes.

68. Shortly after, Alexander III wrote to the chapter prohibiting a bishop-elect from retaining his prebends (*St-Pierre*, 36, no. 27, 1170/71).

69. John of Salisbury, *Letters*, 2: 536–49, no. 288, ca. February 1169, provides an eyewitness account of the meeting. See also Gillingham, "Doing Homage," 72–77.

70. Turner, *Eleanor of Aquitaine*, 205–12, presents a clear account of the issues and events.

71. Herbert of Bosham, *Vita Sancti Thomae*, 418–28; trans. in Staunton, *Lives*, 154–62. See also Barlow, *Becket*, 179–89.

72. John of Salisbury, *Letters*, 2: 608–15, no. 280, July 1168, to Master Lombard of Piacenza, his tutor in canon law while in exile.

73. For the Possesse family, and Jean in particular, see Evergates, *Aristocracy*, 184–84, 240, and Genealogy 8.

74. Guy II of Possesse mortgaged his lands at Tournan to his cousin Guy of Garland and his castle at Possesse to Count Henry in 1155/58 to finance his crusade (*Actes*, no. 108, undated, but see editor's note).

75. *Actes*, nos. 230, 231, 232, all 1165.

76. *Actes*, no. 239, 1166, known from a seventeenth-century copy of documents preserved at Marmoutier (BnF, Lat. 544, 58–59), which states that the original was sealed with yellow wax. It appears that Guy and Anselm deposited the letter at Marmoutier for safekeeping. For the familial relationship of Guy and Anselm of Garlande, see Evergates, *Aristocracy*, 184–85 and Genealogy 8.

77. *Actes*, no. 108, undated: Guy of Garlande and Mathieu of Touquin paid the count 260*l. provinois* and 12*l.* in coin of Châlons to redeem Guy's mortgaged castle. The editors of the *Actes* date Henry's letter to 1158, but I think that this redemption belongs after the decision of the Christmas court in 1166.

78. Similarly at Oudincourt near Vignory, which Henry purchased from Gilbert, viscount of Vesoul, for a 20*l.* fief rent payable at the Fair of Bar-sur-Aube. Henry did not keep the property but instead gave it to Bartholomew of Vignory in augmentation of his fief; in exchange

Bartholomew gave the count a 10l. rent from his house at Bar-sur-Aube during fairs (*Actes*, no. 271, 1168).

79. *Actes*, no. 265, 1168, probably before William's election as archbishop of Sens in late October, delivered in Chartres. A decade later Odo's son, Renaud II of Pougy, claimed castle-guard from the local inhabitants at Marolles "whenever he wanted it" and "for as long as he wanted it," but an inquest among local knights revealed that the men should be allowed to return home each night (*St-Germain-des-Prés*, 1: 243–45, no. 168, 1176, act of Archbishop William of Sens).

80. *Actes*, no. 237, 1165: he then added a privilege that no other mill could be built there without the nuns' permission.

81. Evergates, *Aristocracy*, 28–31.

82. *Actes*, no. 245, 1166: *scripto ipsius Andree et ejusdem sigilli testimonio studiose cartulam illius legens ipse perspexi, proprii autentica impressione sigilli presentem istam diligenter munire curavi.* The letter was probably drafted by a canon of St-Médard (Bur, in *Actes*, 1: xxiv), who added, perhaps quoting, that Count Henry *in conjugio habebam* the king's daughter Marie. André was lord of La Ferté-Gaucher while his mother was still living in her dower castle at Montmirail.

83. *Actes*, no. 280, 1169.

84. *Actes*, no. 261, 1168.

85. *Actes*, no. 274, 1168 (Clairvaux), and no. 282, 1169 (Notre-Dame of Oulchy).

86. *Actes*, no. 270, 1168: Aubert of Landricourt feudalized his allodial land to compensate for alienating his fief (woods) to Hautefontaine without license. Hugh of Chaumuzy exchanged his fief at Cuchery for land he held from the prior of Belval at Athenay, which became a comital fief (*Actes*, no. 281, 1169).

87. *Actes*, no. 255, 1167.

88. Evergates, *Aristocracy*, ch. 3.

89. Thomas Becket, *Correspondence*, 1: 64–77, no. 24, to Becket, undated but probably spring of 1164. The same letter is in John of Salisbury, *Letters*, 2: 2–15, no. 136, dated early 1164.

90. Peter of Celle, *Letters*, 430–33, no. 108, after 29 September 1169.

91. St-Remi of Reims had one of the best Carolingian libraries for both liturgical and intellectual purposes. It survived to the eighteenth century, when Martène saw 500–600 books there, mostly of Carolingian provenance, before the library burned in 1774 (Lesne, *Histoire de la propriété ecclésiastique*, 4: 603).

92. John wrote to his friend Bishop John of Poitiers that he would have forwarded Henry's letter but that he already had sent it to Becket (John of Salisbury, *Letters*, 2: 178–85, no. 177, ca. July 1166).

93. Wood, "The Execution of Papal Justice," 101, 153–99.

94. Ralph was dean (1176–96). See Uruszczak, "Enseignants," 750–51, and Duggan, "The Price of Loyalty," 12 n. 51, and her brief biography in Thomas Becket, *Correspondence*, 2: 1384–85.

95. Uruszczak, "Enseignants," 749–51, and Duggan, "The Price of Loyalty," 15 n. 63. Herbert of Bosham had high praise for Ralph, whom he included among Becket's *eruditi* (*Vita Sancti Thomae*, 526).

96. An otherwise unknown monk, "Robert the Englishman," copied Augustine's *Expositio in Psalmis* at St-Remi; see Caviness, *Sumptuous Arts*, 7.

97. Peter of Celle wrote a rapturous account of the Carthusian way of monastic life at Mont-Dieu during his visit, perhaps ca. 1160, while his old friend Simon Aurea Capra was prior

(Peter of Celle, *Letters*, 92–103, no. 28, to Abbot Hardouin of Larrivour). Mont-Dieu was founded in 1136 on land donated by the chapter of St-Remi, with which the priory maintained close ties.

98. In a letter to Becket, John of Salisbury included Peter of Celle among Becket's "friends," but whether Peter was in fact a personal friend or simply a supporter is not clear (Thomas Becket, *Correspondence*, 1: 482–85, no. 102, July 1166).

99. See Nederman, *John of Salisbury*, 33–34, and Chibnall, "John of Salisbury as Historian," 169.

100. John of Salisbury, *Letters*, 2: 714–25, no. 304, December 1170, to Abbot Peter of St-Remi.

101. For Becket's time at Pontigny, see Barlow, *Thomas Becket*, 117–58.

102. Kinder, "Toward Dating Construction of the Abbey Church."

103. Herbert of Bosham, *Vita Sancti Thomae*, 379; trans. in Staunton, *Lives of Thomas Becket*, 136–37. William Fitzstephen, *Vita Sancti Thomae*, 20–23; trans. in Staunton, *Lives of Thomas Becket*, 48–53, describes Becket's table and company while chancellor. For a concise biography of Bosham, see Smalley, *The Becket Conflict*, 59–86.

104. Bosham explained in his letter of dedication how he aided the reader by varying the size of letters, highlighting in colored ink, and adding comments/corrections in the margins, all the while keeping the text readable rather than erudite (text printed in Delisle, "Traductions de textes grecs," 732–35, no. 1). See also De Hamel, "Manuscripts of Herbert of Bosham," which gives an analysis and photograph (39) of Peter Lombard's gloss on the Psalms with Bosham's corrections. Bosham's "edition" is dated to the mid-1170s, before 1176 and perhaps ca. 1173.

105. The four volumes begun at Pontigny in 1165/66 were originally dedicated to Thomas Becket, but after completing them in the mid-1170s Bosham erased the original dedication and composed a new one to Archbishop William, whom he had known since the 1140s in England and who harbored him in Sens after Becket's murder. For Bosham's prefaces and dedications, see Glunz, *History of the Vulgate*, 341–50. For a brief intellectual history of Bosham, see De Visscher, *Reading the Rabbis*, 1–21.

106. Staunton, *Thomas Becket*, 63–74, stresses the function of invented speeches in Bosham's biography of Becket.

107. Herbert of Bosham, *Vita Sancti Thomae*, 379; trans. in Staunton, *Lives of Thomas Becket*, 136–37.

108. Peyrafort-Huin, *La bibliothèque médiévale de Pontigny*, 18–22, 110.

109. William Fitzstephen, *Vita Sancti Thomae*, 77.

110. James, *Ancient Libraries*, 82–83, prints a later inventory of Becket's books left to Christ Church Canterbury.

111. Herbert of Bosham, *Vita Sancti Thomae*, 404. For Becket's years at Ste-Colombe, see Barlow, *Thomas Becket*, 158–224.

112. Herbert of Bosham, *Vita Sancti Thomae*, 403–4, and 407–8 (for an appreciation of *dulcis Francia*).

113. Stirnemann, "En quête de Sens," reveals the extent of book production in Sens. She identifies 58 books painted in Channel Style that were produced in Sens, rather than in Paris as previously thought, in the years 1165–78.

114. Stirnemann, "En quête de Sens," 307–10, and "Where Can We Go from Here?" 87.

115. Nicholas asked for two barrels of wine, one for himself and one for the abbot of Montiéramey, as the bishop had promised; see Benton, "Nicolas de Clairvaux." The bishop of Auxerre was probably Alan, former abbot of Larrivour, whom Nicholas had known in the 1140s while he was secretary to the bishop of Troyes. They also shared a Clairvaux experience, Alan as a monk in the 1130s and Nicholas as Bernard's secretary in the late 1140s.

116. William Fitzstephen, *Vita Sancti Thomae*, 99–100, 101; trans. in Staunton, *Lives of Thomas Becket*, 65. This encounter took place Easter 1166 in Angers, where Henry II had summoned Becket's clerics to make their peace in return for recovering their confiscated benefices in England.

117. See ch. 5. What follows attempts to integrate what is known about Henry's library with bookmaking and collecting in southern Champagne in the second half of the twelfth century based on the work of Patricia Stirnemann (see bibliography).

118. The inventory of Henry's library lists it as *Item magistri Godefridi* (Lalore, *Inventaires*, 2: 270, no. 2271). That lost volume was possibly made from the copy at Pontigny (Peyrafort-Huin, *La bibliothèque médiévale de Pontigny*, 111), as was Becket's copy (Cambridge University, Trinity College, B.16.17), which contains both Geoffrey of Monmouth's *History* and Bede's *Ecclesiastical History of the English People* (Peyrafort-Huin, 541–42, no. 94), thus providing in one volume the two basic histories of England.

119. John left his Vegetius and his personal copy of the *Policraticus* to the cathedral chapter of Chartres, whose necrology lists his bequest of books "and especially his *Polycraticus*" (*Notre-Dame de Chartres*, 3: 202). Henry's copy has not been identified and does not appear in the 1319/20 inventory of books. But since Becket had a copy, which he brought back from France in 1170 and bequeathed to Christ Church Canterbury (James, *The Ancient Libraries*, 85, no. 852), it seems likely that Henry had a copy made at the same time.

120. John of Salisbury, *Letters*, 2: 336–37, no. 209, ca. 1166/67.

121. Allmand, *The "De Re Militari"*, esp. 84–91, 277–79.

122. John of Salisbury, *Letters*, 2: 315–39, "to his most serene lord Henry, illustrious and glorious count palatine of Troyes," no. 209, undated but likely early in John's exile, probably 1165 or 1166.

123. John of Salisbury, *Letters*, 2: 334–37, no. 209.

124. The volume (BnF, Lat. 9688) was inventoried among Henry's books in 1319/20 (Lalore, *Inventaires*, 2: 270, no. 2283: *Item liber Valerii Maximi*); photograph in *Splendeurs*, 37. Stirnemann, "Quelques bibliothèques," 23–24, describes it as a beautiful, clear English script; see also Stirnemann, "Where Can We Go from Here?," 85–86. For a photograph of the colophon (*Titulus Scriptoris: feliciter emendavi descriptum Pruvini issu illustris comitis Henrici, Willelmus Anglicus, anno incarnati verbi mclxvii indictione xv*), see Stirnemann, in *Splendeurs*, 64, fig. 30. This William may have been the same as "William the Englishman" in Bar-sur-Aube in 1155 and "William the Scribe of Provins" in the 1160s and 1170s (see ch. 5 at n. 64); in 1179, he drew up a pre-crusade bequest for the treasurer Artaud (*Paraclet*, 83–84, no. 64, 1179). Perhaps he was the "third William" in the chancery in 1171 (*Actes*, no. 331).

125. Henry's copy was made from Berne Stadbibliotek, ms. 366, the copy owned and marked by Loup of Ferrieres; see Reynolds, *Texts and Transmission*, 428–30.

126. See ch. 8 ("The Speaking Tomb").

127. William le Mire was one of several monks at St-Denis who were studying and translating Greek works in the 1160s and 1170s, especially works related to the monastery's patron saint; see Nebbiai-Dalla Guarda, *La bibliothèque de l'abbaye de Saint-Denis*, 29–35.

128. Herbert of Bosham, *Epistolae*, 207–17, no. 1, at 217. Herbert's last sentence, regarding *Attic Nights*, was omitted in the *PL* reprint of the letters; see De la Mare et al., "Pietro de Montagnana," 223 n. 22, and Smalley, "A Commentary on the *Hebraica*," 37–39.

129. For the significance of Aulus Gellius for John of Salisbury's ideas, see Martin, "The Uses of Tradition," 57–68.

130. Stirnemann, "Quelques bibliothèques," 24 n. 41, gives the inscription: *Willelmus*

scripsit anno incarnati verbi MCLXX. Indictione III. Concurrente III. Epacta I. Henry's copy of *Attic Nights* is listed in the 1319/20 inventory of his books (Lalore, *Inventaires*, 2: 271, no. 2302: *Item liber Agelli Noctium Aticarum*).

131. Henry's copy (Vatican, Reg. Lat. 1646) and Becket's twin (BnF, Lat. 13038) contain only books 9–20 of *Attic Nights*; see De la Mare et al., "Pietro de Montagnana," 223–24. For the interest of English *literati* in *Attic Nights*, see Thomson, *William of Malmesbury*, 189–98.

132. Stirnemann, "Two Twelfth-Century Bibliophiles," 121, and *Splendeurs*, 39 (photograph). Henry's copy was inventoried as *Item Ciciliani* [read instead: *Titilivi*; see Stirnemann, in *Splendeurs*, 37] *tertia pars* (Lalore, *Inventaires*, 2: 270, no. 2288).

133. Bishop Hugh of Durham (1153–95) had been archdeacon of Winchester under Bishop Henry; see Scammell, *Hugh de Puiset*. Count Henry may have owned a copy of Cyprian's letters because the volume owned by Bishop Hugh was copied by an English hand and decorated by the same painter who executed three of Count Henry's own books (Quintus Curtius Rufus, Freculf, and part of Josephus) as well as a volume owned by Archbishop Henry of Reims (a copy of Sigebert of Gembloux); see Stirnemann, "Un manuscrit de Claudian," 55 n. 10.

134. Stirnemann, "Un manuscrit de Claudian," 55–56.

135. Herbert of Bosham, *Epistolae*, 279–81, no. 24: requests the pope's intervention to repair the disorder in England caused by Becket's exile.

136. Robert of Auxerre, *Chronicon*, 262–65 (a brief biography).

137. Robert of Auxerre, *Chronicon*, 263–64.

138. For the significance of the *romans* of antiquity for the recovery of ancient Latin culture, see Haugeard, "Traduction et essor de la littérature en langue française."

139. Fourrier, "Encore la chronologie," 70–74, argues persuasively that *Erec* was written in 1170, that is, after Henry II of England's Christmas court at Nantes in 1169, which may have served as Chrétien's model for King Arthur's court at Nantes, where Erec and Enide were crowned by the local bishop in the presence of many barons and knights from the Plantagenet realms. The fact that an unnamed archbishop of Canterbury earlier in the story blessed Erec and Enide at their wedding suggests that the romance was composed before Becket's murder on 29 December 1170, after which the office was vacant for three years. Schmolke-Hasselmann, *The Evolution of Arthurian Romance*, 232–44, argues that *Erec* contains several references to Henry II, but Misrahi, "More Light on the Chronology," 90–101, maintains that Chrétien's scenes are entirely imaginary.

CHAPTER 7. COUNT HENRY IN MID-LIFE, 1171–1175

1. *Actes*, no. 336, 24 May 1172: *bonitate et felicitate.*

2. Count Philip's sister Margaret married Baldwin in 1169, shortly after the death of her first husband, Ralph II (the Leper), count of Vermandois; she was thirty-seven at the time and without living children; see Nicholas, "Countesses as Rulers in Flanders," 126–27.

3. Gislebert of Mons, *Chronique*, 102–3 (*Chronicle*, 60), cap. 64. Elizabeth of Hainaut was born in April 1170; her brother Baldwin was born in July 1171 (101–2 [*Chronicle*, 59–60], caps. 61, 63; see Falmagne, *Baudouin V*, 112–14. Marie of Champagne was born in the months before the August 1171 marriage contract.

4. See Joris, "Un seul amor."

5. Guy of Bazoches, *Liber epistularum*, 59–61, no. 16, plausibly dated to ca. 1171/72 and linked to the marriage treaty; see Bur, "L'image de la parenté," 74–81, with a genealogical

reconstruction and commentary on Guy's selective genealogy. For the Bazoches family, see Newman, *Nesle*, 1: 125–39.

6. Gislebert of Mons, *Chronique*, 107–8 (*Chronicle*, 62–63), caps. 68–69, notes that Baldwin took eighty knights on the tournament circuit after Christmas 1171 to the tournament grounds located between Bussy-le-Château (a comital castle-town) and Châlons (an episcopal city), and to Lizy-sur-l'Ourcq, on the Marne northeast of Meaux. He then took one hundred knights to Nevers, where he joined a tournament sponsored by Count Guy of Nevers at a site between Rougement and Montbard (in Burgundy), despite lacking an invitation (Petit, *Histoire*, 2: 186–87, dated between 16 and 23 April 1173).

7. Crouch, *William Marshal*, 192–206.

8. *Actes*, no. 253, 25 October–31 December 1167: *Daniel sacerdos Xpristos scripsit*. Daniel dated Henry's letter "1167 from the incarnation of our lord Jesus Christ; epact 18, concurrent 6, indiction 15; in the thirty-seventh year of the reign of Louis, king of the Franks; and in the 6366th year from Adam" (photograph of the letter in *Actes*, 1: xxxviii). Daniel's script, dating, and self-identification are unique. The Second Lateran Council (1139) prohibited the despoliation of a deceased bishop's property (*Decrees of the Ecumenical Councils*, 197, canon 5).

9. Peter of Celle (*Letters*, 416–19, no. 102, 1176) later commended William for having "elected and consecrated" Bishop Mathieu.

10. *Acta Pontificum Romanorum inedita*, 1: 242–44, no. 263. The subsequent conflict is discussed in Corbet, "Les collégiales comtales," 200–202, and Falkenstein, *La papauté*, 80–85. It should be noted that Henry did not seek St-Étienne's exemption from episcopal authority in 1169; it was the bishop who asserted his authority over the chapel, which the pope confirmed.

11. Henry's nuncios must have presented his case in Rome in the fall of 1169 or early 1170. The pope's letter granting a seven-year exemption is not extant. All this is recounted in Alexander III's letters of 18/20 May 1171 (see n. 14 below).

12. Thomas Becket, *Correspondence*, 2: 1206–11, no. 282, ?April 1170, to Alexander III.

13. The chronology of Herbert of Bosham's life after 1171 is uncertain. He remained in Sens to the mid-1170s while finishing his edition of Peter Lombard's *Great Gloss*, which he dedicated to Archbishop William, and perhaps followed William to Reims in 1176, where he composed (ca. 1184) a biography of Becket (*Vita Sancti Thomae*). For William's interdict, see Barlow, *Thomas Becket*, 252–55.

14. Letter to the bishop: *Acta Pontificum Romanorum inedita* 1: 250–51, no. 271, 18 May 1171; and Falkenstein, *La papauté*, no. xxx (photograph of AD Aube, G 20, no. 3). Letter to the canons of St-Étienne: *Acta Pontificum Romanorum inedita*, 1: 251–52, no. 272, 20 May 1171; and Falkenstein, *La papauté*, 82–83 (text) and no. xxix (photograph of AD Aube, G 20, no. 4). Duggan (Thomas Becket, *Correspondence*, 2: 1401–2) finds that the pope's letters "echo the language of" Becket's letter to the pope (see n. 12 above) defending the rights of bishops against Count Henry's attempt to exempt St-Étienne from "mother church."

15. Pastan, "*Realpolitik* and Artistic Patronage," 534, 536.

16. It is not known how many canons the cathedral chapter had in 1170; there were at least twenty-three in 1146 (see ch. 4 n. 49), and forty were authorized in the fourteenth century (*St-Pierre*, 208, item 28).

17. *Chronique de Saint-Pierre-le-Vif de Sens*, 202–3, which describes how the remains were replaced in tombs of lead and wood. Geoffroy of Courlon (d. 1293) describes the translation (Geoffroy de Courlon, *Le livre des reliques*, 35). About the same time, Abbot Odo of Ste-Colombe asked the pope to certify the authenticity of the body of Saint Loup kept in a reliquary box; the pope directed Archbishop Hugh of Sens and Bishops Manasses of Orléans and Alan of Auxerre

to inspect the body and confirm the archbishop's earlier inspection and authentication. The three prelates inspected the body, declared it authentic, and had it displayed publicly (Geoffroy de Courlon, *Le livre des reliques*, 288–89, no. 10, 24 June 1160).

18. *Actes*, no. 256, 1167. St-Étienne's reliquary for Potentianus was inventoried in 1319 (Lalore, *Inventaires*, 2: 13–14, no. 115). Perhaps the abbot of Ste-Colombe relinquished those relics because he had the newly authenticated relics of Saint Loup (see n. 17 above) transferred to his priory at St-Loup-de-Naud (Geoffroy de Courlon, *Le livre des reliques*, 290, no. 11, ca. 1162).

19. On the significance of the relic translations by Louis VII and Frederick I, see Petersohn, "Saint-Denis-Westminster-Aachen."

20. See ch. 5 at n. 67.

21. Kidson, "Panofsky, Suger and St Denis," 10, and Cothren, "Suger's Stained Glass Masters."

22. Brown and Cothren, "The Twelfth-Century Crusading Window."

23. The Corinthian capital from St-Étienne (photo in *Splendeurs*, 57, fig. 16) resembles the portal capital of St-Quiriace of about the same date (Timbert, "Le chevet de la collégiale Saint-Quiriace," 252, fig. 21). For the column-sculptures of St-Ayoul, see Snyder, *Early Gothic Column-Figure Sculpture*, 28, fig. 1.18 and 43, fig. 1.50; and Blum, "The Statue-Column of a Queen," 229.

24. Arnaud, *Voyage archéologique*, 26, provides a general sketch of the tympanum with Henry presenting a model of his chapel to another figure, presumably Saint Stephen. The date of the tympanum cannot be determined, but I would place it with the portal column-figures and the interior glazing around 1160, before the construction of Henry's tomb in the mid-1170s.

25. See ch. 4 at nn. 33–34.

26. *Actes*, no. 307, 1170: the brothers of St-Jean-en-Châtel would process with the canons of St-Étienne annually and at the death of every canon, for which Henry gave 5*l.* annual revenue to be enjoyed by Prior Nicholas for his lifetime and by the priory for as long as the brothers processed with the count's canons.

27. *Actes*, no. 354, 1173, Henry's confirmation of St-Étienne's endowment.

28. Chapin, *Les villes de foires*, 33.

29. Falkenstein, *La papauté*, 86–87 (text). The duke decided to build Ste-Chapelle of Dijon after returning from a perilous voyage to the Levant in 1172; while passing through Rome on his way home, he told Pope Alexander III about his plan, which the pope approved (Pérard, *Recueil*, 242–46, 8 November 1172 = *GC*, 14: instr. 186–87). It is highly likely that Hugh had seen his uncle Henry's chapel in Troyes. The duke installed about twenty canons (Richard, *Les ducs de Bourgogne*, 398–99, 427).

30. Aubri of Trois-Fontaines, *Chronicon*, 847.

31. *Actes*, nos. 362–63, (foundation of two chaplaincies), both of 1173. *Actes*, no. 400, 1175 (confirmation of the chapel's endowment).

32. Demouy, *Genèse d'une cathédrale*, 628–31 (brief biography) and "Henri de France et Louis VII" offer a sympathetic portrait of Henry as a Cistercian prelate in the mold of Bernard of Clairvaux.

33. Sassier, *Recherches*, 88–89, and Evergates, *Aristocracy*, 22.

34. The pope's curt letters to the archbishop suggest a breakdown of order within episcopal lands (Alexander III, *Epistolae*, 546–47, nos. 575–76). Count Henry II of Grandpré had a long history of violent conduct against monasteries in the diocese (Barthélemy, "Notice historique sur la maison de Grandpré," 98–100). Peter of Celle *(Letters*, 364–67, no. 84), an undated letter to a cardinal, perhaps Albert of Mora, complaining about the depredations and deaths caused by the counts of Roucy and Rethel and by Hugh of Pierrepont, who finally ended their violences by

intermarrying, perhaps consanguineously, says Peter, dispensation being given for the sake of peace.

35. The conflict is described in Arbois de Jubainville, *Histoire*, 3: 76–81, and Demouy, *Genèse d'une cathédrale*, 529–32.

36. After the tower was dismantled, said the archbishop, the knight Boso, *dominus* of the place, sold the village and all that he possessed there "in fief and domain" to the archbishop for 300*l.*, paid through a Templar brother, such that "anyone who held a fief from him will [henceforth] hold from me [the archbishop] and my successors and will do homage to me." Boso's mother, wife, son, daughter, four brothers, two sisters, a brother-in-law, and a nephew consented to that sale (Varin, *Archives administratives*, 1: 362–65, no. 209, 1171). Boso was listed as the count's liegeman in the roll of fiefs for Bussy (*Feoda* 1: 18, no. 518, ca. 1178). Archbishop Henry's obituary remembered him for having acquired the fortress of Sept-Saulx (*RHF* 15: 924).

37. *RHF* 16: 195, no. 195. Abbot Peter (of Celle) of St-Remi also thanked the archbishop for suppressing the brigands, dismantling the fortress at Sampigny, and building a new one at Sept-Saulx for protecting the surrounding countryside (AD Marne, G 109, 1172). Guermond of Châtillon witnessed the count's act in 1170 (*Actes*, nos. 309, 311). In the roll of fiefs Guermond is listed as the count's liegeman and castellan of Bussy (*Feoda* 1, 18, no. 517, ca. 1178).

38. *RHF* 15: 920, no. 331, 16 June 1171.

39. Varin, *Archives administratives*, 1: 365–67, no. 213, 1171.

40. *RHF* 16: 194–95, 1172: the bishop claimed Henry as *homo noster ligius*; trans. in Evergates, *Documents*, 125–27, no. 97A.

41. See Evergates, *Aristocracy*, 182–83.

42. *RHF* 16: 697–89, Frederick Barbarossa's letter, dated by the editors to 1171/72. The archbishops and bishops in attendance were to excommunicate offending lords and interdict their lands.

43. Alexander III, *Epistolae*, 798–800, no. 896, 22 March 1172; trans. in Evergates, *Documents*, 127–28, no. 97B.

44. Alexander III, *Epistolae*, 800–802, no. 897, 22 March 1172.

45. Alexander III, *Epistolae*, 803–4, no. 899, 22 March 1172; trans. in Evergates, *Documents*, 128–29, no. 97C.

46. Thomas Becket, *Correspondence*, 2: 1260–79, no. 300, after 22 July 1170, to the pope.

47. Barlow, *Thomas Becket*, 252–75, and Kemp, "Pope Alexander III and the Canonization of Saints," 19–21.

48. Alexander III, *Epistolae*, 730–31, no. 794, 24 June 1171.

49. John of Salisbury, *Vita et passio Sancti Thome*.

50. Simon Aurea Capra, *Vita et passio sancti Thome*.

51. For the young king and his revolt, see Warren, *Henry II*, 117–45; Strickland, "On the Instruction of a Prince"; and Gillingham, *Richard I*, 41–51.

52. Strickland, "On the Instruction of a Prince," 186–87.

53. Roger of Howden, *Gesta regis Henrici secundi*, 1: 43–45, states that Eleanor "sent" her sons to join the young king's revolt against their father, whereas William of Newburgh, *Historia*, 171, says that she encouraged her son to go to the French court, where the count of Flanders and other unnamed "great men" supported him.

54. Anonymous letter of 1173 to Alexander III; see Weiler, "Kings and Sons," 20–22.

55. Ralph of Diceto, *Ymagines*, 1: 355–68.

56. Roger of Howden, *Gesta regis Henrici secundi*, 1: 43–45. Stephen of Sancerre, widowed by 1169, had just returned from his pilgrimage to Jerusalem (1171–73), where he was supposed to

marry Sybil of Jerusalem; he is mentioned here for the first time as being closely allied with Counts Henry and Thibaut.

57. Jordan Fantosme, *Chronicle*, lines 1–55.

58. Ralph of Diceto, *Ymagines*, 1: 374–75, and Roger of Howden, *Chronica*, 49–51.

59. Ralph of Diceto, *Ymagines*, 1: 394–95. Prince Henry was given two castles in Normandy plus a 15,000*l.* revenue, Richard received two castles and half of the revenues in Poitou, and Geoffrey received half of the revenues in Brittany.

60. Ralph of Diceto, *Ymagines*, 1: 400–401, reproduces King Henry's letter, read at Westminster on 20 May 1175, announcing his son's submission.

61. Roger of Howden, *Gesta regis Henrici secundi*, 1: 14–19.

62. For Odo of Pougy, see ch. 3 at nn. 81–82. William of Dampierre (1151–74) witnessed an act with his father in 1133, and thus was about the same age as Count Henry. He probably went on the Second Crusade in Henry's company, and he later witnessed twenty-four of the count's acts between 1153 and 1172. His brother Guy was elected bishop of Châlons in 1163 but died before being consecrated, and his sister Heloise married the seneschal Geoffroy IV of Joinville. William's son Guy II (1174–1216) witnessed Countess Marie's acts in the 1180s and went on the Third Crusade, but it is uncertain whether he succeeded his father as constable, since neither his letters patent nor his seal ever identified him as constable, only as "Guy of Dampierre" (Baudin, *Les sceaux*, Corpus [CD-ROM], 77–78). See also Savetiez, "Maison de Dampierre-Saint-Dizier," 19–26.

63. The letters of Henry (*Actes*, no. 320) and Marie (Benton, "Recueil," 1171q), both dated 1171, were done in Sézanne. The dower consisted of all Artaud's possessions, present and future, within his newly constructed lordship of Nogent-sur-Marne and in the count's castellanies of Château-Thierry and Sézanne. Everything else he left to his children. The letters are identical in every respect except that Henry appears in his as "count palatinate of Troyes" and Marie states in hers that she is "joined in legitimate marriage to Henry, count of Troyes." Both letters disappeared after being copied in the sixteenth century. For the Nogent-l'Artaud, see Evergates, *Aristocracy*, 182–84.

64. Nicholas of Bazoches had destroyed the village of Cergy belonging to the canons of St-Médard of Soissons (*Actes*, no. 341, 1171). Odo of Vendreuve inflicted similar damage on a village belonging to the monks of Montier-en-Der (*Actes*, no. 375, 1174).

65. *Actes*, no. 402, 1175.

66. Larrivour, 31–32, no. 19, Garnier's undated report. The arbitration is unusual in that the two parties chose four monastics—Alan (former abbot of Larrivour and bishop of Auxerre who retired to Larrivour), two cellarers of Clairvaux, and Nicholas of Montiéramey (prior of St-Jean-en-Châtel in Troyes)—who in turn invited four distinguished personages to join them: Abbots Girard of Montier-la-Celle and Guitier of St-Loup, Jean (former lord of Possesse and currently monk at Clairvaux), and Garnier of Traînel.

67. *Actes*, no. 383, 1174.

68. Quantin, *Yonne*, 2: 249–51, no. 233, 1174. The dispute arose after the count of Nevers refused to do homage for the lands of his wife, the duke's sister Mathilda of Burgundy (see Petit, *Histoire*, 2: 192–93). After a brief armed conflict, Count Guy was captured (30 April 1174); he did homage for several fiefs, and he promised to destroy his recently built fortifications and pay 2,000 marks in compensation, with the bishops of Langres, Autun, Auxerre, and Nevers as his guarantors (Pérard, *Recueil*, 247–48; Quantin, *Yonne*, 2: 249–51). To raise the fine Guy franchised the city of Tonnerre (Quantin, *Yonne*, 2: 259, 1175).

69. For the circulation of fiefs before 1165, see ch. 3 ("The Business of Fiefs).

70. *Actes*, no. 413, 1175.

71. *Actes*, no. 358, 1173. In 1171 Henry consented, after the fact, to the sale by Odo, viscount of Rosnay, of a comital fief (one-quarter of a mill) to the monks of St-Pierre-aux-Monts of Châlons for 30*l.* and permission for his sons to enter the monastery (*Actes*, no. 329, 1171).

72. *Actes*, no. 347, 1177, license for Molême to acquire his fiefs "in any way they are able."

73. Gislebert of Mons, *Chronique*, 174–75 (*Chronicle*, 96), cap. 115, reports that Count Baldwin granted new fiefs and assigned annual incomes as fiefs in the mid-1180s. A chancery scribe in Champagne noted ca. 1178 that John of Hochecourt held in fief the village of Hochecourt, "which the count gave him," suggesting a recent grant (*Feoda* 1, no. 1731).

74. For example, Henry granted the sales tax collected from a commercial building during the Fair of St-Ayoul to Girard of Beauchery as a fief (*Actes*, no. 300, 1170). The building, owned by the mayor Hatto, might have been the one listed in the *censier* of the Hôtel-Dieu of Provins from the 1170s (Verdier, *St-Ayoul*, 146, no. 5). Girard still held the fief in 1178, for which he was liege and owed three months castleguard (*Feoda* 1, 57 no. 1565). St-Ayoul acquired the revenue by January 1223, n.s. (*Montier-la-Celle*, 25–26, no. 21).

75. On the valuation of fiefs in terms of annual revenue, see Evergates, *Aristocracy*, 25–26.

76. *Actes*, no. 372, 1174, done at Pontoise, where Count Henry was with the king's forces, supporting the Plantagenet brothers; Henry explained the delay by saying: "I owed him that amount as a fief (rent)."

77. *Actes*, no. 498, 1179, 1 April–mid May 1179.

78. Matthew of Beaumont's son Jean returned the count's letter in 1215, when he exchanged his father's 25*l.* revenue for a fief rent worth 60*l.* annually from the same tolls (*Cartulary of Countess Blanche*, 290–91, no. 327). Count Henry's letter of 1174 spoke of *libras annui redditus . . . de feodo*, whereas Matthew of Beaumont called his newly assigned revenue *libratas terre . . . pro feudo*.

79. Evergates, *Aristocracy*, 25–26.

80. Higounet, *Défrichements et villeneuves*, 59–203, devotes much of his study to communities within Champagne.

81. *Actes*, no. 258, 1167, and no. 319, 1171.

82. Immigrants in Troyes, Provins, and Pont-sur-Seine fell by default under the canons of St-Étienne (*Actes*, no. 95, item 51, 1157), and those in Bar-sur-Aube came under the lordship of the canons of St-Maclou (*Actes*, no. 197, item 2, 1160).

83. *Actes*, no. 297, 1170, covering all immigrants *de regno gallico*.

84. *Actes*, no. 344, 1172, letter for the residents of Avize, retained until it was copied in the sixteenth century. *Actes*, no. 356, 1173, late thirteenth-century copy of Henry's letter in possession of the community of Maraye-en-Othe.

85. Higounet, *Défrichement et villeneuves*, 141, 203. Henry founded thirteen "new" villages in all: one in 1156, one in 1161, and eleven in the 1170s (Bur, in *Actes*, 2: 23). One of the earliest new communities was at Maurupt, whose tenants had received unspecified privileges before 1171 (*Actes*, no. 332, 1171). We know that only because the count's men there presented Henry's charter in defense of their privileges against a challenge by the monks of Cheminon; see Lusse, "Deux villeneuves," 72–78.

86. Chazan, "The Blois Incident of 1171."

87. Neubauer and Stern, *Hebräische Berichte*, 152.

88. For a map of Jewish communities in Champagne, see Nahon, "Les communautés juives," 49. Indirect evidence suggests that Henry did in fact deal with local Jewish communities; see Fudeman, *Vernacular Voices*, 83.

89. Reiner, "Rabbénu Tam et le Comte Henri de Champagne," 33–35.

90. Robert of Auxerre, *Chronicon*, 253, describes St-Étienne's luxurious furnishings and objects that perished in the fire of 1188.

91. The iron ring (*annulus ferreus*) of "saint Thomas, archbishop of Canterbury," was listed among St-Étienne's treasures in 1319 (Lalore, *Inventaires*, 2: 6, no. 26). Becket's "oil," shirt, cowl, and blood-stained clothing were located in a phylactery in the chapel's small treasury (Lalore, *Inventaires*, 2: 21, no. 175).

92. Paston, "Dating the Medieval Work," 250–51. Anthony's relics appear in St-Étienne's inventory of 1319–20 (Lalore, *Inventaires*, 2: 3, no. 12; 2: 13, no. 108; and 2: 21, no. 170). By that time the chapel's treasuries contained 512 liturgical objects, mostly reliquaries (Lalore, *Inventaires*, 2: 1–170).

93. Pastan, "Fit for a Count," concludes that the panels from Troyes, now dispersed, probably belonged to St-Étienne rather than the cathedral, and that the glass was fired in the 1170s, which accords with the presence of Mosan craftsmen in Troyes building the count's tomb in the early to mid-1170s. If, as argued here, St-Étienne was essentially built by ca. 1160, the fabric of the chapel would have lacked finished windows for a decade. Photographs of the panels are in Pastan, "Fit for a Count," and color photographs are in *Une Renaissance*, 130–31, fig. 69.

94. *Actes*, no. 390, 1174: André's sale of his share of the mills to St-Martin-ès-Aires for 100*l*.; the names of six other witnesses are no longer decipherable. In 1222, Count Thibaut IV freed William, "the son of my dear mason, Master André," from *taille*, tolls, and all exactions as well as guard duty at the city walls and towers; the count also gave 100*s*. annually from the tax on wine entering Troyes during the fairs, "in remuneration for the service that Master André rendered me" (AN, KK 1064, fol. 330v, April 1222). See Stein, "Le maître d'oeuvre André."

95. Dectot ("Les tombeaux des comtes," 5 and 27, fig. 22) links the commission of the tomb to Henry's second confirmation of St-Étienne's endowment in 1173, and concludes that the tomb was completed "shortly before 1180" (23). The suggestion that Countess Marie commissioned the tomb after 1181 is based on an inscription (missing from modern descriptions of the tomb) that states that Marie shrouded Henry's ashes—not that she commissioned his tomb (Morganstern, *Gothic Tombs*, 203 n. 11). An inscription firmly associated with the tomb states, in Henry's words: "I made this tomb for myself" (see ch. 8 at n. 115).

96. For Becket, see Slocum, *Liturgies in Honour of Thomas Becket*, 79–97, and Staunton, *The Lives of Thomas Becket*, 8–13. Alexander III rejected the initial proposal in 1163 to canonize Bernard because the *vita* offered in support lacked sufficient verification of his acts; it was revised accordingly, and in February 1174 the pope announced that, since the subject was raised at a recent meeting in Paris, he was ready to proceed with Bernard's canonization (*PL* 185: 622–24, nos. 1–3, letters to the church of France, to the king, and to the Cistercians). See Bredero, "The Canonization of Bernard of Clairvaux," 84–90.

97. Henry gave a 10*l*. revenue from the table of money changers in Troyes for the support of Marie (*Actes*, no. 374, 1174). The next year he gave Fontevraud an additional 20*l*. revenue assigned on the sales tax in Provins for his two (unnamed) sisters, most likely Marie and Margaret (*Actes*, no. 397, no. 1175).

98. Kidson, "Gervase, Becket, and William of Sens," makes a strong case for arson.

99. Cragoe, "Reading and Rereading Gervase of Canterbury," 47, argues that Gervase was less interested in describing the new architecture of Canterbury cathedral than in describing "the physical and historic space of the cathedral as the *cathedra* and mausoleum of the archbishops of Canterbury. . . . For him the building was primarily a venue for the saints and their shrines." Draper, *The Formation of English Gothic*, 13–33, provides a succinct summary of events and of the building of Trinity chapel.

100. Houben, *Roger II of Sicily*, 133. Roger II's letter of April 1145 explains the purpose of the tombs (Deér, *The Dynastic Porphyry Tombs*, 1), which were temporarily placed in Cèphalu cathedral while the Capella Palatina was being constructed in Palermo.

101. Nees, "The *Fastigium* of Saint-Remi." For a color photograph of the head of "King Lothair," showing vestiges of paint, see *La France romane*, 345, fig. 261

102. Prache, *Saint-Remi de Reims*, describes the architectural renovations.

103. Dionisotti, "Walter of Châtillon," 90–96, argues persuasively that the poem was written between 1170 and 1176, with the dedication to William inserted after his election to Reims. Lafferty, *Walter of Châtillon's "Alexandreis"*, 183–89, prefers a range of dates between 1171 and 1181. Whether Walter was in Sens or Reims when he began the poem is uncertain. It is possible that he was a canon in Reims under Archbishop Henry and identified by John of Salisbury as "Master Walter, a cleric of the archbishop of Reims," who had lent books to Master Peter Helias (John of Salisbury, *Letters*, 2: 92–101 no. 167, to the chancellor of Poitiers, early June 1166). Hence Walter's welcoming dedication of the *Alexandreis* to the new archbishop in 1176. Two anonymous thirteenth-century *vitae* state that Walter became the "notary and orator" of the (unnamed) archbishop of Reims, who requested that Walter write the *Alexandreis*, and that he began it in the year of Becket's death (Traill, in *Walter of Châtillon*, xii–xiv). That ambiguous statement suggests either that Walter was in the service of Archbishop Henry of Reims before 1170, began to write in 1170, and entered Archbishop William's service in 1176; or that Walter already was in service to Archbishop William in Sens before 1170, began to write there in 1170, and followed William to Reims in 1176.

104. See ch. 8 at n. 6.

105. Walter of Châtillon, *Alexandreis*, bk. 1, lines 468–476 (Achilles); bk 4, lines 176–275 (Darius's wife), bk 7, lines 379–420 (Darius); bk 10, lines 450–454 (Alexander). In Rufus, the tomb of Cyrus is mentioned but not described (*History of Alexander*, 2: 476–79, nos. 30–35).

106. Lafferty, *Walter of Châtillon's "Alexandreis"*, 115–40, discusses these ekphrastic tombs. For the inscriptions on Henry's tomb, see ch. 8 ("The Speaking Tomb").

107. Chrétien de Troyes, *Cligés* (in *Romans*), lines 5312–5325. The generally accepted date for *Cligés* is 1176, as argued by Fourrier, *Le courant réaliste*, 160–74, who locates events alluded to in the romance to the years 1170–76. Ciggaar, "Encore une fois Chrétien de Troyes," 267–68, concludes that *Cligés* must have been written before September 1176.

108. Chrétien de Troyes, *Cligés* (in *Romans*), lines 6003–6024. Astute listeners would have grasped Chrétien's double meaning of relics/saintly woman here: Fenice had just endured a virtual crucifixion at the hands of three doctors from Salerno; her ordeal was proof that she actually had died but also proof of her pure love for Cligés.

109. *The Knight of the Cart* (*Lancelot*) is generally dated 1176–81 (concurrent with *Yvain*), but a strong case has been made for ca. 1177, that is, after *Cligés* (Uitti, *Chrétien de Troyes Revisited*, 60–62).

110. Chrétien de Troyes, *Le chevalier de la charrette* (in *Romans*), lines 1856–1943.

111. If Chrétien was in fact the *Christianus*, canon of St-Loup of Troyes in 1163 (*Actes*, no. 195), he would have witnessed the construction of Henry's tomb in the 1170s.

112. Dectot, "Les tombeaux des comtes," 19–32, 51–53, annex 4, which gives the fullest analysis and publishes canon Peschat's early eighteenth-century description of Henry's tomb and its inscriptions (supersedes Arbois de Jubainville, *Histoire*, 3: 311–24).

113. Arnaud, *Voyage archéologique*, 29. The engraving has been widely reproduced, most recently by Dectot, "Les tombeaux des comtes," 27 (who doubts its accuracy) and Morganstern, *Gothic Tombs*, 11.

114. For Bishop Henry of Winchester's plaques, dated ca. 1150–71, see Stratford, "The 'Henry of Blois' Plaques," 33, who suggests that the bishop might have acquired them during his travels through Flanders or Champagne. Riall, *Henry of Blois*, 5 agrees that the bishop's plaques were made in a Continental workshop rather than by Mosan craftsmen living in England. The bishop was, of course, a known collector with a good eye who liked to acquire objects abroad for his residences.

115. St-Étienne, fol. 31r, 1271–73; photograph in *Splendeurs*, 50, fig. 2.

116. Dectot, "Les tombeaux des comtes," 21–22.

117. Hany-Longuespé, "Les vestiges de Saint-Étienne," 34. See also Hany-Longuespé, *Le trésor et les réliques*, inventaire no. 012, which lists 24 semicircular enamel plaques and one semioval one, dated to 1160–1180; her inventory (nos. 013–017) lists other Mosan enamels of the same period but of unknown function. Several color phographs of the plaques are in the exhibition catalogue *Une Renaissance*, 132–37, no. 71, where they are dated to the 1170s.

118. Dectot, "Les tombeaux des comtes," 22–31, gives a close reading of the extant enamels, which he argues were created concurrently with the tomb itself, as part of an integrated design (against Jottrand, "Les émaux," who would have the enamel plaques made in the 1170s before the tomb itself).

119. Dectot, "Les tombeaux des comtes," 31–32, concludes that St-Étienne was intended as a dynastic necropolis.

120. Stirnemann, "Quelques bibliothèques," 24–25, dates the volumes to the 1170s. They are listed in Henry's library (Lalore, *Inventaires*, 2: 270–71, nos. 2280, 2294).

121. The cathedral chapter of Sens remembered Daniel as archdeacon (of St-Quiriace) of Provins (*Obituaires*, 1.1: 11 [16 September]). It is possible that Daniel came over in the entourage of Thomas Becket, and that his presence at Henry's renunciation of the *regalia* represented Becket's position regarding secular intrusion into ecclesiastical affairs. If Daniel was in fact one of the archbishop's *eruditi*—although he is not named in Herbert of Bosham's catalogue of Becket's clerics (Herbert of Bosham, *Vita Sancti Thomae*, 523–32)—he might have stayed on in Champagne after Becket's murder and directed the copying of Old Testament commentaries for Henry.

122. The volume of sermons is dated 1130–50 (Stirnemann, "Quelques bibliothèques, 24–25). The obituary for St-Victor of Paris mentions him twice, as "Daniel the priest" who bequeathed the canons 200*l.*, money of Paris, and as one who "professed as our canon" (*Obituaires*, 1.1: 582, 3 September, and 1.1: 585, 14 October).

123. Stirnemann, in *Splendeurs*, 69, fig. 38 (Peter Lombard, *Commentary on the Psalms*, painted by a Mosan artist); 71, fig. 42 (Peter Lombard, *Commentary on the Epistles of Paul*, painted in the Mosan style). The inventory of Henry's books lists Jerome's *Against Jovian* and *Commentaries* on Jeremiah and Isaiah (Lalore, *Inventaires*, 2: 270, nos. 2279, 2286, 2287).

124. For the glazing in Sens cathedral, which is dated to the 1150s and is regarded as an earlier iteration of the style in Troyes in the 1160s and 1170s, see Pastan, "Fit for a Count," 369–71. For St-Remi of Reims, see Caviness, *Sumptuous Arts*, 36–64, 98–128. Grodecki, *Le vitrail romane*, 129–30, fig. 111, and Morgan, "The Iconography of Twelfth-Century Mosan Enamels," 263–75, link Mosan-inspired topological stained glass at St-Denis (ca. 1145) and Chablis (ca. 1146) with the Stavelot altar and Count Henry's tomb and St-Étienne's glazing (here dated to the 1170s).

125. Glunz, *History of the Vulgate*, 342, dedicatory rubric added to original dedication to Becket.

126. Peter Comestor, *Scolastica historia*, 3.

127. See ch. 3 at n. 87.

128. Walter of Châtillon, *Alexandreis*, xii.

129. Nicholas of Montiéramey, *Epistolae*, 1652–54, no. 57.

130. Wahlgren-Smith, "Editing a Medieval Text."

131. Chrétien de Troyes, *Le chevalier de la charrette* (in *Romans*), lines 1–2, 26–27; trans. Kibler in *Arthurian Romances*, 207.

132. Chrétien de Troyes, *Le chevalier de la charrette* (in *Romans*), lines 24–29.

CHAPTER 8. THE LAST YEARS, 1176–1181

1. Scholastique was born in an undetermined year during the 1170s; see Gouet and Le Hête, *Les comtes de Blois et de Champagne*, 51.

2. Helinand of Froidmond, *Chronicon*, 1038. Helinand, writing in 1211–23, three decades after Stephen's death and six decades after the Council of Reims, identified Stephen as a canon of Beauvais and of St-Quiriace of Provins, but it is not clear when Stephen acquired those prebends.

3. *Actes*, no. 27, 22 May 1153: Stephen of Provins, cathedral canon, was among those who witnessed *ex parte comitis*. In 1161 he appeared among the canons of St-Étienne immediately after the dean Manasses and the chancellor William (*Actes*, no. 159). William of Champagne, after being elected archbishop of Sens, designated Master Stephen to succeed him as provost of St-Quiriace (*St-Quiriace*, no. 23, 1169). Mayer, *Die Kanzlei*, 2: 588–91, gives a brief biography but rejects the identification of Stephen the chancellor with Stephen who attended the Council of Reims in 1148.

4. Peter of Celle, *Letters*, 330–33, no. 73, between 1155 and 1162, to Becket.

5. Henry's new seal first appeared on the Great Charter enlarging St-Quiriace's endowment (*Actes*, no. 425, 1176). Stylistically in advance of the seal he had used since 1152, it depicts Henry wearing a cylindrical helmet and mounted on a horse riding to the right; in his right hand he carries an upheld sword and in his left a shield with the heraldic "band of Champagne." Based on the "seal of 1163" of Count Thierry of Flanders, it adopted the recent fashion of placing the count's heraldic device on his shield. See Baudin, *Les sceaux*, 75–76, 104–5, 127, 239, 246–54, and Illustrations 5 (photo of the document) and 6 (photo of the orange-red seal). See also Chassel, *Sceaux*, 40–41, and Baudin, "Les sceaux du comte Henri Ier," 82–84 and 109–12 (catalogue of Henry's second seal).

6. Walter of Châtillon, *Alexandreis*, bk. 1, lines 17–18: *Quo tandem regimen kathedrae Remensis adeptio/Duriciae nomen amisit bellica tellus* ("When you at last had gained the see of Reims, the warlike land lost its name for harshness").

7. Falkenstein, "Wilhelm von Champagne," 157–73, provides a chronology of William's years in Reims. See also the brief biographies in Demouy, *Genèse d'une cathédale*, 631–35, and Desportes, *Reims et les Rémois*, 151–54.

8. Ralph of Diceto, *Ymagines*, 1: 412–13.

9. Gervase of Canterbury, *Chronica* (in *Opera historica*, 1), 260.

10. Alexander III, in confirming a decision of Archbishop William of Sens, "now archbishop of Reims," states that the decision was made "in the presence of the noble Count Henry" (*St-Germain-des-Prés*, 1: 247–48, no. 171, 16 February 1176).

11. Alexander III, *Epistolae*, 1063–64. For events in the East, see Phillips, *Defenders of the Holy Land*, 225–45. For Peter of Pavia, bishop of Meaux (1172–75), cardinal-priest of S.

Crisogono (October 1173–May 1179), and archbishop of Bourges (4 May 1179–2 August 1182), see Brixius, *Die Mitglieder*, 65, no. 23, and Janssen, *Die päpstlichen Legaten*, 92–108.

12. Alexander III, *Epistolae*, 384–86, no. 360, 14 July 1165, given at Montpellier after he left Sens.

13. For the count of Nevers and his brother, see Lespinasse, *Le Nivernais*, 1: 365–67.

14. William of Tyre, *Chronique*, 2: 962 (*History*, 2: 359–61), bk. 20, ch. 12. On the significance of King Amalric's diplomatic efforts to obtain Western aid, see Phillips, *Defenders of the Holy Land*, 168–208.

15. Alexander III, *Epistolae*, 599–601, no. 62, 29 July 1169.

16. Barlow, *Thomas Becket*, 193–94.

17. Robert of Torigni, *Chronicle*, 249.

18. Petit, *Histoire*, 2: 181–84, and Richard, *Les ducs de Bourgogne*, 158 n. 4. Count Henry's sister Marie served as regent of Burgundy during her son's minority. Richard III of Crissse was bishop of Verdun (1163–71).

19. The three brothers witnessed an act in Provins (*Actes*, no. 342, dated 1172 but most likely in the spring of 1173, since Easter fell on 7 April 1173). Milo was murdered after King Amalric died. Count Stephen of Sancerre was urged by his knights to marry the very young Sibyl of Jerusalem (born 1158/60), but the forty-year-old widow declined. Returning from Jerusalem by way of Antioch, he was captured by Armenians; released after paying a ransom, he returned to France via Constantinople. See Hamilton, "Miles of Plancy" and *The Leper King*, 84–93.

20. Roger of Howden, *Gesta regis Henrici secundi*, 2: 44, quotes the joint letter of Henry II and Louis VII promising to take the cross and swearing to each other. A commission of three prelates and three barons from each side was to oversee the peace; the French king was represented by his brothers, Peter of Courtenay and Robert of Dreux, and his seneschal Thibaut.

21. Gervase of Canterbury, *Chronica*, 274.

22. Gervase of Canterbury, *Chronica*, 262. For Count Philip's expedition, see Hamilton, *The Leper King*, 119–31, and Phillips, *Defenders of the Holy Land*, 231–40.

23. Aubri of Trois-Fontaines, *Chronicon*, 855.

24. *RHF* 16: 166, Abbot Henry to the pope. Henry (of Marcy) was born ca. 1140, entered Clairvaux ca. 1155, and became abbot (16 October 1175–1 January 1179). Pope Alexander III charged him with recruiting crusaders in 1178, and at the Third Lateran Council (14 March 1179) named him cardinal-bishop of Albano. He died 1 January 1180. See Veyssière, "Le personnel de l'abbaye de Clairvaux," 63, no. 223.

25. *Qui tant fu corageus et fiers*
    Que il ne deigna chevaliers
    Devenir en sa region   —Chrétien de Troyes, *Cligés* (in *Romans*), lines 65–67

26. *Que largece est dame et rëine*
    Qui toutes vertuz enlumine   —Chrétien, *Cligés*, lines 193–94

27. *Actes*, no. 464, 1178: he licensed them to acquire his fiefs, provided that he not lose their homages.

28. The editors of the *History of William Marshal* suggest a date of early or mid-1178 for the tournament at Pleurs, while noting that the text loses any sense of chronology at this point (*History of William Marshal*, 3: 77). Since Henry is not known to have sponsored or attended any tournament within his lands, the event at Pleurs (located near Henry's castle-town of Sézanne), if it did occur, was possible only in Henry's absence after May 1179. Gislebert of Mons, *Chronique*, 116–17 (*Chronicle*, 67), cap. 77, remarks that in August 1177 "knights of Champagne" among many others attended a tournament between Soissons and Braine, beyond the count's borders.

29. Crouch, *Tournament*, 49–50. Young Baldwin V of Hainaut, a tournament regular, traveled with a team of eighty knights to two tournaments at the borders of Champagne in 1171: at a field between the count's castle of Bussy and the episcopal city of Châlons on the Marne, and at Lizy-sur-l'Ourcq, also on the Marne northeast of Meaux.

30. *Epistolae Pontificum Romanorum ineditae*, 179–80, no. 308, 1179, letter responding to Marie's request.

31. Lambert of Ardres, *Historia*, 601–2 (*The History*, 120), cap. 87.

32. Ralph of Diceto, *Ymagines*, 1: 425–26.

33. *Die Urkunden Friedrichs I*, 3: 314–15, no. 762, 13 September 1178.

34. Pérard, *Recueil*, 253, 15 September 1178. Witnesses included Duke Hugh III of Burgundy, Count Erard of Brienne, and the castle lords Hugh of Broyes, Simon of Commercy, Girard of Reynel, Simon of Beaufort, Bartholomew of Vignory, and Geoffroy of Vienne. For the significance of these acts, see Parisse, "Présence et interventions de Frédéric Barberousse," 208–10. For Henry of Bar-le-Duc, see Poull, *La maison souveraine et ducale de Bar*, 119–28.

35. See n. 37 below.

36. Pouzet, "La vie de Guichard," 130–38, provides a full analysis.

37. Longnon, *Documents*, 1: 466–67, no. 2, sealed by the papal chancery on 13 April 1179: the confirmation speaks of *castra . . . cum castelaniis eorum*. See Evergates, *Aristocracy*, 23; Falkenstein, "Wilhelm von Champagne," 204–9; and Bur, "La frontière," 156–60.

38. The change in *mouvance* of the four castles (Mailly, Bitry, Bazarnes, Coulanges-la-Vineuse) must have occurred in the 1170s under Bishop William of Auxerre (1167–82), former archdeacon of Sens and younger brother of Archbishop Hugh of Sens, who had cooperated with Henry in the restoration of secular canons at St-Quiriace in 1159; for his life, see Bouchard, *Sword, Miter, and Cloister*, 390. In 1207 Peter, count of Auxerre and Tonnerre, asserted that he did homage to Countess Marie for Mailly (in 1184) on the advice of his fief-holders there, implying that Mailly was by then held in fief from the count of Champagne (*Cartulary of Countess Blanche*, 35–36, no. 4). For the Champenois "intrusion" into Auxerre, see Sassier, *Recherches*, 155–211.

39. Bernard of Clairvaux announces the resolution of a dispute by which the count of Nevers agrees that his four castles will be handed over (*tradentur*) to the bishop of Auxerre at the bishop's will (Quantin, *Yonne*, 1: 393–97, no. 247, 1145).

40. Castle lords, too, transferred the *mouvance* of fiefs held from them; see Evergates, *Aristocracy*, 72–74.

41. *Cartulary of Countess Blanche*, 95–96, no. 72, 1200. Perhaps the duke only heard about it or was alluding in error to Count Thibaut's homage to his grandfather Odo II, an understandable confusion half a century later.

42. Robert of Torigni, *Chronicle*, 350, reports that when he became abbot of Mont-St-Michel in 1154, his barons did homage to him for their *tenementis* held from the abbey. Gislebert of Mons, *Chronique*, 75 (*Chronicle*, 44), cap. 43, states that whoever constructed a new castle in the county of Hainaut had to give fidelity with security and homage for it, which consequently became a fief.

43. Since the four archiepiscopal castles whose *mouvance* the archbishop transferred to Henry were listed in the fief rolls as being held directly from the count, the inquest must have occurred in late fall 1178 or early spring 1179.

44. William, "marshal of Count Henry," sealed a letter endowing anniversary Masses by the monks of St-Mesmin for himself and his wife; it was dated 1179 "during the rule of King Louis and Count Henry" (photograph in *The Knights Templar*, 232–33, cat. 15bis).

45. Robert of Torigni, *Chronicle*, 349–53 (Appendix 8, from the abbey's cartulary, fol. 132), describes the inquest of 1172; see Keefe, *Feudal Assessments*, 1–19.

46. Evergates, *Aristocracy*, 17–21, and 49, fig. 1.

47. I conclude that the resultant rolls of fiefs were deposited in St-Étienne in the same manner that the rolls of 1190 were deposited there before Count Henry II's departure on the Third Crusade, as the marshal Geoffroy of Villehardouin subsequently recalled (see n. 48). Count Henry increased the treasurer's income at the same time (*Actes*, no. 481, 9 April 1178–31 March 1179).

48. *Cartulary of Countess Blanche*, 294–95, no. 333, ca. 1209, letter to Countess Blanche regarding the *scripta feodorum* (= Longnon, *Documents*, 1: xxx, no. 2).

49. Evergates, *Aristocracy*, 46–50, 199–204.

50. Foreville, *Lateran I, II, III et Lateran IV*, 134–58 and 389 (list of prelates attending the Council). The bishop of Langres had just died, and the bishop of Châlons (Guy of Joinville) apparently did not attend.

51. Renaud (of Bar-le-Duc) was the son of Count Henry's sister Agnes (Poull, *La maison souveraine et ducale de Bar*, 117–18). He became bishop of Chartres (1182–9 December 1217) after the death of Bishop Peter of Celle, and went on the Third Crusade.

52. Walter Map, *De nugis curialium*, 450–53.

53. Edbury and Rowe, *William of Tyre*, 28.

54. Peter of Pavia, cardinal legate in France, presented the pope with a list of candidates worthy of being named cardinal (Alexander III, *Epistolae*, 1370). See also Guillemain, "L'épiscopat français à Lateran III," 28.

55. Peter of Celle, *De disciplina claustrali*, 96.

56. In a letter to Alexander III, Peter cited "infirmity" and old age as reasons for not attending Lateran III (Peter of Celle, *Letters*, 350–51, no. 80, 1178).

57. Peter of Celle, *De disciplina claustrali*, 100. The editor dates the text to 1179 (26–27).

58. I take Peter's use of *prosperitas* to be expansive, to subsume an increase in material wealth in the sense that Henry used it at the very beginning of his rule, when he made a gift for his own "*prosperitate* and salvation" (*Actes*, no. 24, 30 March–18 April 1152).

59. The fragmentary inventory of Henry's library does not include a copy of *De disciplina claustrali*. For the two extant copies, see Peter of Celle, *De disciplina claustrali*, 75–78.

60. Henry's acts dated 1179 in the *Actes* should be dated from 1 April (Easter) to the end of May (his departure), except for those acts expressly given en route to Jerusalem.

61. *Actes*, no. 502, 1 April–30 May 1179 (chapel of Notre-Dame of Provins); *Actes*, no. 495, 1 April–30 May 1179 (St-Nicolas of Sézanne), sealed by Henry and Marie.

62. *Actes*, no. 493, 1 April–30 May 1179.

63. *Actes*, no. 507, 1 April–30 May 1179, done in Troyes. For a full analysis of the charter and its context, see Wilmart, *Meaux*, 103–25, and in greater detail his "Les débuts de la commune de Meaux."

64. John of Salisbury, bishop of Chartres, excommunicated the townsmen on 25 October 1180 (*GC*, 7: 1146). But in Count Henry's absence overseas, Bishop Simon of Meaux refused to promulgate the sentence, according to Stephen of Tournai, who complained to the papal notary John of Orléans (Stephen of Tournai, *Lettres*, 94–95, no. 80, November 1180/84). The destruction of the archives in Meaux during the Hundred Years War makes it difficult to reconstruct the city's earlier history.

65. Gislebert of Mons, *Chronique*, 126 (*Chronicle*, 72), cap. 89.

66. Baldwin V was born in 1150 and knighted by his father on 31 March 1168; he married Margaret of Flanders (sister of Count Philip of Flanders) in 1169 and became associated in rule

in 1171, after Baldwin IV fell from scaffolding at Frederick I's new palace in Valenciennes. At his father's death in November 1171, Baldwin succeeded as count of Hainaut. For his exploits at tournaments, see Falmagne, *Baudouin V*, 111–33, and Crouch, *Tournament*, 27–29.

67. Gislebert of Mons, *Chronique*, 112 (*Chronicle*, 72), cap. 89.

68. *Actes*, no. 491, 1179 (probably June). He sealed a second letter at Châtillon, for the hospital of Bar-sur-Aube (*Actes*, no. 490, 1179, probably June), witnessed by Hugh of Plancy, William the marshal, William the almoner, Artaud the treasurer, and Walter of Porta.

69. *Actes*, no. 522, 1179: Henry said that he inspected *diligenter* Count Hugh's charter. His marshal William, treasurer Artaud, scribe Thibaut of Fismes, chancellor Stephen, and Peter of Langres also witnessed.

70. *Actes*, no. 523, 1179: Henry gave 20*l.* from the toll at Pont-sur-Seine, payable by the toll collector in two annual installments. The count's entourage now included Robert of Milly and Alberic, a new notary. Countess Marie confirmed Henry's act (Benton, "Recueil," 1179ff).

71. Brand, *Byzantium Confronts the West*, 24–25. For a biography, see Edbury and Rowe, *William of Tyre*, 13–22.

72. William of Tyre, *Chronique*, 2: 1203 (*History*, 2: 443–44), bk. 21, cap. 30. The *Chronique de Saint-Pierre-le-Vif de Sens*, 210, implies that Peter of Courtenay accompanied Count Henry from the start of the journey in France.

73. Hamilton, *The Leper King*, 145–46.

74. *Actes*, no. 526, 1179, probably in September or October, in Jerusalem. The reference to *custodes terre mee* is not to a regency council but rather to Henry's provosts and other agents, like the *custodes* of his fairs, who were responsible for collecting his revenues.

75. *Actes*, no. 525, 1179, probably in September or October, done in Jerusalem, witnessed by Count Henry's marshal William, treasurers Artaud and Robert of Milly, Thibaud (the Scribe) of Fismes, Masters Philip of Sézanne and Hugh, the chaplain Nicholas of Montiéramey, Peter Bristaud, Milo of Provins, the chancellor Stephen and notary Alberic, and Count Henry of Grandpré and his brother Geoffroy, "and many others." These are the last appearances of Henry's marshal William *Rex* and chaplain Nicholas of Montiéramey. Nicholas had prebends at St-Étienne and at the cathedral of Meaux. He left 60*l.* for St-Étienne's endowment (*Obituaires*, 4: 529, 16 October: *Magister Nicolaus de Monasterio Arremarensi, hujus ecclesie [St-Étienne] canonicus*), and 40*l.* for Meaux's endowment (*Magister Nicolaus, Meldensis canonicus*), as provided by Abbot Garin of St-Victor, his testamentary executor (*Obituaires*, 4: 106, 19 October). The chapter of Meaux remembered him as *Dominus Nicolaus de Monestariis matricularius ecclesie Meldensis* (*Obituaires*, 4: 109, 30 October).

76. Kenaan-Kedar, "The Cathedral of Sebaste," 100–101.

77. Kenaan-Kedar, "The Cathedral of Sebaste," 102–4.

78. Kenaan-Kedar, "The Cathedral of Sebaste," 110–20.

79. *Actes*, no. 527, 1179, for anniversary Masses for his father, mother, and sons. Witnesses included Count Henry of Grandpré, William of St-Maurice, William the marshal, Robert of Milly, Artaud (treasurer), Thibaud of Fismes (scribe), and the Templar brother William.

80. Hamilton, *The Leper King*, 150–58.

81. Henry would have received the letter after Philip's coronation (1 November 1179) and before 28 June 1180, when King Henry II of England made peace between Philip and his mother (Hamilton, *The Leper King*, 150).

82. Alexander III, *Epistolae*, 783, no. 872, 28 February 1171. The pope suggested a better match with a son of John Komnenos and even enlisted Louis's brother, Archbishop Henry, to thwart a German marriage (964, no. 1504, 6 September 1174).

83. Aubri of Trois-Fontaines, *Chronicon*, 847, copying Guy of Bazoches's lost *Chronographia*; see Hamilton, *The Leper King*, 137–38.

84. Hamilton, *The Leper King*, 147–48. She apparently arrived from Genoa, where a fleet of galleys escorted her to Constantinople (Magdalino, *The Empire of Manuel Komnenos*, 101–2 n. 31).

85. Hilsdale, "Constructing a Byzantine *Augusta*" (I thank Michael McCormick for this reference). Agnes/Anne died ca. 1240 after a complicated history; see Van Kerrebrouck, *Les Capétiens*, 97–98, for a brief biography.

86. "Whoever desires to know the canons and name of the [attending] bishops by number and title may read the record that I made at the request of the holy fathers who took part in this synod and which I diligently compiled. I later placed it in the archive of the holy church of Tyre together with other books that I gave to that church over which I have presided for the past six years" (*Chronique*, 2: 998, ch. 21, no. 25 [*History*, 2: 438]). William reached Acre on 12 May 1180 (Brand, *Byzantium Confronts the West*, 25).

87. André of Marchiennes, *Continuatio Aquicinctina*, 418–19. It is not known where Henry was captured or how he reached Constantinople. Map 2 charts an overland route from Caesarea through Asia Minor to Constantinople.

88. See n. 97 below.

89. William of Nangis, *Chronique*, 72, and Robert of Auxerre, *Chronicon*, 249, state that the emperor ransomed Count Henry.

90. An inscription on the Saint Philip reliquary states that Henry brought Peter's tooth from Rome (Lalore, *Inventaires*, 1: cvii).

91. Henry the Lion married Henry II's daughter Mathilda in 1168; see Jordan, *Henry the Lion*, 160–82.

92. André of Marchiennes, *Continuatio Aquicinctina*, 419.

93. Aubri of Trois-Fontaines, *Chronicon*, 856.

94. *Actes*, no. 528, 10–16 March 1181, referring to a tax collected before his departure in the spring of 1179.

95. *Actes*, no. 529, 10–16 March 1181. The prioress later took the letter to Countess Marie for her confirmation (Benton, "Recueil," 1181c).

96. *Actes*, no. 530, 10–16 March 1181 (photograph in *Splendeurs*, 53, fig. 7).

97. Countess Marie later assigned the revenue (*Langres*, 172–74, no. 145, 1182) because in the commotion following Henry's death, Chancellor Haice forgot to draft the letter.

98. The canons of St-Quiriace celebrated his anniversary on 16 March (Verdier, *Saints de Provins*, 211). Benton, "Court," 553–43, concludes that Henry died on 16 March (against Arbois de Jubainville, *Histoire*, 3: 28, 111, who gives 17 March).

99. Dectot, "Les tombeaux des comtes," 6–7, suggests that the record of Count Thibaut III's funeral in 1201 (49–50, annex 1: eighteenth-century copy of an anonymous account; BnF, Collection de Champagne, t. 128) might have applied to Henry's own funeral in 1181.

100. *Obituaires*, 4: 455 (16 March).

101. *Notre-Dame de Chartres*, 3: 64 (17 March): *Henricus dictus Largus*.

102. *Obituaires*, 4: 131, 199.

103. *Obituaires*, 4: 292.

104. *Obituaires*, 4: 322 (16 March).

105. *Obituaires*, 4: 226.

106. *Obituaires*, 4: 546 (17 March).

107. Aubri of Trois-Fontaines, writing in the 1240s, quotes from Guy of Bazoches's (lost) *Chronographia*: *Guido:* <u>*Florebat*</u> *in Francia palatinus Campanie comes Henricus, quin potius Francia per*

illum; vir de quo dubium genere nobilior esset an animo, cui Francie regina soror et filia regis uxor, et in quo constabat regnum sibi constituisse virtutes et reginam plus quam regalis munificentie largitatem. Novum et iocundum in eo spectaculi genus exhibebat invidie pia contentio, laudis certamen inter famam et meritum eius, quod scilicet per agrando circum niterentur invicem prevenire, merito fama tamen vincebatur. Nam quod precedente merito premebatur, a comite preciosis gestorum titulis et sparsis longe lateque beneficium daiis emebatur. Inter insignia suorum operum illud iubare spledidiore refulsit, quod ecclesiam palatio suo contiguam in honore gloriosi prothomatiris Stephani—prout instruxit eum quem erga Deum habebat amor—extruxit, ditavit prediis, ornavit olosericis, honoravit thesauris, clero laudes exultatione divinas spiritali decantante celibriter honoravit. Fateor me non vidisse, legisse non memini tante liberalitatis principem extitisse (Aubri of Trois-Fontaines, *Chronicon*, 847). Aubri balanced Guy's extravagant praise with his own, less than flattering stories about Henry (see ch. 9 at n. 37).

108. Arnaud's engraving locates the tomb between the last two pillars of the choir (Dectot, "Les tombeaux des comtes," 35).

109. Dectot, "Les tombeaux des comtes," 20–22.

110. The tomb cover is described in Dectot, "Les tombeaux des comtes," 19–20, and Morganstern, *Gothic Tombs*, 10. The chapter's cartulary of ca. 1273 contains the same scene of Count Henry (sitting on a horse) presenting a model of his chapel; photograph in *Splendeurs*, 50, fig. 2 (BnF, Lat. 17098, fol. 31): the count holds the right hand of a young figure clothed in a white chemise, who holds in his left hand the hand of a master dressed in an ermine-trimmed blue robe.

111. The tomb inscriptions were recorded by Peschat, an eighteenth-century canon who was in charge of restoring the tomb. His record is published in Dectot, "Les tombeaux des comtes," 51–53, annex 4. The translation here is slightly modified from Morganstern, *Gothic Tombs*, 11.

112. Dectot, "Les tombeaux des comtes," 21, concludes that the inscription reflects Simon's versifications, especially in his epithets.

113. For his life, see Stohlmann, "Magister Simon Aurea Capra," and Godefroy, "Saint-Ayoul," 30–33.

114. *Me meus huc finis protrait de peregrinis*
     Finibus, ut sit in his hic sine fine cinis.   —Dectot, "Les tombeaux des comtes," 52
A variant (?imperfect) reading of those two lines is added to an early thirteenth-century copy of Anselm's works from Pontigny:
     Epitaphum Comitis Henrici
     Me meus hic finis advenit de peregrinis
     Finibus hic, ut in his sim fine sine cinis.   —Indiana University, Lilly Library, Poole MS
                                                              18, fol. 142v

115. Morganstern, *Gothic Tombs*, 11–12 (slightly modified translation here).

116. Morganstern, *Gothic Tombs*, 12 (slightly modified translation here).

117. John of Salisbury, *Policraticus*, 2: 629 (trans. *Policraticus*, 141), bk. 6, ch. 26: *Sol eminet universis ut cuncta videat et diiudicet universa; solem alterum principem esse credo.*

118. Guy of Bazoches, *Liber epistularum*, 56–58, no. 15, written most likely in the mid-1170s, after Guy's installation as a canon at Châlons (he would have been in his midthirties), which Count Henry attended, says Guy. See also Putter, "Knights and Clerics," 258–59.

119. Walter of Châtillon, *The Alexandreis*, bk. 1, lines 468–70, 488–92; trans. in Townsend, *Alexandreis*, lines 449–455, 576–578:
     Et contentus erit sic solo principe mundus
     Ut solo sole hoc unum michi deese timebo
     Post mortem cineri ne desit fama sepulto
     Elisiisque velim solam hanc preponere campis.

120. Morganstern, *Gothic Tombs*, 10.

121. Nolan, *Queens in Stone*, 99–101.

CHAPTER 9. LEGACY AND AFTERLIFE

1. Dunbabin, *France in the Making*, 295–99, puts it just right in characterizing the lands of Louis VI and Louis VII as a "royal principality." Werner, "Kingdom and Principality," 262–63, refers to the rich, "well-ordered principalities" of northern France that were administratively well in advance of the royal domain.

2. For an analysis of the rolls of fiefs of 1178, see Evergates, *Aristocracy*, 17–21, and 203 (Table B.3) for a list of the thirty castellanies.

3. That is, almost half of the count's fiefholders held their comital fiefs in simple homage (*homagium, homagium planum, homagium non ligium*); see Evergates, *Aristocracy*, 18–19. For multiple homages in Reims, see Desportes, *Reims et les Rémois*, 74–75.

4. Odo of Deuil, *De profectione Ludovici VII*, 78–81.

5. *Feoda* 1, 3, no. 73. For Bartholomew of Vignory (1150–91), see Evergates, *Aristocracy*, 29, 92, 171.

6. On the politics of contingency, see Richard, *Les ducs de Bourgogne*, 266–69.

7. *Feoda* 1, 3–7, nos. 62–176.

8. Evergates, *Aristocracy*, 39–40.

9. According to the "customs" of the castellanies of Montereau (*Feoda* 1, 50, no. 1285) and Provins, and by implication Bray-sur-Seine (*Feoda* 1, 58, no. 1643). See M.-Cl. Hubert, "*Consuetudo*."

10. Evergates, *Aristocracy*, 205–6, Table C.2.

11. *Montier-la-Celle*, 270–72, no. 228, 1178: the bishop speaks of celebrating divine offices *militibus in eodem castello manentibus et uxoribus eorum*. I read *manere* here to include the seven resident knights of Villemaur (four owed *estagium* and three an unspecified *custodiam*) as well as the six knights who performed annual castle-guard (*Feoda* 1, 11–12, nos. 330–54). In all, thirteen (48 percent) of the 27 fiefholders in Villemaur owed castle-guard.

12. Evergates, *Aristocracy*, 205–6, Tables C.1–C.3. About a quarter (26.7 percent) of the count's fiefholders, including the viscounts and castellans and a number of castle lords, owed full-time garrison duty (*estagium, mansionem per annum*).

13. *Actes*, no. 226, 1165.

14. *RHF* 16: 119, no. 365, April 1165.

15. Gislebert of Mons, *Chronique*, 75–80 (*Chronicle*, 43–45), caps. 43–45, reports that castles were renderable in Hainaut.

16. In Provins the Templars had a building in the New Market before 1171, when they exchanged it for the stone house and ancillary buildings of Henry Burda (nephew of Bishop Mathieu of Troyes) located in the Old Market; Count Henry exempted all merchants doing business there from his sales tax (*Actes*, no. 318). The Templars also had acquired a residential compound from Henry Bristaud (son of Peter Bristaud, the viscount of Provins) in the commercial quarter of the suburb of St-Ayoul (Verdier, *Saint-Ayoul*, 146, no. 40, 1170). The Templars may have had a house in Troyes by 1159 (see n. 18 below).

17. Bernard, *cambitor* of the Templars in Provins, witnessed Count Henry's act in 1171 (*Actes*, no. 318). On Templar financial transactions, see Barber, *The New Knighthood*, 266–79.

18. The earliest, indirect reference to a Templar house in Troyes is in 1177 when Count

Henry, in his bedroom (*thalamus*), permitted Geoffroy of Mousson to mortgage his revenues from the market of Ramerupt to the Templars for 100*l*. (*Actes*, no. 458). The Templars may have been present in Troyes before 1159, when Count Henry changed the payment his father had granted them (10 marks of silver annually) to 24*l*. payable from his sales taxes in Troyes; presumably the revenue was collected by Templars resident in Troyes (*Actes*, no. 133; photo in *The Knights Templar*, 53, illustration 34, and 220–21, catalogue 8). Five years later, in 1164, the count seems to have reassigned that payment to the sales tax on wool and yarn collected in Provins (*Actes*, no. 223). The Hospitallers had tax-exempt houses and stalls in Bar-sur-Aube in 1163 (*Actes*, no. 194).

19. Desportes, *Reims et les Rémois*, 114–16, and Laurent, *Un grand commerce d'exportation*, 86–91. For Milan, see Bautier, "Provins et les foires," 158, and "Les foires," 106. See also Racine, *Plaisance*, 322, and Reynolds, "Genoese Trade," 380.

20. Chapin, *Les villes de foires*, 77–82, discusses the nascent cloth industry in Troyes. By 1197 cloth merchants from Troyes, Provins, and Lagny were even selling in Genoa (257–58).

21. Bautier, "Provins et les foires,"163–64.

22. The document that mentions a commune in Provins in 1153 (*Actes*, no. 36) is highly suspect and probably a fourteenth-century fabrication; see Verdier, *Saint-Ayoul*, 115.

23. *Actes*, no. 529, 1181. The Fontevrist priory of Fontaines-les-Nonnes also had a number of properties and buildings in Provins (*Actes*, no. 75, 1156).

24. Sivéry, *L'économie du royaume de France*, argues that by the thirteenth century there were "two Frances," a new, essentially urbanized one and an old, essentially rural one. Champagne ranked among the "new" economic regions. Sivéry places the origin of that divide between the two economies at ca. 1180, which is to say that the critical shift in Champagne occurred precisely during Count Henry's rule and resulted in great part from his policies.

25. See Evergates, *Aristocracy*, 28–31.

26. *Bien garda la terre et maintint* (Evrat, *La Genèse*, line 185). I have translated *maintint* as "govern" because I think that Evrat was alluding to her active role in administering the county.

27. *Et doze ans avoit passéz Ke li bons sire est trespasséz*
   De ceste vie en parmanable,
   U il ne dote mais diable.
   C'est li bons cuens ki tans biens fist,
   Ke l'onor Saint Estievene assist
   Riche eglise et bien provendée
   Dont la terre et tote amendée.   —Evrat, *La Genèse*, lines 121–128

28. *Cil Ebron de qu'il est tels joies*
   C'est la riche eglise de Troies
   Que li cuens Henris fist del suen,
   A son voloir et a son buen,
   En l'oneur del premier martir.
   De qu'il ne vout onques partir:
   La est ses chans et sa couture,
   La est se droite sopulture
   La gist ses cors, en ciel est s'ame.   —Evrat, *La Genèse*, lines 20720–20728

29. Jean le Nevelon, *La Venjance Alixandre*, lines 46–55.

30. Guiot of Provins, *La Bible*, lines 300–306, 324–324.

31. Dectot, "Les tombeaux *des comtes*," 54 (an early eighteenth-century description by canon Peschat). Dectot argues (39–41) that Thibaut's tomb was begun ca. 1225 and not

completed until the mid-1260s. Such a dating seems quite out of context, given the circumstances of Countess Blanche's regency (see *Cartulary of Countess Blanche*, 3–10). Morganstern, *Gothic Tombs*, 111–17, interprets Thibaut's tomb, the earliest example of a "tomb of kinship," as having meaning within the context of Blanche's regency, especially its inscriptions in which Blanche declares her abiding love for Thibaut.

32. Pastan and Balcon, *Les vitraux*, 458–63, esp. Bay 210.

33. St-Étienne, fol. 31r; a photograph is in *Splendeurs*, 50, fig. 2.

34. Bourquelot, "Cantique latin."

35. *Actes*, no. 412, 1175.

36. Verdier, *Saints de Provins*, 140–50.

37. Aubri of Trois-Fontaines, *Chronicon*,

38. Verdier, *Saints de Provins*, 149–50.

39. Aubri of Trois-Fontaines, *Chronicon*, 841: *largitate et liberalitate famosus* (a phrase lifted from Guy of Bazoches), and 847: *ecclesiam palatio suo contiguam . . . extruxit, ditavit predis, ornavit olosericis, honorari thesauris* (copied from Robert of Auxerre's description of the fire of 1188 in Troyes; see his *Chronicon*, 253). For Aubri as historian, see Schmidt-Chazan, "Aubri de Trois-Fontaines," and Chazan, "L'usage de la compilation" and *L'empire et l'histoire universelle*, 360–62.

40. Aubri of Trois-Fontaines, *Chronicon*, 847. No trace of such a relic can be found in the 1319 inventory of the chapel's possessions. For the analysis of what seems a fabrication, see Verdier, *Saints de Provins*, 150–56.

41. Constable, "Troyes, Constantinople, and the Relics of St. Helen," and Geary, "Saint Helen of Athyra and the Cathedral of Troyes."

42. Frenken, *Die Exempla des Jacob von Vitry*, 106–7. For values of fiefs, see Evergates, *Aristocracy*, 208, Table C.7.

43. Étienne of Bourbon, *Anecdotes historiques*, 124, no. 146. In two other tales Stephen of Bourbon lifted from Jacques of Vitry, the count was identified as Thibaut II (127, no. 150; 134, no. 157). The editor notes (124–25 n. 2) that both Jacques of Vitry and an anonymous collection of *exempla* from Tours identify the count as Thibaut II.

44. Joinville, *Vie de Saint Louis*, 33 (*The Life of Saint Louis*, 168), caps. 89–90.

45. Evergates, *Aristocracy*, 182–85.

46. Delisle, "Discours [sur un antiphonaire]," 104 (identification of Philip the Chancellor as the author), 127–28. Taylor, "The Eight Monophonic Political Planctus," 14–24, analyzes the poetry and music of *Omnis in lacrimis*, the longest of the eight "political" *planctus* in the Florence manuscript, as a "retrospective collection" of musical composition from the school of Notre-Dame. All eight of the *planctus* are in the tenth fascicle of the manuscript (Rillon-Marne, "Philippe le Chancelier et son oeuvre," 86–87, Table 7, lists the contents). Taylor raises the possibility that the lament for Henry was written by someone who knew him and perhaps was in his employ, but the moralistic ending of *Omnis in lacrimis*, with its stress on the vanities of vanities, fits with Philip's other works.

47. *Largitate vir serenus.*
    gratiarum donis plenus,
    comes flos comitum,
    non impar regibus,
    fatis crudelibus
    exsolvit debitum.

Privatur preside
Campania.
Lugeat ecclesia,
vidua presidio,
clerus patrocinio,
paupereas suffragiis,
Francia consilio.   —Text and trans. in Taylor, "The Eight Monophonic Political
                              Planctus," 15–16, fig. 2

48. Dectot, "Les tombeaux des comtes," 50 (annex 2). Arbois de Jubainville, *Histoire*, 3: 319–20.

49. Dectot, "Les tombeaux des comtes," 5, fig. 2, a late eighteenth-century engraving printed by Arnaud in his *Voyage archéologique*.

50. See Morganstern, *Gothic Tombs*, 13–17; Dectot, "Les tombeaux des comtes," 32–41, 53–56; and Evergates in *Cartulary of Countess Blanche*, 6–7.

51. See Dectot, "Les tombeaux des comtes."

52. Evergates, *Aristocracy*, 56–58.

53. For Jeanne, see Lalou, "Le gouvernement de la reine Jeanne."

54. Evergates, *Aristocracy*, 61–62.

55. Lalore, *Inventaires*, 2: 1–43, 269–70. Henry's cap was item no. 43 (Lalore, *Inventaires*, 2: 5).

56. Lalore, *Inventaires*, 2: 270–71. A fragmentary roll lists forty-nine volumes, of which thirty-one survive in the Bibliothèque Municipale of Troyes (Stirnemann, "Une bibliothèque princière"). A photograph of the inventory roll listing items in the "Old Treasury" is in *Splendeurs*, 36, 59, fig. 20.

57. Evergates, *Aristocracy*, 366, Appendix B, n. 1, describes the surviving rolls.

58. Evergates, *Aristocracy*, 198–204.

59. Three related events suggest that the transfer occurred under Charles IV (1322–28). In 1322–23 the bailiffs of Champagne, responding to the royal ordinance of 10 March 1321, drew up detailed rolls of property alienated since 1285 (Evergates, *Aristocracy*, 199 n. 1). In 1326 the royal chancery translated the feudal inquest rolls of 1265 as if they were the most current (Evergates, "The Chancery Archives," 173 n. 63). By 1328 the bailiffs of Champagne were sending their accounts directly to Paris (Nortier, "Le sort des archives dispersées," 462–63).

60. What follows is taken from Dectot, "Les tombeaux des comtes," 12–13.

61. Arbois de Jubainville, *Histoire*, 3: 318, thought it likely that repairs were made soon after, but that the panels of inscriptions might not have been restored to their original places.

62. Martène, *Voyage littéraire*, 1: 90.

63. Bocher de Coluel, a civil engineer, marked the position of the tombs in the engraving made sometime between 1753 and 1769 (Dectot, "Les tombeaux des comtes," 5, fig. 2). Dectot concludes that the tombs were originally placed in the choir.

64. Martène, *Voyage littéraire*, 1: 90.

65. Martène, *Voyage littéraire*, 1: 90. He seems not to have been interested in specific titles, and ends his list with "etc."

66. Lalore, *Inventaires*, 2: 56, no. 468 (inventory of ca. 1700). See also Hany-Longuespé, *Le trésor et les reliques*, 102–4.

67. Hany-Longuespé, "Les vestiges de Saint-Étienne," 33–34. The names of the cathedral chapter's thirty-eight canons and of St-Étienne's forty-four canons and thirty-one chaplains were listed (Prévost, *Histoire*, 1: 192–97, 197–200, 268–79).

68. Pastan, "Fit for a Count," 364–65.

69. Dectot, "Les tombeaux des comtes," 50–51 (annex 3), report of 27 February 1792, signed by the physician Bouquot.

70. Reproduced by Lalore, "Restes mortels des comtes de Champagne." A color photograph is in Hany-Longuespé, *Le trésor et les reliques*, 106, and in *Splendeurs*, 58, fig. 18.

71. Hany-Longuespé, *Le trésor et les réliques*, 12.

72. Lalore, "Restes mortels," 116–18.

73. Brown, "Burying and Unburying the Kings of France," 252–55.

74. Hany-Longuespé, *Le trésor et les réliques*, 12.

75. Details in Gur, "L'ancien quartier du palais des comtes," 232–35.

76. Evergates, *Aristocracy*, 199–200.

77. Hany-Longuespé, *Le trésor et les réliques*, 102–4.

Bibliography

PRIMARY SOURCES

Abelard, *Carmen. Peter Abelard, "Carmen ad Astralabium": A Critical Edition.* Ed. Joseph Marie Annaïs Ruingh-Bosscher. Groningen: Rijksuniversiteit te Groningen, 1987.

Abelard. *The Letter Collection of Peter Abelard and Heloise.* Ed. David Luscombe, trans. Betty Radice, rev. David Luscombe. Oxford: Oxford University Press, 2013.

Acta Pontificum Romanorum inedita. Ed. J. von Pflugk-Harttung. 3 vols. Stuttgart, 1884. Rpt. Graz: Akademische Druck- und Verlagsamstalt, 1958.

Adrian IV. *Epistolae. PL* 188: 1360–1644.

Alexander III. *Epistolae. PL* 200: 70–1318.

André of Marchiennes. *Continuatio Aquicinctina* of Sigbert of Gembloux. Ed. D. L. Conrad Bethmann. *MGH SS* 6: 405–38.

"Annales de Lagny." Ed. Élie Berger. *BEC* 38 (1877): 477–82.

"Annales de Saint-Denis." Ed. Élie Berger. *BEC* 40 (1879): 261–95.

"Annales sanctae Colombae Senonensis." In *Bibliothèque historique de l'Yonne*, ed. L.-M. Duru. 1: 200–218. Auxerre: Perriquet, 1850.

Anonymous of Laon, *Chronicon. RHF* 13: 677–83; 18: 1181–1219.

Arnaud, Anne-François. F. *Voyage archéologique et pittoresque dans le département de l'Aube et dans l'ancien diocèse de Troyes.* Troyes: Impr. de L.-C. Cardon, 1837.

Aubri of Trois-Fontaines. *Chronicon.* Ed. Paul Scheffer-Boichorst. *MGH SS* 23: 631–950. Hannover, 1874.

Aulus Gellius. *The Attic Nights of Aulus Gellius.* 3 vols. Ed. and trans. John C. Rolfe. Cambridge Mass.: Harvard University Press, 1927. Rev. ed. 1946 (vol. 1), 1952 (vol. 3).

Avenay. Louis Paris. *Histoire de l'abbaye d'Avenay.* 2 vols. Paris: Picard, 1879.

Barthélemy, Édouard de. *Diocèse ancien de Châlons-sur-Marne: histoire et monuments.* 2 vols. Paris: A. Aubry, 1861.

Baudri of Bourgueil. *The Historia Ierosolomitana of Baldric of Bourgueil.* Ed. Steven Biddlecombe. Woodbridge: Boydell, 2014.

Benton, John F. "Recueil des actes des comtes de Champagne, 1152–1197." An unpublished "preedition" (1988) of 732 acts of Henry I, Marie, and Henry II. The acts of Henry I are now published as the *Recueil des actes de Henri le Libéral, 1152–1181.* 2 vols. (2009, 2013). The acts of Marie and Henry II are accessible only in this "pre-edition," available at several major university libraries in the U.S. and France.

Bernard of Clairvaux. *Epistolae.* In *Sancti Bernardi Opera*, vols. 7–8. Ed. J. Leclercq and H. M. Rochais. Rome: Editiones Cisterciensis, 1957–78. Trans. Bruno Scott James as *The Letters of*

St. Bernard of Clairvaux (1953), with a new introduction by Beverley Mayne Kienzle. Collegeville, Minn.: Cistercian Publications, 1998.

————. "Liber ad milites Templi de laude novae militiae." In *Tractatus et Opuscula* (*Sancti Bernardi Opera*), 3: 213–39. Trans. Conrad Greenia as "In Praise of the New Knighthood," in *Bernard of Clairvaux: Treatises III*, 113–67. Kalamazoo, Mich.: Cistercian Publications, 1977.

Bourquelot, Félix. "Cantique latin à la gloire d'Anne Musnier, héroïne du douzième siècle." *BEC* 1 (1839–40): 295–304.

Calendar of Documents Preserved in France Illustrative of the History of Great Britain and Ireland, Vol. 1, *A.D. 918–1206*. Ed. John Horace Round. London: Eyre and Spottiswoode, 1899.

Camuzat, Nicolas. *Promptuarium sacrarum antiquitatum Tricassinae dioecesis*. Troyes: U. Moreau, 1610.

The Cartulary of Countess Blanche of Champagne. Ed. Theodore Evergates. Medieval Academy Books 112. Toronto: University of Toronto Press, 2009.

Champollion-Figeac, J. J., ed. *Documents historiques inédits tirés des collections manuscrites de la Bibliothèque royale et des archives ou des bibliothèques des départements*. 4 vols. Paris: Firmin-Didot, 1841–48.

Chrétien de Troyes. *Chrétien de Troyes: Romans*. Ed. J. M. Fritz, Charles Méla, O. Collet, D. F. Hult, and M.-Cl. Zai. Paris: La Pochothèque, 1994. Trans. William W. Kibler and Carleton W. Carroll in *Arthurian Romances*. London: Penguin, 1991.

Chronicon Universale Anonymi Laudunensis, von 1154 bis zum Schluss (1219). Ed. Alexander Cartellieri, rev. Wolf Stechele. Leipzig: Dyksche Buchhandlung, 1909.

La chronique de Morigny (1095–1152). Ed. Léon Mirot. 2nd ed. Paris: Picard, 1912.

Chronique de Saint-Pierre-le-Vif de Sens, dite de Clarius. Ed. and trans. Robert-Henri Bautier and Monique Gilles. Paris: CNRS, 1979.

Clairvaux. Recueil des chartes de l'abbaye de Clairvaux aux XIIe siècle. Ed. Laurent Veyssière. Paris: CTHS, 2004.

Collection Moreau. vol. 60. BnF.

Decrees of the Ecumenical Councils. Vol. 1, *Nicaea I to Lateran V*. Ed. Norman P. Tanner. Washington, D.C.: Georgetown University Press, 1990.

Delisle, Léopold. "Discours [sur un antiphonaire]." *Annuaire-Bulletin de la Société de l'Histoire de France* (*année 1885*) 22 (1885): 82–139.

Desguerrois, Marie-Nicolas. *La saincteté chrestienne*. Troyes: Jean Jacquard, 1637.

Duchesne, André. *Histoire de la maison de Chastillon sur Marne*. Paris: S. Cramoisy, 1621. The *preuves* are printed separately in part 2.

Épernay. Auguste Nicaise, *Épernay et l'abbaye Saint-Martin de cette ville: Histoire et documents inédits*. 2 vols. Châlons-sur-Marne: J-L Le Roy, 1869.

Epistolae Pontificum Romanorum ineditae. Ed. S. Loewenfeld. Leipzig: Veit, 1885.

Étienne of Bourbon. *Anecdotes historiques, légendes et apologues tirés du recueil inédit d'Étienne de Bourbon, dominicain du XIIIe siècle*. Ed. A. Lecoy de la Marche. Société de l'Histoire de France 185. Paris: Librairie Renouard, 1877.

Evergates, Theodore, ed. *Feudal Society in Medieval France: Documents from the County of Champagne*. Philadelphia: University of Pennsylvania Press, 1993.

Evrat. *Le Genèse d'Évrat*. Ed. Wil Boers. 4 vols. Leiden: Universiteit Leiden, 2002.

Fontevraud. Grand cartulaire de Fontevraud. Ed. Jean-Marc Bienvenu, with Robert Favreau and Georges Pons. 2 vols. Poitiers: Société des Antiquaires de l'Ouest, 2000, 2005.

Foreville, Raymonde, and Gillian Keir, eds. *The Book of St Gilbert*. Oxford: Clarendon Press 1987.

Freculf. *Frechulfi Lexoviensis episcopi Opera omnia*. Ed. Michael I. Allen. 2 vols. Corpus Christianorum. Continuatio mediaevalis, 169, 169A. Turnhout: Brepols, 2002.

Frenken, Goswin. *Die Exempla des Jacob von Vitry: Ein Beitrag zur Geschichte des Erzählungslitteratur des Mittelalters*. Munich: C. Beck, 1914.

Gallia Christiana in provincias ecclesiasticas distributa. 16 vols. Paris, 1739–1877.

Geoffroy de Courlon, *Le livre de reliques de l'abbaye de Saint-Pierre-le-Vif de Sens*. Ed. Gustave Julliot and Maurice Prou. Sens: Ch. Duchemin, 1887.

Gerald of Wales. *De principis instructione liber*. In *Giraldi Cambrensis opera*, ed. George F. Warner, vol. 8. Rolls Series. London: Eyre and Spottiswoode, 1891.

Gervase of Canterbury. *Chronica*. In *Opera Historica*, vol. 1, ed. William Stubbs. *The Chronicles of the Reigns of Stephen, Henry II, and Richard I*. Rolls Series 72. 2 vols. London: Longman, 1879–80.

Gesta Stephani. Ed. and trans. K. R. Potter, intro. R. H. C. Davis. Oxford: Oxford University Press, 1976.

Gislebert of Mons. *La chronique de Gislebert de Mons*. Ed. Léon Vanderkindere Brussels: Kiessling, 1904. Trans. Laura Napran as *Chronicle of Hainaut*. Woodbridge: Boydell, 2005.

Grosse, Rolf. "Überlegungen zum Kreuzzugsaufruf Eugens III. von 1145/46, mit einer Neuedition von JL 8876." *Francia* 18 (1991): 85–92.

Guiot de Provins. *La Bible*. In *Les oeuvres de Guiot de Provins, poète lyrique et satirique*. Ed. John Orr. Manchester: University of Manchester Press, 1915.

Guy of Bazoches. *Liber Epistularum Guidonis de Basochis*. Ed. Herbert Adolfsson. Stockholm: Almquistoch Wiksell, 1969.

Helinand of Froidmond. *Chronicon*. PL 212: 717–1082.

Helmold of Bosau. *Helmoldi presbyteri bozoviensis Chronica Slavorum*, 3rd ed. Ed. B. Schmeidler. *MGH SRG*. 32. Hanover: Hahniani, 1937. Trans. F. J. Tschan as *The Chronicle of the Slavs*. New York: Columbia University Press, 1966.

Herbert of Bosham. *Epistolae*. In *Herbert de Boseham, Opera*, 2 vols., ed. J. A. Gilles, 2: 207–310. Oxford: J.H. Parker, 1846. Rpt. in *PL* 190: 1415–74.

———. *Vita Sancti Thomae*. In *Materials*, 3: 155–534.

Hill, Raymond Thompson, ed. *Two Old French Poems on Saint Thibaut*. New Haven, Conn.: Yale University Press, 1936.

Historia gloriosi regis Ludovici VII. RHF 12: 124–33.

Historia Francorum. RHF 12: 115–17.

History of William Marshal. Ed. A. J. Holden, trans. S. Gregory and D. Crouch. 3 vols. London: Anglo-Norman Text Society, 2002–2006.

Hugh of Poitiers. *Chronique*. In *Monumenta Vizeliacensia: textes relatifs à l'histoire de l'abbaye de Vézelay*, ed. R. B. C. Huygens, 395–607. Corpus Christianorum. Continuatio mediaevalis, 42. Turnhout: Brepols, 1976. Trans. John Scott and John O. Ward as *The Vézelay Chronicle*. Binghamton, N.Y.: Medieval and Renaissance Texts and Studies, 1992.

Jaksch, August, ed. *Monumenta historica ducatus Carinthiae*. 11 vols. Klagenfurt: Kleinmayr, 1896–1972.

Jean le Nevelon. *La Venjance Alixandre*. Ed. Edward B. Ham. Princeton, N.J., 1931. 2nd ed. Ann Arbor: University of Michigan Press, 1946.

John of Salisbury. *The Letters of John of Salisbury*. Ed. W. J. Millor, H. E. Butler, and C. N. L. Brooke. Vol. 1, *The Early Letters (1153–1161)*; vol. 2, *The Later Letters (1163–1180)*. Oxford: Oxford University Pres, 1979, 1986.

————. *The Historia Pontificalis of John of Salisbury*. Ed. and trans. Marjorie Chibnall, London: Thomas Nelson, 1956.

————. *Policraticus. Ioannis Saresberiensis Episcopi Carnotensis Policratici*. Ed. Clement Webb. 2 vols. Oxford: Clarendon, 1909. Trans. Cary J. Nederman as *Policraticus*. Cambridge: Cambridge University Press, 1990.

————. *Vita et Passio Sancti Thome*. In *Materials*, 2: 301–22.

Joinville. *Jean de Joinville: Vie de Saint Louis, Credo et letter à Louis X*. Ed. Natalis de Wailly. 2nd ed. Paris: Firmin Didot, 1874. Trans. Caroline Smith as *The Life of Saint Louis* in *Joinville and Villehardouin, Chronicles of the Crusades*, 137–336. London: Penguin, 2008.

Jordan Fantosme. *Jordan Fantosme's Chronicle*. Ed. R. C. Johnson. Oxford: Oxford University Press.

Lalore, Charles, ed. *Collection des principaux cartulaires du diocèse de Troyes*, 7 vols. Paris: E. Thorin, 1875–90.

————, ed. "Documents pour servir à la généalogie des anciens seigneurs de Traînel." *MSA* 34 (1870): 177–277.

————, ed. *Inventaires des principales églises de Troyes*. Collection des documents inédits relatifs à la ville de Troyes et de la Champagne méridionale. 2 vols. Troyes: Dufour-Bouquot, 1893.

Lambert of Ardres. *Lamberti Ardensis historia comitum Ghisnensium*. Ed. Johann Heller. In *MGH SS* 24: 550–642. Trans. Leah Shopkow as *The History of The Counts of Guines and Lords of Ardres*. Philadelphia: University of Pennsylvania Press, 2001.

Lambert of Wattrelos. *Annales Cameracensis*. In *MGH SS* 16: 509–54.

Langres. Cartulaire du chapitre cathédral de Langres. Ed. Hubert Flammarion. 2nd ed. Turnhout: Brepols, 2004.

Larrivour. Cartulary of Larrivour. AD Aube 4 H 1 (thirteenth-century).

Layettes du Trésor des Chartes. Ed. Alexandre Teulet et al. 4 vols. Paris: Imprimerie Nationale, 1863–1909.

"Léproserie." Harmand, "Notice historique sur la Léproserie de la ville de Troyes." *MSA* 14 (1847–48): 429–669.

Libellus de diversis ordinibus et professionibus qui sunt in aecclesia. Ed. Giles Constable and Bernard S. Smith. Oxford: Oxford University Press, 2003.

Littere Baronum: The Earliest Cartulary of the Counts of Champagne. Ed. Theodore Evergates. Medieval Academy Books 107. Toronto: University of Toronto Press, 2003.

Longnon, Auguste, ed. *Documents relatifs au comté de Champagne et de Brie (1172–1361)*. 3 vols. Paris: Imprimerie Nationale, 1901–1914.

Luchaire, Achille. *Études sur les actes de Louis VII*. Paris: Picard, 1885.

Martène, Edmond and Ursin Duran, eds. *Thesaurus novus anecdotorum*. 5 vols. Paris: F. Delaulne, 1717. Rpt. Farnborough: Gregg, 1968–69.

————, eds. *Veterum scriptorum et monumentorum historicorum, dogmaticorum, moralium Amplissima Collectio*. 9 vols. Paris, 1724–33.

Materials for the History of Thomas Becket, Archbishop of Canterbury. Ed. J. C. Robertson, 7 vols. Rolls Series 67. London: Longman, 1875–85.

Meinert, Hermann, ed. *Papsturkunden in Frankreich. Neue Folge. 1 Bd. Champagne und Lotharingien*. 2 vols. Berlin: Weidmannsche Buchhandlung, 1933.

Montiéramey. Cartulaire de Montiéramey. In Lalore, *Collection* 7 (1890).

Montierender. Chartes de Montierender. In Lalore, *Collection* 4 (1878): 90–137.

Montier-la-Celle. Cartulaire de Montier-la-Celle. In Lalore, *Collection* 5 (1882).

Monumenta Germaniae Historica. Scriptores (MGH SS). 30 vols. Hannover, 1824–1924.

Neubauer, Adolf and Moritz Stern, eds. *Hebraïsche Berichte über die Judenverfolgungen während der Kreuzzüge*. Berlin: L. Simon, 1892.

Newman, William Mendel, ed. *Les seigneurs de Nesle en Picardie (XIIe–XIIIe siècle): leurs chartes et leur histoire*. 2 vols. Philadelphia: American Philosophical Society, 1971.

Nicholas of Montiéramey. *Epistolae*. PL 196: 1593–1654.

Niketas Choniates. *O City of Byzantium: Annals of Niketas Choniates*. Trans. Harry J. Magoulias. Detroit: Wayne State University Press, 1984.

Notre-Dame de Chartres. Cartulaire de Notre-Dame de Chartres. Ed. Eugène de Lépinois and Lucien Merlet. 3 vols. Chartres: Société Archéologique d'Eure-et-Loire, 1862–65.

Notre-Dame de Paris. Cartulaire de l'église Notre-Dame de Paris. Ed. M. Guérard. 4 vols. Paris: Crapelet, 1850.

Obituaires. Obituaires de la province de Sens. Paris: Imprimerie Nationale. 1. *Diocèse de Sens et de Paris*. Ed. Auguste Molinier, 2 vols. 1902. 2. *Diocèse de Chartres*. Ed. A. Molinier, 1906. 4. *Diocèses de Meaux et de Troyes*. Ed. Armand Boutillier du Retail and P. Piétresson de Saint-Aubin. 1923.

Odo of Deuil. *De profectione Ludovici VII in Orientem*. Ed. and trans.Virginia Gingerick Berry as *The Journey of Louis VII in the East*. New York: Norton, 1948.

Orderic Vitalis. *The Ecclesiastical History of Orderic Vitalis*. Ed. and trans. Marjorie Chibnall, 6 vols. Oxford: Oxford University Press, 1969–1980.

Otto of Freising. *Gesta Friderici I imperatoris*. Ed. G. Waitz and B. de Simson. Scriptores rerum Germanicarum in usum scholarum. 3rd ed. Hanover, 1912. Trans. Charles C. Mierow with Richard Emery as *The Deeds of Frederick Barbarossa*. New York: Columbia University Press, 1953.

Paraclet. Cartulaire de l'abbaye du Paraclet. In Lalore, *Collection*, 2 (1878).

Patrologiae cursus completus. Series Latina (PL). Ed. J.–P. Migne. 221 vols. Paris, 1844–65.

Pavillon, B. *La vie du bienheureux Robert d'Arbrissel*. Samur: François Ernov, 1667.

Pérard, Estienne, ed. *Recueil de plusiers pièces curieuses servant à l'histoire de Bourgogne*. Paris: C. Cramoisy, 1664.

Peter Comestor. *Petri Comestoris Scolastica Historia. Liber Genesis*. Ed. Agneta Sylwan. Corpus Christianorum. Continuatio Mediaevalis, 191. Turnhout: Brepols, 2005.

Peter of Celle. *De disciplina claustrali*. In *Pierre de Celle: L'école du cloître: introduction, texte critique, traduction et notes*. Ed. Gérard de Martel. Paris: Éditions du Cerf, 1977.

———. *The Letters of Peter of Celle*. Ed. and trans. Julian Haseldine. Oxford: Oxford University Press, 2002.

Peter the Venerable, *The Letters of Peter the Venerable*. Ed. Giles Constable. 2 vols. Cambridge, Mass.: Harvard University Press, 1967.

The Peterborough Chronicle, 1070–1154. Ed. Cecily Clark. 2nd ed. Oxford: Oxford University Press, 1970.

Petit, Ernest. *Histoire des ducs de Bourgogne de la race capetiene*. 9 vols. Paris: Picard, 1885–1909.

Philip of Harvengt. *Ad Henricum*. PL 203: 151–57, no. 17. Partial trans. Robert Ziomkowski as "Letter to Henry, Count of Champagne," in *Medieval Political Theory: A Reader*, 64–66, ed. Cary J. Nederman and Kate Langdon Forhan. London: Routledge, 1993.

Pontigny. Le premier cartulaire de l'abbaye cistercienne de Pontigny (XIIe–XIIIe siècle). Ed. Martine Garrigues. Paris: Bibliothèque Nationale, 1981.

Preuilly. Chartes et documents de l'abbaye cistercienne de Preuilly. Ed. Albert Catel and Maurice Lecomte. Paris: Imprimerie Claverie, 1927.

Quantin, Maximilien. *Cartulaire général de l'Yonne*. 2 vols. Auxerre: Perriquet, 1854, 1860.

Quintus Curtius [Rufus]. *History of Alexander*. Ed. and trans. John C. Rolfe. 2 vols. Cambridge, Mass.: Harvard University Press, 1946.

Ralph of Diceto. *Ymagines Historiarum*. Ed. W. Stubbs. In *The Historial Works of Master Ralph of Diceto, Dean of London*, 1: 291–440; 2: 2–174. Rolls Series 68. 2 vols. London: Public Record Office, 1876.

Recueil des actes d'Henri le Libéral, comte de Champagne (1152–1181). Vol. 1. Ed. John Benton and Michel Bur, with the collaboration of Dominique Devaux, Olivier Guyotjeannin, Xavier de la Selle, and Rosy Meiron and Michèle Courtois. Académie des Inscriptions et Belles-Lettres. Paris: De Boccard, 2009. Vol. 2. *Indices et addenda*. Ed. Michel Bur, with the collaboration of Michèle Courtois. Académie des Inscriptions et Belles-Lettres. Paris: De Boccard, 2013.

Recueil des actes de Henri II, roi d'Angleterre et duc de Normandie. Ed. Léopold Delisle and Élie Berger. 4 vols. Paris: Imprimerie National, 1907–27.

Recueil des actes de Louis VI, roi de France (1108–1137). Ed. Jean Dufour. 4 vols. Académie des Inscriptions et Belles-Lettres. Paris: De Boccard, 1992–94.

Recueil des actes de Philippe Auguste. Ed. Henri-François Delaborde, Charles Petit-Dutaillis, Jacques Boussard, and Michel Nortier. 4 vols. Paris: Imprimerie Nationale, 1916–79. Vol. 5, *Supplément d'actes, actes perdus, additions et corrections aux précédents volumes*. Ed. Michel Nortier. Académie des Inscriptions et Belles-Lettres. Paris: De Boccard, 2004.

Recueil des Historiens des Gaules et de la France. Ed. Dom Bouquet et al. 24 vols. Paris, 1734–1904.

Robert (of Saint-Marien) of Auxerre. *Chronicon*. Ed. O. Holder-Egger. In *MGH SS* 26: 219–76 [includes a *vita* of Abbot Milo, 262–65], with continuations, 276–87.

Robert of Torigni. *The Chronicle of Robert of Torigni*. Ed. Richard Howlett. In *Chronicles of the Reigns of Stephen, Henry II and Richard I*. Rolls Series 82, vol. 4. London: Longman, 1889. Trans. Joseph Stevenson as *The Chronicles of Robert de Monte*. The Church Historians of England 4.2. London: Seeleys, 1856; rpt. and repaginated Lamyseter: Llanerch, 1991.

Roger of Howden. *Chronica*. Ed. W. Stubbs. Rolls Series 51. 4 vols. London: Public Record Office, 1869–71.

———. *Gesta Regis Henrici secundi*. Ed. W. Stubbs. In *The Chronicles of the Reigns of Henry II and Richard I, A.D. 1169–1192, Known Commonly under the Name of Benedict of Peterborough*. Rolls Series 49. 2 vols. London: Longman, 1867.

St-Étienne. Cartulary of Saint-Étienne of Troyes. BnF, Latin 17098 (ca. 1271). Original foliation cited here.

St-Germain-des-Prés. *Recueil des chartes de l'abbaye de Saint-Germain-des-Prés*. Ed. René Poupardin. 2 vols. Paris: H. Champion, 1909, 1930.

St-Loup. *Cartulaire de l'abbaye de Saint-Loup de Troyes*. In Lalore, *Collection* 1 (1875).

St-Pierre. *Cartulaire de Saint-Pierre de Troyes*. In Lalore, *Collection* 5 (1880): 2–228.

St-Quiriace. Michel Veissière. *Une communauté canoniale au Moyen Age: Saint-Quiriace de Provins (XIe–XIIIe siècles)*. Provins: Société d'Histoire et d'Archéologie de l'Arrondissement de Provins, Documents et travaux, 1. Provins: L'Imprimerie Notre-Dame, 1961.

St-Sépulcre de Jérusalem. *Le cartulaire du chapitre de Saint-Sépulcre de Jérusalem*. Ed. Geneviève Bresc-Bautier. Paris: Librarie Orientaliste Paul Geuthner, 1984.

Sigebert of Gembloux, *Chronica cum continuationibus*. Ed. L. K. Bethmann. *MGH SS*, 6: 268–474. Hannover, 1888.

Simon Aurea Capra. Martha Mary Parrott, "The Ylias of Simon Aurea Capra: A Critical Edition." Ph.D. dissertation, Univeristy of Toronto, 1975.

———. "L'Ilias de Simon Chèvre d'Or: Édition critique et commentaire" by Sébastien Peyrard. Thèse, École des Chartes, 2007.

———. *Versus magistri Symonis cognomento Capra Aurea. PL* 185: 1251–54.

———. *Vita et passio sancti Thome*. In Francis R. Swietek, "A Metrical Life of Thomas Becket by Simon Aurea Capra." *Mittellateinisches Jahrbuch* 11 (1976): 177–95.

Staunton, Michael, trans. *The Lives of Thomas Becket*. Manchester: Manchester University Press, 2001.

Stephen of Tournai. *Lettres d'Étienne de Tournai*. Ed. Jules Desilve. Paris: Picard, 1893.

Suger. *Oeuvres*. Ed. Françoise Gasparri. 2 vols. Paris: Belles Lettres, 1996, 2008.

———. *Vie de Louis VI le Gros*. Ed. and trans. Henri Waquet. 2nd ed. Paris: Belles Lettres, 1964.

Tardif, Jules, ed. *Monuments historiques: cartons des rois*. Paris: J. Claye, 1866. Nendelm: Kraus Reprint, 1977.

Temple. Cartulaire général de l'Ordre du Temple, 1119?–1150. Ed. Marquis d'Albon. Paris: H. Champion, 1913.

Templiers de Provins. Histoire et cartulaire des Templiers de Provins. Ed. Victor Carrière. Paris: H. Champion, 1919.

Thomas Becket. *The Correspondence of Thomas Becket, Archbishop of Canterbury, 1162–1170*. Ed. and trans. Anne Duggan. 2 vols. Oxford: Oxford University Press, 2000.

Tiron. *Cartulaire de l'abbaye de la Sainte-Trinité de Tiron*, ed. Lucien Merlet. 2 vols. Chartres: Imprimerie Garnier, 1883.

Die Urkunden Friedricks I. Ed. Heinrich Appelt. 5 vols. Hannover: Hahn, 1975–1990.

Valerius Maximus. *Memorable Doings and Sayings*. Ed. and trans. D. R. Shackleton Bailey. 2 vols. Cambridge Mass.: Harvard University Press, 2000.

Vallet de Viriville, A. *Les archives historiques du département de l'Aube et de l'ancien diocèse de Troyes*. Troyes: Bouquot, 1841.

Varin, Pierre, ed. *Archives administratives de la ville de Reims*. 5 vols. Paris: Crapelet, 1839–48.

Vegetius, *Epitome rei militaris*. Ed. M. D. Reeve. Oxford: Oxford University Press, 2004.

Vie de Saint Thibaut de Provins: édition critique. Ed. Manuel Nicolaon. Turnhout: Brepols, 2007.

Vita Adalberonis Trevirensis archiepiscopi. RHF 14: 357.

Vita B. Petri Julieacenesis." PL 185: 1255–70.

Vita prima sancti Bernardi. PL 185: 225–386.

Vita tercia sancti Bernardi. PL 185: 523–30.

Walter Map. *De Nugis Curialium. Courtiers' Trifles*. Ed. and trans. M.R. James, rev. C.N.L. Brooke and R.A.B. Mynors. Oxford: Oxford University Press, 1983.

Walter of Châtillon. *Galteri de Castellione Alexandreis*. Ed. Marvin L. Colker. Padua, 1978. Trans. David Townsend as *The Alexandreis of Walter of Châtillon: A Twelfth-Century Epic*. Philadelphia: University of Pennsylvania Press, 1996.

———. *Walter of Châtillon: The Shorter Poems*. Ed. and trans. David A. Traill. Oxford: Clarendon, 2013.

William FitzStephen. *Vita Sancti Thomae*. In *Materials*, 3: 1–154.

William Godel. *Chronicon. RHF* 13: 671–77.

William of Malmesbury. *Historia Novella: The Contemporary History*. Ed. Edmund King, trans. K. R. Potter. Oxford: Oxford University Press, 1998.

William of Nangis. *Chronique latine de Guillaume de Nangis, de 1113 à 1300*. Ed. Hercule Gérard. 2 vols. Paris: Renaud, 1843.

William of Newburgh. *Historia*. In *Chronicles of the Reigns of Stephen, Henry II and Richard I*. Edited by Richard Howlett. Rolls Series 82, vol.1. London: Public Record Office, 1884.

William of Tyre. *Chronique*. Ed. R.B.C. Huygens. 2 vols. Turnhout: Brepols, 1986. Trans. Emily Atwater Babcock and A. C. Krey as *A History of Deeds Done Beyond the Sea*. 2 vols. New York: Columbia University Press, 1943.

SECONDARY WORKS

L'abbaye parisienne de Saint-Victor au moyen âge. Ed. Jean Longère. Paris-Turnhout: Brepols, 1991.

Abbot Suger and Saint-Denis: A Symposium. Ed. Paula Lieber Gerson. New York: Metropolitan Museum of Art, 1986.

Allmand, Christoper. *The "De Re Militari" of Vegetius: The Reception, Transmission and Legacy of a Roman Text in the Middle Ages*. Cambridge: Cambridge University Press, 2011.

Arbois de Jubainville, Henry d'. "Catalogue d'actes des comtes de Brienne, 950–1356." *BEC* 33 (1872): 141–86.

———. "Études sur les documents antérieurs à l'année 1285, conservés dans les archives des quatre petits hôpitaux de la ville de Troyes." *MSA* 21 (1857): 49–116.

———. *Histoire de Bar-sur-Aube sous les comtes de Champagne, 1077–1284*. Paris: A. Durand, 1859.

———. *Histoire des ducs et des comtes de Champagne*. 7 vols. Paris: A. Durand, 1859–69.

———. "Les premiers seigneurs de Ramerupt." *BEC* 21 (1861): 440–58.

———. "Sigillographie." In A. Gaussen, *Portefeuille archéologique de la Champagne*. Bar-sur-Aube: Jardeaux-Ray, 1861.

Armstong-Partida, Michelle. "Mothers and Daughters as Lords: The Countesses of Blois and Chartres." *Medieval Prosopography* 26 (2005): 77–107.

Barber, Malcolm. *The New Knighthood: A History of the Order of the Temple*. Cambridge: Cambridge University Press, 1994.

———. "The Origins of the Order of the Temple." *Studia Monastica* 12 (1970): 219–40.

Barker, Lynn K. "MS Bodl. Canon Pat. Lat. 131 and a Lost Lactantius of John of Salisbury: Evidence in Search of a French Critic of Thomas Becket." *Albion* 22 (1990): 21–37.

Barlow, Frank. *Thomas Becket*. Berkeley: University of California Press, 1986.

Barthélemy, A. "Notice historique sur la maison de Grandpré." *Revue de Champagne et de Brie* 9 (1880): 97–105.

Bartlett, Robert. *Gerald of Wales: A Voice of the Middle Ages*. Stroud: Tempus, 1982.

Baudin, Arnaud. *Les sceaux des comtes de Champagne et de leur entourage (fin XIe–début XIVe siècle): Emblématique et pouvoir en Champagne*. Langres: Dominique Guéniot, 2012.

———. "Les sceaux du comte Henri Ier le libéral: images et usages." In *Recueil des actes d'Henri le Libéral*, 2: 79–112.

Bautier, Robert-Henri. "Les foires de Champagne: recherches sur une évolution historique." In *La Foire*, 97–147. Receuils de la Société Jean Bodin, 5. Reprinted in his *Sur l'histoire économique de la France médiévale: La route, le flueve, la foire* [Collected Articles, VII,]. Great Yarmouth: Variorum, 1992.

———. "Provins et les foires de Champagne." In *De l'histoire de Brie à l'histoire des réformes: mélanges offerts au chanoine Michel Veissière*, ed. Michèle Bardon, Gilbert Robert Delahaye, Jean Jacquart, and Nicole Lemaitre, 153–74. Paris: Féderation des Sociétés Historiques et Archéologiques de Paris et de l'Ile-de-France, 1993.

———. "Quand et comment Paris devint capitale." *Bulletin de la Société de l'histoire de Paris et de l'Île-de-France* 105 (1978): 17–46. Rpt. in his *Recherches sur l'histoire de la France médiévale.* London: Variorum, 1991.

Beech, George T. "The Eleanor of Aquitaine Vase, William IX of Aquitaine, and Muslim Spain." *Gesta* 31 (1993): 3–10.

Benham, Jenny. *Peacemaking in the Middle Ages: Principles and Practices.* Manchester: Manchester University Press, 2011.

Benton, John F. "The Court of Champagne as a Literary Center." *Speculum* 36 (1961): 551–91. Reprinted in his *Culture*, 3–43.

———. "The Court of Champagne Under Henry the Liberal and Countess Marie." Ph.D. dissertation, Princeton University, 1959.

———. *Culture, Power and Personality in Medieval France.* Collected articles. Ed. Thomas N. Bisson. London: Hambledon, 1991.

———. "Nicolas de Clairvaux à la recherche du vin d'Auxerre d'après une lettre inédite du XIIe siècle." 1962. In his *Culture*, 77–81.

———. "Nicolas of Clairvaux and the Twelfth-Century Sequence, with Special Reference to Adam of St-Victor." 1962. In his *Culture*, 45–75.

Berlow, Rosalind Kent. "The Rebels of Vézelay (1152–55)." *Studies in Medieval and Reniassance History* 9 (1987): 135–63.

Bernard de Clairvaux: histoire, mentalités, spiritualité. Sources Chrétiennes 380. Paris: Cerf, 1992.

Bezzola, Reto R. *Les origines et la formation de la littérature courtoise en occident (500–1200). 3. La société courtoise: littérature de cour et liiérature courtoise.* Vol. 2, *Les cours de France, d'outremer et de Sicile au XIIe siècle.* Paris: É. Champion, 1963.

Bibolet, Françoise. "La Bibliothèque des chanoines de Troyes: leurs manuscrits du XIIe au XVIe s." *MSA* 104 (1964–1966): 139–77.

Biddle, Martin. "Wolvesey: The *Domus quasi palatium* of Henry de Blois in Winchester." *Château Gaillard* 3 (1969): 28–36.

Bisson, Thomas N. *Conservation of Coinage: Monetary Exploitation and Its Restraint in France, Catalonia, and Aragon (c. A.D. 1000–c. 1225).* Oxford: Oxford University Press, 1979.

———. *The Crisis of the Twelfth Century: Power, Lordship and the Origins of European Government.* Princeton, N.J.: Princeton University Press, 2009.

Blampignon, Émile-Antoine. *Bar-sur-Aube.* Paris: A. Picard, 1900.

Blum, Pamela Z. "The Statue-Column of a Queen from Saint-Thibaut, Provins, in the Glencairn Museum." *Gesta* 29, 2 (1990): 214–33.

Blumenfeld-Kosinski, Renate. *Reading Myth: Classical Mythology and Its Interpretations in Medieval French Literature.* Stanford, Calif.: Stanford University Press, 1997.

Bony, Jean. *French Gothic Architecture of the Twelfth and Thirteenth Centuries.* Berkeley: University of California Press,1983.

Bony, Pierre. *Un siècle de sceaux figurés (1135–1235).* Paris: Le Léopard d'Or, 2002.

Bouchard, Constance Brtittain. *Sword, Miter, and Cloister: Nobility and the Church in Burgundy, 980–1198.* Ithaca, N.Y.: Cornell University Press, 1987.

Bougard, François, and Pierre Petitmengin, in collaboration with Patricia Stirnemann, *La bibliothèque de l'abbaye cistercienne de Vauluisant: Histoire et inventaires.* Paris: CNRS, 2012.

Boureau, Alain. "Hypothèses sur l'émergence lexicale et théorique de la catégorie de séculier au XIIe siècle." In *Le clerc séculier au moyen âge*, 35–43. XXIIe Congrès de la Société des Historiens Médiévistes de l'Enseignement Supérieur Public. Paris: Publications de la Sorbonne, 1993.

Bournazel, Éric. *Louis VI le Gros.* Paris: Fayard, 2007.

Bourquelot, Félix. *Histoire de Provins*. 2 vols. Provins: Lebeau, 1839–40.

Boutemy, André. "La Geste d'Enée par Simon Chèvre d'Or." *Le Moyen Âge* 1 (1946): 242–56.

———. "Quatre poèmes nouveaux de Simon Chèvre d'Or." *Revue du Moyen Âge Latin* 3 (1947): 141–52.

Brand, Charles M. *Byzantium Confronts the West, 1180–1204*. Cambridge, Mass.: Harvard University Press, 1968.

Bredero, Adriaan H. *Bernard of Clairvaux: Between Cult and History*, Grand Rapids, Mich.: Eerdmans, 1993.

———. "The Canonization of Bernard of Clairvaux." In *Saint Bernard of Clairvaux: Studies Commemorating the Eighth Centenary of His Canonization*. Ed. M. Basil Pennington, 63–100. Kalamazoo, Mich.: Cistercian Publications, 1977.

Brixius, Johannes Matthias. *Die Mitglieder des Kardinalkollegiums von 1130–1181*. Berlin: R. Trenkel, 1912.

Brouillon, Louis. *Recherches sur Vitry-en-Perthois*. 1927. Rpt. Paris: Res Universis, 1993.

Brown, Elizabeth A. R. "Burying and Unburying the Kings of France." In *Persons in Groups: Social Behaviors as Identity Formation in Medieval and Renaissance Europe*, ed. Richard C. Trexler, 241–66. Binghampton: Center for Medieval and Renaissance Studies, 1985. Reprinted in her *The Monarchy of Capetian France and Royal Ceremonial* [collected articles, no. IX], 241–66. Hampshire: Variorum, 1991.

Brown, Elizabeth A. R., and Michael W. Cothren. "The Twelfth-Century Crusading Window of the Abbey of Saint-Denis: Praeteritorum Enim Recordatio Futuorum est Exhibitio." *Journal of the Warburg and Courtauld Institutes* 49 (1986): 1–40 and Plates 1–12.

Brühl, Carlrichard. *Palatium und Civitas: Studien zur Profantopographie Spätantiken Civitas vom 3. bis 13. Jahrhundert. Bd. 1. Gallien*. Cologne: Böhlau, 1975.

Brunn, Uwe. *Des contestaires aux "Cathares": discours de réforme et propagande antihérétique dans les pays du Rhin et de la Meuse avant l'Inquisition*. Paris: Institut d'Études Augustiniennes, 2006.

Buc, Philippe. "Conversion of Objects." *Viator: Medieval and Renaissance Studies* 28 (1997): 101–43.

Bur, Michel. *La Champagne médiévale: recueil d'articles*. Langres: Dominique Guéniot, 2005.

———. *La formation du comté de Champagne, v. 950–v. 1150*. Nancy: Publications de l'Université de Nancy II, 1977.

———. "La frontière entre la Champagne et la Lorraine du milieu de Xe à la fin du XIIe siècle." In his *La Champagne médiévale*, 141–60.

———. "L'image de la parenté chez les comtes de Champagne." In his *La Champagne médiévale*, 59–89.

———. "Meaux dans l'histoire de la Champagne du Xe au XIIe siècle." In his *La Champagne médiévale*, 443–56.

———. "Recherches sur la frontière dans la région mosane aux XIIe et XIIIe siècles." In his *La Champagne médiévale*, 161–80.

———. "Remarques dur le plus anciens documents concernant les foires de Champagne." In his *La Champagne médiévale*, 463–84.

———. *Vestiges d'habitat seigneurial fortifié en Champagne centrale*. Inventaire des sites archéologiques non monumentaux, 3. Reims: ARERS, 1987.

Caviness, Madeline Harrison. *Sumptuous Arts at the Royal Abbeys in Reims and Braine*. Princeton, N.J.: Princeton University Press, 1990.

Cerrini, Simonetta. "Le fondateur de l'ordre du Temple à ses frères: Huges de Payns et le *Sermo*

Christi militibus." In *Gesta Dei per francos: Études sur les croisades dédiées à Jean Richard*, ed. Michel Balard, Benjamin Z. Kedar, and Jonathan Riley-Smith, 99–110. Aldershot: Ashgate, 2001.

———. *La révolution des Templiers: une histoire perdue du XIIe siècle*. Paris: Perrin, 2007.

Chagny, Dom. "L'abbaye royale de Saint-Pierre de Lagny." *Revue de Champagne et de Brie* 1 (1876): 246–50.

Chapin, Elizabeth. *Les villes de foires de Champagne des origines au début du XIVe siècle*. Paris: H. Champion, 1937.

Chassel, Jean-Luc. "L'usage du sceau au XIIe siècle." In *Le XIIe siècle: mutations et renouveau en France dans la première moitié du XIIIe siècle*, ed. Françoise Gasparri, 61–101. Paris: Le Léopard d'Or, 1994.

———, ed. *Sceaux et usages de sceaux: Images de la Champagne médiévale*. Paris: Somogy, 2003.

Chazan, Mireille. *L'empire et l'histoire universelle: De Sigebert de Gembloux à Jean de Saint-Victor (XIIe–XIVe)*. Paris: H. Champion, 1999.

———. "L'usage de la compilation dans les chroniques de Robert d'Auxerre, Aubri de Trois-Fontaines et Jean de Saint-Victor." *Journal des Savants* (1999): 261–94.

———. *See also* Schmidt-Chazan.

Chazan, Robert. "The Blois Incident of 1171: A Study in Jewish Intercommunal Organization," *Proceedings of the American Academy for Jewish Research* 36 (1968): 13–31.

Cheney, Mary G. "The Recognition of Alexander III: Some Neglected Evidence." *English Historical Review* 84 (1969): 474–97.

Chibnall, Marjorie. "John of Salisbury as Historian." In *The World of John of Salisbury*, ed. Michael Wilks, 169–77. Oxford: Blackwell, 1989.

Ciggaar, Krijnie. "Encore une fois Chrétien de Troyes et la 'matière byzantine': la révolution des femmes au palais de Constantinople." *Cahiers de Civilisation Médiévale* 38 (1995): 267–74.

Civel, Nicolas. *La fleur de France: Les seigneurs d'Ile-de-France au XIIe siècle*. Turnhout: Brepols, 2006.

Clanchy, M. T. *Abelard: A Medieval Life*. Oxford: Blackwell, 1997.

———. *From Memory to Written Record: England, 1066–1307*. Oxford: Blackwell, 1979; 2nd ed., 1993.

Clark, W. B. "Art and Historiography in Two Thirteenth-Century Manuscripts from Northern France." *Gesta* 17 (1978): 37–48.

Cline, Ruth Harwood. "Abbot Hugh: An Overlooked Brother of Henry I, Count of Champagne." *Catholic Historical Review* 93 (2007): 501–16.

Constable, Giles. *Crusaders and Crusading in the Twelfth Century* [collected articles]. Farnham: Ashgate, 2008.

———. "The Disputed Election at Langres in 1138." *Traditio* 17 (1957): 119–52.

———. *The Reformation of the Twelfth Century*. Cambridge: Cambridge University Press, 1996.

———. "The Second Crusade as Seen by Contemporaries." In his *Crusaders and Crusading*, 229–300.

———. "Troyes, Constantinople, and the Relics of St. Helen in the Thirteenth Century." In *Mélanges offerts à René Crozet*, ed. Pierre Gallais and Yves-Jean Rion, 2: 1035–42. 2 vols. Poitiers: Société d'Études Médiévales, 1966.

Corbet, Patrick. "Les collégiales comtales de Champagne (v. 1150–v. 1230)." *Annales de l'Est* 29 (1977): 195–241.

Cothren, Michael W. "Suger's Stained Glass Masters and Their Workshop at Saint-Denis." In *Center of Artistic Enlightenment*, ed. George Mauner, Jeanne Chanault Porter, Elizabeth

Bradford Smith, and Susan Scott Munshower, 47–75. State College: Pennsylvania State University Press, 1988.

Cotts, John D. *The Clerical Dilemma: Peter and Blois and Literate Culture in the Twelfth Century.* Washington, D.C.: Catholic University of America Press, 2009.

———. "Monks and Clerks in Search of the *Beata Schola*: Peter of Celle's Warning to John of Salisbury Reconsidered." In *Teaching and Learning in Northern Europe, 1000–1200*, ed. Sally N. Vaughn and Jay Rubenstein, 255–77. Turnhout: Brepols, 2006.

Cowdrey, H. E. J. "Peter, Monk of Molesme and Prior of Jully." In *Cross Cultural Convergences in the Crusader Period: Essays Presented to Aryeh Graboïs on his Sixty-Fifth Birthday*, ed. Michael Goodrich, Sophia Menache, and Sylvia Schein, 59–73. New York: Peter Lang, 1996.

Cragoe, Carol Davidson. "Reading and Rereading Gervase of Canterbury." *Journal of the British Archaeological Association* 154 (2001): 40–53.

Crouch, David. *The Reign of King Stephen, 1135–1154.* Harlow: Longman, 2000.

———. *Tournament.* London: Hambledon and Continuum, 2005.

———. *William Marshal: Knighthood, War and Chivalry, 1147–1219.* London: Longman, 1990. 2nd ed. 2002.

Dahan, Gilbert, ed. *Pierre le Mangeur ou Pierre de Troyes: Maître du XIIe siècle.* Bibliothèque d'histoire culturelle du Moyen Âge, 12. Turnhout: Brepols, 2013.

Daly, Saralyn R. "Peter Comestor: Master of Histories." *Speculum* 32 (1957): 62–73.

Dectot, Xavier. "Les tombeaux des comtes de Champagne (1151–1284): Un manifeste politique." *Bulletin Monumental* 162 (2004): 1–62.

———. *Sculptures des XIe–XIIe siècles: Roman et premier art gothique.* Paris: Réunion des Musées Nationaux, 2005.

Deér, József. *The Dynastic Porphyry Tombs of the Norman Period in Sicily.* Cambridge, Mass.: Harvard University Press, 1959.

De Gryse, Louis M. "Some Observations on the Origin of the Flemish Bailiff (Bailli): The Reign of Philip of Alsace." *Viator* 7 (1976): 243–94.

De Hamel, Christopher. "Manuscripts of Herbert of Bosham." In *Manuscripts at Oxford: An Exhibition in Memory of Richard William Hunt (1908–1979)*, ed. A. C. de la Mare and B. C. Barker-Benfield, 39–41. Oxford: Bodleian Library, 1980.

De Hamel, C. F. R. *Glossed Books of the Bible and the Origins of the Paris Booktrade.* Bury St Edmunds: D.S. Brewer, 1984.

De la Mare, A. C., P. K. Marshal, and R. H Rouse. "Pietro da Montagnana and the Text of Aulus Gellius." *Scriptorium* 30 (1976): 219–25.

Delisle, Léopold. "Traductions de textes grecs faites par des religieux de Saint-Denis au XIIe siècle." *Journal des Savants* (1900): 725–37.

Demouy, Patrick. "Les archevêques de Reims et les foires (XIe–XVe siècles)." In *Le marchand au moyen âge*, 81–94. Preface by Michel Balard. 19e Congrès de la Société des Historiens Médiévistes de l'Enseignement Supérieur Public, Reims, juin 1988. St-Herblain: S.H.M.E.S, 1992.

———. *Genèse d'une cathédrale: Les archevêques de Reims et leur église aux XIe et XIIe siècles.* Langres: Dominique Guéniot, 2005.

———. "Henri de France et Louis VII: L'évêque cistercien et son frère le roi." In *Ses serviteurs de l'état au moyen âge*, 47–61. 29e Congrès de la Société des Historiens Médiévistes de l'Enseignement Supérieur Public, Pau, mai 1998. Paris: Publications de la Sorbonne, 1999.

Depreux, Philippe. "L'actualité de Freculf de Lisieux: à propos de l'édition critique de son oeuvre." *Tabularia* [on-line journal] (2004): 1–9.

Dereine, Charles. "Chanoines." *Dictionnaire d'histoire et de géographie ecclésiastique* 12 (1951): 354–405.

Desportes, Pierre. *Reims et les Rémois aux XIIIe et XIVe siècles.* Paris: Picard, 1979.

Devailly, Guy. *Le Berry, du Xe siècle au milieu du XIIIe.* Paris: Mouton, 1973.

De Visscher, Eva. *Reading the Rabbis: Christian Hebraism in the Works of Herbert of Bosham.* Leiden: Brill, 2014.

Diggelmann, Lindsay. "Marriage as Tactical Response: Henry II and the Royal Wedding of 1160." *EHR* 119 (2004): 954–64.

Dionisotti, A.C. "Walter of Châtillon and the Greeks." In *Latin Poetry and the Classical Tradition: Essays in Medieval and Renaissance Literature*, ed. Peter Godman and Oswyn Murray, 73–96. Oxford: Clarendon, 1990.

Draper, Peter. *The Formation of English Gothic: Architecture and Identity.* New Haven, Conn.: Yale University Press, 2006.

Dubois, Henri. "Les institutions des foires médiévales: protection ou exploitation du commerce?" In *Fieri e mercati nella integrazione delle economie europee, secc. XIII–XVIII.* Atti della "Trentaduesima Settimana di Studi," 8–12 maggio 2000. Ed. Simonetta Cavaciocchi, 161–84. Florence: Le Monnia, 2001.

Dufour, Francesco. *Le strade cristiane per Roma.* Milan: Mondadori, 1998.

Dufour, Jean. "Adèle de Champagne, troisième femme de Louis VII, une reine méconnue." In *Reines et princesses au moyen âge*, 1: 35–41. 2 vols. Montpellier: Université de Paul-Valéry, 2001.

Duggan. Anne J. "Alexander *ille meus*: The Papacy of Alexander III." In *Pope Alexander III*, 13–49.

———. "The Price of Loyalty: The Fate of Thomas Becket's Learned Household." In her *Thomas Becket: Friends, Networks, Text and Cult*, 1–18. Aldershot: Ashgate, 2007.

Dunbabin, Jean. *France in the Making, 843–1180.* Oxford: Oxford University Press, 1985; 2nd ed. 2000.

———. "Henry II and Louis VI." *In Henry II: New Interpretations*, 47–62.

Edbury, Peter W. and John Gordon Rowe. *William of Tyre: Historian of the Latin East.* Cambridge: Cambridge University Press, 1988.

Erlande-Brandeburg, Alain. "La cathédrale Saint-Étienne de Sens: La première cathédrale gothique." In *Les laïcs dans les villes de la France du Nord du XIIe siècle*, ed. Patrick Demouy, 29–39. Turnhout: Brepols, 2008.

Eschapasse, M. "La trésor de la cathédrale de Troyes." *Monuments Historiques de la France* (1956): 33–38.

Everard, J. A. "Lay Charters and the *Acta* of Henry II." *Anglo-Norman Studies* [2007] 30 (2008): 100–116.

Evergates, Theodore. *The Aristocracy in the County of Champagne, 1100–1300.* Philadelphia: University of Pennsylvania Press, 2007

———. "The Chancery Archives of the Counts of Champagne: Codicology and History of the Cartulary-Registers." *Viator: Medieval and Renaissance Studies* 16 (1985): 159–79.

———. *Feudal Society in the Bailliage of Troyes Under the Counts of Champagne, 1152–1284.* Baltimore: Johns Hopkins University Press, 1975.

———. "Louis VII and the Counts of Champagne." In *The Second Crusade and the Cistercians*, ed. Michael Gervers, 109–17. New York: St. Martin's, 1992.

Falkenstein, Ludwig. "Alexandre III et Henri de France: conformités et conflits." In *L'église de France et la papauté, Xe–XIIIe siècle*, ed. Rolf Grosse, 103–76. Bonn: Bouvier, 1993.

———. "Alexander III. und der Streit um die Doppelwahl in Châlons-sur-Marne (1162–1164)." *Deutsches Archiv für Erforschung des Mittelalter* 32 (1976): 444–94.

———. "Étienne la de Chapelle als Vertrauter Ludwigs VII. und Delegate Alexanders III." *Archivum Historiae Pontificiale* 26 (1988): 375–92.

———. *La papauté et les abbayes françaises aux XIe et XIIe siècle: exemption et protection apostolique.* Paris: H. Champion, 1977.

———. "Wilhelm von Champagne, Elekt von Chartres (1164–1168), Erzbischof von Sens (1168/69–1176), Erzbischof von Reims (1176–1202), Legat des apostolischen Stuhles, im Spiegel päpstlicher Schreiben und Privilegien." *Zeitschrift der Savigny-Stiftung für Rechtsgeschichte.* Bd. 120. *Kanonistische Abteilung* 89 (2003): 107–284. Summarized in his "Guillaume aux Blanches Mains, archevêque de Reims et légat du siège apostolique (1176–1202)." *Revue de l'Histoire de l'Église de France* 91 (2005): 2–25.

Falmagne, Jacques. *Baudouin V, comte de Hainaut, 1150–1195.* Montréal: Presses de l'Université de Montréal, 1966.

Fassler, Margot E. *Gothic Song: Victorine Sequences and Augustinian Reform in Twelfth-Century Paris.* Notre Dame, Ind.: University of Notre Dame Press, 1993, 2nd ed. 2011.

———. *The Virgin of Chartres: Making History Through Liturgy and the Arts.* New Haven, Conn.: Yale University Press, 2010.

Faugeras, Jacques. *Étienne de Champagne, premier comte de Sancerre.* Sancerre: J. Faugeras, 1991.

Flori, Jean. *L'essor de la chevalerie, XIe–XIIe siècles.* Paris: Droz, 1986.

Foreville, Raymonde. *Latran I, II, III et Latran IV.* Histoire des Conciles Oecuménique 6. Paris: Éditions de l'Orante, 1965.

Fourrier, Anthime. *Le courant réaliste dans le roman courtois en France au moyen âge. 1. Les débuts (XIIe siècle).* Paris: A.G. Nizet, 1960.

———. "Encore la chronologie des oeuvres de Chrétien de Troyes." *Bulletin Bibliographique de la Société Internationale Arthurienne* 2 (1950): 69–88.

———. "Retour au *Terminus.*" In *Mélanges de langue et de littérature du moyen âge et de la renaissance offerts à Jean Frappier,* 1: 299–311. 2 vols. Geneva: Droz, 1970.

La France romane au temps des premiers Capétiens (987–1152). Exhibition catalogue, Musée du Louvre, 10 mars–6 juin 2005. Paris: Musée du Louvre, 2005.

Frenken, Goswin. *Die Exempla des Jacob von Vitry: Ein Beitrag zur Geschichte des Erzählungs litterature des Mittelalters.* Munich: Beck, 1914.

Friend, Albert C. "Chaucer's Version of the Aeneid." *Speculum* 28 (1953): 317–23.

Fudeman, Kristen. *Vernacular Voices: Language and Identity in Medieval French Jewish Communities.* Philadelphia: University of Pennsylvania Press, 2010.

Gaborit-Chopin, Danielle. "Suger's Liturgical Vessels." In *Abbot Suger and Saint-Denis: A Symposium,* 283–93.

Gandil, Pierre. "Pierre le Manguer, doyen du chapitre cathédral de Troyes." In Dahan, *Pierre le Mangeur,* 17–25.

Gasparri, Françoise. "Bibliothèque et archives de l'abbaye de Saint-Victor de Paris au XIIe siècle." *Scriptorium* 55 (2001): 275–84.

———. "*Scriptorium* et bureau d'écriture de l'abbaye Saint-Victor de Paris." In *L'abbaye parisienne de Saint-Victor,* 113–39.

Geary, Patrick J. "Saint Helen of Athyra and the Cathedral of Troyes in the Thirteenth Century." *Journal of Medieval and Renaissance Studies* 7 (1977): 149–76. Rpt in his *Living with the Dead in the Middle Ages,* 221–42. Ithaca, N.Y.: Cornell University Press, 1994

Geiger, Ari. "Historia Judaica: Petrus Comestor and his Jewish Sources. In Dahan, *Pierre le Mangeur*, 125–45.

Gillingham, John. "Doing Homage to the King of France." In *Henry II: New Interpretations*, 63–84.

———. *Richard I*. New Haven, Conn.: Yale University Press, 1999.

Glunz, H. H. *History of the Vulgate in England, from Alcuin to Roger Bacon*. Cambridge: Cambridge University Press, 1933.

Godefroy, J. "L'histoire du prieuré Saint-Ayoul de Provins et le récit des miracles du saint." *Revue Mabillon* 28 (1938): 29–48.

Gouet, Jean and Thierry Le Hête. *Les comtes de Blois et de Champagne et leur descendance agnatique: Généalogie et histoire d'une dynastie féodale, Xe–XVIIe siècle*. St-Sebastien de Morsent, 2004.

Graboïs, Aryeh. "The Crusade of King Louis VII: A Reconsideration." In *Crusade and Settlement*, ed. Peter W. Edbury, 94–104. Cardiff: University College Cardiff Press, 1985.

———. "De la trêve de Dieu à la paix du roi: Étude sur la transformations du mouvement de la paix au XIIe siècle." In *Mélanges offerts à René Crozet*, ed. Pierre Gallais and Yves-Jean Riou, 1: 185–96. 2 vols. Poitiers: Société d'Études Médiévales, 1966.

Grant, Lindy. *Abbot Suger of St-Denis: Church and State in Early Twelfth-Century France*. London: Longman, 1988.

———. "Suger and the Anglo-Norman World." *Anglo-Norman Studies* 19 (1996): 51–68.

Grill, P. Leopold. "Heinrich von Kärnten, Bischof von Troyes." *Cistercienser-Chronik* 37/38 (1956): 33–53.

Grodecki, Louis, with Catherine Brisac and Claudine Lautier. *Le vitrail romane*. Fribourg: Office du Livre, 1977.

Guillemain, Bernard. "L'episcopat français à Lateran III." In *La Troisième Concile de Lateran (1179): Sa place dans l'histoire*, ed. Raymonde Foreville, 23–31. Paris: Études Augustiniennes, 1992.

Gullick, Michael. "How Fast Did Scribes Write? Evidence from Romanesque Manuscripts." In *Making the Medieval Book: Techniques of Production*, ed. Linda L. Brownrigg, 39–58. Proceedings of the Fourth Conference of the Seminar in the History of the Book to 1500, Oxford, July 1992. Los Altos Hills, Calif.: Red Gull Press, 1995.

Gur, Edmond. "L'ancien quartier du palais des comtes de Champagne et le quartier actuel de la préfecture," *MSA* (1946): 225–36.

Guyotjeannin, Olivier. *Episcopus et comes: affirmation et déclin de la seigneurie épiscopale au nord du royaume de France (Beauvais-Noyon, Xe–début XIIIe siècle)*. Geneva: Droz, 1987.

Hagger, Mark. "Theory and Practice in the Making of the Twelfth-Century Pipe Rolls." In *Records, Administration and Aristocratic Society in the Anglo-Norman Realm: Papers Commemorating the 800th Anniversary of King John's Loss of Normandy*, ed. Nicholas Vincent, 1–28. Woodbridge: Boydell, 2009.

Hamilton, Bernard. *The Leper King and his Heirs: Baldwin IV and the Crusader Kingdom of Jerusalem*. Cambridge: Cambridge University Press, 2000.

———. "Miles of Plancy and the Fief of Beirut." In Kedar, *The Horns of Hattin*, 136–46.

Hany-Longuespé, Nicole. *Le trésor et les reliques de la cathédrale de Troyes, de la Quatrième Croisade à nos jours*. Troyes: Maison du Boulanger, 2005.

———. "Les vestiges de Saint-Étienne au trésor de la cathédral de Troyes." In *Splendeurs*, 30–35.

Haseldine, Julian. "Friends, Friendship and Networks in the Letters of Bernard of Clairvaux." *Cîteaux: commentarii cistercienses* 57 (2006): 243–79.

————. "Friendship, Intimacy and Corporate Networking in the Twelfth Century: The Politics of Friendship in the Letters of Peter the Venerable." *English Historical Review* 126 (2011): 251–80.

Haugeard, Philippe. "Traduction et essor de la littérature en langue française: l'état d'esprit des premiers auteurs de romans (XIIe siècle)." In *Une conquête des savoir: les traductions dans l'Europe latine (fin du XIe siècle–milieu du XIIIe siècle)*, ed. Max Lijbowicz, 25–41. Turnhout: Brepols, 2009.

Heinemeyer, Walter. "Die Verhandlungen an der Saône im Jahre 1162," *Deutsches Archiv für Erforschung des Mittelalters* 20 (1969): 155–89.

Helias-Baron, Marlène. "Ferveur des laïcs ou précaution monastique? Étude des pics documentaires observés dans les chartriers Cisterciens à la veille des deuxième et troisième croisades." *Revue Mabillon* n.s. 19 [80] (2008): 77–97.

Héliot, Pierre. "Sur le résidences baties en France du Xe au XIIe siècle." *Le Moyen Âge* 61 (1955): 27–61, 291–317.

Héliot, Pierre and Marie-Laure Chastang. "Quêtes et voyages de reliques au profit des églises françaises du moyen âge." *Revue d'Histoire Ecclésiastique* 59 (1964): 789–823.

Helmerichs, Robert. "*Ad Tutandos Patriae Fines*: The Defense of Normandy, 1135." In *The Normans and their Adversaries at War: Essays in Memory of C. Warren Hollister*, ed. Richard P. Abels and Bernard S. Bachrach, 129–48. Woodbridge: Boydell, 2001.

Henriet, Jacques. "La cathédrale Saint–Étienne de Sens: la parti du premier maître et les campagnes du XIIe siècle." *Bulletin Monumental* 140 (1982): 81–176.

Henry II: New Interpretations. Ed. Christopher Harper-Bill and Nicholas Vincent. Woodbridge: Boydell, 2007.

Higounet, Charles. *Défrichements et villeneuves du bassin parisien (XIe–XIVe siècle)*. Paris: CNRS, 1990.

Hilsdale, Cecily J. "Constructing a Byzantine *Augusta*: A Greek Book for a French Bride." *The Art Bulletin* 87 (2005): 458–83.

Houben, Hubert. *Roger II of Sicily: A Ruler Between East and West*. Trans. G.A. Loud and D. Milburn of *Roger II. von Sizilien*, 1997. Cambridge: Cambridge University Press, 2002.

Hubert, Jean. "La vie commune des clercs et l'archéologie." In *La vita comune del clero nei secoli XI et XIIe*, 1: 90–111. Atti della Settimana di studio Mendola, settembre 1959. Milan, 1962. Reprinted in his *Arts et vie sociale de la fin du monde antique au moyen âge: études d'archéologie et d'histoire*, 125–11 [cited here]. Geneva: Droz, 1977.

Hubert, Marie-Clotilde. "*Consuetudo*, service d'estage, et recensement des vassaux en Champagne vers 1172." In *Auctoritas: Mélanges offerts au professeur Olivier Guillot*, ed. Giles Constable and Michel Rouche, 479–88. Paris: Presses de l'Université de Paris, Sorbonne, 2006.

Jacob, Robert. "Le pape, l'enquête et la coutume: sur un voyage de Vézelay à Rome en 1151." In *L'enquête au moyen âge*, ed. Claude Gauvard, 89–120. Rome: École Française de Rome, 2008.

Jaksch, August. *Geschichte Kärntens bis 1335*. 2 vols. Klagenfurt: Ferd. Kleinmayr, 1928–29.

James, M.R. *Ancient Libraries of Canterbury and Dover*. Cambridge: Cambridge University Press, 1903.

Janssen, Wilhelm. *Die Päpstlichen Legaten in Frankreich von Schisma Aneklets II. zum Tode Coelestins III. (1130–1198)*. Cologne: Böhlau, 1961.

Jordan, Karl. *Henry the Lion: A Biography*. Trans. P. S. Falla. Oxford: Clarendon, 1986.

Jordan, William Chester. "*Quando fuit natus*: Interpreting the Birth of Philip Augustus." In *The Work of Jacques Le Goff and the Challenges of Medieval History*, ed. Miri Rubin, 171–88. Woodbridge: Boydell, 1997.

Joris, André. "Un seul amour . . . ou plusiers femmes?" In *Femmes-Mariages-Lignages, XIIe–XIVe siècles: Mélanges offerts à Georges Duby*, ed. Jean Dufournet, André Joris, and Pierre Toubert, 197–214. Brussels: De Boeck, 1992.

Jottrand, Mireille. "Les émaux du trésor de la cathédrale de Troyes: décoraient-ils les tombeaux des comtes de Champagne?" *Gazette des Beaux-Arts* 6, 65 (1965): 257–64.

Kalavreza, Ioli. "Helping Hands for the Empire: Imperial Ceremonial and the Cult of Relics at the Byzantine Court." In *Byzantine Court Culture from 829 to 1204*, ed. Henry Maguire, 53–79. Washington, D.C.: Dumbarton Oaks, 1997.

Keefe, Thomas K. *Feudal Assessments and the Political Community Under Henry II and His Sons.* Berkeley: University of California Press, 1983.

Kemp, E. W. "Pope Alexander III and the Canonization of Saints." *Transactions of the Royal Historical Society* 27 (1945): 13–28.

Kenaan-Kedar, Nurith. "The Cathedral of Sebaste: Its Western Donors and Models." In *The Horns of Hattin*, ed. B. Z. Kedar, 99–120. London: Variorum, 1992.

Kidson, Peter. "Gervase, Becket, and William of Sens." *Speculum* 68 (1993): 969–91.

———. "Panofsky, Suger and St-Denis." *Journal of the Warburg and Courtauld Institutes* 50 (1987): 1–17.

Kienzle, Beverly M. *Cistercians, Heresy and Crusade in Occitania, 1145–1229: Preaching in the Lord's Vineyard.* York: York Medieval Press, 2001.

Kinder, Terryl N. "Toward Dating Construction of the Abbey Church of Pontigny." *Journal of the British Archaeological Association* 145 (1992): 77–88.

King, Edmund. *King Stephen.* New Haven, Conn.: Yale Unievsrity Press, 2010.

———. "Stephen of Blois, Count of Mortain and Boulogne." *English Historical Review* 115 (2000): 271–96.

The Knights Templar: From the Days of Jerusalem to the Commanderies of Champagne. Catalogue of the Exhibition, 16 June–31 October 2012. Ed. Arnaud Baudin, Ghislain Brunel, and Nicolas Dohrmann. Troyes: Somogy, 2012.

Lachaud, Frédérique. *L'éthique du pouvoir au moyen âge: l'office dans la culture politique (Angleterre, vers 1150–vers 1330).* Paris: Garnier, 2010.

Lafferty, Maura K. *Walter of Châtillon's "Alexandreis": Epic and the Problem of Historical Understanding.* Turnhout: Brepols, 1998.

Lalore, Charles. "Restes mortels des comtes de Champagne." *Revue de Champagne et de Brie* 13 (1992): 113–20.

Lalou, Elisabeth. "Le gouvernement de la reine Jeanne (1285–1305)." *Cahiers Haut-Marnais* 167 (1986): 16–30.

Laudage, Johannes. *Alexander III. und Friedrich Barbarossa.* Cologne: Böhlau Verlag, 1997.

Laurent, Henri. *Un grand commerce d'exportation au moyen âge: la draperie des pays-bas et dans les pays méditeranéens (XII–XVe siècle).* Paris: Librairie E. Droz, 1935.

Leclercq, Jean. "Gébuin de Troyes et S. Bernard." In his *Recueil d'études sur saint Bernard et ses écrits*, vol. 2., 83–93. Rome, Edizioni di Storia e Letteratura, 1962

———. "Les collections de sermons de Nicolas de Clairvaux." *Revue Benedictine* 66 (1956): 269–302.

Lemarignier, J.-F. *Recherches sur l'hommage en marche et les frontières féodales.* Lille: Bibliothèque Universitaire, 1945.

Leroy, Thierry. *Hugues de Payns: chevalier champenois, fondateur de l'Ordre des Templiers.* Troyes: Maison du Boulanger, 1999, 2nd ed. 2001.

———. "The Organization of the Champagne Templar Network, 1127–1143." In *The Knights Templar*, 116–21.

Lesne, Émile. *Histoire de la prorpieté ecclésiastique en France*. vol. 4. *Les livres: scriptoria et biblio-thèques au commencement du VIIIe à la fin du XIe siècle*. Paris: H. Champion, 1938.

Lespinasse, René. *Le Nivernais et les comtes de Nevers*, 2 vols. Paris: H. Champion, 1909–11.

Lewis, Andrew W. *Royal Succession in Capetian France: Studies on Familial Order and the State*. Cambridge, Mass.: Harvard University Press, 1981.

Leyser, Karl J. "Frederick Barbarossa and the Hohenstaufen Polity." *Viator* 19 (1988): 153–76.

Locatelli, René. " 'L'expansion de l'ordre cistercien.' In *Bernard de Clairvaux: histoire, mentalités, spiritualité*, 103–40.

LoPrete, Kimberly A. *Adela of Blois: Lord and Lady, c. 1067–1137*. Dublin: Four Courts, 2007.

Luscombe, David. "Peter Comestor." In *The Bible in the Medieval World: Essays in Memory of Beryl Smalley*, ed. Katherine Walsh and Diana Wood, 109–29. London: Blackwell, 1985.

———. "The Place of Peter Comestor in the History of Medieval Theology." In Dahan, *Pierre le Mangeur*, 27–45.

Lusse, Jackie. "D'Etienne à Jean de Joinville: l'ascension d'une famille seigneuriale champe-noise." In *Jean de Joinville: de la Champagne aux royaumes d'outre-mer*, ed. Danielle Quéruel, 7–47. Langres: Dominque Guéniot, 1998.

———. "Deux villeneuves de la forêt de Trois-Fontaines au XIIe siècle: Maurupt et Sermaize (Marne)." *MSM* 116 (2001): 67–87.

Magdalino, Paul. *The Empire of Manuel Komnenos, 1143–1180*. Cambridge: Cambridge University Press, 1993.

Maillé, Marquise de. *Provins: les monuments religieux*. 2 vols. Paris, 1939. Rpt.Chartres: Librairie des Arts et Metiers, 1975.

Maines, Clark. "Good Works, Social Ties, and the Hope for Salvation: Abbot Suger and Saint-Denis." In *Abbot Suger and Saint-Denis*, 77–94.

Martène, Edmund. *Voyage littéraire de deux religieux bénédictines de la Congregation de Saint-Maur*. 2 vols. Paris: F. Delaulne, 1717.

Martin, Janet. "Uses of Tradition: Gellius, Petronius and John of Salisbury." *Viator* 10 (1979): 57–76.

Mathieu, Jean-Noël. "Recherches sur les premiers seigneurs de Moëlain-Dampierre." *MSM* 116 (2001): 37–66.

Mathorez, Jules. "Guillaume aux Blanches-Mains, éveque de Chartres." *Archives Historiques du Diocèse de Chartres* (1912): 187–340.

Mayer, Hans Eberhard. *Die Kanzlei des lateinischen Könige von Jerusalem*. 2 vols. *MGH SS* 40. Hannover: Hahnsche Buchhandlung, 1996.

McGuire, Brian Patrick. *Friendship and Community: The Monastic Experience, 350–1250*. Ithaca, N.Y.: Cornell University Press, 1988; Rpt. with a new introduction, 2010.

McKitterick, Rosamond. *Charlemagne: The Formation of a European Identity*. Cambridge: Cambridge University Press, 2008.

Meijns, Brigitte. "L'ordre canonial dans le comté de Flandre depuis l'époque mérovingienne jusqu'à 1155: typologie, chronologie et constantes de l'histoire de fondation et de réforme." *Revue d'Histoire Ecclésiastique* 97 (2002): 5–58.

Mesqui, Jean. "Notes sur la topographie de Provins à l'époque des foires." In *Provins et sa region*. [= *Bulletin de la Société d'Histoire et d'Archéologie* 135] (1981): 47–54.

———. "Les palais des comtes de Champagne à Provins (XIIe–XIIIe siècles)." *Bulletin Monumental* 151 (1993): 321–55.

———. "Les ponts sur la Seine et ses affluents entre Troyes et Montereau au XIIIe siècle." In *Mélanges d'archéologie et d'histoire médiévales dans l'Aube*, no. 2, 27–55. Troyes, 1985.

———. *Provins: la fortification d'une ville au moyen âge.* Paris: Arts et Métiers Graphiques, 1979.

Mews, Constant J. "The Council of Sens (1141): Abelard, Bernard, and the Fear of Social Upheaval." *Speculum* 77 (2002): 342–82.

Misrahi, Jean. "More Light on the Chronology of Chrétien de Troyes?" *Bulletin Bibliographique de la Société Internationale Arthurienne* 11 (1959): 89–120.

Morgan, Nigel. "The Iconography of Twelfth-Century Mosan Enamels." In *Rhein und Maas: Kunst und Kultur, 800–1400,* 2 vols. 2: 263–75. Köln: Schnütgen-Museum, 1973.

Morganstern, Anne McGee. *Gothic Tombs of Kinship.* University Park: Pennsylvania State University Press, 2000.

Mory, James M. "Peter Comestor, Biblical Paraphrase, and the Popular Medieval Bible." *Speculum* 68 (1993): 6–35.

Nabbiai-Dalla Guarda, Donatella. *La bibliothèque de l'abbaye de Saint-Denis à France du IXe au XVIIIe siècle.* Paris: CNRS, 1985.

Nahon, Gérard. "Les communautés juives de la Champagne médiévale (XIe–XIIe siècles)." In *Rachi: ouvrage collectif,* ed. Manes Sperber, 33–78. Paris: Service technique pour l'Éducation, 1974.

Nazet, Jacques. *Les chapitres de chanoines séculiers en Hainaut du XIIe au début du XVe siècle.* Brussels: Académie Royale de Belgique, 1993.

Nederman, Cary J. *John of Salisbury.* Tempe: Arizona Medieval and Renaissance Studies, 2005.

———. "Textual Communities of Learning and Friendship Circles in the Twelfth Century: An Examination of John of Salisbury's Correspondance." In *Communities of Learning: Networks and the Shaping of Intellectual Identity in Europe, 1100–1500,* ed. Constance J. Mews and John N. Crossley, 73–83. Turnhout: Brepols, 2011.

Nees, Lawrence. "The *Fastigium* of Saint-Remi ("the Tomb of Hincmar") at Reims." In *Representing History, 900–1300: Art, Music, History,* ed. Robert A. Maxwell, 31–52, 211–21. University Park: Pennsylvania State University Press, 2010.

Nicholas, Karen. "Countesses as Rulers in Flanders." In *Aristocratic Women in Medieval France,* ed. Theodore Evergates, 111–37. Philadelphia: University of Pennsylvania Press, 1999.

Nolan, Kathleen. *Queens in Stone and Silver: The Creation of a Visual Imagery of Queenship in Capetian France.* New York: Palgrave Macmillan, 2009.

Nortier, Michel. "Étude sur un recueil de lettres écrites par Suger ou à lui adressées (1147–1150)." *Journal des Savants* (2009): 26–102.

———. "Le sort des archives dispersées de la Chambre des Comptes de Paris." *Bibliothèque de l'École de Chartes* 123 (1965): 460–537.

Oury, G.M. "Recherches sur Ernaud, abbé de Bonneval, historien de Saint Bernard." *Revue Mabillon* 59 (1977): 97–127.

Pacaut, Marcel. "Louis VII et Alexandre III (1159–1180)." *Revue d'Histoire de l'Église de France* 39 (1953): 5–45.

———. *Louis VII et son royaume.* Paris: SEVPEN, 1964.

———. *Louis VII et les élections épiscopales dans le royaume de France.* Paris: J. Vrin, 1957.

Parisse, Michel. "Croix autographes de souscription dans l'Ouest de la France au XIe siècle." In *Graphische Symbole in mittelalterlichen Urkunden: Beiträge zur diplomatischen Semiotik,* ed. Peter Rück, 143–55. Sigmaringen: Thorbecke, 1996.

———. "La frontière de la Meuse au Xe siècle." In *Haut Moyen Âge: Culture, éducation et société: études offerts à Pierre Riché,* 427–37. Nanterre: Éditions Publidix, 1990.

———. "Les relations (de Saint Bernard) avec l'empire." In *Bernard de Clairvaux,* 401–27.

———. "Présence et interventions de Frédéric Barbarousse en Lorraine." In *Friedrich*

Barbarossa: *Handlungsspielräume und Wirkungsweisen des Staufischen Kaisers*, ed. Alfred Haverkamp, 201–23. Sigmaringen: Thorbecke, 1992.

Pastan, Elizabeth. "Dating the Medieval Work: The Case of the Miracles of Saint Andrew Window from Troyes Cathedral." In *Feud, Violence and Pracice: Essays in Medieval Studies in Honor of Stephen D. White*, ed. Belle S Tuten and Tracey L. Billado, 239–57. Farnham: Ashgate, 2010.

———."Fit for a Count: The Twelfth-Century Stained Glass Panels from Troyes." *Speculum* 64 (1989): 338–72.

———. "*Realpolitik* and Artistic Patronage in Twelfth- and Thirteenth-Century Troyes." In *Four Modes of Seeing: Approaches to Medieval Imagery in Honor of Madeline Harrison Caviness*, ed. Evelyn Staudinger Lane, Elizabeth Carson Pastan, and Ellen M. Shortell, 530–46. Farnham: Ashgate, 2009.

Pastan, Elizabeth, and Sylvie Balcon. *Les vitraux du choeur de la cathédrale de Troyes (XIIIe siècle)*. Corpus Vitrearum, vol. 2. Paris: CTHS, 2006.

Petersohn, Jürgen. "Saint-Denis-Westminster-Aachen: Die Karls-Translatio von 1165 und ihre Vorbilder." *Deutsches Archiv für Erforschung des Mittelalter* 31 (1975): 420–54.

Petit, Ernest. *Histoire des ducs de Bourgogne de la race capetienne*. 9 vols. Dijon: Imp. Darantiere, 1885–1909.

Peyrafort-Huin, Monique, in collaboration with Patricia Stirnemann, with a contribution by Jean-Luc Benoit, *La bibliothèque médiévale de Pontigny (XIIe–XIXe siècles): histoire, inventaires anciens, manuscrits*. Paris: CNRS, 2001.

Phillips, Jonathan. *Defenders of the Holy Land: Relations between the Latin East and the West, 1119–1187*. Oxford: Oxford University Press, 1996.

———. *The Second Crusade: Extending the Frontiers of Christendom*. New Haven, Conn.: Yale University Press, 2007.

Picard, Jean-Charles, ed. *Les chanoines dans la ville: recherches sur la topographie des quartiers canoniaux en France*. Paris: De Boccard, 1994.

Pietresson de Saint-Aubin, Pierre. "La fourniture de la pierre sur les grands chantiers Troyens du moyen âge et de la renaissance." *Bulletin Archéologique du Comité des Travaux Historiques et Scientifiques* 1928–1929 (1932): 569–601.

Pithou, Pierre. *Le premier livre des mémoires des comtes héréditaires de Champagne et de Brie* (1572, reprinted in 1581). In his *Opera sacra, iuridica, historica, miscellanea*, 453–510. Paris: Cramoisi, 1609.

Pontal, Odette. *Le conciles de la France capétienne jusqu'en 1215*. Paris: Cerf, 1995.

Pope Alexander III (1159–81): The Art of Survival. Ed. Peter D. Clarke and Anne J. Duggan. Farnham: Ashgate, 2012.

Poull, Georges. *La maison souveraine et ducale de Bar*. Nancy: Presses Universitaires de Nancy, 1994.

Pouzet, Ph. "La vie de Guichard, abbé de Pontigny (1136–1165) et archevêque de Lyon (1165–1181)." *Bulletin de la Société Littéraire de Lyon* 10 (1926–28): 117–50.

Prache, Anne. *Saint-Remi de Reims: L'oeuvre de Pierre de Celle et sa place dans l'architecture gothique*. Geneva: Droz, 1978.

Prévost, Arthur Émile. *Histoire du diocèse de Troyes pendant la Révolution*. vol. 1. Troyes: Gustave Frémont, 1908.

Putter, Ade. "Knights and Clerics at the Court of Champagne: Chrétien de Troyes's Romances in Context." In *Medieval Knighthood, V*, ed. Stephen Church and Ruth Harvey, 243–66. Papers from the Sixth Strawberry Hill Conference, 1994. Woodbridge: Boydell, 1995.

Racine, Pierre. *Plaisance du Xe à la fin du XIIIe s.* 3 vols. Paris: Librairie H. Champion, 1979.

Reiner, Avraham (Rami). "Rabbénu Tam et le Comte Henri de Champagne." In *Héritage de Rachi*, ed. René-Samuel Sirat, 27–39. Paris: Éditions de l'Éclat, 2006.

Renoux, Annie. "Espaces et lieux de pouvoirs royaux et princiers en France (fin IXe–début XIIIe siècle): changement et continuité." In *Palais royaux et principères au moyen âge*, ed. A. Renoux, 18–42. Le Mans: Publications de l'Université du Maine, 1996.

Reynolds, L. O. *Texts and Transmission: A Survey of the Latin Classics.* Oxford: Oxford University Press, 1983.

Reynolds, Robert. L. "Genoese Trade in the late Twelfth Century, Particularly in Cloth from the Fairs of Champagne." *Journal of Economic and Business History* 3 (1931): 662–81.

Riall, Nicholas. *Henry of Blois, Bishop of Winchester: A Patron of the Twelfth-Century Renaissance.* Portsmouth: Hampshire County Council, 1994.

Richard, Jean. "Le 'conduit' des routes et la fixation des limites entre mouvances féodales." *Annales de Bourgogne* 94 (1952): 85–101.

———. *Les ducs de Bourgogne et la formation du duché du XIe au XIVe siècle.* Dijon: Imprimerie Bernigaud et Privat, 1954.

Rillon-Marne, Anne-Zoé. "Philippe le Chancelier et son oeuvre: Étude sur l'elaboration d'une poetique musicale." 2 vols. Thèse de Doctorat: Université de Poitiers, 2008.

Robertson, Lynsey E. "An Analysis of the Correspondence and Hagiographical Works of Philip of Harvengt." Ph.D. thesis. University of St. Andrews, 2007.

Roserot, Alphonse. *Dictionnaire historique de la Champagne méridionale (Aube) des origines à 1790.* 3 vols. Langres: Imprimerie Champenoise, 1942–48. Rpt. Marseille: Laffitte, 1983.

Rouse, Mary A. and Richard A. Rouse. *Authentic Witnesses: Approaches to Medieval Texts and Manuscripts.* Notre Dame, Ind.: University of Notre Dame Press, 1991.

———. "*Potens in opere et sermone*: Philip, Bishop of Bayeux, and His Books." In their *Authentic Witnesses*, 33–60.

———. "The *Florilegium Angelicum*: Its Origin, Content, and Influence." In *Authentic Witnesses*, 101–88.

Rubaud, Roger. "Bar-sur-Aube au temps des foires." In *Mélanges d'archéologie et d'histoire médiévales dans l'Aube*, no. 2, 65–103. Imprimerie de la Renaissance, 1985.

Rudolf, Conrad. "Inventing the Exegetical Stained-Glass Window: Suger, Hugh, and a New Elite Art." *Art Bulletin* 93 (2011): 399–422.

Sassier, Yves. *Louis VII.* Paris: Fayard, 1991.

———. *Recherches sur le pouvoir comtal en Auxerrois du Xe au début du XIIIe siècle.* Auxerre: Publications de la Société des fouilles archéologique et des monuments historiques de l'Yonne, 1980.

Savetiez, Charles. "Maison de Dampierre-Saint-Dizier." *Revue de Champagne et de Brie* 17 (1884): 10–26.

Scammell, G. V. *Hugh de Puiset: Bishop of Durham.* Cambridge: Cambridge University Press, 1956.

Schenk, Jochen. *Templar Families: Landowning Families and the Order of the Temple in France, c. 1120–1307.* Cambridge: Cambridge University Press, 2012.

Schmale, Franz-Josef. "Friedrich I. und Ludwig VII. Im Sommer des Jahres 1162." *Zeitschrift für Bayerische Landesgeschichte* 31 (1968): 315–68.

Schmidt-Chazan, Mireille. "Aubri de Trois-Fontaines, historien entre la France et l'Empire." *Annales de l'Est* 36 (1984): 163–92. See also Mireille Chazan.

Schmolke-Hasselmann, Beate. *The Evolution of Arthurian Romance: The Verse Tradition from*

Chrétien to Froissart. Trans. Margaret and Roger Middleton. Cambridge: Cambridge University Press, 1998.

Severens, Kenneth W. "The Early Campaign at Sens, 1140–1145." *Journal of the Society of Architectural Historians* 29 (1970): 97–107.

———. "The Continuous Plan of Sens Cathedral." *Journal of the Society of Architectural Historians* 34 (1975): 198–207.

Sigal, Pierre-André. "Les voyages de reliques aux onzième et douzième siècles." In *Voyage, quête, pèlerinage dans la littérature et la civilisation médiévales,* 75–104. Senefiance, 2. Paris: Librairie Honoré Champion, 1976.

Sivéry, Gérard. *L'économie du royaume de France au siècle de Saint Louis.* Lille: Presses Universitaires de Lille, 1984.

Slocum, Kay Brainerd. *Liturgies in Honour of Thomas Becket.* Toronto: University of Toronto Press, 2004.

Smalley, Beryl. "A Commentary on the *Hebraica* by Herbert of Bosham." *Recherches de Théologie Ancienne et Médiévale* 18 (1951): 29–65.

———. *The Becket Conflict and the Schools: A Study of Intellectuals in Politics.* London: Blackwell, 1973.

Snyder, Janet E. *Early Gothic Column-Figure Sculpture in France: Appearance, Materials, and Significance.* Farnham: Ashgate, 2011.

Somerville, Robert. *Pope Alexander III and the Council of Tours (1163): A Study of Ecclesiastical Politics and Institutions in the Twelfth Century.* Berkeley: University of California Press, 1977.

Soria, Myriam. "Alexander III and France: Exile, Diplomacy and the New Order." In *Pope Alexander III (1159–81): The Art of Survival,* 181–201.

Splendeurs de la cour de Champagne au temps de Chétien de Troyes. Exhibition catalogue. Bibliothèque municipale de Troyes, 18 June–11 September, 1999. Troyes: Archives Départementales de l'Aube, 1999.

Spufford, Peter. *Handbook of Medieval Exchange.* Woodbridge: Boydell, 1986.

Staunton, Michael. *Thomas Becket and his Biographers.* Woodbridge: Boydell, 2006.

Stein, Henri. "Le maître d'ouevre André, architecte des comtes de Champagne, 1171–1222." *Nouvelle Revue de Champagne et de Brie* 9 (1931): 181–85.

Stirnemann, Patricia. "Une bibiothèque princière au XIIe siècle." In *Splendeurs de la cour de Champagne,* 36–42.

———. "En quête de Sens." In *Quand la peinture était dans les livres: mélanges en l'honneur de François Avril,* ed. Mara Hofmann and Caroline Zöhl, 303–11. Turnhout: Brepols, 2007.

———. "Gilbert de la Porrée et les livres glosés à Laon, à Chartres et à Paris. In *Monde médiéval et société chartraine,* ed. Jean-Robert Armogathe, 83–95. Paris: Picard, 1997.

———. "Où one été fabriqués les livres de la glose ordinaire dans la première moitié du XIIe siècle?" In *Le XIIe siècle: mutations et renouveau en France dans le première moitié du XIIe siècle,* ed. Françoise Gasparri, 257–301. Paris: Le Léopard d'Or, 1994.

———. "Private Libraries Privately Made." In *Medieval Manuscripts, Their Makers and Users.* Special Issue of *Viator* in Honor of Richard and Mary Rouse, 185–98. Turnhout: Brepols, 2011.

———. "La production manuscrite et la bibliothèque de Saint-Victor, 1140–1155." In *L'abbaye parisienne de Saint-Victor,* 140–41.

———. "Quelques bibliothèques princières et la production hors scriptorium au XIIe siècle."

Bulletin Archéologique du Comité des Travaux Historiques et Scientifiques n.s. 17–18. Années 1981–82. Fascicule A. Antiquités Nationales, 7–38. Paris: CTHS, 1984.

———. "Reconstitution des bibliothèques en langue latine des comtes de Champagne." In *Le moyen âge à livres ouverts*. Actes du Colloque (Lyon, 24 et 25 septembre 2002), 37–45. Lyon: Bibliothèque municipale de Lyon, 2002.

———. "Le témoinage des manuscrits: scribes et enlumineurs (1140–1220)." In Peyrafort-Huin, *La bibliothèque médiévale de Pontigny*, 55–78.

———. "Two Twelfth-Century Bibliophiles and Henry of Huntingdon's *Historia Anglorum*." *Viator* 24 (1993): 121–42.

———. "Un manuscrit de Claudian fabriqué à la cour de Champagne dans le années 1160." In *Bibliologia* 20 [= Mélanges d'histoire des textes en l'honneur de Louis Holtz] (2003): 53–57.

———. "Where Can We Go from Here? The Study of French Twelfth-Century Manuscripts." In *Romanesque: Art and Thought in the Twelfth Century: Essays in Honor of Walter Cahn*, ed. Colum Hourihane, 82–94. University Park: Pennsylvania State University Press, 2008.

Stirnemann, Patricia and Dominique Poirel. "Nicolas de Montiéramey, Jean de Salisbury et deux florilèges d'auteurs antiques." *Revue d'Histoire des Textes* n.s. 1 (2006): 173–88.

Stohlmann, Jürgen. "Magister Simon Aurea Capra: Zu Person und Werk des späteren Kanonikers von St. Viktor." *Latomus: Revue d'Études Latines* [*Homages à André Boutemy*] 145 (1976): 243–66.

Stratford, Neil. "The 'Henry of Blois' Plaques in the British Museum." *British Archaeological Association Conference* 6 (1983): 28–37.

Strickland, Matthew. "On the Instruction of a Prince: The Upbringing of Henry, the Young King." In *Henry II: New Interpretations*, 184–214.

Taylor, Leslie Anne. "The Eight Monophonic Political *Planctus* of the Florentine Manuscript." MA thesis, University of British Columbia, 1994.

Thomas, Heinz. "Die Champagnemessen." In *Frankfurt im Messenetz Europas: Erträge des Forschung*, ed. Hans Pohl, 13–36. Frankfurt am Main: Historisches Museum, 1991.

Thompson, Kathleen Hapgood. "The Formation of the County of Perche: The Rise and Fall of the House of Gouet." In *Family Trees and the Roots of Politics: The Prosopography of Britain and France from the Tenth to the Twelfth Century*, ed. K. S. B. Keats-Rohan, 299–314. Woodbridge: Boydell, 1997.

———. *Power and Border Lordship in Medieval France: The County of Perche, 1000–1226*. Woodbridge: Boydell, 2002.

Thomson, Rodney M. *William Malmesbury*. Woodbridge: Boydell, 1987, rev. 2003.

Tibber, Peter. "The Origins of the Scholastic Sermon, c. 1130–c. 1210." D. Phil., Oxford, 1984.

Timbert, Arnaud. "Le chevet de la collégiale Saint-Quiriace de Provins: l'oeuvre d'Henri le Libéral," *Bulletin Monumental* 164, 3 (2006): 243–60.

———. "Le déambulatoire de la collégiale de Saint-Quiriace de Provins." *Bulletin Monumental* 162, 3 (2004): 163–73.

Touati, François-Olivier. *Maladie et société au moyen âge: le lèpre, les lépreux et les léproseries dans la province ecclésiastique de Sens jusqu'au milieu du XIVe siècle*. Brussels: De Boeck, 1998.

Toubert, Pierre. "Une des premières vérifications de la loi de Gresham: la circulation monétaire dans l'état pontifical vers 1200." Rpt. in his *Études sur l'Italie médiévale (IXe–XIVe s.)*, 180–89. London: Variorum, 1976.

Tronzo, William. *The Cultures of His Kingdom: Roger II and the Capella Palatina in Palermo.* Princeton, N.J.: Princeton University Press, 1997.

Türk, Egburt. *Pierre de Blois: Ambitions et remords sous les Plantagenêts.* Turnhout: Brepols, 2006.

Turner, Ralph V. *Eleanor of Aquitaine.* New Haven, Conn.: Yale University Press, 2009.

Uitti, Karl D., with Michelle A. Freeman. *Chrétien de Troyes Revisited.* New York: Twayne, 1995.

Ulrich, Pierre. "Guy de Joinville, évêque de Châlons (1164–1190)." *MSA* 77 (1962): 48–57.

Une Renaissance: L'art entre Flandre et Champagne, 1150–1250. Exhibition catalogue. Saint-Just-la-Pendue: Imprimerie Chirat, 2013.

Uruszczak, Waclaw. "Enseignants du droit à Reims au XIIe siècle." In *Excerptiones iuris: Studies in Honor of André Gouron,* ed. Bernard Durand and Laurent Mayali, 741–58. Berkeley: University of California Press, 2000.

Vacandard, Elphège. *Vie de Saint Bernard, abbé de Clairvaux.* 2 vols. Paris: J. Gabalda, 1895.

Van der Hosrt, Koert et al., eds. *The Utrecht Psalter in Medieval Art: Picturing the Psalms of David.* London: Harvey Miller, 1996.

Van Kerrebrouck, Patrick. *Les Capétiens, 987–1328.* Nouvelle histoire généalogique de l'auguste maison de France 2. Villeneuve d'Ascq: Patrick van Kerrebrouck, 2000.

Verdier, François. *Une prieuré au temps des foires de Champagne: Saint-Ayoul de Provins.* Langres: Dominique Guéniot, 2009.

———. *Saints de Provins et Comtes de Champagne: essai sur l'imaginaire médiéval.* Langres: Dominique Guéniot, 2007.

Verhulst, A. E. "Flemish Financial Institutions from the Eleventh to the Thirteenth Century." In *Medieval Finance: A Comparison of Financial Institutions in Northwest Europe,* ed. Bryce Lyon and A. E. Verhulst, 12–40. Providence, R.I.: Brown University Press, 1967.

Vernet, André and J-F Genest, *La Bibliothèque de l'abbaye de Clairvaux du XIIe au XVIIIe.* Vol. 1: *Catalogues et répertoires.* Paris: CNRS, 1979.

Veyssière, Laurent. "Le personnel de l'abbaye de Clairvaux au XIIe siècle." *Cîteaux* 51 (2000): 17–90.

Von Simson, Otto. *The Gothic Cathedral: Origins of Gothic Architecture and the Medieval Concept of Order.* 1956; 2nd rev. ed. New York: Pantheon, 1962.

Voss, Lena. *Heinrich von Blois, Bischof von Winchester (1129–71).* Berlin: E. Ebering, 1932.

Wahlgren-Smith, Lena. "Editing a Medieval Text: The Case of Nicholas of Clairvaux." In *Challenging the Boundaries of Medieval History: The Legacy of Timothy Reuter,* ed. Patricia Skinner, 173–83. Turnhout: Brepols, 2009.

Warren, W. L. *Henry II.* Berkeley: University of California Press, 1973.

Weiler, Björn. "Kings and Sons: Princely Rebellions and the Structures of Revolt in Western Europe, c.1170–c. 1280." *Historical Research* 82 (2009): 17–40.

Werner, Karl Ferdinand. "Kingdom and Principality in Twelfth-Century France." In *The Medieval Nobility: Studies on the Ruling Classes of France and Germany from the Sixth to the Twelfth Centuries,* ed. and trans. Timothy Reuter, 243–90. Amsterdam: North-Holland, 1979.

West, Charles. "Count Hugh of Troyes and the Territorial Principality in Early Twelfth-Century Western Europe." *English Historical Review* 127 (2012): 523–48.

Willems, Eugène. "Cîteaux et la seconde croisade." *Revue d'Histoire Ecclésiastique* 49 (1954): 116–51.

Williams, John R. "William of the White Hands and Men of Letters." In *Anniversary Essays in Mediaeval History by the Students of C. H. Haskins,* ed. John L. La Monte and Charles H. Taylor, 365–87. Boston: Houghton Mifflin, 1929.

Wilmart, Mickaël. "Les débuts de la commune de Meaux (1179–1184)." *Bulletin de la Société Littéraire et Historique de la Brie* 55 (2000): 108–30.

———. *Meaux au Moyen Âge: une ville et ses hommes du XIIe au XVe siècle.* Montceaux-lès-Meaux: Fiacre, 2013.

Wood, Emily Katherine. "The Execution of Papal Justice in Northern France, 1145–1198." Ph.D. dissertation, Harvard University, 2009.

Wurm, Hermann Joseph. *Gottfried, Bischof von Langres (†1165): Ein biographischen Versuch als Beitrage zur Geschichte des zwölften Jahrhunderts.* Würzburg: Druck von F. X. Bucher, 1886.

Index

Unless otherwise noted, the spelling and identifcation of placenames follow the *Index Nominum* in Benton-Bur, *Receuil des actes d'Henri le Libéral*, vol. 2. The count's castle-towns are signaled by an asterisk.

Acknowledgments

I have enjoyed the support of several institutions and colleagues over the many years I have lived with Henry the Liberal. Membership at the Institute for Advanced Study, Princeton, allowed me the opportunity to frame the project not far from where John F. Benton produced the first modern study on Henry, his circle, and his "court." Fellowships at All Souls College, Oxford, and at Clare Hall, Cambridge, were critical to my understanding the European-wide stage on which Henry and his family and friends acted. I am grateful to Patricia Stirnemann for freely sharing her groundbreaking work on Henry's library and for stimulating my thinking about Henry's culture. I thank Elizabeth Paston and Lindy Grant for discussions on the architecture and glazing of St-Étienne of Troyes, which extended my reading of the new comital campus in Troyes. Michel Bur aided the completion of this book by graciously sending me advanced copies of his superb edition and indexes of Henry's acts. Two anonymous readers for the Press provided invaluable suggestions for sharpening the focus of the book, which acquired a new life. I thank Gordon Thompson for the maps and illustrations, and for his patience in their several iterations. Finally, I thank Jerry Singerman, my editor at Penn Press, for being such an empathetic and encouraging patron of my projects on medieval Champagne.